English Language Education

Volume 21

More information about this series at http://www.springer.com/series/11558

Tae-Young Kim

Historical Development of English Learning Motivation Research

Cases of Korea and Its Neighboring Countries in East Asia

 Springer

Tae-Young Kim
Department of English
College of Education
Chung-Ang University
Seoul, Republic of Korea

ISSN 2213-6967   ISSN 2213-6975   (electronic)
English Language Education
ISBN 978-981-16-3291-4   ISBN 978-981-16-2514-5   (eBook)
https://doi.org/10.1007/978-981-16-2514-5

This Springer imprint is published by the registered company Springer Nature Singapore Pte Ltd.
The registered company address is: 152 Beach Road, #21-01/04 Gateway East, Singapore 189721, Singapore

Preface

Most researchers majoring in second language (L2) acquisition do not usually take historical approaches, and this trend seems to be more noticeable in recent years. This academic trend is not an exception in the field of motivation, and researchers endeavor to describe the current status of learner motivation or the contribution of L2 learners' motivation to their ultimate success in L2 learning. Thus, the present and future of L2 learning and teaching may be the primary concern for most L2 motivation researchers.

However, L2 learning/teaching motivation is not created and terminated in a short period of time. As L2 learning/teaching takes place for many years or even decades, L2 motivation goes through multiple levels of psychological fluctuation. Students and teachers will experience many ups and downs. Such historicity of each L2 learner and teacher is now attracting the attention of many L2 motivation researchers. With academic proposals emphasizing the social turn in applied linguistics and dynamic systems theory, the longitudinal changes in L2 learning motivation are now one of the central topics in this field.

Although the above-stated academic changes are certainly a welcome move, I believe that we also need to extend the scope of scholarly investigation in L2 learning motivation beyond the individual learner level. Their social environment and family background influence L2 learners' motivation. Suppose the learner's family prioritizes the role of L2 education and believes in the efficacy of education for the family's economic prosperity. In that case, this student will create implicit, practical views on language learning and schooling experience, and the next level of investigation would be identifying the reason for emphasizing L2 learning in the family, in the region, and even in a nation. Why and how have they created such an attitude toward L2 learning? This question may seem an intriguing one, but in the case of English learning in (South) Korea and many other nations in Asia, this may be opening up Pandora's box as it involves complicated socioeconomic and political factors. English had been introduced rather abruptly after the trade treaties with the USA and the UK were ratified in the nineteenth century in the modernization process of Korea and other East Asian nations. The USA and the English language's influence cannot be ignored in twentieth-century history in this region.

Considering such intricate history regarding English learning in Korea and its neighboring nations in East Asia, it would be necessary to analyze Korean students' English learning motivation not from synchronic but from macro, diachronic viewpoints. I believe that the genesis of English learning motivation in Korea and East Asia can be adequately addressed with the lens of longitudinal perspectives where various sociohistorical events affected the general public's opinions of learning a foreign, particularly English, language. During the past century, Korea had undergone dramatic changes from a poverty-stricken agricultural nation to one of the world's mid-sized industrial and cultural powerhouses. Given this unprecedented upward transformation, it would be an academically intriguing topic to trace the history of English learning and teaching and how the motivation to learn this language in Korea has evolved through successive generations.

In this regard, the first part of this book truthfully follows the historical transition of English learning in Korea. Starting with nineteenth-century English learning, this book covers Korean students' English education and its related motivational aspects in the twentieth century and finally explains the most recent changes in English learning and its motivation in the twenty-first century. Through a series of historical investigations, I believe readers can reach a clear understanding of the creation, maintenance, fluctuation, and sometimes termination of English learning motivation among students in Korea. I endeavored to introduce various but related topics to Korean students' English learning in the latter part. Thus, the cases of China, Japan, and North Korea are presented in Chap. 5. Recent advances in EFL (de)motivation theory are also explained in Chap. 6 to facilitate the readers' more profound understanding of the status quo of English learning motivation in Korea. Chapter 7 reframed English learning in Korea by utilizing different socio-psychological concepts such as competitive motivation, alter-ego familism, *kitsch*, cultural capital, and amotivated English learning.

By publishing this project, it is hoped that similar lines of investigation focusing on the sociohistorical genesis of L2 learning/teaching motivation can soon be pursued further. Once again, when learning another language, our psychological affairs, particularly motivation, are continuously influenced by our personal history and social surroundings. For this reason, macro, longitudinal perspectives are essential to complete our scientific inquiry into language learning motivation.

Seoul, Republic of Korea   Tae-Young Kim

Acknowledgments

First of all, I would like to express my sincere appreciation to Springer for granting an extension of manuscript submission. As this book project was affected by many unforeseen obstacles, including the COVID-19 pandemic, the publication process was indeed rocky. Without their generous support, this project would have been either suspended or aborted entirely. This work was supported by the Ministry of Education of the Republic of Korea and the National Research Foundation of Korea (NRF- 2018S1A6A4A01036484). Without the financial support from NRF, many data collection trips to North American libraries having rare documents of English teaching/learning in Korea would not have been possible. I am immensely thankful to Cheng Yu Tung East Asian Library at the University of Toronto, where I spent productive days in the summer of 2018. My colleagues and friends in Korea and overseas enthusiastically supported my book proposal and drafting. My dear family deserves my sincere appreciation, and without the perseverance of my wife, Jungyeon (Tanya), and son, Young June, my academic time travel tracing back to nineteenth-century Korea could not have been embarked on at all. Thank you all for your love and unconditional support.

Contents

Chapter 1
Introduction

1.1 Central Issues of This Book: Motivation Engraved in the Nation's Collective History

In our daily lives, we often use expressions such as "I'm not motivated to do this work" or "Brad is so motivated to learn how to play the new PlayStation game." The word motivation, in these cases, is not different from the person's desire or willingness to start (and also continue) the task at hand. Because the use of motivation is often related to the on-the-spot, here-and-now situation, a historical analysis of the origin of any particular type of motivation is not usually conducted. For example, although Sumin, an EFL (English-as-a-foreign language) student in South Korea, may say, "I'm quite motivated to learn English," the reason for Sumin's motivation is not sought. Instead, teachers and parents have often used the student's motivation to increase the student's levels of learning engagement and eventual proficiency in a foreign language. The fundamental reason for wanting to or not wanting to learn English is not usually the main theme of investigation. Sumin may not want to learn English because she does not imagine herself going abroad. She may not be motivated to learn English because she does not particularly like the current president of the U.S. We can find various reasons for generating, maintaining, or terminating the motivation to learn English.

Most of the previous practical handbooks on second language (L2) learning motivation, however, have focused on how to enhance students' motivation in class and aimed to increase learner participation in L2 classrooms (e.g., Dörnyei & Kubanyiova, 2014; Hadfield & Dörnyei, 2013). Increasing students' L2 learning motivation has been a major educational issue, because, for the past half a century, motivation has consistently been believed an essential psychological factor for students predicting L2 proficiency (Dörnyei & Ushioda, 2021; Gardner, 1985, 2010). Motivation, as a psychological construct, encompasses complicated subfactors, and in order to address these intricacies in motivation, various researchers have tried to (re-)define its nature, mainly during the 1990s (e.g.,

© Springer Nature Singapore Pte Ltd. 2021

T.-Y. Kim, *Historical Development of English Learning Motivation Research*,
English Language Education 21, https://doi.org/10.1007/978-981-16-2514-5_1

Crookes & Schmidt, 1991; Dörnyei, 1994; Oxford & Shearin, 1994). Nonetheless, since the learners have a unique history as human beings in a specific learning context, their particular historicity needs to be addressed. Moreover, learners in the same-speech community often share a similar mindset in creating the attitude and motivation for learning a foreign language. For instance, as Oller et al. (1977) and Oller and Perkins (1978) have reported, the learner with a high level of antipathy toward the target language community may create negative attitudes toward the target language speakers, and this will provide strong motivation for these speakers to excel, leading to a higher degree of L2 learning motivation. Thus, learners' personal experience, be it positive or negative, can exert a substantial influence on their L2 learning motivation and attitudes.

Moreover, the collective memory of the learners, the community, and the nation can have an impact on individual students' motivation. For example, the frequent use of English in the global market is clearly related to the increasing power of the U.S. in the twentieth century (and that of the British Empire in the nineteenth century), resulting in an increasing numbers of countries bestowing a special status on the English language as de facto the only foreign language, or a dominant second language (Marlina, 2014). Undoubtedly, this contributed to the creation of the discourse of English as an international language (Crystal, 1997; Graddol, 1997; McKay, 2002) academically, and consolidated students' external reasons for learning English. Given this, collective historicity surrounding an L2 results in the generation and maintenance of an individual student's L2 learning motivation. Despite this observation, most research on L2 learning and teaching motivation has not focused on this historical aspect while developing their theories of L2 motivation.

In the literature of L2 learning motivation, researchers have not adequately addressed the above-mentioned historical nature of L2 learning and teaching motivation. For example, in Edward Deci and Richard Ryan's Self-Determination Theory (SDT) (Deci & Ryan, 2012), the degree of learners' internalization was highlighted from intrinsic motivation, where learners wanted to continue learning for the sake of learning, to four types of extrinsic motivation. In these extrinsic motivations, learners do not initiate learning, for it is inherently exciting for a variety of reasons. In the case of intrinsic motivation, learners do not have an internal struggle because they would like to conduct the activity. However, when extrinsic motivation is involved, they experience different levels of internal struggle, due to the perceived disparity between their own hearts (aspiration of things they would like to do instantly) and the rational decision to concentrate on the imposed work that they must do for themselves or others around them (e.g., family, parents, or teachers). In this line of investigation, the ontogenetic and phylogenetic history of learning an L2 was not considered systematically. Instead, cross-sectional, temporal aspects of motivation occurring at the moment of investigation became the subject of scientific inquiry; each learner's unique history (or that of the members of the society) was not viewed as the key factor affecting various degrees and types of motivation.

The current situation in the field of L2 learning and teaching motivation is not different. In recent years, Dörnyei (2005, 2009) proposed the L2 Motivational Self

System (L2MSS), where two types of L2 self were suggested: the ideal L2 self and the ought-to L2 self. When L2 learners imagine a desirable future state wherein they can achieve what they aspire to become, these bright future self-images are represented by the ideal L2 selves. On the contrary, in the case of the ought-to L2 selves, once they embark on L2 learning activities, they feel inner urges to do the work because they are either afraid of not attaining their ideal future upholding their social status or obliged to do the L2 learning due to other close persons' persuasion or nudges. In the ideal L2 self, a more internalized form of self-image is assumed; in the ought-to L2 self, a less internalized self-image is supposed. In the L2MSS, Dörnyei (2005, 2009, 2019) also stated the third component: L2 learning experience, which "concerns situated 'executive' motives related to the immediate learning environment and experience (e.g., the impact of the teacher, the curriculum, the peer group, the experience of success)" (Dörnyei, 2009, p. 29). He further stated that this concept is "conceptualized at a different level from the two self-guides, and future research will hopefully elaborate on the self aspects of this bottom-up process" (p. 29). Although L2 learning experience is included as the third component in the L2MSS, only a few qualitative or mixed-methods studies have been conducted (e.g., Asker, 2012; Shoaib & Dörnyei, 2005). Learner history through in-depth qualitative inquiries is still not the primary concern in L2 motivation studies. The most recent literature connecting L2 motivation and L2 selves influenced by the complex dynamic systems theory (e.g., Larsen-Freeman, 2015) considers different levels of timescale, but the primary concern centers on the present and its immediate past and future. For example, Mercer (2015), arguing for the necessity of multilevel nested systems approaches in understanding the concept of self, distinguished levels of self, which last from seconds (level 1) to months (level 4). Given the cross-sectional nature of previous literature, her inclusion of different levels of timescale in understanding learner motivation is an academic advancement. However, comprehensive efforts to encompass an extended period of time including months or years will be needed for us to fully understand the complexities in the motivation, attitudes, perception, and evaluation of a foreign language.

In summary, previous literature on L2 learning and teaching motivation is based on an ahistorical approach. Collective psychology in a community, a region, and even a nation can affect an individual learner's desire to learn (or not to learn) a specific foreign language. For example, as succinctly described by Diamond (2019), it is highly unlikely for an Indonesian student to hold a favorable attitude toward Dutch, the language of the Netherlands, their oppressor in the previous century. The nation's history is taught to the next generation mainly through public education; antipathy or penchant toward a specific nation influences the motivation to learn its language. Similarly, Koreans may experience complicated emotions when learning Japanese, the language of their colonizer in the early twentieth century. Given this, the current volume primarily concerns the macro undercurrents formulating the overall attitudes toward a specific language. Specifically, the historical approach toward the English language in Korea is the focus of this book, and it is hoped that this historical phylogenetic approach brings academic vigor in investigating L2 learning and teaching motivation more holistically.

1.2   Learning English in Korea: A Brief Historical Retrospection

The central theme of this book is to investigate Korean English as a foreign language (EFL) learners' motivation. The investigation will focus on how various types of EFL learning motivation have evolved as sociopolitical milieus have changed during the last two centuries (since English was first introduced after Korea [formerly the Joseon Dynasty] and the U.S. Treaty of Justice, Amity, Commerce, and Navigation was ratified on May 22, 1882. As explicated in the following chapter, the Joseon Dynasty (lasted from 1392 to 1910) had extremely limited exposure to the Western society via China (formerly the Qing Dynasty from 1644 to 1912). No Korean could speak and understand the English language, which resulted in the use of double translation at the time of the Treaty (Kim, 2016; Kwon & Kim, 2010); Tang Xiaoyi (唐紹儀),[1] a junior Chinese diplomat who had stayed in the U.S. and studied at New York University and Columbia University, was invited as a mediating interpreter because he could understand both English and classical Chinese. Korean diplomats, having superb literacy only in classic written Chinese, expressed their opinions and wrote the conditions of the treaty on a sheet of paper in Chinese letters. Reading those letters, Mr. Tang translated the Korean government's opinions into oral English to the U.S. diplomats.

To compensate for the lack of foreign language skills (which was regarded as a national disgrace), King Gojong ordered the establishment of *Yookyeong'gongwon* (育英公院), the Royal English School. The school was a foreign language academy funded by the government in 1886 after a short transitional period of *Dongmunhak* (同文學), a 1-year fast-track translation school in 1883. After the Korea and U.S. Treaty of 1882, the English language has been actively instructed across Korea due to the close political and economic relations between the two nations. For the last two centuries, English has constantly been instructed in Korea. With only a short noticeable exception from 1939 to 1945 (when the Government-General of Korea, the chief colonial administration established by Imperial Japan, officially prohibited the instruction of English at all educational levels), English has taken the central place in both public and private education in Korea.

Since its official arrival to the Korean peninsula in 1882, the English language has been taking the starring role for the learners to enable them to ascend the social hierarchy. Learning and using English has been acclaimed as the acquisition of worldly success, with direct links to the idealistic affluence and savviness of the Western world (most notably represented by the U.S. and the U.K.). Notable public figures, including Dr. Rhee Syngman, the first president of the Republic of Korea, during the first half of the twentieth century acquired proficiency in English through

---

[1]This book follows the order of the family name followed by the given name for East Asian names (usually names of China, Japan, and Korea). For example, in "Tang Xiaoyi," "Tang" refers to the family name and "Xiaoyi" to the given name. In all other cases, traditional Western naming convention (i.e., given name followed by family name) was observed.

studying abroad in the U.S. and the U.K. After the Korean War (1950–1953), the political and economic ties with the U.S. consolidated the favoritism toward English in South Korea. Often, the desire to be employed in a secure workplace represented Korean EFL learners' motivation. For this reason, internal competition among Koreans vying for employment explains a large portion of their EFL learning motivation.

As described in subsequent Chaps. 2, 3, and 4, the origin of English learning motivation among Koreans can be attributed to the concept of *hakbul* (學閥), or academic credentialism, where the name of the university an individual graduated from largely determines their chance of employment and promotion in their occupation. The establishment of Kyungsung Imperial University (京城帝國大學) in 1924, and the so-called SKY (i.e., the acronym of Seoul National, Korea, and Yonsei Universities) cartel after the 1950s also intensified the rivalry among Korean secondary school students. In this academic competition, English had always been considered the crucial school subject; for generations, English was taught and tested for the preparation of college entrance examinations. The test format primarily focused on the test takers' knowledge of English morphosyntax and reading comprehension until 1992. Thus, Korean students did not have the opportunity to develop English listening and speaking proficiency, which is a negative washback effect of a high-stakes national test.

The competition among Korean compatriots in learning English became fierce as Korea was passing through a period of rapid economic expansion (for nearly four decades, starting in the 1960s). The EFL learning motivation originating from the desire to outperform the proficiency of other Korean students in college entrance exams was reported to create a unique motivational component: competitive motivation (Kim, 2006, 2010; Kim & Kim, 2016). Note that the competition is related not only to English but also to all school subjects included in the college entrance exam (officially, the College Scholastic Ability Test; CSAT, 大學修學能力試驗). In South Korea, educational fever (Seth, 2002) surrounding the widespread interest in college admission has been closely associated with the idea of subliming one's family's reputation and its collective prosperity. For ages, in the traditional Confucian society such as China and Korea, an offspring's success had often been decided by the result of *gwageo* (in Korea) or *keju* (in China), the Royal Civil Service Examination, in the central bureaucratic system (Yu & Suen, 2005). Only a limited number of government officers were selected (annual average: 29 persons, according to Han, 2014) after taking *gwageo* in Korea. Against this historical backdrop, Korea still leaves a trace of this Confucian tradition; in this regard, Korea's college entrance exam is similar to the traditional *gwageo* exam. The day the CSAT is taken, for example, is prominent in the headlines of newspapers and TV media. On exam day, which is usually Thursday in the second week of November every year, flight departure and arrival schedules are adjusted, and planes are grounded during the English listening comprehension test, so as not to disturb the test takers' performance (Moon, 2018).

In understanding EFL learning motivation in South Korea, the nature of this exam's orientation needs to be scrutinized. This psychology toward obtaining higher scores in L2 exams may also be explained by Gardner's (1985, 2010) instrumentality. While explaining the complex nature of instrumentality, Gardner (2010) stated:

> [O]ne individual might study a second language to "get a good job," while another might do it "to please a parent or some other significant person," and another to "satisfy a university requirement," etc. These are distinct reasons and thus it is possible that an individual who feels strongly that one is appropriate may not feel the same way about others. (p. 127)

As presented in the above excerpt, the desire for employment, pleasing the family members, and satisfying a university requirement may be perceived as different subtypes of motivational constructs. However, in the case of EFL learning, these distinctive motivations may be merged in the lives of individual learners. For example, 3rd-year high school students, who aspire to be admitted to a prestigious university, may enthusiastically study English to both satisfy their university admission requirements and please their parents. Because the name of the university and the students' undergraduate major are commonly perceived as determining factors for employment after graduation, high school students' EFL learning motivation also includes occupational instrumentality. On the contrary, learning any other foreign languages in South Korea presents an entirely different aspect. As illustrated above, English learning motivation found among Korean high school students fulfills dual or even triple functions mentioned by Gardner (2010). However, learning Chinese, a second dominant foreign language in Korea, does not serve such multiple functions, and the motivation of Chinese language learners are distinct and rarely merged. An office worker learning Chinese in Seoul, Korea, would like to be promoted at his or her workplace. The desire for university admission or pleasing family members is not usually the primary concern of Korean learners of Chinese. Similarly, high school students learning Japanese do not expect their knowledge in Japanese to be directly linked to their successes in university admission or employment.

In summary, the motivation toward learning English in South Korea has served multiple functions, and the nature of EFL-learning motivation has been closely associated with South Korea's modern history. The increasing influence of English as an international language has also strengthened the role of English in Korea. Therefore, learning English involves multiple levels of motivation within an individual, which is not commonly identified in the learning of other foreign languages.

1.3   Organization of the Book

The organization of the current volume is as follows. The introduction (this chapter) presents the meaning of learning English in South Korea and how it differs from learning other foreign languages. With a brief critique of previous L2 motivation theories, the introduction reviews the historical progression of English learning in South Korea.

The brief history of English learning in Korea is explicated in Chaps. 2, 3, and 4. Chapter 2 highlights the historical overview of English learning in Korea in the nineteenth century and during the Japanese Colonization Period (from 1910 to 1945). In this chapter, by anchoring major historical events often marked by a series of political upheavals, it will be highlighted that the attitudes Koreans have toward English are closely related to the Confucian tradition in the Joseon Dynasty, which has remained the case into the twenty-first century. In the late nineteenth century, English was considered a crucial tool for enhancing one's social status, and this chapter investigates how such a positive social value on English was intensified in the Japanese Colonization Period, which ended in 1945 when Japan surrendered in World War II.

Chapters 3 and 4 focus on the southern part of Korea (south of 38° of northern latitude); only South Korea's situations surrounding English education and learners' motivation are explained. In the northern part of the Korean peninsula, Kim Il-Sung (1912–1994) established the Democratic People's Republic of Korea (DPRK) on September 9, 1948, and invaded South Korea after an extended period of civil war preparation. Young General Kim, supported by the Soviet Union, gradually gained political power after a fierce power struggle with other leaders having different ideas about the ideological sovereignty of North Korea. Kim held the position of Premier of North Korea from 1948 to 1972 and its President from 1972 until his death in 1994. During and after the Korean War (1950–1953), the English language was not taught in North Korea because it was regarded as the language of the "supreme enemy," the U.S. For this reason, in Chaps. 3 and 4, the historical overview of English learning in South Korea (officially the Republic of Korea) will be highlighted.

In Chap. 3, the role of English among South Korean people during the Korean War and the post-war reconstruction period until the 1980s will be explained. In the process of post-war industrialization from the 1950s to the 1980s, English became the most critical school subject, directly linked to university entrance exams across Korea. Moreover, at the workplace, English functioned as the primary tool for promotion. Together with *hakbul*, or "academic credentialism," having its origin in the Confucian tradition in East Asia, English learning motivation became increasingly instrumental and competitive for admission to higher educational institutions, and promotion to a higher ranking at work or social organizations. President Park Chung-hee, who maintained his presidency from 1960 to 1979, expedited government-led economic development. South Korea witnessed rapid economic expansion during this period, and English was prioritized at both educational institutions and workplaces across South Korea. This chapter illustrates the conceptual connection between *hakbul*-orientation and competitive motivation.

Chapter 4 deals with the changing nature of English learning in the past three decades. In the 1990s and 2000s, English was increasingly regarded as a useful device for communication among non-native English speakers around the world. This chapter focuses on how such changes have influenced Korean students' English learning motivation. This chapter also explains how the role of English as an international language in the era of economic and cultural prosperity in Korea after the 1990s influenced Gardner's integrative/instrumental orientation and Korean students' competitive motivation. At the turn of the century, English was no longer regarded as one of the essential school subjects only; it is now seen as a useful device for international communication. Oral presentation skills and speaking proficiency in English are increasingly regarded as adequate linguistic, cultural capital (Bourdieu, 1974) among Koreans. Parents who can provide their children with the opportunity to learn English believe that they are creating a better competitive edge, which will function as distinctive cultural capital. This chapter illustrates various English-related social phenomena, often called "English fever" (Park, 2009), including English education at kindergarten, studying abroad in an English country, and teaching English in English (TEE) movement after the 1990s.

To provide a comprehensive view of English learning motivation, in Chap. 5 the learning of English in East Asian countries is introduced. The similarities and differences in L2 learning motivation in China, Japan, and North Korea will be discussed. In the case of China, English learning had been expedited through the modernization process in the nineteenth and early twentieth centuries. However, the civil war between the National Party and the Communist Party prevented a steady development in English education. Moreover, the establishment of the People's Republic of China and the Cold War suppressed the instruction of English for decades. The Economic Reform after Deng Xiaoping's reign from 1978, however, was the turning point in English education. The historical expansion of the English language in China and its recent educational policy, such as the introduction of the College English Test (CET), will be explained. Japan's English education presents differences compared with that of China. The success of the Meiji Restoration transformed the nation into a centralized national system, and the Ministry of Education systematically controlled English education. Similar to China, English was regarded as the language of modernization and advanced technology in Japan. The Japanese government until the early twentieth century embraced the English language by hosting British linguists, including Dr. Harold Palmer, and establishing the Institution for Research in English Teaching (IRET) in 1923. However, during World War II, until Japan's surrender to Allied Nations in 1945, English was regarded as the language of the enemy nations and thus suppressed. During the reconstruction period after the U.S. Military Government in Japan and its subsequent economic prosperity in the latter half of the twentieth century, Japan re-emphasized the importance of English learning. Similar to the case of South Korea, English was considered a crucial school subject, and was included in the college entrance exams. Japan's recent movement toward English education at the elementary school level is also included in this chapter. This chapter concludes with a summary of English education in North Korea. The notion of *Juche*, or self-reliance, will be explained to provide a pivotal understanding of the general educational atmosphere in North Korea. The traditional socialist ideology and the justification of the dictatorial regime represented by the Kim family have constituted a significant portion of North Korean English textbooks. In this chapter, the recent changes after 2012, during the reign of Kim Jong-un, are explained with representational practical section contents from their English textbooks.

After comparing the similarities and differences in EFL learning motivation in East Asian countries, Chaps. 6 and 7 focus more on Korea-specific concepts such as competitive motivation and amotivated English learning. In Chap. 6, after surveying dominant theories of L2-learning motivation, including Dörnyei's (2005, 2009) L2 motivational self-system and its three subcomponents—the ideal L2 self, the ought-to L2 self, and the L2 learning experience—recent advancements in this field are explained with close reference to the Korean educational contexts. This chapter encompasses relatively new concepts in the field: demotivation, teacher motivation, and L2 teachers' emotional labor. Moreover, the origins of competitive motivation will be explained with close reference to recent research (e.g., Kim, 2006, 2010; Kim & Kim, 2016). Vygotskian sociocultural theory and activity theory (Engeström, 1987, 1999a, 1999b; Leont'ev, 1978), as well as their application to the field of L2 motivation will be presented in the latter half of this chapter; Motivational Languaging Activities (MLAs) are introduced to enhance students' low level of L2 learning motivation in L2 classrooms.

Chapter 7 focuses on the socio-psychological factors inherent in English learning motivation among Koreans. Five different but conceptually related factors are found in approaching Korean students' EFL learning motivation: competitive motivation, alter ego familism, English learning as "Kitsch," English as cultural capital, and amotivated English learning. From these multifaceted approaches, it will be argued that EFL learning needs to be understood as a social, cultural, and historical phenomenon, not merely as individual learners' characteristics or propensities. For example, this chapter covers the paradox of amotivated English learners and their unexpectedly high level of English proficiency. Because of the psychological pressure from parents, teachers, and friends, many school-aged children in South Korea experience varying degrees of stress when learning and studying English. The intense competition for university admission and better job placement leads most Korean students to be amotivated English learners. This means that in many cases, particularly in the case of high school students in South Korea, students' English proficiency is relatively high even though they are in an amotivated state, when they experience severe demotivation. To explain such amotivated but highly proficient EFL students in Korea, multilayered approaches highlighting the sociocultural heritage among the students, regional communities, and the nation are scrutinized.

Chapter 8 summarizes the arguments and findings in the previous chapters, and provides future prospects of English learning and teaching, educational implications, and practical suggestions, alleviating an overly competitive socio-educational atmosphere in South Korea. While minding the potential dangers of the ahistorical approach in the field of L2 motivation, the chapter re-emphasizes the useful contribution of sociohistorical perspectives to this field.

References

Asker, A. (2012). *Future self-guides and language learning engagement of English-major secondary school students in Libya: Understanding the interplay between possible selves and the L2 learning situation.* Unpublished doctoral dissertation, University of Birmingham, England. Retrieved November 9, 2019, from https://etheses.bham.ac.uk/id/eprint/3486/

Bourdieu, P. (1974). Cultural reproduction and social reproduction. In R. Brown (Ed.), *Knowledge, education and social change* (pp. 71–84). London: Taylor & Francis.

Crookes, G., & Schmidt, R. W. (1991). Motivation: Reopening the research agenda. *Language Learning, 41*, 469–512.

Crystal, D. (1997). *English as a global language* (2nd ed.). Cambridge, England: Cambridge University Press.

Deci, E. L., & Ryan, R. M. (2012). Motivation, personality, and development within embedded social contexts: An overview of self-determination theory. In R. M. Ryan (Ed.), *The handbook of human motivation* (pp. 85–107). Oxford, England: Oxford University Press.

Diamond, J. (2019). *Upheaval: Turing points for nations in crisis.* New York: Little, Brown.

Dörnyei, Z. (1994). Motivation and motivating in the foreign language classroom. *The Modern Language Journal, 78*, 273–284.

Dörnyei, Z. (2005). *The psychology of the language learner: Individual differences in second language acquisition.* Mahwah, NJ: Lawrence Erlbaum.

Dörnyei, Z. (2009). The L2 motivational self system. In Z. Dörnyei & E. Ushioda (Eds.), *Motivation, language identity and the L2 self* (pp. 9–42). Bristol, England: Multilingual Matters.

Dörnyei, Z. (2019). Towards a better understanding of the L2 learning experience, the Cinderella of the L2 Motivational Self System. *Studies in Second Language Learning and Teaching, 9*(1), 19–30.

Dörnyei, Z., & Kubanyiova, M. (2014). *Motivating learners, motivating teachers: Building vision in the language classroom.* Cambridge, England: Cambridge University Press.

Dörnyei, Z., & Ushioda, E. (2021). *Teaching and researching motivation* (3rd ed.). London: Routledge.

Engeström, Y. (1987). *Learning by expanding: An activity-theoretical approach to developmental research.* Helsinki, Finland: Orienta-Konsultit.

Engeström, Y. (1999a). Activity theory and individual and social transformation. In Y. Engeström, R. Miettinen & R.-M. Punamaki (Eds.), *Perspectives on activity theory* (pp. 19–38). New York: Cambridge University Press.

Engeström, Y. (1999b). Innovative learning in work teams. In Y. Engeström, R. Miettinen & R.-M. Punamaki (Eds.), *Perspectives on activity theory* (pp. 377–404). New York: Cambridge University Press.

Gardner, R. C. (1985). *Social psychology and second language learning: The role of attitudes and motivation.* London: Edward Arnold.

Gardner, R. C. (2010). *Motivation and second language acquisition: The socio-educational model.* New York: Peter-Lang.

Graddol, D. (1997). *The future of English.* London: The British Council.

Hadfield, J., & Dörnyei, Z. (2013). *Motivating learning.* London: Pearson.

Han, Young-Woo. (2014). *Gwageo, Choolse'eui sadari [Gwageo, the ladder toward worldly success].* Seoul, Korea: Jisiksaneupsa.

Kim, Tae-Young. (2006). Motivation and attitudes toward foreign language learning as socio-politically mediated constructs: The case of Korean high school students. *The Journal of Asia TEFL, 3*(2), 165–192.

Kim, Tae-Young. (2010). Socio-political influence on EFL motivation and attitudes: Comparative surveys of Korean high school students. *Asia-Pacific Education Review, 11*, 211–222.

Kim, Tae-Young. (2016). An investigation of socio-educational aspects of English education during Japanese colonial period: Focusing on Chosun Ilbo and Dong-A Daily articles. *Studies in English Education, 21*(1), 179–210.

Kim, Tae-Young, & Kim, Yoon-Kyoung. (2016). A quasi-longitudinal study on English learning motivation and attitudes: The case of South Korean students. *The Journal of Asia TEFL, 13*(2), 138–155.

Kwon, Oryang, & Kim, Jeong-Ryeol. (2010). *Hankook yeong'eogyoyooksa [History of English education in Korea].* Seoul, Korea: Hankookmunwhasa.

Larsen-Freeman, D. (2015). Ten 'lessons' from complex dynamics systems theory: What is on offer. In Z. Dörnyei, P. D. MacIntyre & A. Henry (Eds.), *Motivational dynamics in language learning* (pp. 11–19). Bristol, England: Multilingual Matters.

Leont'ev, A. N. (1978). *Activity, consciousness, and personality.* Englewood Cliffs, CA: Prentice-Hall.

Marlina, R. (2014). The pedagogy of English as an international language (EIL): More reflection and dialogues. In R. Marlina & R. A. Giri (Eds.), *The pedagogy of English as an international language* (pp. 1–19). Cham, Switzerland: Springer.

McKay, S. L. (2002). *Teaching English as an international language.* Oxford, England: Oxford University Press.

Mercer, S. (2015). Dynamics on the self: A multilevel nested systems approach. In Z. Dörnyei, P. D. MacIntyre & A. Henry (Eds.), *Motivational dynamics in language learning* (pp. 139–163). Bristol, England: Multilingual Matters.

Moon, K. (2018, November 15). BBC Worklife: The Korean CSAT is the exam that stops a nation. Retrieved November 11, 2019, from https://www.bbc.com/worklife/article/20181114-the-korean-csat-is-the-exam-that-stops-a-nation

Oller, J., Baca, L., & Vigil, A. (1977). Attitudes and attained proficiency in ESL: A sociolinguistic study of Mexican Americans in the Southwest. *TESOL Quarterly, 11,* 173–183.

Oller, J., & Perkins, K. (1978). Intelligence and language proficiency as sources of variance in self-reported affective variables. *Language Learning, 28,* 85–97.

Oxford, R. L., & Shearin, J. (1994). Language learning motivation: Expanding the theoretical framework. *The Modern Language Journal, 78*(1), 12–28.

Park, Jin-Kyu. (2009). 'English fever' in South Korea: Its history and symptoms. *English Today, 25* (1), 50–57.

Seth, M. J. (2002). *Education fever: Society, politics, and the pursuit of schooling in South Korea.* Honolulu, HI: University of Hawai'i Press.

Shoaib, A., & Dörnyei, Z. (2005). Affect in life-long learning: Exploring L2 motivation as dynamic process. In P. Benson & D. Nunan (Eds.), *Learners' stories: Difference and diversity in language learning* (pp. 22–41). Cambridge, England: Cambridge University Press.

Yu, L., & Suen, H. K. (2005). Historical and contemporary exam-driven education fever in China. *KEDI Journal of Educational Policy, 2*(1), 17–33.

Chapter 2
Historical Overview of English Learning in South Korea: The Nineteenth Century and Japanese Colonization

This chapter presents the progress of English education before August 15, 1945, when the Korean people were liberated from the former Japanese Empire. The chapter begins with the Western influence in Korea during the nineteenth century and the first encounter with English speakers. The rapid spread of English education is explained with reference to the concept of modernization and the desire to "get rank" or be employed in the public sectors in Korea. Based on these historical accounts, a discussion on the nature of English learning motivation in the late nineteenth century and the subsequent Japanese colonial period follows.

2.1 Background: The Nineteenth-Century Joseon Korea and the Western Influence

Yi Seong-gye, former General of the Goryeo Dynasty (高麗, AD 918–1392), founded the Joseon Dynasty with political support from the new literati class in Goryeo, ascended the throne himself, and later became King Taejo. Although King Taejo was a part of the militia and came to the throne under the auspices of the armed forces, he had to comply with the ruling political party composed of avid supporters of the neo-Confucian school of thought established by Zhu Xi (朱熹, 1130–1200, also known Master Zhu 朱子) during the Song Dynasty in China. The neo-Confucians in the former Goryeo Dynasty, with a few exceptions, participated in the foundation of the new Joseon Dynasty. These neo-Confucians were well versed in classical Chinese literature and philosophy from the Confucian school of thought. Since *gwageo*, the Royal examination for the appointment of officers, was administered from AD 958 in the Goryeo Dynasty, all test takers learned the esoteric philosophy of neo-Confucianism and classical Chinese literature. Most neo-Confucians endeavored to hold government officer positions and had varying degrees of practical knowledge about the operation of the political regime and the

© Springer Nature Singapore Pte Ltd. 2021
T.-Y. Kim, *Historical Development of English Learning Motivation Research*,
English Language Education 21, https://doi.org/10.1007/978-981-16-2514-5_2

nation. Thus, King Taejo had no other choice but to place a high value on their talent. These neo-Confucians consolidated their political power in the new Joseon Dynasty in Korea.

The Joseon Dynasty survived for more than 500 years from 1392 to 1910, which is a relatively long period. As a point of reference, the current British Windsor monarch inherited the Hanover monarch, which started reigning over the U.K. from 1714, over 300 years ago. In China as well, the Ming Dynasty lasted less than 300 years (1363–1644), and the Qing Dynasty, the latest imperial dynasty in China, was not an exception (1636–1912). Despite the notable nationwide catastrophic warfare caused by the Japanese invasion in the late sixteenth century and the Qing China in the early seventeenth century, Joseon, as an independent nation, could sustain her regime and enjoyed political longevity. This remarkable sustainability as a nation contributed to consolidating the authority of the neo-Confucians, who still upheld the philosophical remnants of Zhu Xi, reiterated over hundreds of years.

However, the industrial revolution that began in the U.K. in the eighteenth century had expedited the expansion of Western colonialism, and the British empire expanded her territory. The success of the British empire was emulated and hastily followed by other European countries. The fact that the British empire was the vanguard in the expansion of Western colonialism is important in the history of English education in Korea because China, a neighboring country sharing the northern borderline with Korea, was affected by the British expansion. The first and second Opium Wars (1839–1842 and 1856–1960, respectively), or the U.K. and China War, resulted in the Treaty of Nanking—the first "unequal treaty"—which granted indemnity and extraterritoriality to Britain and ceded Hong Kong to the British Empire. Compared to Britain's 69 war casualties in the first Opium War, those of the Qing Dynasty were estimated to be more than 18,000 (Martin, 1847). This remarkable difference is primarily accountable for the notable difference in the degree of industrialization in ammunition and weaponry between the U.K. and China (Platt, 2018). It must have been inevitable to find the Chinese army troops turn agape, immobilized upon facing the British naval bombardment from modern warships. Having endured this diplomatic disgrace, the Qing Dynasty gradually reached a consensus that the modernization ignited by the industrial revolution also needed to be introduced to China. To expedite the commercial trade and learning of the Western civilization, the Qing Dynasty founded *Tongwen Guan* (同文館) in Beijing in 1863, and the children of merchant families were selected to learn English, French, and Russian (see Chap. 5 for more details on English education in China).

The political context in Japan was also going through a series of significant transitions, from feudal *Edo Bakufu* (江戸幕府) or *Tokugawa Bakufu* (徳川幕府) to modern imperial Japan, which culminated in the Meiji Restoration (明治維新). *Edo Bakufu*, founded by Shogun (i.e., General) Tokugawa Ieyasu (徳川 家康, 1543–1616) in 1600, was inherited by only those from the Tokugawa clan. The Japanese emperor, a titular head of the nation, did not have any actual political power, and Shogun from the Tokugawa clan functioned as the de facto ruler of all Japanese islands. Throughout the *Edo Bakufu* period, foreign trade with the West was minimal, and only merchant ships from the Netherlands were selectively admitted to the port of Nagasaki from 1639 to 1854. However, the U.S. Commander Matthew C. Perry (1794–1858), after lengthy negotiations with the *Tokugawa Bakufu*, succeeded in opening the port of Kanagawa (now Yokohama) on March 8, 1854. The modern technology and the foreign influence represented by the U.S. were readily accepted by a group of young politicians, including Saigo Takamori and Kido Takayoshi. They were enthusiastic in accepting the Western civilization that contributed to the Meiji Restoration. With support from these social reformists, young Emperor Meiji succeeded in restoring the Japanese emperor's political power and put an official end to *Tokugawa Bakufu*. After the Restoration, Imperial Japan established the centralized system and accelerated the modernization of Japan under the slogan "Enrich the Country, Strengthen the Military" (富国強兵).

Despite these rapid geopolitical changes in its neighboring countries, Korea did not initiate diplomatic relations with nations other than China, which was the only traditional partner for foreign exchange.[1] The official policy of the Joseon Dynasty was *Swaegook* (鎖国), the seclusion policy. This policy had been maintained throughout the Joseon Dynasty, but in the nineteenth century, the *Swaegook* policy was further consolidated after a series of bloody conflicts with French troops and with U.S. commercial vessels. The Western countries, which, by the mid-nineteenth century, were nearing the completion of the industrial revolution, actively tried to expand their overseas territory for trade, to increase their national revenue, and for missionary purposes (Ross, 2017).

It is noteworthy that Christianity was vigilantly propagated in the Korean peninsula and ordinated the persecution of all types of Christian missionary work including both Roman Catholicism and Protestantism. As mentioned, the official political philosophy adopted in the Joseon Dynasty was Confucianism—that of Confucius, but particularly the neo-Confucianism established by Zhu Xi. In (neo-) Confucianism, the political system is represented by the monarch, and the king is often equated with one's father and master teacher, which means that the national identity emphasized both loyalty (toward the king) and filial piety (toward one's parents). The former was on the public level and the latter on the personal level (Park & Müller, 2014). For the neo-Confucian scholars, most of whom were also politicians, the basic Christian concepts such as God and the Trinity were often perceived as an outright subversion of the traditional concepts prioritizing the loyalty to the king and the filial duty to parents. Thus, Christianity was considered an imminent peril to the maintenance of the dynasty.

Consequently, the national level of persecution continued throughout the nineteenth century. At first, the persecution mainly targeted the early Roman Catholics in Korea. At the initial stage of Catholicism, Christianity was studied by scholars in

---

[1]However, although unofficial, because of geographical proximity, international trade with Japan, Mongolia, the Uyghur Kingdom, the Manchu, and the Ryukyu Kingdom (now Okinawa in Japan) was also necessary. Thus, interpreters for these languages were educated in *Sayeokwon* (司譯院) in the Joseon Dynasty (Chung, 2014).

Joseon who were interested in the advanced Western technology. Books on Western civilization, culture, and geography were imported via the Qing Dynasty, and Catholicism was also introduced to Korea in the seventeenth century (Lee, 2003). Although the kings in the sixteenth and seventeenth centuries were not officially against Western influence, the propagation of Catholicism in Korea was increasingly perceived as a grave threat to the monarch. As such, the Western influence, often equated with Christianity, was prohibited in the Joseon Dynasty.

The *Swaegook* policy in the nineteenth century was further strengthened by a series of war states with France and the U.S. The nationwide, systematic persecution toward Roman Catholicism in Korea resulted in large-scale martyrdom. The Byeong'in Persecution in 1866 ended in the execution of nine out of 12 French priests in Korea, and Father Felix-Clair Ridel took refuge from Korea in China and reported this confrontation to France. To protect French missionaries in Korea, a naval fleet of seven warships from Indochina occupied Ganghwa Island, west of Korea, in October 1866. They requested punishment for the persecution of French priests and a commercial treaty between France and Korea. However, Daewongun, the regency on behalf of the then young King Gojong, ignored the French request and ordered a military campaign against the French navy stationed in Ganghwa Island. The French navy, attacked by surprise, reported three war casualties and retreated from Korea. In the same year, the General Sherman incident occurred. An American armed merchant marine steamer, named General Sherman, was burnt and destroyed by Koreans in Pyeongyang (currently the capital city of North Korea) in August 1866. This vessel demanded trade with Koreans in Pyongyang, but this was evidently a violation of Korea's official seclusion policy. Despite a couple of diplomatic negotiations between the U.S. crew members and the Korean officers, Daewongun, the regency, ordered the vessel leave immediately or all crew aboard would face execution. However, the regency's order was not delivered to the crew members in the vessel, and General Sherman kept demanding trade. As a result, the vessel was sunk after 4 days of fierce battle between the two parties. From 1866 to 1868, the U.S. continued their demand for repatriating the crew of General Sherman in the case of their survival and signing a commercial treaty between the U.S. and Korea, which was refused by the Joseon Dynasty. Under these aggravating mutual relations, to initiate diplomatic relations with Korea and demand an official apology for the General Sherman incident, a fleet of five warships were dispatched from the port of Nagasaki, Japan, to Ganghwa Island. Disregarded by Korea, on June 10, 1871, the U.S. Navy attacked various locations in Ganghwa Island. It did not take long for the U.S. to win the battle with their superior modern weaponry. However, the official seclusion policy of the Joseon Dynasty was unflagging, and the U.S. Navy left for China on July 3, 1871. This incident was later called Sinmiyangyo (辛未洋擾, literal meaning "Western disturbance in the Shinmi year," i.e., 1871), or the U.S.-Korea War of 1871.

Sinmiyangyo saw Korea utterly defeated. It was also a symbolic incident showing the omnipotence of the industrial revolution represented by the U.S. naval weaponry. However, Daewongun responded to the Western power by erecting the monument of Cheokhwa (斥和), meaning "Repel Foreign Nations," in 1871. He believed that the

Western civilization must be demolished in Korea. By erecting such monuments in more than 200 places across the Korean peninsula, he reaffirmed his unflagging volition to adhere to the seclusion policy in order to maintain Korean sovereignty and independence.

Although the Joseon Dynasty endeavored to isolate Korea from the Western countries and remained "the hermit nation" (Griffis, 1882), Daewongun, the regency, could not keep disregarding the frequent requests from the U.S., either directly or diplomatically, through China. As a result, from April to May 1882, diplomatic efforts were commenced between the U.S. and Korea, and finally the 14 Article Treaty was approved by Commodore Robert William Shufeldt, the U.S. representative, and Plenipotentiary Shin Heon and Deputy-plenipotentiary Kim Hong-jip, the Korean representatives. The Treaty of Peace, Amity, Commerce, and Navigation was effective from May 22, 1882, till the moment of annexation of Korea by Japan on August 29, 1910. As explained in the introduction, because of the lack of competent English-Korean translators in Korea, double translation by Tang Xiaoyi (唐紹儀) was used at the time of the treaty (Kim, 2016; Kwon & Kim, 2010). The two Korean representatives wrote their conditions and terms on a sheet of paper in classical Chinese characters. Mr. Tang translated them into English for the U.S. representative.

2.2   The Spread of English Language in the Late Nineteenth Century Korea

Immediately after the Treaty between Korea and the U.S. was ratified, Korea was forced to begin diplomatic negotiations to establish similar treaties with other European nations such as the U.K., Germany, Russia, and France. It did not take long for Koreans to realize the need to learn foreign languages for diplomacy and commerce with these Western nations. The Joseon Dynasty, at the governmental level, had educated a small number of translators for Chinese, Japanese, Mongol, and Jurchen (Chung, 2014). However, these translators were mostly for trades with Korea's neighboring countries. Despite the fact that Korea initially made contact with Westerners in the Qing Dynasty China in the sixteenth century and scholarly knowledge of the alphabet letters was spread in the mid-nineteenth century (Kim, 2011), no systematic training in English or any other European languages began until the establishment of Dongmunhak (同文學), the Government English Translation School.

Inspired by China's *Tongwenguan* (同文館) established in Beijing in 1863 after the defeat of the Opium War, P. G. von Mülledorf (1848–1901), a German scholar and diplomat and the advisor on foreign policy to Korea, took the lead on the foundation of Dongmunhak, mainly for training foreign language translators working at customs offices. Mr. T. E. Halifax, a British telegraphic engineer, was appointed as the head teacher, and two U.K.-born Chinese teachers assisted Halifax

(Choi, 2006; Park, 1974). According to Choi (2006), the education in Dongmunhak was 1 year long, and the students were mainly instructed with British textbooks. It is assumed that the students at Dongmunhak learned both written and spoken English in four sub-skills (reading, writing, speaking, and listening). Choi (2006) states that the students had to intensively study English sentence structures along with vocabulary and spellings for 1 day, and the next day an intensive vocabulary lesson followed. Based on this information, it seems that the main teaching method used in Dongmunhak was the Grammar-Translation Method (GTM).

Mr. George W. Knox, a missionary of the U.S. Presbyterian Church, reported the Korean situation regarding Dongmunhak in his letter to the U.S. in 1883 as follows:

> ... Advice from Corea states that an English school has been established in the capital, with English-Chinamen as teachers, and already had seventy students. It is purposed to engage Americans or Englishmen as teachers as soon as possible. Evidently the Coreans feel the importance of Western learning. (cited in Kim, 2011, p. 240)

However, given the primary purpose of Dongmunhak, the graduates needed to perform accurate translation between English and Korean to measure the right amount of foreign trade tax and expedite customs declaration. Thus, intensive training in the correct interpretation of English sentences and an extensive vocabulary must have been required for the 1 year, fast-track interpreter training language course. In this regard, English education at Dongmunhak can be considered an example of English for specific purposes (ESP).

Although Dongmunhak adopted the GTM, it should be noted that this teaching method was welcomed by foreign teachers such as Mr. Halifax, Mr. Tang Xiaoyi, and Mr. Oh Joonghyun, who were all very fluent in English. Despite the heavy emphasis on formal sentence structure and the memorization of the English word list due to the characteristics of the GTM, the communication between the instructors and the students was conducted in English, since the instructors did not have Korean language skills. This implies that the instruction at Dongmunhak shows a similarity to English immersion.[2]

In retrospect, Dongmunhak paved the way for the establishment of Yookyeong'gongwon (育英公院), or the Royal English School, in 1886 (see below). The primary purpose of Dongmunhak was to train English-Korean translators and allocate them to various public offices where English communication was required. Therefore, it had a compact curriculum emphasizing hands-on practical translation. For example, Mr. Namgung Eok (1863–1939), the first graduate of Dongmunhak, attended this English school from September 1883 to January

---

[2]Kim (2011) argued that Dongmunhak adopted the Direct Method as the instructors were fluent English speakers. However, Mr. Ko Yeong-chul, the first English learner in Korea, after completing his basic English training in China, was hired as a government officer at Dongmunhak (Kim, 2011, p. 182), and his role was to facilitate the communication between English instructors and the students enrolled in Dongmunhak. In this process, Mr. Ko needed to use Korean with the students to resolve any potential miscommunication between the instructors and the students. Besides, the heavy emphasis on practical English for the customs office seems to have placed an inherent limitation on the systematic instruction through the direct method in its original form.

30, 1884—that is, only for 4 months—before graduation (Moon, 1976). In general, the Dongmunhak graduates worked as government officers in various government offices, including customs' offices. Moreover, several of them were selected to serve as teaching assistants in Yookyeong'gongwon. Thus, despite its short duration, Dongmunhak succeeded in functioning as an interim institution for English-Korean translators (Moon, 1976).

King Gojong, unlike his father, Daewongun, the regent, had a keen interest in the modernization of Korea. Immediately after the ratification of the Treaty between Korea and the U.S., he dispatched His Excellency Min Yeong'ik (1860–1914) as a goodwill ambassador to the U.S. Mr. Min and his fellow subordinates, starting from San Francisco, visited major cities across the U.S., met President Chester Allen Arthur in New York, and traveled to Europe. Having experienced Western civilization, upon arrival to Korea, Min Yeong'ik strongly urged the king to establish a regular, Western-style language school. As a result, King Gojong approved the establishment of the Royal English School in September 1884 (Moon, 1976). At the same time, King Gojong's subordinates also proposed the selection of young, talented boys from among his subjects to extensively study and acquire knowledge in Western languages and civilizations (Kim, 1997).

Yookyeong'gongwon, the Royal English School, is the first official, comprehensive English language institute. As stated above, Dongmunhak did not provide comprehensive English language instruction. It was mainly for training English-Korean interpreters working at the custom's offices at major ports in Korea. King Gojong and his Korean government sent a diplomatic letter to the U.S. requesting young educated Americans who could teach English to selected Korean youths. After the U.S. reviewed this request, three college graduates were selected and dispatched to Seoul, Korea. G. W. Gilmore, D. A. Bunker, and H. B. Hulbert, all graduates of the Union Seminary in New York, arrived in Korea in July 1886 and took a leading role in opening Yookyeong'gongwon on September 23 (Kim, 1997).

Compared to Dongmunhak, the curriculum of this school was more systematic. According to the Charter of Yookyeong'gongwon Curriculum, this school had two Chambers—Left and Right. In the Left Chamber, only ten junior officers who had already passed *gwageo*—the Royal officer appointment exam—and were adroit in language were granted admission. In the Right Chamber, 20 talented youths between 15 and 20 years of age from a high social class (all *Yangban*, or the ruling gentry class) were admitted. The educational expenses at Yookyeong'gongwon were fully covered by the Korean government; thus, education was free for the students. The duration of the study was flexible; once they passed the "Grand Exam" administered every 3 years, they were considered to have sufficient knowledge of English.

Choi (2006) reported that not only the three American missionary teachers but an English teacher from China and the interpreters who graduated from Dongmunhak supported the foreign language education in Yookyeong'gongwon. King Gojong was enthusiastic about establishing this school and selected the students himself. Gilmore, one of the teachers, reported that since the students were well versed in memorizing Chinese characters and had cultivated principled study habits while preparing for *gwageo,* they learned English words at a remarkably fast speed, memorizing 3000 words in the first 10 months. Noticing the students' accomplishment, all the teachers exerted great efforts in their teaching (Park, 1974). Upon his arrival in Korea, remarking on the students at Yookyeong'gongwon, Gilmore (1892) stated:

> Houses had been bought and partly prepared for our occupation, school-buildings and quarters for the scholars [i.e., students] were well underway, and everything looked promising. However, the proverbial slowness of the Orient harassed us, and it was the last week in September before we got to work. The pupils belonged to the nobility and were appointed by the king. Thirty-five were named as our first class, of whom thirty began attendance on the exercises. We found that not one of them knew a word of English so that we had to begin with the alphabet. Three interpreters were attached to the school, one for each of the teachers [i.e., Mr. Gilmore, Mr. Bunker, and Mr. Hulbert]. There we found helpful at the start, though we could soon have dispensed with their services. ... The scholars learned very rapidly. Their memories had been developed by the study of Chinese. Our teaching was by daily praxis. As soon as the scholars had learned a small vocabulary, natural science and mathematics were brought before them, and they learned English through these channels. (Gilmore, 1892, pp. 229–230).

As indicated above, it needs to be noted that all the English education adopted in Yookyeong'gongwon was conducted in English because the three American teachers had barely any knowledge of Korean. Although there were interpreters in the school, who were former Dongmunhak students, it seemed that their role was fairly limited because the education conducted in Yookyeong'gongwon aimed at comprehensive tertiary education. For the interpreters who learned English in Dongmunhak only for a year or less, it would be beyond their capability to engage in simultaneous interpretation for the various subjects instructed in Yookyeong'gongwon and translate them into Korean for the students. It is also notable that English immersion was found in the form of content-based instruction. As Gilmore stated, once the students acquired the essential English words, English was adopted as the instructional language in various school subjects, including mathematics and natural sciences.

In addition to Gilmore's (1892) comments above, Kim (1997) also reported that the curriculum at Yookyeong'gongwon was not limited to English language instruction but included "Western studies" as well. As the students' English proficiency increased, the school curriculum was expanded to include economics, history, politics, and geography. Textbooks for these subjects were imported directly from the U.S. Based on the historical information above, it seems that the education in Yookyeong'gongwon was similar to the Direct Method (Richards & Rodgers, 2014) or Immersion education (Cummins, 1992), where the target language is taught in the target language per se.

However, English education at the school did not last long. It was discontinued in 1893 and was merged into the English School founded by Mr. Hutchinson, a British teacher (Kim, 1997). As stated above, the students, particularly in the Left Chamber, were already government officers, and they did not have to learn English for employment purposes. Further, the students in the Right Chamber did not have to study hard and graduate from Yookyeong'gongwon. At the time of modernization in Korea, the demand for English-educated students far exceeded the supply. Thus, once these students acquired a moderate level of English proficiency, they were offered various profitable jobs.

Thus, the initial zeal toward the English language gradually waned in Yookyeong'gongwon. Students' high level of instrumental motivation (Gardner, 1985) for "getting rank" or occupying a high social status in public venues and leading an affluent life, paradoxically, functioned as a strong demotivator to continue their English learning once they were hired by a governmental bureau and their instrumental needs were met. Besides, the tight budget of the Korean government could not sustain the Royal English School. Disheartened, all three American teachers, first Gilmore, then Hulbert, and finally Bunker, resigned from the school and returned to the U.S. (Paik, 1929).

In summary, Yookyeong'gongwon had fulfilled its historic role in that it boasted a much more systematic and comprehensive curriculum than that of Dongmunhak. Furthermore, the establishment of this Royal English School was the first governmental effort to introduce Western-style education to Koreans. It is noteworthy to find a prototype of English immersion education for the students in this school. Yookyeong'gongwon was succeeded by the English School by Mr. Hutchinson, and subsequently by Public Hansung (i.e., Seoul) Foreign Language School.

2.3   The Early Contribution of Protestant Missionary Schools to English Education

Together with the public, governmental effort to establish the Royal English School, the active role of Christian missionaries in the nineteenth century English education in Korea should be noted. The first Christian mission can be traced back to 1794 when Chinese Catholic Father, Joo Mun-mo (周文谟, Zhou Wenmo Jacob), entered Korea. The monotheism of Christianity was regarded as a potential threat to the maintenance of the Joseon Dynasty, which officially accredited Confucianism as the only national ideology. As a result, early Catholicism met enormous persecution from the Joseon government. According to Catholic Bishops' Conference of Korea (2018), it is estimated that at least 1800 Koreans suffered martyrdom in four major persecutions in Korea: the Sinyu Persecution in 1801, Kihae in 1839, Byeong'o in 1846, and Byeong'in in 1866.

Compared to the active propagation of Roman Catholicism in Korea, it was not until the 1880s that the Protestants became active. After the Korea-U.S. Treaty in 1882, a group of American Christian missionaries entered Korea and started propagating Christianity. The propagation of Protestant Christianity in Korea evolved in a different way from that of Roman Catholics. Instead of establishing churches, the missionaries endeavored to found Western schools for education and medicine, and thus many mission secondary schools were established from the 1880s onward (Kim, 1997). These included Paichai Hakdang (founded by H. G. Appenzeller in 1885), Ewha Hakdang (by Mary F. Scranton in 1886), and Kyeongsin School (by H. G. Underwood in 1886). Chejungwon, the first Western medical clinic, was also established in 1885 by Horace Newton Allen (1858–1932), an American doctor and missionary.

Note that these missionary schools used English as the medium of communication and instruction. The missionaries did not have sufficient Korean proficiency, and terms and technical words, particularly in the field of medicine, did not have corresponding Korean words since the contents and concepts did not exist in Korea before. Consequently, similar to Yookyeong'gongwon, established in the same period, English became the language of instruction within these missionary schools, adopting the Direct Method and English immersion approaches. As the early Christian missionaries tried to use education and medicine as the tools for propagating Christianity, Bible study was usually included in their school curricula. In all cases, English, both oral and written, was used, which significantly contributed to English education in Korea. Various high school subjects were introduced in these schools, including mathematics, physics, chemistry, and hygiene education—all instructed in English. According to Lee (2014), these missionary schools aimed to educate and train Korean youths as future missionaries in Korea. Additionally, class discussion was encouraged in these schools, which reflects the influence of American school culture.

It should be noted that King Gojong was also supportive of establishing Western-style educational institutions. He showed personal favor toward American missionaries, and this seems related to the report from His Excellency Min Yeong'ik and other high-ranking officers. While the reasons for this favorable attitude are unclear, two significant factors can be attributed to the king's favoritism toward the U.S. and the English language used in this potential amicable country. The first factor was "the good offices" condition included in the Korea-U.S. Treaty of 1882. The contents of Article I in the Treaty are as follows:

ARTICLE I.
    There shall be perpetual peace and friendship between the President of the United States and the King of Chosen and the citizens and subjects of their respective Governments.
    If other powers deal unjustly or oppressively with either Government, the other will exert their good offices on being informed of the case, to bring about an amicable arrangement, thus showing their friendly feelings.

King Gojong seemed to have emphasized the good offices condition above and expected that the U.S. would protect Korea in the case of warfare (Han, 2006). He believed that the U.S. would dispatch its armed forces to Korea even before the time of forceful annexation with Japan in 1910. However, contrary to his (naïve) expectation, the U.S. government considered the above condition as a diplomatic cliché that did not have tangible binding forces between the two nations.[3]

---

[3]History demonstrates the fact that among the foreign nations that opened their legations in Korea, the U.S. was the first nation to withdraw it, which was due to the result of the Teft-Katsura Secret Agreement between the U.S. and Japan in the aftermath of Japan's victory in the Russo-Japanese War in 1905. The U.S. sanctioned Japan's occupying Korea, and in return Japan sanctioned the U.S. occupation of the Philippines (Esthus, 1959).

Moreover, advanced Western medical practice saved the life of Mr. Min Yeong'ik, the high-ranking officer and kin to the Queen. The U.S. expertise impressed the king and contributed to his preference for the U.S. over other nations. Dr. H. N. Allen, the doctor who saved Mr. Min Yeong'ik, reported the incident in detail in his diary entries as follows.

December 5, Friday, 1884
    ... We retired about 10:30 but had barely gotten... in bed when a great shout of many men was heard. Our gate here was violently rung, and a foreigner kept calling for me.
    I went into the sitting room and found Mr. Scudder, Secretary to the U.S. Legation, with a note for me from Mr. Paul G. von Moellendorf urging me to come to his place at once as he had a dying man on his hand. Mr. Scudder then explained that that evening the foreign officials were all in attendance upon a dinner party at the foreign office (Moellendorff) and that an alarm of fire was heard and Min Yong Ik, one of the most prominent Corean nobleman, cousin to the Queen, ran out to see where the fire was and was cut down with a sword by an unknown person. This Min Yong Ik was the Ambassador to the U.S., a progressive man and one in favor of foreign relations.
    ... I found the patient [Min Yong Ik] in a horrible condition all blood and gore and attended by fourteen Corean doctors who made great objections to my hemic measures. ... I tied the bleeding temporal artery, put a silk suture in the divide temple, two in the cartilage of the ear, four in the neck, and two deep silver ones in the back. (pp. 407–409)

March 27, Friday, 1885
    Today I was called to treat the King and Queen for the first time. They are just recovering from the varioloid and asked me to remove the sequence, which in the King is a trouble of his throat, and the Queen has a swelling in her ear. It was not satisfactory as I could not see them. Having simply to depend upon the statement of a nobleman who came for them. (p. 457)

May 29, Friday, 1885
    This morning I have on a dressing gown made of quilted silk of a changeable bronze color sent as a present from the King and Queen. ...
    The hospital is doing well. The petition which I sent in was kindly granted in a spirit very favorable to me. ... (pp. 466–467)

As described in Allen's (1991) diary, King Gojong had a favorable attitude toward U.S. medicine after the recovery of Min Yeong'ik. Under the auspices of the throne, Allen's hospital and, by extension, the Western civilization represented by the U.S. thrived in Korea in the late nineteenth century. It did not take more than a decade for Koreans to realize that English is the language of commerce and international communication. The following excerpt from Ko Young-Hee, Deputy-Minister of Education of the Korean Empire, recognizes the power of the English language.

Regarding the Western languages used in different European countries, English is widely used for international trade, French is for diplomacy, and German is for military system and law... (Hansungsoonbo, September 17, 1898 cited in Kim, 2011, p. 82)

Lew (1994) also highlighted the positive attitude toward the U.S. in the early newspapers published in Korea at the turn of the century. As a method of enlightenment for Korea, Seo Jae-pil (1864–1951), who acquired U.S. citizenship and was renamed as Dr. Philip Jaisohn, organized *Dongnip Hyeophoe* (meaning The

Independence Association) and published its newspaper, titled *Dongnip Shinmun*, or The Independent, in 1896. The publication of this newspaper lasted for 3 years and 8 months from April 7, 1896, to December 4, 1899. Since it was published by Dr. Seo Jae-pil and then by Mr. Yun Chi-Ho, both of whom stayed and studied in the U.S. for a considerable period of time, The Independent maintained a positive attitude toward the U.S. According to Lew (1994), the following excerpt from the editorial of The Independent epitomized the pro-American attitude.

> In this nation (i.e., the U.S.), people's argument is based on the sense of honor. In addition, there are a multitude of social custom and businesses following the disposition of Providence and compassion when they manage every aspect of worldly affairs including political matters and human right. Thus, with the auspices of the heaven, this nation became the most prosperous in the globe and the foremost nation enjoying its peaceful blessings. (The Independent, October 16, 1897, cited in Lew, 1994, p. 73)

Undoubtedly, the influence of the Korean newspapers during this period must have contributed to the creation of a pro-American attitude among Koreans and a positive attitude toward English, the language used in this nation.

With the growing popularity of English, many Koreans in major cities across Korea started to attend these missionary schools mainly to learn English, rather than for Christianity itself. As Koreans who learned English from these schools graduated and worked as teachers in the same schools, the emphasis on English education gradually decreased in these missionary schools; the language of instruction tended to be replaced from English to Korean gradually. The primary purpose of the missionary schools was not English education but the teaching of Western civilization, and through the enlightenment they intended to indirectly propagate Christianity. Paichai Hakdang, one of the first missionary schools, decided to decrease the proportion of English instruction in 1902 and remove English classes in 1903 entirely. As a consequence, the enrollment of Korean students in this school decreased dramatically, to the extent of risking the normal operation of Paichai. In the end, they changed the school policy of free education for all, and students who wanted to learn English began paying tuition fees (Paik, 1929).

Given the above anecdotal episodes and historical facts, the primary motivation for Koreans who learned English in the nineteenth century from the missionaries in Protestant schools across Korea was primarily instrumental. In other words, they learned English to get a secure, well-paid, stable job. In the late nineteenth century, according to Cho (2017), the Joseon Dynasty was strictly operated by a hierarchical caste system, "in which commoners, or *sangmin*, made up 90% of the population and constantly suffered from the tyranny of aristocrats" (p. 46). He continues:

> [U]nder such circumstances, mobility desires continued to grow, and English was one of the very few tools available to commoners to change their future. With an increasing number of English-Korean interpreters achieving both a title and wealth through English alone, English was legitimatized and validated as a golden tongue for the general public. (Cho, 2017, p. 46)

The ultimate goal of Western (mostly American) English teachers was to propagate Christianity by means of education; however, they kept teaching English by using English immersion or the direct method and contributed to the spread of secondary school education to Korean youths. For this reason, the missionary schools at the turn of the twentieth century in Korea played a significant educational role in the modernization process in Korea. The following subsections summarize the curriculum and education in three primary missionary schools: Paichai Hakdang, Ewha Hakdang, and Kyeongsin Schools.

2.3.1   Paichai Hakdang (培材學堂)

Henry G. Appenzeller (1858–1902), a Methodist missionary, established the first missionary school for boys, Paichai Hakdang (currently Paichai High School and Paichai University), in Seoul in February 1885. Kim (1997) stated that the primary purpose of this school was to teach English to Korean youths, but according to Appenzeller (n.d.), this school aimed to educate and graduate students well versed in liberal education. Since this school was the first of its kind, in 1887, 2 years after its establishment, the number of students rose to 67, and in 1889 there were 82 students (Paik, 1929, p. 129). It is noteworthy that King Gojong officially approved this school and named it Paichai Hakdang, which literally means "Hall of Rearing Useful Men." The Korean government selected several talented students from this school and appointed them to official posts (Paik, 1929). The king's special auspices soon spread among Koreans, which was beneficial for the steady growth of student enrollment in Paichai Hakdang.

The principal subject instructed was English. The Korean students in Paichai Hakdang were keen on learning English to be successful or to "get rank" in the hierarchical Korean society. Contrary to the fact that Yookyeong'gongwon, the Royal English school, was established and the students were either government officers currently holding positions or sons of ruling *yangban* class, learning English language at Paichai Hakdang was open to the general public. Learning English at Paichai must have been regarded as a convenient tool to secure employment and promotions, and eventually revive one's fortunes. In 1886, reporting Koreans' enthusiasm toward English, Appenzeller himself remarked:

> The enthusiasm for the study of English has always been great among the Koreans. A little knowledge of the new tongue [i.e., English] was and still is a stepping stone to something higher. Ask a Korean 'why do you wish to study English?' and his invariable answer will be 'to get rank.' (cited in Paik, 1929, p. 129).

2.3.2   Ewha Hakdang (梨花學堂)

Ewha Hakdang (currently Ewha Girls' High School and Ewha Womans University) was established by Mary F. Scranton (1832–1909) in Jeong-dong, Seoul, on May 31, 1886. This school is recorded as the first modern educational institute for Korean women. Scranton left the following memoir at the foundation of this school.

> It began with one scholar. She was the concubine of an official who was desirous his wife should learn English, with the hope that she might sometime become an interpreter for the Queen. (The Korean Repository, January 1896, cited in Paik, 1929)

The curriculum at Ewha Hakdang was, at first, primarily about the Lord's Prayer or various hymns in English but soon expanded to include English grammar, mathematics, Korean, music, history, and calligraphy. The language of instruction was mainly English, and Korean was used for supplementary purposes. Moon (1976) mentioned that English-medium instruction at Ewha was conducted not because this school emphasized English education but because the instructors (mostly missionaries) did not have sufficient command of Korean. This was corroborated by the memoir of Kim Rosa, a graduate of the early-stage Ewha Hakdang:

> Once admitted to the school, I started to play house. They taught me the Lord's Prayer or hymns in English, and we had an increasing number of teachers. From the beginning, the missionaries [i.e., teachers] taught all the contents in English without using an interpreter. (cited in Moon, 1976, p. 631)

This school continued emphasizing English education in the early twentieth century, and according to *Hwangseong Shinmun* on September 17, 1908, the recruitment of Ewha Hakdang students stated that this school had offered comprehensive education for Korean women encompassing elementary, secondary, and tertiary school levels; English was included as the school's subject both at the elementary and secondary levels, and English literature was at the tertiary level. Thus, Ewha Hakdang seems to have continued English instruction at the turn of the twentieth century.

2.3.3   Kyeongsin School (儆新學校)

Kyeongsin School, commonly known as Underwood School, was established in Jeong-dong, Seoul, in 1886 by Horace G. Underwood (1859–1916), an American Presbyterian missionary, for the propagation of Christianity and youth education. He recruited 20 orphans for this boarding school and began teaching Chinese letters and simple English conversation. Unlike Paichai and Ewha Hakdangs, English did not seem to be the main focus of the curriculum in this school. Lillias Horton Underwood, the wife of Horace G. Underwood, left the following memoir:

> ... After breakfast follow a few English lessons (we have decided to teach very little English, as the best experience of the oldest missionaries in the field is against it), and a Bible lesson. These recitations are interspersed with short recesses and the afternoons are given to play and study hours, and Chinese, which is the most important factor in the education of Koreans. (Underwood, 1890, cited in Paik, 1929, p. 131)

Although Kim (1997) stated that English was one of the most important school subjects, Paik (1929) highlighted that the fundamental function of this school was to educate orphans in the modern school system. In 1901, Kyeongsin School placed more emphasis on secondary education where English continued to be taught (Kim, 1997).

As shown in the three modern schools, to varying degrees, English was taught as one of the crucial school subjects, and in many cases was used as the language of instruction. The writing of Lillian Horton Underwood in 1890 reveals that the U.S. missionaries were already aware of the shortcomings of instructing English language first at their educational institutions. As the case of Paichai Hakdang shows, for most Korean youths the primary purpose of school enrollment was to learn English, and after reaching communicative level in English, they often voluntarily quit attending school. Given that the founding year of Paichai Hakdang was 1885 and that of Ewha was 1886, for less than 5 years, Korean youths' primary motivation for school enrollment seems to have been widely known to Protestant missionaries in Korea.

2.4 English Learning Motivation at the Turn of the Twentieth Century

The utilitarian nature of English learning had been consolidated at the turn of the twentieth century when the Korean Empire gradually came under the control of Japan and other Western countries. English instruction at the turn of the century became relatively stable and systematic compared with that conducted in Dongmunhak or Yookyeong'gongwon in previous decades. Nonetheless, throughout the following two decades in the 1890s and 1900s, the desire to be successful in pre-modern Korean society was reflected in English learning.

In the nineteenth century, *yangban*, the ruling class in Korea, consolidated and inherited their higher social status and economic prosperity through *gwageo*. Since the *gwageo* system tested the applicants' knowledge in Chinese classics in a series of essay tests, the system per se was regarded fair as long as it was administered and monitored meticulously. In the stratified social hierarchy in Joseon, the *gwageo* test was the only means to rise from humble beginnings and maintain their current status as *yangban*. For this reason, young Korean men prepared for this exam over decades.

However, in the late decades of the Joseon Dynasty, the overall management of this high-stakes test lost its rigor. The ruling *yangban* class used various illegal means, which included using substitute exam-takers, cheating on the test after bribing the proctors, and marking a special memo at the margin of the paper to reveal the test takers' identity. All these measures were possible only for the wealthy ruling class, and those intelligent but born to a low-income family could not pass the exam.

Ushered in by the Korea-U.S. Treaty in 1882, the modernization process was expedited in Korea, and a few pioneers such as Mr. Kim Hongjip (the lieutenant officer at the Korea-U.S. Treaty of 1882), Rhee Syngman, and Yun Chi-ho, who were sympathetic to the Western civilization, endeavored to introduce a government-initiated, top-down reform. *Gwageo*, maintained for approximately a thousand years from the Goryeo Dynasty, was perceived as the symbol of *Ancien Régime* inhibiting the immediate industrialization. Thus, by implementing the Gabo Reform in 1894, the *gwageo* examination was abolished entirely.

Abolishing the *gwageo* system resulted in a remarkable aftermath in the Joseon society. The ruling *yangban* class, represented by the successful passing of this exam and appointment as a government officer, suddenly fell in their standing. The means to inherit their prestige and wealth was the *gwageo* exam, which was entirely abandoned. In this political turmoil, however, the graduates of the public English institutes (e.g., Yookyeong'gongwon) or the missionary schools (e.g., Paichai Hakdang) rapidly gained access to government positions. As mentioned above, even when the *gwageo* was maintained, because of the high volume of demand, most students who started to learn English in either a public foreign language school or a private school ended up discontinuing their English learning to pursue the numerous English-related job offers. Several prominent figures in the period could ascend to high ranks in the transitional Korean society. In this subsection, His Excellency Lee Ha-Young's life will be introduced first, and Dr. Rhee Syngman's story about English learning will be explained, followed by Mr. Yun Chi-Ho's contribution to the enlightenment of Korea.

2.4.1   Lee Ha-Young, Korean Deputy-Ambassador to the U.S.

It would not be a hyperbole to state that a modicum of knowledge in English in the transitional era in nineteenth-century Korea would lead to a high-ranking social status. The story of Mr. Lee Ha-Young (1858–1929) had long been regarded as an exemplary case demonstrating the powerful efficacy of the English language. His unprecedented rise through English would be beyond the description of any movie or novel. Lee Ha-Young, born in 1858, was from a humble origin; it is even reported that he was an illiterate *mochi* (i.e., Japanese rice cake stuffed with red bean paste) vendor (Cho, 2017) and once begged at *Tongdosa*, a Buddhist temple located in southern Korea (Jeon, 2006). While working as a clerk at a Japanese-owned store in Busan, Korea, for 8 years, Mr. Lee Ha-Young started his own business in 1884 in Nagasaki, Japan, but his colleague betrayed him and fled with his business investment. Disheartened, Mr. Lee was onboard heading back to Busan from Nagasaki. It was a mere coincidence that he met Dr. H. N. Allen on the ferry. He recounted this as follows:

> In the fall of 1884, I encountered an extraordinarily talented man in a foreign land. I met a doctor called Allen on board on my way back from Nagasaki, Japan. Dr. Allen approached me warm-heartedly, although we were total strangers. He said he was dispatched to the Orient to promote Western medicine. . . . Befriended as if old friends, we landed on the port of Incheon. I was the first close friend that Allen made in Joseon. (Lee, 1926, cited in Jeon, 2006)

Although it is unclear how the two young fellows of the same age (both born in 1858) could communicate, Dr. Allen must be the symbol of fortune for Mr. Lee Ha-Young. He began working as a cook helper for Allen, whose status in Joseon was also quite unstable. However, Dr. Allen suddenly advanced in his profession because of the failed assassination of His Excellency Min Yeong'ik (see Dr. Allen's diary in Sect. 2.3). As stated above, Allen was called upon to conduct an emergency operation on him on December 5, 1884, and Mr. Min Yeong'ik survived with his help. Lee Ha-Young accompanied the doctor to aid translation, and despite his lack of proficiency in English, Mr. Lee Ha-Young, in the eyes of English illiterates, was regarded as an elite scholar who was also proficient in Western civilization. His Excellency Min Yeong'ik soon introduced Dr. Allen and Mr. Lee Ha-Young to King Gojong and the queen. For his medical finesse, Dr. Allen was appointed as the court physician in 1885, and Mr. Lee Ha-Young accompanied the new court physician. As the royal law prohibited the access of humble men to the palace, Mr. Lee Ha-Young was granted an official rank of Oi'amoon Joosa (外衙門 主事, meaning, the seventh rank officer at the Ministry of Foreign Affairs).

Mr. Lee Ha-Young began his government position as an examination administrator at Yookyeong'gongwon in 1885, where the sons of *yangban* class and the current government officers learned English. In the Joseon Dynasty, it was a true rarity for a person from a humble social class to have a higher status in government than the *yangban* class. With the recommendation of Min Yeong'ik, Mr. Lee was promoted to the position of royal translator of the king. With His Excellency Park Jung-Yang, the first Korean ambassador to the U.S. and his entourage, he was dispatched to the U.S., granted an audience with President Cleveland at the White House in January 1888 and subsequently, contributed to the establishment of the Korean Legation in Washington D.C. in 1889 (Old Korean Legation, 2019).

After staying in D.C. for a year and a half, Lee Ha-Young returned to Korea and continued to seize fast-track opportunities. After serving as a local governor, he was appointed as the Deputy Vice Minister of the Ministry of Foreign Affairs in 1894, and eventually as the Minister of Foreign Affairs in the Korean Empire in 1904 at the age of 47. Within two decades, Mr. Lee witnessed a sea of change in his own fortune—from an obscure cook helper to the head of foreign affairs at the Korean Empire.

However, the historical verdict toward the chronicle of Mr. Lee Ha-Young is not positive by any means. In 1905, he collaborated with other government officers and ceded the diplomatic sovereignty of the Korean Empire to the Japanese Empire. For this act and related matters that expedited the annexation between Korea and Japan, he was knighted baron in 1910, and officially retired from office. He was even more successful after his retirement; in 1922, he established *Daeryook* (i.e., Continental) Rubber Corporation and started producing rubber shoes, which made him a billionaire.

From the perspective of English education, Mr. Lee's success story was spread across Korea and functioned as a living proof of the colossal power of English. In traditional Korean society, where social class was rigidly stratified, this resounding success from humble origins to an authority figure of the nation substantially consolidated the instrumental motivation to learn English. In this success story, other types of motivation, such as integrative and/or intrinsic ones, could hardly be created and considered among Koreans.

2.4.2   Dr. Rhee Syngman, the First President of the Republic of Korea

The life of Rhee Syngman (1875–1965) would be noteworthy not because he was the first president of the Republic of Korea but because he delivered the first public speech in English and was the first Korean to receive a Ph.D. from the West. Throughout his life, he spent almost 40 years in the U.S. while serving as President of the Provisional Government of the Republic of Korea, which was founded overseas in 1919. Born to a remote relative family of the Joseon Dynasty, Dr. Rhee initially learned Chinese classics and prepared for the *gwageo* exam in his late teens. The uncontrolled disorder surrounding the *gwageo* administration resulted in Rhee's continual failure in the royal exam, and he spent all his late teen life (from the age of 13 to 19) in the futile effort of taking this exam (Kang, 2010).

The abolition of *gwageo* from the Gabo Reform in 1894 must have been a groundbreaking threat to Rhee, nullifying the time and energy spent on preparing for the *gwageo*. However, he swiftly modified his career path by deciding to attend Paichai Hakdang, operated by Appenzeller (see Sect. 2.3.1), in November 1894 (Kim, 2011). In the aftermath of the Gabo Reform, talented Korean youths started to learn foreign languages, mainly the English language. Because of his talent and previous Chinese classic learning, it is reported that Rhee Syngman's learning progress in English was extraordinary. Starting from the alphabet with W. A. Noble, the chemistry teacher, Mr. Rhee's English was the best among all Paichai students. In July 1895, within 7 months, with a strong recommendation from D. A. Bunker, another teacher and later the principal of Paichai Hakdang, Rhee Syngman was hired as an English teacher for beginners (Kim, 2011). According to Kim (2011), to make a living while attending the school, Rhee began working as a Korean tutor for Georgiana E. Whiting, a doctor at *Chejungwon*, the Royal Medical Institution. He was paid 20 dollars per month for his Korean tutoring (Kang, 2014). Through this opportunity to have English conversations with native speakers, Rhee developed his English proficiency rapidly.

Rhee Syngman's early career in English is represented by his English public speech at the commencement ceremony of Paichai Hakdang on July 8, 1897. Since Paichai was operated rigorously by a group of U.S. missionaries, 600 guests, including senior officials and the royal family of the Joseon Dynasty, foreign envoys and diplomats, and their families, were all invited. It is reported that among the various programs during the ceremony, Mr. Rhee distinguished himself by making an impassioned English speech (Kim, 2011) on the topic of the independence of

Korea. Owing to the relevance of this topic and the superb logic he advocated, Rhee Syngman was acclaimed by the audience.

After graduation from Paichai, Rhee Syngman was arrested for his radical independence movement and imprisoned in Seoul for more than 4 years. His enthusiasm toward English was not quenched in prison; he kept reading, studying, and memorizing English magazines and the English Bible, which missionaries had sent as personal belongings in custody. After being granted a special pardon in 1904, he went to the U.S. and earned a Bachelor's degree at the George Washington University, an M.A. degree at Harvard, and a Ph.D. at Princeton in June 1910.[4]

Dr. Rhee Syngman's public English speech in 1897 is recorded as the first public speech in English in Korea, and his doctoral degree earned in 1910 is also marked as the first Ph.D. in the Korean history. Dr. Rhee Syngman stayed in the U.S. and exerted his diplomatic effort for Korean independence. After liberation from Japan, Dr. Rhee returned to Korea and was elected as the first president of the Republic of Korea in 1948. Given Dr. Rhee's path of life, his penchant for English would appear to be a natural consequence. He spent most of his life in the U.S., got married to Francesca Donner, an Austria-born American, in 1933, published English books such as *Japan Inside Out,* criticizing the negative consequences of Japanese Imperialism (Rhee, 1941),[5] and kept an English diary for 40 years from 1904 to 1944 (Lew et al., 2015). Thus, one can see that most of the first cabinet members during his presidency were graduates from the U.S. or the U.K.—15 from the U.S. and three from the U.K.

For most Koreans, the lesson from Dr. Rhee Syngman's story was evident: English is the "golden tongue" for success (Cho, 2017). Without his English proficiency, Dr. Rhee Syngman would not have been a prominent figure in the late Joseon Dynasty, and could not have visited the U.S. nor have become the first doctoral degree holder in Korea. The rise of English speakers in Korea in the late nineteenth century and the first half of the twentieth century germinated the idea that the English language was the golden key replacing classical Chinese in the previous *Ancien Régime*. This meant that knowledge of classical Chinese was tested through *gwageo* before the Gabo Reform, but after the abolition of this old exam, proficiency in English and related foreign experiences replaced the role of classical Chinese and the passing of the *gwageo* exam. Therefore, Dr. Rhee Syngman's ultimate success— being elected the founding president of Korea—consolidated the bias toward the efficacy of learning English among Koreans.

---

[4]His Ph.D. dissertation, titled *Neutrality as influenced by the United States*, was published by the Princeton University Press in 1912 (Rhee, 1912), two years after his degree conferment.

[5]After the publication of this book in June 1941, Japan attacked Pearl Harbor in Hawaii in December 1941. As Dr. Rhee had stated that the U.S. would be on warfare with Japan in this book, the book became an instant bestseller.

2.4.3   Mr. Yun Chi-Ho: The Foreign Language "Genius" in Korea

Since the lives of pioneering Koreans who learned English took different career paths, some Koreans devoted themselves to the independence movement of Korea in the early twentieth century, whereas others converted to pro-Japanese ideology or immigrated to the U.S. and acquired its citizenship (e.g., Dr. Seo Jae-pil, or Philip Jaisohn). Perhaps, Mr. Yun Chi-Ho (1865–1945) would be counted as the most talented Korean in foreign languages; he was known to be able to speak English, Chinese, Japanese, and French (Kim, 2006a). After acquiring sizable knowledge in classical Chinese, in 1881, Mr. Yun Chi-Ho was dispatched to Japan as a member of *Sinsayooramdan*, or the Royal Inspection Group to Japan, to understand the Western civilization adopted in Japan. Mr. Yun learned Japanese there in 1882. Besides, he started to learn English from January 16, 1883, with the support of Ernest Francisco Fenollosa at Tokyo University (Kim, 2011). Mr. Yun Chi-Ho also began language exchange with a Dutch officer in Yokohama; in exchange for teaching Korean, he learned English from the officer. According to Kim (2006a), Yun Chi-Ho learned English for one hour every day from January to May 1883 and could complete the first volume of the English textbook titled "English Premier."

However talented Mr. Yun was, his English in 1883 was not at an advanced level by any means. In Joseon at that time, however, he received an opportunity to be hired as a Korean-English translator. Mr. Lucius H. Foote (1826–1913), the first U.S. Envoy Extraordinary and Minister Plenipotentiary to Korea, was desperately looking for a translator, and among Koreans no one but Mr. Yun Chi-Ho had learned English in both Korea and Japan. Thus, hired as an English translator by the U.S. Legation to Korea, he accompanied Mr. Foote when he met King Gojong in the Royal Palace. Kim (2006a) stated that since Yun's Japanese proficiency was far better than his English, another Japanese-English translator translated Mr. Foote's English into Japanese, and then Mr. Yun translated it into Korean for the king, for the first 3 months at the Royal Palace.

Mr. Yun Chi-Ho's fortune continued. On the occasion of Foote's return to the U.S., Yun accompanied him and went to Shanghai to learn English at the Anglo-Chinese College, where he learned English systematically for 4 years. Then he left Shanghai with a recommendation letter from Young J. Allen, the dean of the Anglo-Chinese College, and arrived in Nashville, Tennessee, in November 1888. He studied theology at Vanderbilt University for 2 years (1888–1890) and learned the humanities and natural sciences at Emory University. He left the U.S. in 1893 and returned to the Anglo-Chinese College in Shanghai to start his teaching career.

The Joseon Dynasty soon acknowledged Mr. Yun Chi-Ho's superb English proficiency, and when he returned to Korea he was appointed as the Vice Minister of Education in 1895 and actively participated in a series of enlightenment movements in Korea. During the Japanese colonization, he worked as a secretary general of the YMCA, as the principal of Songdo Higher General School, and as a member of the board of directors at Ewha Womans' College.[6] He is also assumed to have written the lyrics of the National Anthem of Korea (Kim, 2001a).

2.4.4 The Contributions of Early Pioneers of English Learning in Korea

During the period of modernization in Korea, these figures, both from public English institutes and private missionary schools alike, consolidated an excessively strong level of instrumental motivation to learn English among Koreans. Favorable attitudes toward English must have facilitated modernization by educating young students to be competent in understanding the Western civilization and culture in English. Lee (2002) stated that those who learned English at the turn of the century not only served as professional translators and interpreters but were also appointed as government officers in various bureaus in the Joseon Dynasty. In particular, King Gojong tried to consolidate his political power through pro-American diplomacy after the Korea-U.S. Treaty of 1882. Those with a command of working-level English, particularly from Dongmunhak or Yookyeong'gongwon (both public English institutes), were prioritized during the reign of King Gojong (Lee, 2002).

This close connection to the central political power strengthened the instrumental nature of learning English. As Appenzeller commented (cited in Paik, 1929), the primary reason for learning English was employment or "to get rank," not scholarly or religious reasons. After achieving a communicative level of English proficiency, most students quit their learning and sought proper occupations. Governmental positions were the most coveted, notably after the Gabo Reform in 1894, when the *gwageo* exam for selecting officers was abolished officially. Aligned with the king's pro-Americanism, those who graduated from English-related institutes were considered the top candidates for filling government job postings.

Given this sociopolitical milieu, it would be natural to find enthusiasm toward English in the late nineteenth and early twentieth century in Korea. Nobuo Junfei (信夫 淳平), who worked as a Japanese diplomat in Korea in 1900, stated as follows in his book, *The Korean Peninsula*:

> The British Minister to Korea reported the financial situation of Korea two years ago, and among them, mentioning tuition fees spent on foreign languages, he stated that "Koreans have the superb linguistic ability in the East and their enthusiasm toward foreign language education must be second to none. Thus, only 14 years have passed since foreigners have entered Seoul, but Koreans' command of English is incomparable to that of Beijing people. Chinese and Japanese cannot exceed Koreans in terms of excellent command of English." I believe this is by no means a hyperbole. (Nobuo, 1901, p. 126)

Nobuo continues explaining the reason for Koreans' effort to learn foreign languages.

---

[6]The "Womans" in "Ewha Womans' College" is not a typo.

Imagine that Spanish, Italian, Turkish, or Greek embassies are established in Korea. In this case, foreign language schools teaching the above languages will be founded immediately. It is also extremely odd to find the fluctuation in the number of students enrolled in one specific language school. If Japan exerts influence on the Korean government, the Japanese language school is inundated with students, and if Russian power is on the rise, the Russian school is favored. Thus, perhaps the best way to measure the differential influence according to power nations surrounding Korea would be to analyze the vicissitudes of the foreign language schools. . . . Can we educate outstanding individuals in this atmosphere? It would only result in training mediocre interpreters. (Nobuo, 1901, p. 127)

At a macro level, the English fever in the late Joseon Dynasty can be explained from the perspective of Social Darwinism, defined as "an ideology that suggests only the strongest and best-adapted humans should excel in society" (Cho, 2017, p. 44). The historical verdict of this ideology already proved its catastrophic impact in the twentieth century, most notably in the rise of Adolf Hitler and the Holocaust. However, at the turn of the century, Social Darwinism had provided a convenient theoretical justification for imperialism in the West and Japan toward so-called less-developed Third World countries. Japan was also influenced by Social Darwinism, and it would be a natural consequence for Japan to annex Korea on the pretext of developing its society and enlightening the illiterate, less-civilized East Asians.

Note that Social Darwinism seems to have acquired full recognition in the mindset of the pioneers of English learning in Korea. For example, Yun Chi-Ho began writing an English diary from December 7, 1889, a year after arriving in the U.S. to October 1943. For more than 50 years, Yun persistently maintained this habit of English writing. It is not a mere coincidence that Rhee Syngman also kept English logbooks from 1904 to 1944 (Lew et al., 2015). To many Koreans, English was considered the language of civilization represented by the U.S., the most powerful nation in the world. All of these ideas may be related to Social Darwinism. An extreme form of it is presented in the following excerpt from Yun Chi-Ho's English diary written in 1893.

To me a tremendous and interesting fact is that 10 millions of Africans through circumstances beyond their control, have come in possession of one of the richest and noblest languages in the world-the English. Perhaps they have been amply paid, as a race, for their servitude in this one invariable gift. (Yun Chi-Ho Diary, February 17, 1893, cited in Cho, 2017, p. 49)

Cho (2017) attributed Yun Chi-Ho's politically incorrect opinion above to the influence of Social Darwinism. Yun justified that the African Americans' extreme adversity during their slavery could be sufficiently compensated for by the simple fact that they acquired the English language, "one of the richest and noblest languages in the world." In his view, the Joseon Dynasty must have been an under-developed, uncivilized, and powerless feudal nation. In Cho's (2017, p. 49) remark, "English was a medium for Yun to connect him to the idealized 'imagined community' (Norton & Kanno, 2003), away from the helpless and hopeless homeland of which he did not wish to be part."

Additionally, King Gojong's favorable attitude toward the U.S. influenced the love of English, the language of the U.S. King Gojong endeavored to adjust the imperial power relationships between China and Japan through diplomatic interventions from the U.S. As mentioned above, King Gojong developed his preference for the U.S. in the hope of securing the good offices conditions in the Korea-U.S. Treaty of 1882, even to the extent of dispatching the U.S. armed forces to Korea. Jeon (2006), in this regard, argued that Mr. Lee Ha-Young was sent to the U.S. Congress under the secret order of the king to request that the U.S. Army be sent to Korea to stabilize and untangle the unduly interference from the foreign powers infringing the national sovereignty. Although this might not be a historical record, Jeon's argument presents King Gojong's unconditional trust toward the U.S. Cho's (2017) analysis regarding the king's preference toward the U.S. wrote:

> Having reached its zenith of power and influence, the Qing Dynasty of China began to decline due to external wars and internal conflicts while English was growing in Korea. As America came on the scene as a new Elder Brother for Korea, an image largely shaped by pro-American King Gojong, English became strongly attached to "power" which was badly needed not only by commoners suffering from the abuse of the ruling class but also by the country that had been reduced to an arena of competition among great imperial powers. (Cho, 2017, p. 46)

2.4.5 Interim Summary: The Desire to Get Rank and Live Without Starvation

Yookyeong'gongwon was reorganized and reformulated into a Public English Language School in 1894. Public schools teaching other foreign languages were gradually established in Seoul at the turn of the century: the Japanese Language School was established in 1891; the Chinese Language School in 1891; the French Language School in 1895; the Russian Language School in 1896; the German Language School in 1898 (Lee, 2014). These foreign language schools were all merged and renamed as *Hansung Oegookeo Hakgyo* (漢城外國語學校), or Hansung Foreign Language School, which included Hansung (i.e., Seoul) in their school name in 1906. However, this newly established school did not last long after the annexation treaty between the Korean Empire and Japan in 1910. Public Foreign Language School was abolished on November 1, 1911, by Japanese Bylaw 257.

In Public Foreign Language School, students received English instruction for 5 years, and this was the same as other Western languages such as German, French, and Russian (Lee, 2014). It should be noted that compared to the number of newly admitted students and existing students, the number of graduates was remarkably low. Lee (2014) attributes this disparity to the social atmosphere in the 1900s. Students had a high level of instrumental motivation to learn English rather than having intrinsic motivation to sustain their learning process. This means that most students did not find strong motivation to continue studying English if they were offered a better job opportunity while enrolled in the school. During the period of modernization, command of foreign languages was urgently needed in various industries and public offices, and even a little knowledge of English was appreciated in these jobs. In this regard, at the turn of the twentieth century, English learning motivation was clearly related to instrumental motivation reflecting better employment opportunities and job security, all of which enabled them to escape absolute poverty.

2.5   The Japanese Colonization Period

During the period of imperialist Japanese occupation (1910–1945), the Japanese Governor General of Korea (朝鮮総督) rigorously controlled the education system, leading to drastic changes in language learning and its related English learning motivation (Kim, 2016; Kwon, 2000). Learning Japanese became mandatory, and the opportunities for learning English-speaking skills decreased in general. Grammar skills became the main focus of teaching and testing, requiring sophisticated knowledge of English vocabulary and morphosyntactic features (Kim-Rivera, 2002). For those aspiring to attend secondary schools, acquiring English grammar knowledge became necessary. During the colonial period, secondary education for Koreans was restricted, let alone tertiary education, and enrollment in professional colleges and Kyungsung Imperial University[7] through fierce internal competition with compatriots was considered the surest way to a stable life. Thus, competition for college entrance became severe (Seth, 2002).

Kim (2011) argued that Imperial Japan imposed an implicit discrimination policy in English education between Mainland Japan (i.e., 内地 [naichi], inner land) and the annexed Korea (i.e., 外地 [gaichi], outer land). After the deprivation of diplomatic sovereignty in 1905, Japan intervened in education policy in protectorate Korea. In 1906, the Foreign School Act promulgated by the Japanese Resident-General to Korea (統監府) adjusted the goal of educating Koreans to raising practitioners and reduced the duration of English Language School from a 5-year curriculum to a 3-year curriculum, like that in Japanese and Chinese language schools. According to Kim (2011), of the 19 hours spent by 1st-year students weekly, 7 hours were devoted to English reading-translation, 6 hours to English dictation, and 4 hours to English composition-calligraphy. English conversation, where pronunciation was emphasized, was only for 2 hours per week. For 2nd- and 3rd-year students, the situation worsened. The school hours allotted to English reading and grammar were increased, and by contrast, English conversation was taught only 1 hour per week. Thus, English conversation constituted only 5% of the entire curriculum of English School.

---

[7]Kyungsung (or Keijo) Imperial University (京城帝國大學), founded in 1924, was the only comprehensive four-year university in Korea at the time and was also one of the imperial universities across Japan. After the liberation from Japan in 1945, most of the university's facilities were annexed to Seoul National University. Besides Kyungsung Imperial University, quite a few technical colleges had been established either by Korean educators or by foreign missionaries, but none of them were officially accredited by the Japanese Governor General's office.

This worsening situation was closely related to the "Illiteracy Policy" applied to Koreans, particularly imposed during the first decade of the Japanese Colonization Period (from 1910 to 1919).[8] The first decade during the period of Japanese colonization has often been referred to as the Military Control Period. The duration of primary education was shortened to 4 years, that of secondary school was for 2–4 years, and that of tertiary school was for 3–4 years. No comprehensive university education was allowed, and only practical technical college education was conducted. English was instructed as an optional course at secondary schools, and for girls' secondary schools, English was not included in the school curriculum. Since the appointment of secondary school teachers mandated fluency in Japanese, Korean teachers before the colonization period were replaced with Japanese teachers. This meant that Korean secondary school students learned English by using the Japanese language through English teachers coming from Japan. Compared with this illiteracy policy imposed on Korea, the situation in the Japanese archipelago, or mainland Japan, presented a drastically different picture. The English teaching method was surveyed at the national level in 1910, and the first English teaching contest was held in Kyoto in 1913, all of which were intended to increase the overall English proficiency across mainland Japan (Kim, 2011). Additionally, the Ministry of Education in Japan actively invited renowned British scholars to Japan; Harold E. Palmer was invited in 1922, stayed for 14 years, and established the Institute for Research in English Teaching (IRET); A. S. Hornby also joined Palmer's IRET in 1931 and succeeded Palmer's position in 1936 (Smith, 1998). Both made significant contributions to English education in the early twentieth century Japan (see Chap. 5 for detailed information on English education in Japan).

Contrary to the communicative orientation in Japan, in Korea, the meaning of English learning had changed fast from the acquisition of communication skills to memorizing vocabulary and complicated grammar rules for English exams in college admission tests (Kim, 2016). With the increasing level of difficulty, the priority in learning English changed from developing practical oral proficiency to enhancing test-taking techniques, an inevitable wash-back effect of the test format. The instrumentality during the Japanese colonization related more to the desire to obtain a higher English test score than one's peers, a desire not closely related to authentic communicative needs (Hwang, 2014; Kim, 2011). English tests functioned

---

[8]The term "illiteracy policy" would invite a cautious interpretation. The overall literacy rate represented by the primary school enrollment rate was remarkably increased during the Japanese Colonization Period. Based on the annual statistics published by the Government-General of Korea, Kimura (1993) argued that the enrollment rate for boys had risen from 20% in 1912 to 70% in 1940, whereas that for girls had risen from almost nil in 1912 to above 20% in 1940. However, the opportunities to receive either secondary or tertiary education was still fairly limited among Koreans compared with their Japanese counterparts. This indicates that basic literacy education was the main focus during the Japanese colonization period. Kimura (1993, p. 649) also acknowledges that "it seems unlikely that every element of Korean living conditions improved under colonial rule. . . . [T]he strict Japanese-first colonial policy depressed most Koreans." Also, the expansion of primary education in Korea during the 1930s could be attributed to the strategic plan of the Japanese military to transform colonial Korea as the land of logistical support to continue war in Asia (Chung, 2002).

as a tool for stimulating fierce internal competition among compatriots, consolidating competitive motivation, gaining superiority over others. When learners have only one chance annually in the national exam, the test tends to exacerbate social competition and family commitment to education, found in the traditionally "Confucian" education nations such as Korea, China, Hong Kong, and Singapore (Marginson, 2011). Under the normative evaluation, the way to gain a high score is repetitive practice; through this tenacious practice, learners can boast guaranteed high scores on the national exam.

In this regard, competitive motivation, identified from the Japanese Colonization Period, seems to share similarities with performance goals in its focus on proving one's ability by surpassing the standards set up by others, as discussed by Ames (1992). However, competitive motivation does not simply imply surpassing the normative standards but also securing higher ground than others (Kim, 2006b, 2010). Those with competitive motivation aim to outperform others, and they do not mind exerting excessive efforts in practicing already familiar knowledge to minimize mistakes (Kim et al., 2008). In this competitive atmosphere, the learning of English often ends up comprising exclusively individual tasks rather than collaborative ones (Gan, 2009).

2.5.1 Suppression Period in English Education (1910–1919)

As stated above, the first decade of the period of Japanese colonization is called the Military Control Period. Terauchi Masatake (寺内 正毅, 1852–1919), a Japanese military officer and the first Governor General of Korea (tenure: 1910–1916) appointed by Imperial Japan, employed military force to maintain control in Korea, where many Koreans plotted a rebellion against Japanese colonial rules. To expedite the assimilation of Korea into Japan and combine two nations into one, Governor Terauchi promulgated the First Ordinance on Chosun Education (OCE, 朝鮮教育令) in August 1911. He ordered the establishment of thousands of primary and secondary schools across Korea and intended to provide literacy-oriented primary education to Korean youths (Kang, 2015). The spread of primary education was a welcome gesture in Korea and positively contributed to the introduction of systematic general education for the Korean public (Kimura, 1993). The curriculum was geared toward Japanese language and history since the main intention was the assimilation policy and rearing "loyal subjects of the Japanese Empire (皇国臣民)."

In terms of English education, Korean English teachers were rapidly replaced by Japanese teachers. The first OCE renovated the entire educational structure in Korea, and English became an elective school subjects for boys' secondary school and the instructional language was Japanese not English. In addition, the Government-General of Korea (朝鮮総督府; i.e., the chief administration of the Japanese colonial government in Korea from 1910 to 1945) abrogated the Hansung Foreign Language School, which succeeded the English education conducted in

Yookyeong'gongwon, and English education at tertiary educational institutions was abolished during this era of military control (Lee, 2014; Lee & Yeo, 2001; Park, 2008). These measures contributed to the significant regression of English education from the era of the Korean Empire (i.e., before the annexation). Not surprisingly, according to the Private School Act amended in 1915, all educational institutions were to be approved by the Government-General of Korea, and all newly appointed teachers had to prove fluency in the Japanese language. Thus, many Korean English teachers could not hold their position because of their lack of Japanese fluency (Kim, 2011).

The overall trend in the first decade of Japanese colonization was a decrease in English education, particularly in public education. Hours of English instruction at public schools decreased, whereas the Japanese language instruction increased. Mr. Lee Tae-gyu, a graduate from Kyungsung Higher General School (京城高等普通學校) in 1919, stated as follows in an interview conducted in 1964:

> After completing fourth year at Gyeonggi [High School], which had been called Kyungsung Higher General School at that time, I kept attending the Department of Instruction in the same school for one year, where English was not instructed. They said that teachers at normal school did not need to know it. . . . After I started to attend Hiroshima High Teachers School (廣島高等師範學校) [in Japan], I found that I knew A, B, C, D, E, F, G, H, I only but didn't know J and after. How did I know until the alphabet I? These letters were needed to study calculus or algebra. . . . So, for the lack of English education, I had an unfathomable hardship after being admitted to Hiroshima High Teachers School. At that time, Japanese students used original textbooks. These books were written in English. I couldn't read these books, couldn't understand the technical terms in English, couldn't write after what had been written on the blackboard [in English]. . . . I was nearly a dead man for almost a year. (cited in Park, 2003, p. 70)

As poignantly illustrated in the above recount, during the 1910s in Korea, English was not actively instructed, whereas in Japan the situation was very different (Kim, 2011). It is also noteworthy that many English "self-study" books were published during this period in Korea. For example, Lee Ki-Yong, a graduate of Hansung Foreign Language School and former English teacher in the same school, published *English Grammar for Middle School* in 1911. Yun Chi-Ho (see Sect. 2.4.3), in the same year, published *A Shortcut to English Grammar* (영어문법첩경[英語文法捷徑]). Moon Myung-Jin, an English teacher who graduated from Hansung Foreign Language School, published *Self-study for Mastering English Without a Teacher* (무사자통영어독학[無師自通英語獨學]) in 1915, and Jang Doo-Chul published *Mastering English Without a Teacher* (무선생영어자통[無先生英語自通]) in 1917. The book titles, particularly in the latter half of the 1910s, indicate the nature of self-study in the English language. This reflects the educational context at this time; deprived of educational opportunities, particularly at the tertiary level, Koreans still endeavored to learn English. This might be because most Koreans still believed that proficiency in English is a golden key to employment opportunities and a higher salary than that of peers.

During the period of modernization from 1882 to 1910, Koreans came to realize that the acquisition of the English language can establish a useful connection with the U.S. and the modern Western civilization. This was corroborated by the diaries of Mr. Yun Chi-Ho and Dr. Rhee Syngman, both of whom underwent U.S. education at the turn of the century. Besides, for a few wealthy Koreans, the desire to experience the modern lifestyle resulted in an increase in studying abroad in Japan and the U.S. According to Park (1974), Japan was regarded as more Westernized and civilized than Korea, and many Koreans desired to study abroad in Japan instead of going directly to the U.S. Such a trend is reflected in the contents of novels published in Korea at the same period, where the main characters aspire to study abroad in the U.S. For example, in Mr. Lee In-Jik's *Hyeol'eui Nu* (meaning: Bloody Tears), the first "new novel" published in 1906, *Okryeon*, the female character, meets a man who was preparing to study in the U.S., and she goes there with him. *Mujeong* (meaning: Without Affection), the first modern novel written by Yi Kwang-su (Chunwon) in 1917, also portrays its two main characters studying in the U.S. Therefore, in the 1910s, it seems that Koreans exhibited strong fondness for the U.S. because this nation was the symbol of Western lifestyle and modernization.

As stated above, the preference for English, the language of the U.S., is initially identified in King Gojong's pro-American attitude. English had consolidated its status as the language of social success, particularly after the abolition of *gwageo*, the traditional royal examination for government officers, and the English fever was promulgated by the success stories of a few Korean pioneers who were proficient in English at the turn of the twentieth century. In the 1910s, despite the colonial status and the deprivation of learning opportunities, Koreans continued to emphasize the benefits of learning English, and this social consensus is represented by the increase in students studying abroad.

2.5.2 Revitalization of English Education (1920–1922)

Under the de facto military rule of the Governor General of Korea, the continued oppression of freedom of expression and the deprivation of educational opportunities escalated anti-Japanese sentiment among Koreans. The Samil Independence Movement, or March First Movement, was the first massive resistance from Korean people against harsh Japanese military rules. This nationwide uprising was ignited by the sudden demise of former King Gojong. It was widely suspected among Koreans that the Government-General of Korea was involved in his death. At first, the Japanese government tried to repress the movement and dismiss it as simply a public disorder incident. However, as the number of participating Koreans increased and the Government-General of Korea felt threatened by a series of anti-Japanese political movements, this resulted in the resignation of Hasegawa Yoshimichi (長谷川 好道), the second Governor General (tenure: 1916–1919). Saito Makoto (斎藤 実) replaced him, and subsequently implemented the "Cultural Policy" as a series of measures to ameliorate Japan's policies on Koreans. The military police were replaced by a civilian force, and a limited level of press freedom was permitted.

The political change also influenced English education in Korea. The second OCE effective from 1922 mandated English as a mandatory subject in higher general schools and became an elective course in girls' higher general schools. Further, English instruction at the tertiary level was approved (Dong-A Ilbo, 1921b, March 4). The weekly hours of English instruction (6 h) became similar to those of Japanese (i.e., national language) instruction (8 h) for 1st-year higher general school students. In the case of 2nd and 3rd-year students, the situation was the opposite; the weekly hours of English instruction were 7 hours per week, while Japanese was taught for 6 hours per week.

These changes following the implementation of the "Cultural Policy" need careful interpretation. First, Park (2015) emphasizes that the meaning of culture, at least in Japan in the 1910s, imposes a remarkably different connotation. "Culture" had roughly been interpreted as "controlling by laws, educating people (文治教化)," or more precisely as enlightening the public without implementing military force or oppressive authority. Thus, "Cultural Policy" cannot be interpreted using the current usage of "culture." This means that the political regime by Governor Saito did not show revolutionary changes from military dictatorship to sophisticated and elegant constitutionalism. For this reason, although forceful repression by military police has been replaced by civil police control, the educational opportunities for Koreans were still fairly limited compared with those for their Japanese counterparts.

The following statistics are a summary of applicants for the schools in Pyeong-yang in 1921.

As presented in Table 2.1, there were 1574 students in total who aspired to be admitted to the primary school, called general school (普通學校), but the opening in 1921 only allowed 860 students. This means that only half of Korean children at that time were admitted into basic education, which is often considered a human right. The situation was worse in secondary school education, where only a third of the applicants were offered admission to secondary schools, or higher general schools (高等普通學校). Across Korea, the overall competition rate for primary schools

Table 2.1 Application of school in Pyeongyang

School level School name	Number of seats	Number of actual applicants
General School (Primary Education)		
First Public General School	150	200
Second Public General School	120	250
Third Public General School	120	210
Girls' General School	200	314
Soongdeuk General School	120	300
Gwangsung General School	150	300
Total	860	1574
Secondary School (Secondary Education)		
Soongsil Middle School	225	390
Gwangsung Higher General School	150	450
Public Higher General School	150	489
Total	525	1329

was 1:2 and that for secondary schools was 1:10, that for technical colleges and universities varied from 1:3 to 1:20 (Jeon, 2005). The reasons for such high competition among Korean students were (1) the lack of educational opportunity and (2) the Japanese policy on salary discrimination based on the jobseekers' educational background. The dearth of educational opportunities in the Japanese Colonization Period had often been justified by the exam results; individual students, rather than the Ministry of Education, were blamed for their laziness and the lack of intelligence or effort to pass the exam (Kang, 2009).

The lack of opportunity for learning, particularly that of learning English, was temporarily supplemented by *yahak* (야학; 夜學), or Night School, voluntarily organized by Koreans. In newspaper articles, we can find the evidence of the establishment of English night school and English-learning social gatherings. English-speaking Christian missionaries, medical doctors, and Koreans having working knowledge of English volunteered at these night schools. The following newspaper articles by Dong-A Ilbo in 1921 report that six night schools were established only within 3 months.

English-Learning Meeting in Dongrae: Following the need of the present era, youths in Dongrae village who perceived the urgent need of English opened English-learning meeting by inviting Mr. Hyun Yang-Woon, the English instructor at Dongrae Higher General School. (Dong-A Ilbo, 1921a, April 16)

Congratulating on the Establishment of Night School and Wishing Its Continuity: Recently, six night schools were established. Labor Night School and English Night School, which are under the management of Pusan Youth Organization, are boasting a healthy and steady growth in student enrollment. And Pusanjin Girls' Night School, established less than two months ago, has already more than 70 applicants and now experiences the lack of classroom ... (Dong-A Ilbo, 1921e, November 8)

During this period, the educational opportunity for women rapidly increased. This is a notable change given that most educational institutions in the previous era were only for boys, except Ewha Hakdang, which was devoted to girls' education in Korea. In the traditional system, women did not have the chance to receive primary or secondary school education. However, in the Revitalization Stage from 1920 to 1922, various efforts were made to provide educational opportunities to women. Dong-A Ilbo newspaper article reports the opening of a night class in Taewha Girls' Institute.

In order to cultivate general knowledge to average housewives who did not have schooling opportunity, it had already been reported that Taewha Girls' Institute opens lecture meetings and teaches English, Japanese, Chinese character, and arithmetic. This institute could not hold all the students because of the influx of applicants. They establish night classes and plan to teach ... (Dong-A Ilbo, 1921d, May 18)

In general, Governor Saito's so-called "Cultural Policy" expanded educational opportunities for Koreans. However, as shown in Table 2.1, the opportunities were still limited, and the competition among students became fiercer as they advance from primary to secondary schools. Recovering from Terauchi's and Hasegawa's military oppression in the previous decade, Koreans regained the opportunity to learn English, and English was included again in the secondary school curriculum.

However, the lack of competent English teachers prevented Korean students from acquiring fluency in English speaking and listening. Moreover, many Korean teachers of English were replaced by their Japanese counterparts, which deprived Koreans of the chance to authentically experience English.

The aftermath of the Samil Independence Movement also exerted a negative influence on English education in Korea. The intelligence bureau of the Government-General of Korea concluded that many foreign (mostly American) missionaries were involved in or actively espoused this movement and plotted to expel them from the Korean peninsula. According to Park (1974), the number of foreign missionaries was 460 before the Samil Independence Movement in 1919, but it plummeted to 173 in 1922. This meant that the opportunity to receive English immersion education through English-speaking missionaries in private schools dramatically decreased, and consequently the grammar-translation method from Japanese English teachers came to the fore in Korea after the 1920s.

The changing situation in English education in Korea before and after the period of Japanese colonization is of key interest in this book. Before the annexation of Korea and Japan, English learning motivation was largely instrumental, emerging from the learners' personal desire for increased opportunity in employment and/or promotion. This personal level of instrumental motivation was consistently supported by the king and a few Korean pioneers who shared pro-American attitudes. The modernization process also expedited the learning of English through public institutional support (e.g., Yookyeong'gongwon) or through the U.S.-influenced missionary schools (e.g., Paichai and Ewha Hakdang). However, the deprivation of diplomatic sovereignty by the Eulsa Treaty in 1905 and the consequent annexation in 1910 seem to have awakened political awareness and heightened the importance of enlightenment aligned with Korean patriotism. Compared to the previous era, the learning of English added another dimension of patriotic enlightenment as the Japanese control of Korea was consolidated—the enlightenment of the Korean masses. Learning English could function as a direct channel for importing the Western civilization; instead of taking an indirect route through Japan, Koreans endeavored to learn about advanced civilization from the U.S. and the U.K. In order to facilitate this enlightenment process and spread its benefits, English learning was encouraged. English was increasingly regarded as the symbol of an educated person.

> English has now become the world language. If we do not understand commerce, politics, and sciences, it is generally regarded as the lack of common knowledge. This also means that the difficulty [of not knowing English] is not negligible in participating in the civilization of many nations and creating a powerful culture. . . . Thus, we would like to proclaim to you, brethren. . . . In order to import the quintessence of civilization around the world to our best, you must exert your very best to learn English. (Dong-A Ilbo, 1921c, March 23)

Interestingly, on the same day, Dong-A Ilbo, one of the most influential Korean daily newspapers, also enthusiastically encouraged study-abroad in America.

> In analyzing the history of Japanese civilization, we can extract unique principles of progress, but the number one principle will be the system of study abroad. . . . Particularly, Japan decided to seek knowledge around the globe, and this became the grand scheme of

prospering their nation. They dispatched study-abroad students to the U.K., the U.S. France, or Germany and did their best to learn their cultures every day. . . . This gives us an important lesson. Now, we would like to recommend study-abroad, particularly to the U.S. to graduating students across Korea today. (Dong-A Ilbo, 1921c, March 23)

Thus, although we can identify the instrumental nature of English learning motivation in the first decade of Japanese colonization, it was different from the previous era, when an individual's desire to be successful in life was the dominant reason for learning English. As shown in the above newspaper articles, in the early 1920s, English learning acquired a more altruistic meaning for the Korean community in general; the learning of English was often associated with direct importation of advanced Western technology, and this was believed to benefit the Korean compatriots. In this regard, English learning motivation at the initial stage of colonization was instrumental at both individual and community levels.

In summary, the second OCE mandated an increase in educational opportunities from 1920. However, these opportunities were still relatively limited for most Koreans, and not all students aspiring to learn English could learn it on their own authority. Although a window of opportunity was somehow opened by the Korean people's voluntary establishment of *yahak*, or night school, this type of education was temporary and did not have a systematic curriculum. At the same time, the opportunity to learn English through English immersion education by English-speaking foreign missionaries rapidly shrank because of the Japanese policy of deporting foreign missionaries from Korea. This resulted in the dependence on the grammar-translation method. In addition, the lack of opportunity for higher education was often attributed to students' lack of efforts or diligence, not to the insufficient educational infrastructure. In order to acquire educational opportunities by passing the entrance exam at every school level from primary to secondary, and eventually to tertiary educational institutions, students' competitive motivation to outshine other students was exacerbated.

2.5.3 Stagnation of English Education (1922–1937)

Undoubtedly, the role of English education during this stagnant period was centered on the college admission test. After the promulgation of the second OCE, public secondary school English instruction was revived, albeit with limited access for the general public. Moreover, as 10 years had passed since Japanese colonization began in 1910, the need for offering higher education for the Japanese citizens living in Korea had been escalated. It is estimated that the population of Seoul in 1924 was approximately 300,000, among which the Japanese were 80,000 (Jeon, 2005). As stated in the introduction of this chapter, the Governor General of Korea established Kyungsung (or in Japanese pronunciation: Keijo, 京城) Imperial University in Seoul in 1924. Including the Japanese archipelago (often referred to as the inner land), only nine 5-year (2 years of pre-department [豫科], 3 years of the main department [本科]), comprehensive, imperial universities were established.[9]

The foundation of Kyungsung Imperial University was closely related to the Samil Independence Movement. As mentioned above, the missionaries, primarily Americans, were regarded as potential instigators or sympathizers for this independence movement. Thus, the Government-General of Korea was not welcoming of these missionaries and they were forced to leave Korea. The evictions of the foreign missionaries also meant that English learning in missionary schools including Soongsil in Pyongyang, and Ewha and Yonhi in Seoul drastically decreased (Yoon, 2014). In order to suppress students' and parents' protest against the lack of English education, Kyungsung Imperial University put an emphasis on English language and literature. In this university, in 1926, 2 years after the establishment of the pre-department, the departments "Studies in Law and Literature" and "Studies in Medicine" began offering academic courses. Two courses were offered for Japanese linguistics and literature, and an equal number of courses for English linguistics and literature. In comparison, in 1928, Tokyo Imperial University conducted three courses on Japanese linguistics and literature and two in English linguistics and literature (Yoon, 2014). Therefore, English education offered in Kyungsung Imperial University reflected political consideration and addressed Koreans' enthusiasm toward learning English at tertiary higher educational institutions.

Throughout the operation of this university until the day of liberation on August 15, 1945, graduates had been offered incommensurably better occupational opportunities such as central positions in the Government-General of Korea, with decent salaries. As these positions were considered "dream jobs" by most Koreans, the admission to Kyungsung Imperial University was extremely competitive. Only 810 Koreans were admitted in 22 years from 1924 to 1945 (Jeon, 2005), constituting less than one-third of the entire graduate population. In retrospect, Japanese, not Korean, students in Korea benefitted in every aspect while entering university, given the structure of the admission exam. Students applying for humanities and social sciences, took sub-tests including national language (i.e., Japanese) and Classical Chinese, foreign language (either English or German), math, and history. For applicants of natural sciences, the sub-tests included national language (i.e., Japanese) and Classical Chinese, foreign language (either English or German), math, and biology. All the questions in the exam were in Japanese, and the students needed to respond in Japanese. Thus, Korean students were, from the outset, in unduly disadvantageous positions in the entrance exam. For example, all applicants were required to translate *Genji Monogatari* (The Tale of *Genji*, 源氏物語), a classic novel of Japanese middle age literature in the twelfth century, into modern Japanese. The biggest challenge for Korean applicants, however, was not national language but foreign language (English). The English exam had two translation tasks: English

---

[9]The name and foundation year of each imperial university: Tokyo (1886), Kyoto (1897), Tohoku (1907), Kyushu (1911), Hokkaido (1918), Kyungsung (or Keijo, 1924), Taihoku (in Taiwan, 1928), Osaka (1931), and Nagoya (1939).

into Japanese (national language) and Japanese into English. This meant that although Koreans understood the message in the original passage written in English perfectly, its translation into Japanese could be problematic. Their score in translation was strictly assessed by Japanese assessors, and in the case of spelling error or grammatical mistakes in Japanese, they were penalized. As Japanese was an L2 to Korean applicants, this translation test put them at a disadvantage. According to Jeon (2005), for example, the total number of applicants for admission to Kyungsung Imperial University in 1924 was 647; among them, 241 were Koreans and 406 were Japanese. The initial student recruitment number was 160 (which was expanded to 180 later) and the competition ratio was more than 3:1. Among the 241 Korean applicants, only 44 (18.2%) were granted admission, whereas 136 Japanese students (33.5%) out of 406 applicants were admitted.

These circumstances surrounding the entrance exam at Kyungsung Imperial University exerted undeniable influence on English education in Korea. As the exam adopted English-Japanese and Japanese-English translation formats, the grammar-translation method was firmly established in Korea. English education changed from communication with English speakers (mostly American missionaries) to the pencil-and-paper exam preparation for admission to Kyungsung Imperial University.

Again, Korean students' admission to and their subsequent graduation from this university were largely equated with their success in job selection, promotion, and salary. Other colleges including Yonhi (now Yonsei University) and Bosung (now Korea University) soon adopted similar exam formats (Park, 2003). Therefore, English education during this period was quickly replaced by the memorization of English vocabulary and grammar, and fast and accurate reading comprehension and translation skills were prioritized. Criticizing this situation, Horace Horton Underwood (1890–1951), a professor at Yonhi College,[10] wrote the following:

> Under this sort of plan, it is not surprising that 'the best teacher of English Grammar in the city of Seoul' should be an individual who cannot speak English intelligently but who has thoroughly mastered the puzzles and trick questions of the examinations for the advanced school in this subject. (Underwood, 1926, p. 237)

The zeal toward English education spread from the university entrance exam to the general public. The desire to learn English is also related to having more opportunities to enter higher education. Since the Government-General of Korea limited educational opportunities for Koreans (see Table 2.1 in the previous section), all Korean students experienced a series of entrance exams even before attending elementary school. For example, the following magazine article describes the anguish of a heartbroken father whose son failed to gain admission to a general school, which is equivalent to elementary school.

> I have a son who is turning 7 years old this spring. Six-year-old means the proper age for general school admission, so I wanted to enroll my son in a public general school in Susong-

---

[10]He was the son of Horace Grant Underwood (1859–1916) who founded Kyeongsin School (儆新 學校), or the Joseon Christian College, the predecessor of Yonsei University.

dong (in Seoul) last year (i.e., 1933). However, unfortunately, my son failed the entrance exam last year. That poor little thing was disheartened at the result and felt so ashamed. My heart was torn with sorrow. Actually, my son is slower than his peers in his age, slow in body growth, and has the weak physique. Maybe he was spoiled by his grandmother who always endears him. . . . Isn't it ironic that I have to have my son re-take an entrance exam even for general school teaching an elementary curriculum? I also have to admit that I felt uncomfortable to witness my son's bitterness. He was basically only a little six-year-old kid with a runny nose. (Shin Kyung-Whan, *Agonistic tale of entrance exam preparation*, from Joong-Ang, April issue, 1934, cite in Jeon, 2008)

The extreme competition in entering elementary schools was a nationwide phenomenon for decades during the Japanese Colonization Period. Dong-A Ilbo reports the sorrowful scene of young kids who failed the entrance exam held in Gwangju, Jeolla Province.

At 1:00 PM, on the 29th of last month, a heartbreaking scene was witnessed. The sound of the wailing of approximately 400 kids of ages 6 and 7 resounded in the playground. It was the wailing of kids who submitted the application form [to Gwangju Public General School] but were turned down because of the school's limited capacity to hold students. (Dong-A Ilbo, 1922, April 2)

Given this socio-educational context throughout the period of Japanese colonization, the enthusiasm to receive a better education at a higher educational institution continued. As stated above, having secondary or preferably tertiary education represented by Kyungsung Imperial University was the most secure means to employment and promotion, particularly in government offices. The existence and operation of Kyungsung Imperial University seems to have a strong relationship with the high level of academic credentialism in Korea, some of which still exists (Kim 2001b; Seth, 2002).

Yoon (2014) described the graduates of the department of English linguistics and literature at Kyungsung Imperial University. From 1930 to 1934, among the 24 graduates whose career path was identified, five chose to attend graduate school or became teaching assistants in the same department, 15 became English teachers at secondary schools, and four chose other careers such as working at the Government-General office of Korea or at Kyungsung Broadcasting Service (pp. 174–175). These career paths all strongly indicate that the graduation from this university guaranteed stable, if not the best, job opportunities after graduation.

The above statistics of the graduates of Kyungsung Imperial University indicate that the department of English linguistics and literature had functioned as an English teacher-training center. According to Park (1974), the zeal toward learning English had been continually accelerated during the Japanese Colonialization Period until its absolute abrogation in 1939. The Cultural Policy of Governor General Saito Makoto resulted in the establishment of private higher educational institutions. Following the establishment of Ewha Womans' College (now Ewha Womans' University) in 1905 and Yonhi College (now Yonsei University) in 1917, under the Cultural Policy, Bosung College (now Korea University) was approved by the Government-General of Korea in 1921 and Soongsil College (now Soongsil University) in 1925. This successive approval of higher educational institutions meant that the demand for English teachers continuously increased.

In this urgent demand for English teachers across Korea, the department of English linguistics and literature at Kyungsung Imperial University functioned as the most authoritative outlet for the provision of English teachers. Therefore, in this social atmosphere, 15 out of 24 graduates from this department chose teaching as their profession. Park (1974) states that before the establishment of Kyungsung Imperial University, English instructors in Korea were either English-speaking foreign missionaries or Koreans who had studied abroad, particularly in the U.S. In some cases, Koreans who majored in English language and literature in Japan became English teachers after returning to Korea. However, these cases did not have a positive effect on the educational contexts in Korea. Foreign missionaries and Koreans who graduated from U.S. universities did not have comprehensive knowledge of English education in Korea. Being a native speaker of English or being a graduate from a U.S. university, regardless of undergraduate major, could not be a sufficient condition for teaching English. Koreans who graduated from Japanese universities were not different either. Thus, as indicated in the number of graduates who became English teachers at secondary schools, Kyungsung Imperial University had a positive role in enhancing the quality of English education in Korea given the quality of its graduates (Park, 1974).

In the 1920s and 1930s, motivated by the enthusiasm toward studying abroad in English-speaking countries, many students aspired to major in English. As early as 1926, Dong-A Ilbo reports that English was the most favored major among Korean students who studied in Tokyo, Japan, stating that 486 students among approximately 2000 chose English-related majors.

> In Tokyo and its vicinity, Korean students are estimated at approximately 13,000, and among them, only 2,021 students were enrolled in accredited educational institutions. Their majors and enrolled students are as follows.
> Department of English: 486, Department of Law: 351, Department of Sociology: 121, Department of Politics and Economics: 24, Department of Philosophy, Religion, and Physics (combined): 32. (Dong-A Ilbo, 1926, January 29)

Park (1974) and Yoon (2014) stated that it is worth noting that most students majored in English at a time when Korea was under Japanese colonization, and there was an evident power imbalance between Japanese and Koreans as the oppressor and the oppressed. In this case, the oppressed people endeavored to gain political and economic power, choosing either law or economics as their college major. However, as reported by Dong-A Ilbo (1926) above, English outnumbered law in terms of enrolled students in Tokyo. This fact indicates that Korean students studying abroad perceived English as a more effective tool for their success in employment than any other undergraduate majors in the 1920s.

As presented in the previous section, although Cultural Policy was administered in Korea from the 1920s, educational opportunities for learning English, let alone learning other school curricula, were extremely limited. Moreover, the Direct Method, where English is used for instruction and communication, had been used in the English education conducted before the deprivation of diplomatic sovereignty by Japan in 1905 (Eulsa Treaty, or Japan-Korea Treaty of 1905) and the annexation of Korea by Japan in 1910. On the contrary, the lack of communication focus during the Japanese Colonization Period came to the fore of problems. For example, the students in Bosung Higher General School were on strike to urge the replacement of a Japanese English teacher with a Korean English teacher who was often seen as providing more authentic English pronunciation (Kim, 2011).

As English education in the colonization period was mostly conducted by Japanese teachers of English, particularly at the public schools, the students did not have the chance to experience authentic British or American pronunciation of English. In his book titled "Korea on the Japanese" (1930), Mr. Henry B. Drake, who worked as an English teacher in Seoul in the late 1920s, explained his odd experience of being unable to successfully communicate with Korean students who already had many years of English learning, which clearly lacked verbal emphasis.

> The boys [i.e., students] came to me with anything from five to ten years of English study behind them, but under the Japanese. To build on this foundation would have been like building on a ditchful of loose rubble. Their pronunciation was so original that to make me understand they were obliged to repeat their remarks to me two or three times and word by word, even letter by letter; and my pronunciation seemed to them so ludicrous that it sent them into violent fits of laughter. So it took us quite a long time to adjust ourselves to each other, on a basis of mutual forbearance. There was on unpleasantness. The students were very considerate. After all, coming from the outside world it was natural that I should have picked up some curious habits of speech. And we drifted finally into the tacit agreement that I might pronounce in my own insular way, provided I did not insist on their imitating me. But it was all very jolly, because when the fog of dullness was settling over a lesson I would fix on something a student had said, and say, "Now in England we would pronounce it like this"; and the gush of unintelligible noises that I emitted would dissipate the dullness on a roar of delight. (Drake, 1930, p. 127)

Since the English education provided in the public institutions such as higher general schools and Kyungsung Imperial University focused more on literacy-related aspects in English (i.e., reading, writing, and morphosyntactic rules), Koreans did not have the chance to develop their oral competence. Thus, voluntary organizations teaching English speaking and listening continued to flourish. For example, Korea Central Christian Youth Association invited native English speakers and opened a class for teaching English pronunciation, and Hamheung Christian Youth Association also organized similar seminars (Kim, 2016).

> Korea Central Christian Youth Association will hold a seminar of authentic English pronunciation with Mr. Crawley, English teacher at Kyungsung Higher Commercial School, at their building this Friday. For those whose English knowledge is equivalent to 3rd year at a higher general school or above, auditing will be granted. Admission is free. (Dong-A Ilbo, 1924, September 26)
>
> Hamheung Christian Youth Association invited Mr. H. S. Crawley, English instructor at Kyungsung Higher Commercial School and traveler to Korea to a seminar on English pronunciation held at Haehoegwan at 19:30 from 19th to 21st every night. (Dong-A Ilbo, 1925, March 20)

However, it did not resolve the inherent problem in Korea: the lack of opportunity to learn English in a communicative way. The option was to go and study abroad in English-speaking countries. If that was not possible, most Koreans could not develop oral/aural English proficiency and experienced "the exam hell" (Lee &

Fig. 2.1 Inoue English advertisement in Dong-A Ilbo on November 16, 1929

Fig. 2.2 Inoue English LP record advertisement in Chosun Ilbo on March 29, 1936

Larson, 2000) and extreme competition for admission to a higher educational institution.

Noticeable technological advances are found in English education in the mid-1920s: namely, the introduction of the radio broadcasting system and the Long Play (LP) record. On February 16, 1927, Kyungsung Broadcasting Service was opened, which heralded the new era of radio English lecture. According to Lee (2012), it is a breakthrough that English lesson was included in the radio program. Given that the entire airtime at the broadcast company was six and a half hours, the inclusion of English lessons is evidence that this language was prioritized over other foreign languages.

The newly invented LP record also contributed to alleviating the lack of opportunities in English education. Mr. Inoue Jukichi (井上十吉, 1862–1929), lexicographer and English scholar in the early twentieth-century Japan, advertised his distance English learning method in newspapers across Korea. His advertisement used aggressive catchphrases such as "English is the Best Tool for Dragon Gate," "We Can't Achieve the Best Level Without Knowing English," and "Conquer English This Fall" (see Figs. 2.1 and 2.2). The Inoue method was basically Korean students' sending their English writing samples from Korea to Japan, and the writing samples were proofread and corrected by English instructors in Japan and returned to Korea to the students.

Even after Mr. Inoue's death in 1929, his distance learning methods continued to be advertised actively, and the main contents of his English curriculum were recorded in LP records (see Fig. 2.2). The English LP records were dispatched to Korean subscribers. In Fig. 2.2, it is advertised as "You, Young Folks! This Spring Is the Best Time to Conquer English, the Tool for Success," and states that anyone can read English in a month, write it in 2 months, and speak it in 3 months.

In the 1930s, the enthusiasm toward English continued. Newspaper articles, advertisements, and those who returned after studying abroad fueled this enthusiasm toward English learning. The voluntarily organized English pronunciation seminars in the 1920s mentioned above were developed into English public speech contests in the 1930s. The popularity of English speech contests was also related to the new traditions in missionary schools in Korea. As stated above, missionary schools such as Yonhi College and Ewha Womans' College emphasized English learning and continued English instruction by adopting the Direct Method from American missionaries. Park (1974) highlighted that for Ewha Womans' College, at the initial stage of its accreditation in 1905, only two departments were granted: Departments of Music and Liberal Arts. However, foreign missionaries called the Department of Liberal Arts as the Department of English Literature; this is evidence that English was considered the major language of instruction and the representative field of academic study.

Influenced by such an enthusiastic attitude toward English, various English speech contests were held in different places across Korea. Dong-A Ilbo reported that the Pan-Korea English Speech Contest for boys and girls was held, and a total of 16 schools participated in this contest in 1932. In addition, Chosun Ilbo reported that similar English contests were held first at Yonhi College in 1933 and at Ewha Womans' College in 1934. Moreover, English drama performance was frequently announced in the newspaper. The leading educational institutions for English performance were Yonhi and Ewha Womans' Colleges (Kim, 2016).

Held by Yonhi College and funded by the present newspaper, the first Pan-Korea English speech contest for boys and girls in Korea will be held at 7:30 on the 19th of November. As reported before, a total of 16 schools will participate in this contest, which has proved a huge success already. (Dong-A Ilbo, 1932, November 17)

Ehwa Womans' College will hold Korean and English speech contests for girls attending secondary schools across Korea. English contest will be held on September 28th and Korean one on September 29th. Only one speaker should be selected from each participating school, and the allotted time will be 10 minutes. The participating school must submit the participant's name, date of birth, title of speech, and the overall contents by the end of June to the Ministry of Education. (Chosun Ilbo, 1934, May 23)

Compared to the trend of English education in the 1920s, a series of new phenomena in the 1930s illustrated above indicate that the educational opportunities to learn English steadily increased. At the same time, the general public's interest in English and their motivation to learn this language were also on the rise.

Note that the enthusiasm toward English learning is not separable from the overall zeal for better education to lead a better life. The competition for a higher academic degree and education was consistently aggravated (Park, 2003). Under this social milieu, the success or failure in school entrance exam was often regarded as the most important lifetime event even for the family members. It is unfortunate to find that newspaper articles continually reported the tragic suicide cases related to failing various entrance exams. For example, Chosun Ilbo reported a suicide case on October 18, 1923, and cited Mr. Park Kyung-Bok's suicide note.

> I don't have talent that I can't keep on studying. I feel so ashamed that I can't meet my parents. I'd rather take my own life. (Chosun Ilbo, 1923, October 18).

Mr. Park was only 18 years old when he committed suicide, depressed after failing to be admitted to a higher general school 2 years in a row. Thus, it was not uncommon to find similar suicide cases in daily newspapers throughout the colonial period.

Dong-A Ilbo reports another tragic choice on March 25, 1928.

> On March 20th, after borrowing 10 Won [i.e., Korean currency unit] from his parents, Lee Jong-Hee headed toward Jeonju to take the entrance exam of Jeonju Agricultural School. He walked into Ganggyeong with the hope of taking the train bound for Jeonju. However, he was not confident about passing the exam this time again and was agonized to realize his lack of study talent. Full of pessimism, he finally decided to take his own life, bidding farewell to the world. Out of 10 Won he had brought, he sent 7 Won back home, ran and crashed into a train. We could not watch this with our own eyes and witness the anguish of the bereaved family. (Dong-A Ilbo, 1928, March 25).

2.5.4   Abrogation of English Education (1938–1945)

The negative sociopolitical atmosphere from the end of the 1930s loomed over English education in Korea. The second Sino-Japanese War (中日戰爭) from 1937 sparked dramatic changes in English education. The unstable economic situation ignited by the Great Depression in New York in 1929 also exerted a negative influence on the Japanese economy. From 1929 to 1931, the Japanese economy shrank by 8%, but compared to other European nations, Japan could recover from the impact of the Great Depression by first abandoning the gold standard in their foreign currency policy and by expediting the export of cotton textiles and general merchandise (Seo, 2003). As a consequence, most Western nations blamed Japan for their unfair trade practices and raised tariffs on all Japanese goods in the 1930s. This tension in international trade soon adversely affected the Japanese economy, resulting in a nationwide negative reaction from nationalists, particularly from those in the army. From 1934, the military influence on the Japanese government continued to grow, and the Japanese army endeavored to regain their economic vigor by expanding its territory and importing goods from foreign colonies other than Korea and Taiwan.

The outbreak of the second Sino-Japanese War on July 7, 1937, resulted in the amendment of the second Ordinance on Chosun Education (OCE). As stated in the previous section, the second OCE reflects the "Cultural Policy" granting limited autonomy in English education to secondary schools in Korea and establishing various technical colleges and Kyungsung Imperial University. From 1920 to 1937, for 18 years, English education at various grassroot levels flourished, albeit with limitations, and the opportunity to learn English at secondary and tertiary educational institutions steadily increased. However, the second Sino-Japanese War rapidly changed the educational atmosphere in Korea (and also in Japan). Despite the warning from the League of Nations, the organization for resolving international disputes, Japan did not retreat from China, and the U.S. and the U.K. provided economic and military support for China.

Since the Manchurian Incident in September 1931, when the Japanese army attacked the northern part of China, the diplomatic isolation of Japan became aggravated, and Japan withdrew from the League of Nations in 1933. However, until the attack on the Chinese army in Beijing in 1937 ignited the second Sino-Japanese War, the campaign from the Japanese army was regarded as a series of local incidents, and both the U.S. and the U.K. stayed aloof from Japan. However, from the second Sino-Japanese War, the U.S. and the U.K. gradually increased the level of diplomatic and military intervention in China, and Japan increasingly perceived these nations as potential threats to its empire. The political tension culminated at the Pearl Harbor Attack of Japan in 1941. Until Japan's unconditional surrender on August 15, 1945, the political circumstance was not supportive of English education.

These political upheavals influenced the lives of many Koreans. To encourage Japanese patriotism, the Governor General of Korea forcefully expedited the Assimilation Policy under the slogan of "Japan and Korea Are One Body (内鮮一体)" or "Japan and Korea Share the Same Ancestry (日鮮同祖)." The education, particularly after the outbreak of the second Sino-Japanese War in 1937, was geared toward rearing loyal subjects of the Japanese emperor while self-denigrating Korean identity among Koreans. In March 1938, the Government-General of Korea proclaimed the third OCE, which reflected the newly appointed Governor General Minami Jiro (南次郎; tenure: 1936–1942), former commander in chief of the Japanese army stationed in Korea and minister of the Japanese armed forces. He was known as a belligerent war promulgator who enthusiastically supported extended warfare across East Asia.[11] The amended OCE was influenced by the Governor General and had the following characteristics.

First, Japanese became the language of education, and Korean was prohibited. Second, the curriculum explicitly stated that the main goal of education was to rear loyal and productive subjects of the Japanese empire. Third, only public schools

---

[11]During his tenure, a series of retrograde measures were taken in education. Minami outlawed the Korean language newspapers, including Chosun and Dong-A Ilbo, in 1940. He also enforced the policy of *changsi gaemyeong* (or in Japanese pronunciation: *soshi-kamei*; 創氏改名), which literally means "creation of one's family name, change in one's given name." Many Koreans were forced to renounce their previous family name and re-create a new one, self-denying their Korean heritage.

were permitted, and private schools lost their legal status. Fourth, bible study in missionary schools was prohibited.

In terms of language education, Korean and English were the most negatively affected by the third OCE. Under the second OCE, Korean, along with the Japanese language, was a mandatory school subject, but its status changed into an elective subject in the third OCE. Further, the hours of instruction for English were reduced (Park, 1974; Son, 1971).

As illustrated in Figs. 2.1 and 2.2 on the Inoue English advertisement, we can see that until the mid-1930s, English was advertised and coveted by many Koreans. However, the third OCE changed the status of English as one of many foreign languages. In the previous era, English was perceived as the only de facto foreign language, but after 1938, the foreign languages instructed in secondary schools were redefined as "Chinese, German, French, or English," and Chinese instead of English began to be instructed as the main foreign language. It seems to reflect the political need of the Chinese language to continue the war against China after the second Sino-Japanese War in 1937. Therefore, although English was still one of the major foreign languages, its status suffered qualitative differences compared to that specified in the second OCE.

Moreover, a major change in the college entrance exam was implemented during this period. The bureau of education in the Government-General of Korea formulated a policy to exclude English in college entrance exams. This appears to have been related to the rising anti-sentiment toward the U.S. and the U.K. In 1939, government-instigated protests were organized nationwide against the U.K, the enemy nation not supporting the idea of establishment of Greater East Asia Co-prosperity (大東亜共栄). Chosun Ilbo's article reports the Government-General of Korea's consideration of excluding English from secondary and tertiary school entrance exams.

> English takes the most hours of instruction in secondary school subjects and has the most important status among the subjects in entrance exams. Thus, students are so obsessed with studying English, turn neurotic, or become myopic for the search of English words in dictionaries. This all makes them experience plenty of learning difficulties. Now it is time for us to research all kinds of sciences without borrowing the knowledge in a foreign language. This means that we do not need to have any favoritism toward English. This leads to the reduction of hours of English instruction at secondary schools, but this would require amendments in educational laws. Therefore, the Government-General of Korea now considers excluding English from school entrance exams. (Chosun Ilbo, 1939, June 16).

As the diplomatic relations between Japan and the U.S., as well as with the U.K., worsened, the anti-English sentiment was also aggravated. Spearheaded by the arrest of the "spy network," which eulogized the U.K. in Japan, the Bureau of Education at the Government-General of Korea systematized the purification of the national language movement aiming at eradicating English words that had already infiltrated into everyday words. On August 3, 1940, Mr. Shiobara (鹽原), Chief of Bureau of Education, asserted that "the enthusiasm toward English among the learned are the flowerbed of espionage [for the U.S. and the U.K.]" (Chosun Ilbo, 1940, August 3).

Most English classes at colleges in Korea started to close. For example, in 1941, English education as well as the use of this language was entirely abrogated at Ewha Womans' College. Korean professors with experience of studying abroad in English-speaking countries were forced to retire from their professorship and were expelled from the college; the statue of Ms. Scranton, the founder of Ewha, was demolished; and in the end, Ewha Womans' College was renamed as Kyungsung Women's College (Park, 1974). The situation at Yonhi College was not different. Under the leadership of Dr. Horace Horton Underwood (元漢慶, 1890–1951), Yonhi College could continue to provide English education. However, under the tremendous political oppression from the Government-General of Korea, Yonhi College could not gain approval from the government for the renewal of the employment contracts for English-speaking board members and foreign faculty members on December 17, 1941. According to Park (1974), the reason for dismissal was "the British and American faculty members were citizens of enemy nations." After this incident, the English education at Yonhi shrank to 2 hours a week except for students majoring in liberal arts. Yonhi College also faced the externally imposed name change into Kyungsung Industrial Management College (京城工業經營專門 學校).

In comparison to the active oppression at the college level across Korea, particularly missionary schools, English instruction at the secondary school level did not face total closure. According to Park (1974), despite the reduced class hours for English, Korean English teachers could continue their job until the liberation from Japan on August 15, 1945.

However, despite the suppression of English education until 1945, it should be noted that the pursuit of success through education continued in Korea. Although English education decreased substantially in secondary schools and was excluded from college entrance exams, the competition for school admission continued to be a serious social problem. It seems that *hakbul,* or academic credentialism, found in the present Korean society can be traced back to this period. The pursuit of academic degrees was perceived as the "golden gate" to the upper social class, ruling society in Korea (Kim 2006b, 2010; Zeng, 1995).

Regarding the overall trend of educational competition during the last phase of the colonial period, Jeon (2008) summarized Korean students' academic ordeals as following:

> To reform the practice of secondary school entrance exam format which mainly adopted paper-and-pencil written tests, the Government-General of Korea controlled secondary school exams not to include difficult, interdisciplinary question items. This trend toward easy, simple questions resulted in a surge of applicants who marked perfect scores in the entrance exams whereby each school usually needed to select only 1 out of 10 applicants. In Whimoon Higher General School entrance exam of 1938, the number of applicants who earned perfect score exceeded that year's student quota. Thus, the school had to run through the second round of selection process only for the best of the best.
>
> In October 1939, the Government-General of Korea banned all subject exams except that of the National Language (i.e., Japanese). Banning exam-centered education and paper-and-pencil-based school subject exams resulted in the selection of students fluent in Japanese, faithful to militaristic ideals, and physically sturdy. Undoubtedly, the competition ratio at

that time was over 1:10, and dozens of young students who failed the secondary school entrance exams either committed suicide or ended up becoming pariahs.

The foremost reason for this brutal competition in the entrance exams was the lack of schools in Korea. It was useless to revamp the format of entrance exams without renovating the fundamental problems, which only aggravated the students' stress level. The Government-General of Korea was acutely aware of this but only kept revamping the entrance exam format. This only added Korean students' misery.

In August 1940, the Government-General of Korea made a political decision to outlaw Dong-A Ilbo and Chosun Ilbo, two major daily newspapers published in Korean, in order to expedite the assimilation of Korea into Japan and to suppress the exchange of information promoting patriotic nationalism among Koreans. The suppression of English education culminated after the attack of the Pearl Harbor on December 8, 1941. The attack meant the expansion of warfare with the U.S., and consequently the instruction of English was equated with the act of espionage. As mentioned previously, English instruction at the tertiary level was entirely abolished, and that at the secondary level shrank substantially. All foreign Christian missionaries were expelled from Korea because they did not pay a due tribute to the Japanese Shrine in Korea, which was evidently seen as idol worship for Christians. After Horace Horton Underwood, former dean of Yonhi College, left in June 1942, there were no native speakers of English in Korea until the liberation from Japan in August 1945. The import of English books and study abroad in the U.S. were all strictly banned from 1942 onwards. Thus, for approximately 4 years, English instruction faced the darkest period in the history of English education in Korea.

2.6   Chapter Summary

In this chapter, the historical progression of English education in Korea was explained in tandem with the sociohistorical events following the Korea-U.S. Treaty of 1882. English had been regarded as the golden key to social success. In the late nineteenth century, oral fluency was emphasized and students who enrolled in public or private schools to learn English soon acquired secure jobs. However, the period of Japanese colonization that started from 1910 involved significant changes in English education in Korea. Instead of speaking and listening skills, students' accurate translation skills, primarily related to morphosyntactic knowledge and reading ability, were prioritized. The academic competition also became fierce because of the firm belief in the efficacy of a higher academic degree in gaining job opportunities. The establishment of Kyungsung Imperial University was a catalyst for this academic competition, which is the prototype of competitive motivation found in twenty-first century English learning in Korea (Kim 2006b, 2010). Thus, the introduction and development of English in Korea from 1882 to 1945 could be represented as the transitional phase from communicative orientation to literacy orientation, combined with academic competition.

References

Allen, H. N. (1991). *H. N. Allen's diary* (Trans. Kim, Won Mo.). Dankook University Press.

Ames, C. (1992). Classrooms: Goals, structures, and student motivation. *Journal of Educational Psychology, 84*(3), 261–271.

Catholic Bishops' Conference of Korea. (2018). Hankook gyohoi'eui yeoksa [History of Korean church]. Retrieved August 8, 2018, from http://www.cbck.or.kr/page/page.asp?p_code=K3112.

Cho, Jinhyun. (2017). *English language ideologies in Korea: Interpreting the past and present.* Cham, Switzerland: Springer.

Choi, Yeon-Hee. (2006). Impact of political situations on the early history of English language education in Korea. *Journal of Research in Curriculum Instruction, 10*(1), 235–259.

Chosun Ilbo. (1923, October 18). Nakjero jasal [Committing suicide for failing exams]. Retrieved October 25, 2019, from http://cdb.chosun.com/search/pdf/i_archive/read_pdf.jsp?PDF=19231018203&Y=1923&M=10

Chosun Ilbo. (1934, May 23). Joseon'eo yeong'eo yeohaksaeng woongbyeondaehoi [Female student speech contest in Korean or English]. Retrieved October 25, 2019, from http://cdb.chosun.com/search/pdf/i_archive/read_pdf.jsp?PDF=19340523002&Y=1934&M=05

Chosun Ilbo. (1939, June 16). Yeong'eogwa siheom pyejiseol [Rumors of abolishing English exams]. Retrieved October 25, 2019, from http://cdb.chosun.com/search/pdf/i_archive/read_pdf.jsp?PDF=19390617001&Y=1939&M=06

Chosun Ilbo. (1940, August 3). Baeyeongsasang'eul ilso, soonjeongkook'eo woondongjeongae [Obliterating pro-British sentiment, upholding movement toward pure national language]. Retrieved October 25, 2019, from http://cdb.chosun.com/search/pdf/i_archive/read_pdf.jsp?PDF=19400803202&Y=1940&M=08

Chung, Kwang. (2014). *Joseonsidae'eui oikook'eo gyoyook [Foreign language education in the Joseon Dynasty].* Seoul, Korea: Gimyeongsa.

Chung, Kyo-Young. (2002). Wartime-mobilization and the transformation of colonial education: Education in Korea, 1937-1945. *Korean Journal of Educational Research, 40*(2), 35–64.

Cummins, J. (1992). Bilingual education and English immersion: The Ramirez report in theoretical perspective. *Bilingual Research Journal, 16*(1/2), 91–104.

Dong-A Ilbo. (1921a, April 16). Dongrae yeong'eo gangseuphoe [English-learning meeting in Dongrae]. Retrieved October 25, 2019, from https://newslibrary.naver.com/viewer/index.nhn?articleId=1921041600209204023&editNo=1&printCount=1&publishDate=1921-04-16&officeId=00020&pageNo=4&printNo=231&publishType=00020

Dong-A Ilbo. (1921b, March 4). Hakgyoe iphakhalkka Yeonheejeonmunhakgyo [Shall we go to Yeonhee Technical College]. Retrieved August 14, 2018, from http://newslibrary.naver.com/viewer/index.nhn?articleId=1921030400209202044&editNo=1&printCount=1&publishDate=1921-03-04&officeId=00020&pageNo=2&printNo=188&publishType=00020

Dong-A Ilbo. (1921c, March 23). Hakgisigam [Feelings at the seasons of opening semester]. Retrieved October 25, 2019, from https://newslibrary.naver.com/viewer/index.nhn?articleId=1921032300209201002&editNo=1&printCount=1&publishDate=1921-03-23&officeId=00020&pageNo=1&printNo=207&publishType=00020

Dong-A Ilbo. (1921d, May 18). Taehwayeojakwan yahakgwa gaeseol [Opening of night school at Taehwa Girls' Building]. Retrieved October 25, 2019, from https://newslibrary.naver.com/viewer/index.nhn?articleId=1921051800209203004&editNo=1&printCount=1&publishDate=1921-05-18&officeId=00020&pageNo=3&printNo=263&publishType=00020

Dong-A Ilbo. (1921e, November 8). Yahakhoe balheung'eul choolhamyeo jisok'eul manghanora [Congratulating on the establishment of night school and wishing its continuity]. Retrieved October 25, 2019, from https://newslibrary.naver.com/viewer/index.nhn?articleId=1921110800209204001&editNo=1&printCount=1&publishDate=1921-11-08&officeId=00020&pageNo=4&printNo=437&publishType=00020

Dong-A Ilbo. (1922, April 2). Gyojeong'e gokseong [Wailing at the campus]. Retrieved October 24, 2019, from https://newslibrary.naver.com/viewer/index.nhn?articleId=1922040200209207003&editNo=1&printCount=1&publishDate=1922-04-02&officeId=00020&pageNo=7&printNo=582&publishType=00020

Dong-A Ilbo. (1924, September 26). Yeong'eobal'eumgyosoo cheonggang'eun mooryo [Teaching English pronunciation: Free auditing allowed]. Retrieved October 25, 2019, from https://newslibrary.naver.com/viewer/index.nhn?articleId=1924092600209203003&editNo=1&printCount=1&publishDate=1924-09-26&officeId=00020&pageNo=3&printNo=1490&publishType=00020

Dong-A Ilbo. (1925, March 20). Yeong'eobal'eum gangjwa [Lecture of English pronunciation]. Retrieved October 25, 2019, from https://newslibrary.naver.com/viewer/index.nhn?articleId=1925032000209203040&editNo=1&printCount=1&publishDate=1925-03-20&officeId=00020&pageNo=3&printNo=1665&publishType=00020

Dong-A Ilbo. (1926, January 29). Yeong'eojeongong choeda [English major is the majority]. Retrieved October 25, 2019, from https://newslibrary.naver.com/viewer/index.nhn?articleId=1926012900209202018&editNo=1&printCount=1&publishDate=1926-01-29&officeId=00020&pageNo=2&printNo=1980&publishType=00020

Dong-A Ilbo. (1928, March 25). Haksaeng cheoldo jasal [A student committed suicide on the railroad]. Retrieved October 25, 2019, from https://newslibrary.naver.com/viewer/index.nhn?articleId=1928032500209202017&editNo=1&printCount=1&publishDate=1928-03-25&officeId=00020&pageNo=2&printNo=2721&publishType=00020

Dong-A Ilbo. (1932, November 17). Jeilhoe jeonjoseon namnyeojoongdeunggyo yeong'eo woongbyeondaehoe [First Pan-Korea boys' and girls' secondary school English speech contest]. Retrieved October 25, 2019, from https://newslibrary.naver.com/viewer/index.nhn?articleId=1932111700209202011&editNo=1&printCount=1&publishDate=1932-11-17&officeId=00020&pageNo=2&printNo=4281&publishType=00020

Drake, H. B. (1930). *Korea of the Japanese*. London: The Bodley Head.

Esthus, R. A. (1959). The Taft-Katsura agreement: Reality or myth? *Journal of Modern History, 31*(1), 46–51.

Gan, Z. (2009). 'Asian learners' re-examined: An empirical study of language learning attitudes, strategies and motivation among mainland Chinese and Hong Kong students. *Journal of Multilingual and Multicultural Development, 30*(1), 41–58.

Gardner, R. C. (1985). *Social psychology and second language learning: The role of attitudes and motivation*. London: Edward Arnold.

Gilmore, G. W. (1892). *Korea from its capital*. Philadelphia: The Presbyterian Board of Publication. Retrieved September 6, 2018, from https://archive.org/details/koreafromitscap00gilmgoog.

Griffis, W. E. (1882). *Corea: The hermit nation*. New York: Charles Scribner's Sons.

Han, Hong-Koo. (2006). *Daehanminkooksa [History of the Republic of Korea]*. Seoul, Korea: Hangyeorye.

Hwang, Young-Soon. (2014). The history of American English education in Korea: Reflection and new direction. *The Korean Journal of American History, 40*, 201–238.

Jeon, Bong-Gwan. (2005). Kyungsungjedae ipsi daesodong [Turmoil in the university entrance exam of Kyungsung Imperial University]. Retrieved August 17, 2018, from http://shindonga.donga.com/Library/3/02/13/105035/5.

Jeon, Bong-Gwan. (2006). Lee Ha-Young daegam'eui yeong'eo choolsegi [chronicle of His Excellency Lee Ha-Young's success in English learning]. Retrieved October 25, 2019, from https://shindonga.donga.com/Library/3/02/13/105895/1.

Jeon, Bong-Gwan. (2008). 'Yujeon iphak mujeon nakje' ipsijiokeui tansaeng ['Plutocracy in entrance exam' The birth of exam hell]. Retrieved August 18, 2018, from http://shindonga.donga.com/3/all/13/107537/8.

Kang, Joon-Mann. (2009). *Ipsi jeonjaeng janhoksa [Atrocious history of school exam war]*. Seoul, Korea: Inmulgwasasangsa.

Kang, Joon-Mann. (2014). *Hankook'ingwa yeong'eo [Koreans and English]*. Seoul, Korea: Inmulgwasasangsa.

Kang, Joon-Sik. (2010, March 19). Daetongryeong story Rhee Syngman [The story of President: Rhee Syngman]. Retrieved October 13, 2019, from https://news.joins.com/article/4069146.

Kang, Myung-sook. (2015). *Sariphakgyo'eu kiwon [Origin of private school]*. Seoul, Korea: Hakisiseup.

Kim, Myung-Bae. (2006a). *Gaehwagi'eui yeong'eo iyagi [The story of English in the era of enlightenment]*. Seoul, Korea: International Graduate School of English Press.

Kim, Sung-il, Yoon, Misun, & So, Yeonhee. (2008). Academic interests of Korean students: Description, diagnosis, and prescription. *Korean Journal of Psychological and Social Issues, 14*(1), 187–221.

Kim, Sung-Tae. (Ed.). (2001a). *Yun Chi-Ho ilgi: 1916-1943 [The diary of Yun Chi-Ho]*. Seoul, Korea: Yeoksabipyeongsa.

Kim, Tae-Young. (2006b). Motivation and attitudes toward foreign language learning as socio-politically mediated constructs: The case of Korean high school students. *The Journal of Asia TEFL, 3*(2), 165–192.

Kim, Tae-Young. (2010). Socio-political influences on EFL motivation and attitudes: Comparative surveys of Korean high school students. *Asia Pacific Education Review, 11*, 211–222.

Kim, Tae-Young. (2016). An investigation of socio-educational aspects of English education during Japanese colonial period: Focusing on Chosun Ilbo and Dong-A Daily articles. *Studies in English Education, 21*(1), 179–210.

Kim, Terri. (2001b). *Forming the academic profession in East Asia: A comparative analysis*. London: Routledge.

Kim, Young-Chul. (2011). *Yeong'eo, Joseon'eul kkaewooda [English awakens Joseon]*. Seoul, Korea: Illy.

Kim, Young-Woo. (1997). *Hankook gaehwagi'eui gyoyook [Education at the period of modernization in Korea]*. Seoul, Korea: Gyoyookgwahaksa.

Kim-Rivera, E. G. (2002). English language education in Korea under Japanese colonial rule. *Language Policy, 1*(3), 261–281.

Kimura, M. (1993). Standards of living in colonial Korea: Did the masses become worse off or better off under Japanese rule? *The Journal of Economic History, 53*(3), 629–652.

Kwon, Oryang. (2000). Korea's education policy changes in the 1990s: Innovations to gear the nation for the 21st Century. *English Teaching, 55*(1), 47–91.

Kwon, Oryang, & Kim, Jeong-Ryeol. (2010). *Hankook yeong'eogyoyooksa [History of English education in Korea]*. Seoul, Korea: Hankookmunwhasa.

Lee, Bok-Hee, & Yeo, Do-Soo. (2001). Hankook'eui yeong'eogyoyook'e gwanhan yeoksajeok gochalgwa jeongaebanghyang'e gwanhan yeongu [Study of historical investigation and progression of English education in Korea]. *Gongjuyeongsangjeongbodaehak Nonmunjip, 8*, 377–392.

Lee, Duk-Il. (2003). *Lee Dul-Il'eu yeoin yeoljeon [Lee Duk-Il's women chronicle]*. Seoul, Korea: Gimyeongsa.

Lee, Ha-Young. (1926). Hanmigookgyowa hae'asageon [The national relation between Korea and the U.S. and the Hague incident]. *Sinmin, 6*.

Lee, Kwang-Sook. (2014). *Gaewhagi'eu oikook'eo gyoyook [Education of foreign languages in the Era of Enlightenment]*. Seoul, Korea: Seoul National University Press.

Lee, M. & Larson, R. (2000). The Korean "examination hell": Long hours of studying, distress, and depression. *Journal of Youth and Adolescence, 29*(2), 249–271.

Lee, Sang-Gil. (2012). Kyungsung bangsongguk'eui chochanggi yeonyeprogram'eul jejakgwa pyeonseong [The production and programming of entertainment programs of the early JODK]. *Media and Society, 20*(3), 5–74.

Lee, Sun Mi (2002). *The training of English interpreter of the Chosun Dynasty in 1880's*. Unpublished master's thesis. Graduate School of Korea National University of Education.

Lew, Seok-Choon, Oh, Young Seob, Fields, David P., & Han, Ji Eun. (2015). *The diary of Syngman Rhee*. Seoul, Korea: National Museum of Korean Contemporary History.

Lew, Young Ick. (1994). Korean perception of the United States during the Enlightenment Period. In Young Ick Lew, Byung-kie Song, Ho-min Yang & Hyssop Lim (Eds.), *Korean perception of the United States: A history of formation* (pp. 55–142). Seoul, Korea: Minumsa.

Marginson, S. (2011). Higher education in East Asia and Singapore: Rise of the Confucian model. *Higher Education, 61*(5), 587–611.

Martin, R. M. (1847). *China: Political, commercial, and social: In an official report to her majesty's government* (vol. 2). London: James Madden.

Moon, Yong. (1976). Hankook yeongeogyoyooksa (1883-1945) [History of English education in Korea (1883-1945)]. *Sunggoknonchong, 7*, 618–654.

Nobuo, J. (1901). *Kanhanto [韓半島, The Korean Peninsula]*. Tokyo Book Store (東京堂書店).

Norton, B., & Kanno, Y. (2003). Imagined communities and educational opportunities: Introduction. *Journal of Language, Identity, and Education, 2*(4), 241–249.

Old Korean Legation. (2019). History of the Old Korean Legation. Retrieved October 12, 2019, from https://www.oldkoreanlegation.org/timeline.

Paik, L. G. (1929). *The history of protestant missions in Korea*. Pyeongyang, Korea: Union Christian College Press.

Park, Chan-Seung. (2015). 1920nyeondae Saito chongdok'eui munhwa jeongchiran [What is cultural policy by Governor General Saito?] Retrieved August 13, 2018, from http://blog.daum.net/_blog/BlogTypeView.do?blogid=0NOWR&articleno=241&categoryId=35&regdt=20150725225905.

Park, Chul-Hee. (2003). Sikminjihakryeokgyeongjaenggwa iphaksiheom joonbigyoyook'eui deungjang [Competition of academic credentials and the advent of preparatory education for entrance exam]. *Asian Journal of Education 4*(1), 65–92.

Park, D. M., & Müller, J. C. (2014). The challenge that Confucian filial piety poses for Korean churches. *Theological Studies, 70*(2), 1–8.

Park, Geo-Yong. (2008). Yeongeo sinhwa'eui yeojewa oneul [Yesterday and today of English myth]. *Naeil'eul Yeonun Yeksa, 32*, 77–88.

Park, Pugang. (1974). *Hanguk yeong'eo gyoyooksa yeongu (1883-1945) [A study of the history of English education in Korea (1883-1945)]*. Unpublished master's thesis, Seoul National University, Korea.

Platt, S. R. (2018). *Imperial twilight: The Opium War and the end of China's last golden age*. New York: Knopf.

Rhee, Syngman. (1912). *Neutrality as influenced by the United States*. Unpublished doctoral dissertation. Princeton, NJ: Princeton University Press.

Rhee, Syngman. (1941). *Japan inside out: The challenge of today*. New York: Fleming H. Revell.

Richards, J. C., & Rodgers, T. S. (2014). *Approaches and methods in language teaching* (3). Cambridge, England: Cambridge University Press.

Ross, C. (2017). *Ecology and power in the age of empire: Europe and the transformation of the tropical world*. Oxford, England: Oxford University Press.

Seo, Jung-Ick. (2003). Segyedaegonghwanggi (1929-1936nyeon) ilbon'eui mooyeokgoojowa mooyeokjeongchaek [The Japanese trade structure and policy in the age of the Great Depression]. *Applied Economics, 5*(1), 55–89.

Seth, M. J. (2002). *Education fever: Society, politics, and the pursuit of schooling in South Korea*. Honolulu, HI: University of Hawai'i Press.

Smith, R. C. (1998). The Palmer-Hornby contribution to English teaching in Japan. *International Journal of Lexicography, 11*(4), 269–291.

Son, In-Soo. (1971). *Hankook geundaegyoyooksa [Modern education in Korea].* Seoul, Korea: Yonsei University Press.

Underwood, H. H. (1926). *Modern education in Korea.* New York: International Press.

Yoon, Soo-An. (2014). *'Jegook'ilbon'gwa yeong'eo, yeongmoonhak [Imperial Japan and English language education, English literature].* Seoul, Korea: Somyung.

Zeng, K. (1995). Japan's Dragon Gate: The effects of university entrance examinations on the educational system and students. *Compare, 25,* 59–83.

Chapter 3
Historical Overview of English Learning in South Korea: The U.S. Military Government, Korean War, and Post-War Reconstruction Period

This chapter focuses on the role of English language among Korean people[1] after the liberation from Japan in 1945 and the Korean War, to the post-war reconstruction period until the 1980s. In the process of post-war industrialization from the 1950s to the 1980s, English became the most crucial school subject that directly affected university entrance exams across South Korea. Moreover, it was the key to initial job screening and promotion in work environments. This chapter will argue that this continual trend surrounding English education reflects the concept of *hakbul*, or "academic credentialism," having its origin in the Confucian tradition practiced during the Joseon Dynasty. With the rapid industrialization since the 1960s, Koreans have gradually started to believe that education, particularly academic degrees at prestigious universities, can break the current poverty-stricken status quo and gain access to savvy, affluent, and urbane lifestyles. In this general atmosphere, the motivation to learn English among Korean students acquired an increasingly instrumental and competitive nature. In this backdrop, this chapter surveys the overall English-related social behavior and academic curriculum, and how these phenomena could be consistently explained by the concept of *hakbul* orientation and competitive motivation.

3.1 The U.S. Military Government Period from 1945 to 1948

After the liberation from Japan on August 15, 1945, in order to disarm the Japanese army in the Korean peninsula, the U.S. military troops stationed themselves in the southern part of 38° of north latitude from September 8, 1945; in the northern part of

---

[1]From this chapter on, Korea refers to "South Korea," except Sect. 5.3 in Chap. 5 explaining the situation in North Korea.

© Springer Nature Singapore Pte Ltd. 2021
T.-Y. Kim, *Historical Development of English Learning Motivation Research*,
English Language Education 21, https://doi.org/10.1007/978-981-16-2514-5_3

the Korean peninsula, the Soviet Army quickly took control of Pyeongyang (capital city of North Korea) as early as August 23. The U.S. Army stationed in the southern part established the U.S. Military Government (USMG) and functioned as a *de facto* government until the establishment of the Government of South Korea by democratic national election on August 15, 1948. Therefore, the interim 3-year period following the liberation from Japan until the establishment of South Korea's own government is named the USMG Period. Since the USMG took complete control of South Korea, elite Koreans who had studied abroad in the U.S. were appointed to prime positions in the USMG while supporting the U.S. Army officers in the military cabinet. American officers were relatively young and did not have in-depth knowledge of education in Korea. Thus, the small number of chosen elite Koreans functioned as liaison between the U.S. Army officers having official positions at the USMG and the Korean public who did not know English. To argue that these Koreans controlled the newly established South Korean government in 1948 would not be an overstatement (Lee, 2003; Son, 1992). Those who were able to speak a moderate level of English were hired by the USMG immediately. For example, Peter Hyun, who was born in Hamheung city, North Korea, and later worked as an editor at Doubleday in the U.S., obtained his English job in 1945, immediately after the establishment of the USMG.

> After the liberation from Japan, I could only think of working as an interpreter for the U.S. military personnel stationed in Seoul. I loved and had confidence in English when I attended secondary school in Hamheung. I have to admit that I had never learned spoken English though. So, I thought my speaking ability was not very good. But what's the big deal? I just wanted to test my luck and face it. I was young and foolishly brave. I visited H.R. office at the U.S. Army 8th Division. When a tall and chubby army major sitting on the desk asked my age, and perhaps he thought I was too young to work. I just added three years more than my real age. That's all ... I couldn't believe I could get hired this easy. Without being asked for my resume or qualifications! Having this experience, I began to love America and Americans. (translated by the author, Hyun, 1996, pp. 29–30)

As explained in Chap. 2, during the Japanese Colonization Period, secondary and tertiary education in Korea were extremely elitist, and only a select few who passed the highly competitive entrance exams had the opportunity to receive higher education. As the country had been through 35 years of colonization, Koreans who demonstrated fluent English communication skills were a rarity, and as such they were fast-tracked toward the government office and the monopoly of national wealth under the control of the USMG (Kang, 2009). For example, Mr. Shin Sung-Mo, who had formerly been part of the resistance to the Japanese rule and worked as a navigator, was appointed as Minister of National Defense, and his English ability had been regarded as a factor in his appointment (Kang, 2011, 2014). Many educated Koreans endeavored to be hired not only for high-ranking officer positions, but also for minor jobs related to English interpreting. According to Cho and Lee (1995), the wage for the USMG interpreters was minimal; however, as the USMG officers had the decisional power over the sales of so-called "enemy property," which included the seized properties of Japanese inhabitants in Korea, interpreters were the first persons to obtain such information from the USMG.

The sociopolitical incidents at the inception of the Government of South Korea in the second half of the 1940s indicate the high status of the English language in the country. Under the control of the USMG, English took the prime role: it became the only official language, and, in the case of disparity or miscommunication between English and Korean, the former was prioritized over the latter (Oh, 2000; Son, 1992). Oh (2000, p. 234) explains the behavior toward the English language during the USMG as follows:

> The demand for English speakers showed a rapid increase after the U.S. Headquarter in South Korea and the USMG began to control South Korea. At that time, only a modicum of Koreans had the experience of study abroad in the U.S. Based on their academic credentials from U.S. educational institutes, they were offered high-ranking positions at the USMG. This phenomenon consolidated South Koreans' belief that English proficiency is the prime tool to succeed in Korean society. According to Proclamation No. 1 by General of the U.S. Army Douglas MacArthur,[2] the USMG officialized the use of English language, adopted English as the first foreign language in the middle school curriculum, and increased the weekly hours of instruction of English to the same degree or more as those of Korean. Due to these measures, the English test score became the crucial determinant to be admitted to the upper-level school and started to function as the vital factor to be successful in life.

> Different from today's circumstance, public schools were the only educational institution where Koreans could learn English at the time of liberation. The fact that a person can speak English well connoted two things. First, at the superficial level, it meant that the person had a good standing in English classes. However, this also meant that he or she had a friendly attitude and heartfelt longings toward the U.S., where the English language is used as a de facto national language. During the transition period from the Japanese Colonization to the USMG, while rejecting the language and culture of Japan, the English language and American culture replaced them. The U.S. culture and ways of thinking were rapidly spread in the Korean society often associated with the American dreams. *Mikooktong* (미국통), a new jargon meaning the gateway to America, was created to represent the Koreans who could speak English, had working knowledge of the States, and had the aspiration to the States.

For this reason, short-term English language training programs were widely established across South Korea, mainly targeting police officers and military personnel. For example, a December 28 newspaper article reported the establishment of a Military English School to train 144 military personnel to become army interpreters (Dong-A Ilbo, 1945, December 28).

Dr. Rhee Syngman[3] (1875–1965), the first President of the Republic of Korea (tenure: 1948–1960), contributed to the revival of English in South Korea. Dr. Rhee was the recipient of a missionary scholarship to the U.S.; while studying there, he

---

[2]Article V in Proclamation No. 1 reads as follows:

  Article V: For all purposes during the military control, English will be the official language. In event of any ambiguity or diversity of interpretation or definition between any English and Korean or Japanese text, the English text shall prevail (The United States Department of States, 2019).

[3]He was a former graduate of Paichai Hakdang, established by Rev. Appenzeller. He moved to the U.S., earned a Ph.D. degree in Politics from Princeton University, and took part in the Korean Independence Movement. He was elected as the first President of the Republic of Korea (South Korea).

married Francesca Donner, an Austrian-American, and was fluent in English himself (Critical Studies on Modern Korean History, 1998). Dr. Rhee's favoritism toward English can be considered one of the many reasons for English vogue in the 1940s and onward. In major Korean newspapers, for example, trivial events such as high school or college English speech contests were introduced and widely advertised. Kim and Kim (2018) reported that among the 68 newspaper articles on English education published during the USMG, 56% of them were related to English speech contests, English plays, and English classes, which corroborates the nationwide interest in English.

Kang (2009) pointed out that Rhee Syngman should be criticized as the person who aggravated excessive pro-Americanism and academic credentialism in South Korea. In most Korean newspapers during his tenure, he was addressed as "Dr. Rhee" more frequently than as "President Rhee." The fact that he was conferred a Ph.D. degree at Princeton was acclaimed by most Koreans, which consolidated the naivety that a U.S. degree from an Ivy League university bestowed political authority. While experiencing the USMG, Koreans witnessed that a U.S.-educated, doctoral degree holder had risen to power, and rapidly conferred renewed attention to the importance of an academic degree. Moreover, they realized that the amalgamation between the U.S. and an academic degree maximized the opportunity to succeed in South Korea.

However, during the USMG, the education fever was fueled by U.S. policies in Korea; in fact, the USMG did not exert excessive control over the establishment of higher educational institutions. During the Japanese Colonization Period, opportunities within secondary and tertiary education for Koreans were limited. According to Oh (2000), before liberation, the total number of secondary students in Kyungsung (now Seoul) was 29,748, of which 37% was Japanese, which meant that 18,741 Korean youth attended secondary schools. Furthermore, Lee (2017) reported that in 1944 the entire population in Kyungsung was 988,537. It is estimated that the percentage of Japanese in Kyungsung was around 28 (Park, 2017), which concludes that 711,746 Koreans lived in Seoul. Therefore, population-wise, merely 2.63% of Koreans in Kyungsung could attend secondary school. Considering that these statistics only deal with secondary school attendance, the number of students receiving tertiary education was even lower.

For this reason, the enthusiasm to achieve higher education increased exponentially after the liberation from Japan. As Oh (2000) noted, the educational fever could not be satisfied easily because only a small number of institutions for tertiary education existed. Moreover, during the Japanese Colonization Period, college education in Japan was a viable option for upper(-middle) class in Korea; yet, after the liberation and during the transitional turmoil thereon, the lack of diplomatic relations between the defeated Japanese government and the USMG precluded that option. In addition, studying abroad in English-speaking countries such as the U.S. and the U.K. was not possible for most Koreans given their adverse financial circumstances.

It was a natural consequence that an impressive number of tertiary educational institutions were established during the USMG period. During the 3 years of the USMG (1945–1948), 23 universities were either newly established or restructured

Table 3.1 Percentage of Japanese and Korean Officers in the Government-General of Korea in 1945

Level	Japanese	Korean	Total
1st level (highest)	2 (33.3%)	4 (66.7)	6 (100.0)
2nd level	148 (82.2)	31 (17.8)	174 (100.0)
3rd level	3848 (86.0)	624 (14.0)	4472 (100.0)
4th level (lowest)	46,664 (61.8)	28,891 (38.2)	75,555 (100.0)
Total	50,657 (63.2)	29,550 (36.8)	80,207 (100.0)

Note: Unit—number of persons (percentage in parenthesis)
Adapted from Oh (2000), p. 233

and promoted from their previous technical college status. For instance, private technical colleges were promoted to 4-year comprehensive universities: Bosung, Yonhi, Severance Medical, and Ewha Womans Colleges became Korea, Yonhi, Severance Medical, and Ewha Womans Universities (Oh, 2000).

Because of the aspiration to have educational opportunities, South Korea experienced a considerable expansion of the learning population. The Korean Educational Development Institute (1994) reported that the quantitative expansion was remarkable during the 3-year USMG period in terms of the number of schools, school instructors, and students. Notably, the number of elementary school students showed an increase of 77.6% from 1,366,024 to 2,426,113; that of middle school (i.e., the combination of junior high and high school) students showed an increase of 244.6% from 80,828 to 278,512. Regarding university statistics, for the 2 years from 1945 to 1947, the increase was 74.7%, from 7819 to 13,661.

Oh (2000) pointed out that this surge in education was not merely related to the aspiration to educational opportunity but also to the increasing opportunities for employment. Since the Government-General of Korea controlled occupied Korea, the liberation from Japan meant that these former Japanese rulers were expelled and repatriated. It was estimated that 883,576 Japanese were forced to leave Korea from 1945 to 1947. The Japanese repatriation resulted in the loss of social control when the USMG commenced in 1945. Table 3.1 presents the percentage of Japanese and Koreans in the Government-General of Korea at the time of liberation in 1945 (Oh, 2000, p. 233).

It was entirely dependent on the USMG's decision as to who would be appointed to the key position in the job vacancy. Oh (2000) emphasized that, during the transition period from the Japanese control to the USMG, the U.S. Army Korean headquarters asked for advice from the former Japanese officers before their repatriation, and these high-ranking Japanese officers recommended pro-Japanese Koreans in order to guarantee their safe repatriation to Japan. Therefore, previous pro-Japanese Koreans working at the Government-General of Korea were offered better positions; in order to fill the vacancy in public offices, pro-Japanese background, as well as the aforementioned English abilities, were prioritized.

3.2   During the Korean War and English Education in South Korea: 1950–1953

The interest in English was intensified during the Korean War (the so-called "Fatherland Liberation War" [祖國解放戰爭] in North Korea's nomenclature) from 1950 to 1953. The Soviet Union and China supported the North Korean army, and the North attacked South Korea on June 25, 1950. With the allied forces composed of 16 United Nations members, the South Korean government defended most of its territory, but the war casualties resulted in 1.2 million (Lacina & Gleditsch, 2005). In the following reconstruction period, economic support from the U.S. was crucial, and the role of English was even more emphasized. Most Koreans who endured the poverty-stricken period poignantly recall the economic support from the U.S. The following account is from Kim (2009a):

> The "gracious" U.S. lend a hand on those of us who entered elementary school the next year (i.e., 1951). While licking over the lead of a stubby pencil, we studied sitting on the bitterly cold floor in the classroom. The classroom barely stood with four lean pillars after continued bombardment from the U.S. jet bombers. Having no food during lunchtime, we just got together sunbathing in the sunlight like sunflowers. One day, in such a shabby place, "powdered milk" from the U.S. started to be distributed as war supply. The milk powder bag clearly showing the emblem of the handshake between the Stars and Stripes and *Taegeukki* (Korean national flag) was, in fact, the best nutrition provider for both children and adults in South Korea. Feeling hunger, we devoured the powder in a flurry; sometimes, we steamed and ate it at our leisure. Many years later, rumor said that the milk was for stock feed. But for the starving people, it was "salvation food." (original emphasis, translated by the author)

In this period, Christianity is also used for learning English. As explained in Chap. 2, during the nineteenth century, missionary schools contributed to modern education in Korea—particularly to English education. Similarly, in the 1950s, churches and the Young Men's Christian Association (YMCA) in South Korea functioned as English language schools. It is estimated that more than 200,000 Koreans attended English classes offered by the YMCA. In most cases, the protestant churches, particularly the YMCA, are associated with the headquarters in the U.S., and those who were introduced to this Christian association could have the opportunity to study there and be assisted during their stay (Kang, 1996).

The outbreak of the war aggravated the overreliance on the U.S. even after the conflict. During the USMG and the First Republic led by President Rhee Syngman, the need for Koreans who could speak and understand English had surged to the degree that it overshadowed one's misbehavior during the Japanese Colonization Period; this meant that, even though one may have voluntarily collaborated with the Japanese oppressors, the person's English ability had the power to nullify his or her pro-Japanese activities (Son, 1992). For most Koreans, this had also consolidated the belief of English as the (only) key to success.

During the Korean War, the demand for English was in a dire shortage, and numerous English lessons were organized and offered. Dong-A Ilbo (1951) reports an English lesson offered to police officers:

There exist many miscommunications between foreign troops and Koreans for the lack of communication skills, Gyeongnam Police Academy invites American teachers and Korean English instructors and offers summer English lesson to police officers for one month from August 1. This lesson welcomes all Koreans, not only police officers. For information, please contact Yeongdong Police Academy. (Dong-A Ilbo, 1951, July 31)

Compared with the outbreak of public interest toward the English language, public education was severely limited during warfare—English textbooks were not revised, and most students did not own textbooks. Before the Korean War, the situation was rather similar; as English was officially banned from teaching during World War II under the Japanese Colonization (Kim & Kim, 2018), English textbooks were hard to find. Because of the lack of English education policy in the late 1940s and 1950s during the Korean War, despite the significant difference between U.S. students (L1) and Korean students (EFL), U.S. textbooks were imported and distributed to Korean secondary school students (Dong-A Ilbo, 1948). Moreover, Sunday worship bulletins were also imported from U.S. churches to learn English (Kyunghyang Shinmun, 1948)—these bulletins were perhaps unused and meant to be recycled if not imported to South Korea.

Following the plan to distribute civilian supplies from the U.S., English textbooks are now in stock and will be distributed to secondary schools across South Korea. These textbooks are now being used in U.S. secondary schools and contain contents such as fairy tales and current issues. Fifty copies are allotted to every lower secondary school, and 40 to every high secondary school. (Dong-A Ilbo, 1948, July 6)

The Ministry of Education now distributes easy Sunday bulletins written in English to use for English textbooks. It is said that the contents include fairy tales and current issues. (Kyunghyang Shinmun, 1948, July 6)

Note that the education zeal continued even during the civil war. To Koreans, the best and most reliable way to enhance their quality of life and escape poverty was to continue to receive education. As illustrated above, the knowledge of English was, more than anything else, a convenient way to secure employment during the USMG period and the Korean War. Academic credentials were also imperative to have a job. Furthermore, the opportunity to learn at school was severely suppressed during the Japanese Colonization Period, and only a few select Koreans could be offered educational opportunities at the tertiary level (see Chap. 2). Therefore, even during the war, the aspiration to learn was not quenched; teaching and learning continued incessantly by accommodating more than 100 students in a class and offering morning, afternoon, and night classes (Kang, 2011). The New York Times reported this exceptional aspiration toward education—the following newspaper article, for example, illustrated the adverse educational situation in South Korea (MacGreggor, 1951).

Regardless of other shortcomings, the Republic of Korea has made an earnest and coura-geous effort to continue and improve its educational system.

Even during the worst part of the winter when starvation, cold and disease were taking a toll in hundreds of thousands, means were found by the South Korean Government and the

United Nations to continue the schooling of many children. Now, most of the school-age children are getting regular instruction. ...

As could be expected in a war-torn country, the shortage of textbooks presents a serious problem. But throughout the countryside knots of students sit under trees with perhaps a single blackboard nailed to a tree trunk, sharing and holding together tattered pages of paper-bound volumes. As many as six or eight children share each book and pass it back and forth for recitations as the teacher, often in rags, directs and advises with a pointer torn from a low-handing bough overhead.

Progressive members of the South Korean Government realize that the future of the country rests to a considerable extent on bringing up the educational standards and lowering the high illiteracy rate that has held back the Koreans for centuries. (MacGreggor, 1951, June 8)

As noted in the article, the high illiteracy rate was considered a severe social problem in the early 1950s. Although the GDP per capita of South Korea was less than $100 a year in the 1950s (e.g., $67 in 1953) (Korea Herald, 2015), the Rhee Government had spent an average of 10.5% of the total national expenses on education from 1948 to 1960; as a result, the literacy rate rapidly increased from 22% in 1945 to 75% in 1952, and 78% in 1959.[4]

The outbreak of the Korean War was a national catastrophe resulting in devastation and numerous casualties. However, in terms of social reconstruction, this tragedy caused a complete social reshuffle. The destruction across the nation had made most Koreans start from ground zero. Having their wealth destroyed by the warfare, Koreans had to start from scratch, which strengthened the sense of egalitarianism—meaning that "we Koreans" are equally living in penury, and all Koreans had the equal opportunity to start over. Kang (2011) highlighted that this sense of egalitarianism turned into an overemphasis on education, which was regarded as the key to (re-)climbing the social ladder. This point will be further explained in Sect. 3.7 on *hakbul* or academic credentialism in South Korea.

3.3   Post-War Reconstruction, Education, and English Education: 1954–1960

After more than 3 years of atrocious civil war in Korea, the armistice treaty was ratified in July 1953, and the Rhee Syngman government expedited the reconstruction process. As stated in the previous section, Koreans' aspiration to receive education continued during the war. After the war, the need to have such opportunity increased. Oh (2000) emphasized that, in terms of quantitative aspects, education in South Korea had expanded exponentially. For instance, the number of elementary schools in Korea increased from 2834 in 1945 (at the time of liberation from Japan) to 4602 in 1960, an increase of 62.49%, whereas the number of elementary school

---

[4]UNESCO (2019) data show that 99.4% of South Koreans complete primary education, which means that virtually no Koreans are now illiterate.

Table 3.2 Number of elementary schools, teachers, and students in 1945, 1953, and 1960

Year	Number of schools	Number of teachers	Number of students		
			Boys	Girls	Total
1945	2834	19,729	825,013	541,011	1,366,024
1953	4007	37,320	1,378,874	868,183	2,247,057
1960	4602	61,749	1,966,069	1,633,558	3,599,627

Note: Unit—number of persons

students was 1,366,024 in 1945, but reached 3,599,627 in 1960 (a 163.5% increase). The statistics show that approximately 95% of Korean children attended elementary school in 1960; however, the number of students per school did not improve: 482 in 1945, 561 in 1953, and 782 in 1960. Table 3.2 shows the number of elementary schools, teachers, and students in 1945, 1953, and 1960 (Oh, 2000, p. 251).

Oh (2000) argued that the extension of women's rights represented the main reason for this rapid growth in the number of elementary school students. The increased awareness in women's education caused a chain reaction in secondary and tertiary education, which led the quantitative expansion of education in South Korea in the post-war period.

In the case of middle school, the increase was even more dramatic. At the time of liberation in 1945, middle schools adopted a 5-year system; there were a total of 97 schools and 50,343 students enrolled. In 1960, however, the number of middle schools spiked to 1053, hosting 528,614 students—a ten-time increase within a 15-year period. A noticeable trend was the gender difference in the number of students attending middle school. The ratio of girls to boys was 47.1% (23,721 vs. 50,343) in 1945, but fell to 22.7% in 1953, eventually becoming 24.4% in 1960. Even compared to the liberation period in 1945, the gender imbalance aggravated in the 1950s. In explaining the degeneration in gender balance, Oh (2000) referred to the established tradition of preferring sons to daughters in Korea. In a patriarchal, agricultural society such as that of traditional Korea, there is an easily identifiable, unilateral preference for male offspring and masculinity (cf. An & Kim, 2007; Hofstede, 1991). It appears that the reason for less gender disparity in 1945 may have been the lack of secondary education in colonized Korea. In fact, only girls with a wealthy family background could have had the opportunity to attend 5-year-long middle schools. After the war, however, the opportunity to attend secondary school was extended to the middle class, and more Korean parents decided to have their children attend middle school. In this case, the preference was given to their sons rather than to their daughters because of their limited financial resources for education. Thus, the expansion of educational opportunity had aggravated gender disparity. Nonetheless, the gap showed a rapid decrease from the 1960s onward as the number of children per household decreased, and the social awareness of gender equality rapidly spread.

Regarding the extension of educational opportunities after the Korean War, Oh (1964), who had made significant contributions to establishing the educational system in the 1940s and 1950s, pointed out ten plausible reasons: (1) education fever (教育熱), (2) expansion of educational institutions, (3) introduction of mandatory education, (4) exponential increase in student enrollment, (5) the influence of the agrarian reform (establishing private educational institutions escaping the government's confiscation of private land after the liberation from Japan), (6) high demand of university education, (7) precluded opportunity to study abroad in Japan, (8) the simplification of the school establishment law, (9) postponing the enlistment of male university students, and (10) aggravation of the unemployment crisis. Among these reasons, education fever may be relevant in explaining the English vogue in Korea. Oh (1964) summarized education fever as follows:

> Traditionally, influenced by the Chinese culture, particularly by Confucianism, Koreans have emphasized education and cherished the power of literature. Therefore, the policymakers had established educational institutions, provided the opportunity to receive education for young men, and tried to select talented government officers through this educational system. In addition, Koreans regarded becoming the literati class after learning literature as the idealistic life. Having inherited this tradition, they could not satisfy their aspiration toward education during the oppressive Japanese Colonization Period. With the liberation from Japan, they enthusiastically embraced the opportunity to satisfy this overly suppressed desire to learn. Thus, parents vehemently educated their children despite their unfavorable economic circumstance, and as a result, schools were inundated with Korean youths. Old generations tried to provide their offspring with the chance to succeed in life through the benefit of education, which they did not receive previously. New generations, armed with the power of education, tried to make this unmet dream realized. (Oh, 1964, p. 498)

When attempting to examine the situation surrounding English education during the 1950s and onward, Oh's (1964) explanation about education fever proves relevant. The primary reason for education was to increase the opportunities for success in life; in other words, Koreans had consolidated the belief that the academic degree assures "employment, higher earnings, and most importantly, upward social mobility" (Mok & Neubauer, 2015, p. 1). It could be argued that the belief in the importance of English proficiency served the same purpose as the education fever. From repeated exposure through media and social discourse (DellaVigna & Gentzkow, 2010), the role of education and English had been emphasized and strengthened among Koreans.

It was not until 1954 that the Ministry of Education of Korea announced the establishment of the National Curriculum, which can be referenced for the making of textbooks used in primary and secondary schools across South Korea. Because of the political turmoil and the Korean War, any systematic teaching and learning of school subjects was nearly impossible. Only unsystematic, discontinuous education amalgamated with Korea's zeal toward education could be offered before 1954. However, on April 20, 1954, the First National Curriculum of Korea was announced (Kwon & Kim, 2010). This was a critical historical moment in Korean education— following the systematic outline of the curriculum, English education in Korea could be revised and developed. In this regard, the First National Curriculum was the founding stone in South Korea's English education.

In the First National Curriculum (NC), which lasted from 1954 to 1963, American English was specified as the standard English (Lee, 2011), and the introduction of new vocabulary items was controlled as follows: 400 new words for 1st-year middle-school students, 500 words for 2nd year, and 600 words for 3rd year. Notably, since most English teachers had been trained during the Japanese Colonization Period, it was imperative to remove the Japanese-style English pronunciation among them (Moon, 2005). Moreover, the First NC implemented a mixture of Grammar Translation Method (GTM) and the Audio-lingual Method. As presented in Chap. 2, the GTM had been widely used during the Japanese Colonization Period, when reading comprehension and grammar knowledge were regarded as crucial skills in English. However, this method did not develop necessary oral proficiency in English and could not be of much help during the USMG period. Thus, behavioristic pattern practice and drills were incorporated in the First NC, influenced by the U.S.-based behavioristic pedagogy (Kwon & Kim, 2010).

Although the First NC mandated incorporating U.S. educational psychology—significantly reflecting Skinner's (1957) behaviorism—the educational context in Korea in the 1950s did not provide fertile ground to introduce the behavioristic principle. In fact, English teachers still held a strong belief that the GTM was the best method for them to prepare their students for the entrance exam of higher educational institutions; this may be paradoxical because of the disparity between the imminent need for oral English proficiency and the school-based English exam. Proficiency in English speaking and listening was required to expedite the communication between the U.S. Army, which was mostly still stationed there after the Korean War, and the Korean people. However, the needs for school exam preparation could not be ignored. All Korean middle schools and high schools administered entrance exams on their own before 1968, meaning that all graduating students from elementary and middle schools in the 1950s and 1960s were required to take entrance exams. Since English tests were administered to high school entrance exams, most students prepared for English test. As explained in Chap. 4, it was not until 1993 that the listening comprehension component was included in the Korean college entrance exam system, which meant that the English test remained the same as that administered in the previous generation; the knowledge of reading, grammar, and vocabulary was still prioritized in the 1950s.

For this reason, despite the need to enhance oral proficiency in English among Korean students, the educational system did not support the use of audio-lingualism in the 1950s and repeated the GTM used in previous generations (Hwang, 2014; Kim, 2016). Dong-A Ilbo (1957) criticized the English education method used during the previous Japanese Colonization Period and particularly the GTM in the following article.

> It would be a nationwide phenomenon that the methods which English and other foreign language teachers use are what they had used during the Japanese Colonization Period. It is the worst heritage that Imperial Japan had left on us. [...] Why cannot a college student who studied English start simple English conversation or write a letter in English? The responsibility would be entirely on English teachers because of the ineffective teaching method failing to satisfy students' needs. [...] First of all, it is a tragedy that most English teachers cannot communicate in English. (Dong-A Ilbo, 1957, October 4)

The abovementioned newspaper article, which a professor from Seoul National University contributed to, criticized the lack of English communication skills among English teachers, as well as the ineffective teaching methods carried on from the previous Japanese Colonization Period. Similar critiques continued following the establishment of the First National Curriculum. Chosun Ilbo's (1955) article also pointed out the futile effort to repeat the GTM in enhancing English-speaking proficiency while criticizing the English textbooks mostly used for translation purposes.

> Moving forward or backward? [...] The students during the Japanese Colonization Period paid most attention to vocabulary and interpretation of difficult English passages. [...] However, the new direction in English education presents a substantial difference. [...] It would be sometimes required to have practices in interpretations, but more often than not, it would result in ineffective instruction results if English teachers teach their students esoteric English passages. [...] Are English teachers aware of the shortcomings of their pronunciation? [...] Like first-year beginners, they may need to practice their English pronunciation sitting in front of the audio-recorder or English experts. (Chosun Ilbo, 1955, July 10)

However, opposing opinions reflecting the educational system in South Korea in the 1950s are equally found (Moon, 2005). Because of the prevalent entrance exams in Korea, many English teachers still focused on grammatical aspects and reading comprehension. The following article included in Chosun Ilbo shows advice on English testing provided by Mr. Kim Sook-Dong, an in-service English teacher at Ewha Girl's High School.

> I will highlight important points that all test takers should keep in mind in the English grammar section comprising a third of the entire English test. Usually, in terms of the verb in the English grammar, the question on tense, [...] for the auxiliary verb, proper usage of "should" and "would" [...] for the items asking passive voice, [....] In the case of "If-deletion" [...] (Chosun Ilbo, 1959a, January 26).

Given the educational system in the 1950s, the advice from an English teacher would be practical and timely. In a close examination of the college entrance exam format in use at that time, it is revealed that English conversation and colloquial expressions were not the focus of the test. Figure 3.1 presents parts of the English test items from the National College Qualification Test administered during the First NC period. As shown in Fig. 3.1, the English tests were composed of English pronunciation (i.e., primary accent), orthography, vocabulary and idioms, selecting the correct English sentence, filling in the blank (inferencing), and reading comprehension (Chosun Ilbo, 1962, December 14).[5] As such, for the washback effect, students and teachers alike did not prioritize English speaking and listening.

The resistance to oral proficiency was also raised by the Korea Association of English Linguistics and Literature, a university-based scholarly organization. In the war-torn economic situation of the 1950s, only a modicum of university students

---

[5]This type of national test was administered only for 2 years, in 1962 and 1963. Although the year of first administration had been after the 1950s, this test still belonged to the period of the First National Curriculum. Thus, it would provide useful insights into the typical English testing format throughout the First NC overlapping the 1950s.

could study abroad, meaning that virtually all university students in South Korea did

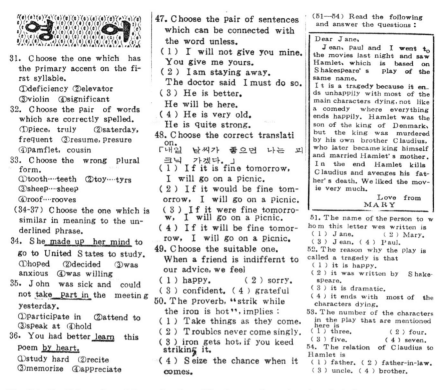

Fig. 3.1 English section of the national qualification test for university admission

not (and could not) have the chance to speak English. Instead, a moderate level of English literacy—mainly English for academic purposes—was required for most of them. For these practical needs, the imminent need for enhancing college students' reading skills in English was argued in the conference organized by this association in 1959.

> It is only a few persons who can use English for practical purposes. [...] The most urgent need would be making students understand the essential books for their undergraduate majors written in English. To make this happen, we should give priority to the ability in reading comprehension. [...] Then, it was pointed out that in terms of curriculum and textbooks, it is imperative to revise middle school and high school English textbooks. Besides, it was criticized that the difficulty level of college English textbooks was too high, given the enormous difference in English proficiency among high school graduates. (Chosun Ilbo, 1959b, July 2)

Note that this article was included in Chosun Ilbo, the Korean national newspaper with the most significant number of subscribers. In the twenty-first-century newspaper articles, such type of articles reporting scholarly discussion on English learning would be a rarity. However, as shown in the excerpt above, it appears that the interest of the general public toward the English language was exceptionally high during this specific period as it was during the USMG and the Korean War periods (Kim & Kim, 2018).

To summarize English education in the post-war reconstruction period during the 1950s, the introduction of the First NC was the historical cornerstone for the development of education in Korea (Moon, 2005). English education also showed a moderate level of progress, which differed from the previous generation. American English was prioritized over British or Japanese English, and the Audio-lingual Method influenced by U.S. behaviorism was incorporated (Kwon & Kim, 2010). However, because of the practical need to prepare for the entrance exams of higher educational institutions, the influence of GTM did not decrease. Both students and teachers still relied on English grammar, vocabulary, and reading comprehension, all of which were emphasized in the GTM method. The fact that the new approach based on Skinner's (1957) behaviorism did not have an impact on English education in the 1950s proves that Korean students and their families had the practical desire to use English, or more precisely English test scores, to be admitted to higher educational institutions such as high schools or universities. As Oh (1964) emphasized, it should be noted that the aspiration to receive education is the heritage of traditional Korean society. As explained in Chap. 2 (and Chap. 5 as well), the Confucianism practiced during the late Joseon Dynasty was suppressed during the Japanese Colonization Period. However, after the liberation from Japan, the expansion of educational opportunities and the establishment of public and private universities fueled the desire to ascend the social ladder through education.

3.4   English as a Tool for College Entrance in the 1960s

The reliance on the U.S. did not change after the political regime changed in the 1960s. President Rhee Syngman lost his political power after the April 19 Student Revolution in 1960, which was ignited by his unconstitutional intervention into the national election. He soon sought political asylum to Hawaii and died there in 1965. In the Second Republic of South Korea established after the collapse of President Rhee's Liberal Party, those who were fluent in English came to compose the cabinet. President Yoon Bo-sun was a graduate of the University of Edinburgh, U.K., and Prime Minister Jang Myeon was the first Korean Ambassador to the U.S., where he had stable personal relations with influential figures. General Jang Do-Young was appointed as the Army Chief of Staff, and it was widely believed that both his and his wife's superb command of English had attracted positive evaluation from many U.S. generals who were stationed in South Korea (Cho, 1998).

The military coup on May 16, 1961, led by Major General Park Chung-hee, resulted in the collapse of the short-lived Second Republic and placed the nation under military control. Kang (2009) provides an interesting analysis of the elite military officer group after the Korean War. Because of the Korean War, the expenses for national defense were approximately 40% of the total national budget in the 1950s and 30% until the 1980s (Han, 2003). Moreover, given the general lack of educational opportunity in the devastated Korea of the 1950s, military officers had expert knowledge in various branches of military service. According to Han (2001), until at least the 1970s, military officers were the most educated elite group in South Korea. He explains the nature of the elite officers in South Korea as follows.

> From 1953 to 1966, the total number of civilians who passed the National Qualifying Examination for Study Abroad was 7,398, and 86 percent of them studied in the U.S. However, the percentage of returnees was only 6 percent. On the contrary, in the 1950s only, approximately 9,000 Korean military officers were selected and dispatched to various military academies and schools in the U.S. and returned to South Korea. Their short duration of study abroad should be considered, but clearly, the Korean armed forces held a high number of study-abroad elites, which is beyond comparison to any other groups in South Korea. (Han, 2003, p. 273)

President Park Chung-hee was a former army general and had actively supported the elite military officers. It should also be noted that the military officers' practical utilitarianism balanced the traditional emphasis on literature. The advanced Western technology was imported through the U.S.-trained Korean military officers and then spread to other social structures across South Korea. By citing a former army general's recollection, Kang (2009) diagnosed that the expansion of elite military officers in Korea might have resulted in the military coup of 1961. Compared with the available human resource in the Korean Army, that of the private sectors, including the political regime in the Rhee government (First Republic) and the Jang Myeon government (Second Republic), was inferior. This circumstance imbued confidence and ignited the ambition to overthrow the political system.

The education fever Oh (1964) criticized was related to the deep-rooted Confucian tradition. However, education fever, often associated with college admission, can also be attributed to the desire to exempt or postpone military enlistment. Given the social atmosphere immediately after the Korean War, most, if not all, healthy Korean young men were subject to military enlistment and were required to serve more than 30 months in the armed forces. However, for college students, the enlistment was postponed. By taking advantage of this sentiment, private universities tried to give admission to as many young men as possible. In academically rigorous universities, including Yonsei University, there were cases of illegal admission in exchange for donations (Underwood, 2002).

The military coup in 1961 did not tolerate such social malaise. The Minister of Education, Mr. Moon Hee-Seok, a former colonel of the Korean Marine Corps, criticized the current practices in Korean universities as they yielded more college graduates than required while making excessive financial profits, and reduced the national admission quota from 91,920 to 62,040 at the end of 1961 (Kang, 2009). The reduction in university quota had resulted in the increase in competition for university admission.

Thus, although the Second National Curriculum (NC), which lasted from February 1963 to January 1973, emphasized speaking and listening in English, the practices in English learning, particularly in high school, did not change due to the negative washback from college entrance exams. According to Kwon and Kim (2010, p. 91), the curriculum objectives of middle school English in the Second NC were as follows:

1. To develop listening and speaking abilities in simple English used in daily life.
2. To make students familiar with basic patterns and usage, and develop reading and writing abilities in English.

3. To make students understand the everyday life and social practices of English-speaking people and develop international understanding and cooperativeness through learning English.

The curriculum objectives of high school English were similar, with "developing listening and speaking abilities in simple English used in daily lives" listed as the first objective (Kwon & Kim, 2010, p. 91). These aims presented in the Second NC were the reflection of criticisms leveled against the First NC. In general, the English textbooks used in the First NC were considered too difficult for students to understand; furthermore, they did not present meaningful connections among subsections like listening, speaking, reading, and writing, but mostly focused on reading comprehension (Kim & Oh, 2019). Taking these aspects into consideration, English textbooks during the Second NC period were designed to incorporate various colloquial English expressions, as well as to provide authentic sample sentences for students to memorize and practice (Kim, 2009b). In addition, Lee (2011) stated that in the middle school English curriculum, the number of new vocabulary items was controlled: 300–400 words for 1st year, 350–450 words for 2nd year, and 400–600 words for 3rd year. The total number of new vocabulary words was downsized from 1450 to 1050.

While explaining the major characteristics of the Second NC, Pae (2000) argued that the Audio-lingual Methods established for this curriculum emphasized the speaking and listening components and the correct English pronunciation. However, as Kwon and Kim (2010) pointed out, the Second NC was still strongly influenced by the GTM.

Major newspapers in South Korea during the Second NC period often criticized the lack of innovation in English teaching, primarily disapproving of the overemphasis on reading, translation, and grammar knowledge, which cannot lead to oral fluency in English.

> At the beginning years [i.e., after liberation from Japan], the objective of English education was to use English as a tool to accept Western cultures. This was not different from that of Japan, and the central focus was the sheer emphasis on reading comprehension, and the teaching method focused on grammar and translation. Unless we include sound training, listening, and expression test in the college entrance exam, it would take an infinite number of years for us to introduce the English teaching method focusing on conversation and production. (Dong-A Ilbo, 1966, September 1)

Kyunghyang Shinmun (1970), another major newspaper in South Korea, also raised severe concerns about the lack of English conversational skills, stating that "although Koreans had learned English for more than 10 years from secondary schools to university, they become embarrassed and cannot make themselves understood in English when they meet foreigners." This newspaper attributed the lack of conversational skills to the educational practices in English classes in Korea, arguing that "most English education at school is allotted English grammar and reading comprehension, ... and we should increase the percentage of time allocation to English conversation" (Kyunghyang Shinmun, 1970, March 20).

The continuous use of GTM could be mainly attributed to the English testing format of higher educational institutions, including college entrance exams. Unless these English tests measured the test takers' speaking and listening abilities, any substantial innovation in English teaching and learning would not have been possible. However, as Kim and Oh (2019) highlighted, the disparity between the Second NC and the instructional capacity among English teachers could be another reason for the widespread use of GTM. Since many, if not most, English teachers were trained during the Japanese Colonization Period, they did not have listening and speaking proficiency in English, although they may have been experts in English grammar, vocabulary, and reading comprehension.

To enhance the oral proficiency of in-service English teachers, the Ministry of Education of Korea selected in-service teachers and dispatched them to the U.S.

> The Ministry of Education finalized the selection of secondary school English teachers dispatched to the U.S. [. . .] They will have the opportunity to attend an orientation session in New York, attend four-week English teaching method seminars in participating universities in Eastern U.S., and stay with host families for two weeks to learn live English. (Dong-A Ilbo, 1971, July 19)

Another social issue during the 1960s was teaching English to elementary school students. It was not until 1997, when elementary English education officially commenced in Korea, that all types of elementary school English education in the official educational system were regarded as illegal. The following newspaper article reports illegal English instructions in private elementary schools in Seoul in 1969.

> The Board of Education in Seoul City made an official recommendation for the dismissal of Mr. Kang Hee-Joon, Principal of Kyonggi Elementary School, and Mr. Kim Kyung-Hee, Vice-principal of Gyeseong Elementary School, from the school foundations of the two private schools respectively. These two private elementary schools kept offering their students over Grade 3 two hours of English classes weekly. . . . Upon receiving intelligence about covert English instructions in most private elementary schools and in some public counterparts for sixth graders, the school supervisors of the Board were mobilized to control the illegal English instruction. The Board warned of canceling the position of the English teachers and principals involved in this illegal activity. (Kyunghyang Shinmun, 1969, December 8)

Of particular interest is the fact that elementary English education was not only suppressed but also subject to legal punishment upon detection. The main reason for punishing early English education was related to the nature of excessive competition to be admitted to higher educational institutions. Although the teaching of English commenced in middle school, early exposure would favor a head start in middle school; for this reason, it was regarded as favoritism toward the recipients. The shared egalitarianism in South Korea (Song, 2006) aims to improve their life conditions; most members in Korea endeavor to occupy the high social ground and improve their conditions in life. Administrating elementary school English education in only a few select elementary schools violated such shared egalitarianism among Koreans. If a student attended a private elementary school teaching English, other students attending a different—most likely public—elementary school that did not provide English education would be at a disadvantage after starting to learn English in middle school. Concerned about such negative consequences, most Korean parents who did not have the financial means to have their children attend private elementary schools regarded early English education in some elite private elementary school as a severe violation of social justice; they wanted to maintain the same social and material standards as wealthier Koreans, despite their financial circumstances not favoring their aspiration.

In order to explain this sentiment of upward social mobility, it may be useful to adopt the concept of "uterine family" by Wolf (1972). While investigating Taiwanese kinship structure and the role of the mother within the family, Wolf (1972) argued that in the traditional patriarchal society where fatherly attitude and primogeniture represent the social norm, the wife, whose status may be tainted, reaffirms it by giving birth to a son and educating him by providing every means to succeed at school and in society. By presenting her offspring's social success, the woman proves her worth in the family, and the implicit dynamics counterbalance the patriarchal system. In this traditional Confucian organization, a woman's "uterine family"—her sons and sometimes daughters—is her real family.

In many cases, in explaining the excessive education fever that intensified during the industrialization of Korea in the 1960s, this concept of "uterine family" may be a useful perspective. The Korea of the 1960s (and that of the following several decades as well) still bore a resemblance to the previous generation. The eldest son was expected to take the initiative within the family; his success usually represented glory for the entire family. For this reason, the other siblings were required to sacrifice their education to support the eldest son, both financially and emotionally. This was the basic functioning of primogeniture in Korea. In the previous decade of war-torn, poverty-stricken South Korea, parents did not have the means to support their children's education, including that of their eldest son. However, as the economic condition improved, primogenitary priority was established, immediately followed by that of the second oldest son. Daughters were usually the last children to invest on—in twenty-first-century Korea, this is not the case anymore.

In the backdrop of 1960s' Korea, illegal English education at elementary schools provoked the anger of many Korean mothers deprived of the opportunity to receive such high-quality English education. This facilitated their self-censorship in order to suppress the elementary school English education in the 1960s and for the following three decades.

Korean mothers' excessive involvement in their children's education led to the coinage of a new term: the "skirt whirlwind" (치맛바람) was used to denote it. Kang (2009) noted that this phenomenon reflected the family aspiration to ascend the social ladder in Korea. As mentioned above, the Korean War temporarily ended in 1953, allowing most Koreans to start over from an egalitarian status. Depending on parental support, their children, primarily the eldest son, could be admitted to a prestigious educational institution, which was supposed to lead to a secure job. Thus, as Kang (2009) stated, labor was actively divided between parents: the father earned money at the workplace, while the mother did her best to support her children and husband. The "skirt whirlwind" was most frequently found in children's education[6]; as a means to consolidate their family status, many Korean mothers began to form a clique to share secret information regarding private tutoring and inviting tutors.

English testing and English instruction in the 1960s did not present a qualitative difference from the 1950s and reiterated the use of GTM mainly for test preparation. However, military control on university admission significantly reduced its quota, and the competition among students for a place in upper-level educational institutions intensified. The "skirt whirlwind" among many Korean mothers, similar to the concept of "uterine family" (Wolf, 1972), was prominent in the 1960s, based on the belief that the children's education guaranteed their social success, which in turn was directly related to the fate of the family. Following this perspective, a child's educational success in South Korea is not an individual matter but the whole family's business. This particular position will be investigated as the phenomenon of "alter-ego familism" in Chap. 7.

Undoubtedly, not all students could thrive at school. Academic success was represented by admission to top universities, including Seoul National University (formerly Kyungsung Imperial University[7]), Korea University (formerly Bosung Technical College), and Yonsei University (formerly Yonhi Technical College), three universities in Seoul. However, most high school students could not gain admission into these universities. Elementary school students endeavored to be admitted to a first-class middle school, middle school students to be admitted to a first-class high school, and high school students to a first-class university. Competition began in the final year of elementary school; in the worst case scenario, the graduating elementary school students who failed to be admitted to the best middle school that they had applied for delayed their graduation and repeated their final year, attempting the middle school entrance exam a second time (Kang, 2009). This excessive competition resulted in the total abrogation of the middle school admission test. From February 1969, all elementary graduates were subject to a random selection system and were allotted to one of the middle schools geographically close to their homes. Since the random selection system resembled the manual lottery spin wheel (see Fig. 3.2), middle school students after 1969 were attributed the nickname "the wheel of fortune generation" (빵빵이 세대).

---

[6]The "skirt whirlwind" was often criticized as a social malaise in South Korea. For example, in 1966, a social campaign was conducted to remove skirt whirlwind from private education. Also, in 1967, a movie titled "Skirt Whirlwind" was released across Korean cinemas (Kang, 2009). Although this term is most often used for the mothers' involvement in their children's education, it is sometimes used for the wife's active (often excessive, illegal) intervention in her husband's workplace, or her working a part-time job.

[7]It should be noted that Seoul National University officially denies the link with Kyungsung Imperial University. During the USMG, Seoul National University was established in 1946 by incorporating many technical colleges including Kyungsung Teachers' College, College of Medicine, and College of Commerce. However, Kyungsung Imperial University was also merged into Seoul National University, and most of its graduates regard that Seoul National University had inherited the traditions of their university.

Fig. 3.2 The random selection of middle schools in February 1969 (source: National Archives of Korea from http://theme.archives.go.kr/next/photo/exam01List.do)

This random selection policy had alleviated the excessive competition among elementary school students. The desire to attend the best university, however, did not fade after 1969. Although the extreme rivalry ended at the elementary level, it was aggravated among middle school students aiming to be admitted to prestigious high schools. The critical factor causing the tight competition for these schools was the number of high school graduates admitted to distinguished universities such as Seoul National University. For their preparation, many, if not most, middle school students relied on private education, including private tutoring. If a student attended one of the top high schools (e.g., Kyonggi and Seoul High School), this fact alone was already a source of pride for their family, which relates to the concept of "uterine family" expressed by Wolf (1972). Korean media raised their concerns about the excessive competition among middle school students in the pursuit of academic credentialism.

3.5   The Yushin Regime by President Park and English Education in the 1970s

On November 13, 1970, Mr. Chon Tae-il, a 22-year-old young tailor working at a garment company at *Pyongwha* (meaning "peace") market in Seoul, poured gasoline over himself and self-immolated while shouting "Observe the labor law! We are not machines!" This tragic incident marked the symbolic moment that raised public awareness of "the darker side of the ongoing Korean economic miracle" and human rights within the Korean Labor Movement (Lankov, 2011). In the process of rapid economic development under the strong leadership of President Park Chung-hee, most laborers were facing dire work conditions. Most of them came from a low-income family living in rural areas and were forced to work overtime even during weekends. Because of their sacrifice, South Korea had rapidly transformed from a poor agricultural economy to a major manufacturer in Asia. As Kim (1991) stated, "in the period of 1962–1979, Korea's real GNP and exports grew at the average annual rates of 9.3 and 33.7%, respectively," and "the growth performance was more spectacular in terms of real GDP per capita which showed an 18-fold increase to $1,481 in 1980 from $87 in 1962" (p. 6). He continues that "primary activities which accounted for as much as 40% of total economic activities in 1962–64 declined to 18.3% by 1980 while manufacturing and mining rose from 18.1% to 30%" (Kim, 1991, p. 6).

The outward-looking, export-focused economy was planned in the 1960s, but substantial export accelerated in the 1970s. The government-subsidized *chaebols* or conglomerates, such as Samsung, Hyundai, and LG Corporation, spearheaded the export of industrial goods. President Park aggressively encouraged the export-oriented economic restructuring. Under the national motto of "Export is the only way to survive," the President supported CEOs in establishing large-sized exporting companies, sometimes even pardoning trade-related crimes such as smuggling. Kang (2014) reiterated that English proficiency became even more critical than in the previous era because of the nation's strong drive toward export. To address the rapid increase in demand for English, many trading companies started to organize in-house English classes, and private English conversation classes were inundated with office workers.

Another major political turmoil to be noted was the start of the ironclad dictatorship by President Park. Under the pretext of the (potential) threat of communism from North Korea and the intensifying Vietnam War, President Park self-proclaimed a new term after his reelection by a narrow margin over his opposing democrat rival, Mr. Kim Dae-jung. This retroactive self-coup took place in October 1972, and is often referred to as the October Yushin (十月維新), or the October Restoration. Since then, until the assassination of President Park on October 26, 1979 (the "10.26 Incident"), the Yushin regime lasted for 7 years. During this period, freedom of expression was severely suppressed; anyone questioning or criticizing the legitimacy of the regime could be executed for treason. The establishment of the Yushin regime in 1972 put an official end to the Third Republic of Korea—which had lasted for 12 years from the military coup in 1961—and started the Fourth Republic.

Such rapid sociopolitical change resulted in further revision of the National Curriculum (NC). Considering the Yushin regime established in 1972, the Third NC (1973–1981) tried to address the Korea-specific context, as well as the emerging U.S.-based educational theories. The ideological competition with North Korea necessitated emphasizing anti-communism within the regular school curriculum, resulting in the establishment of a new school subject, ethics, in elementary and middle schools. At the same time, discipline-centered and spiral curricula (Bruner,

1960) were incorporated in the Third NC, resulting in an increase in the difficulty level of every school subject. Given the sociopolitical situation in South Korea, where liberal, creative criticisms were overshadowed by the ruthless censorship from the Park regime, the U.S.-based ideas reflected in the Third NC had their inherent limitations from inception and only resulted in the students' passive memorization of confusing learning contents in various school subjects.

English education in the Third NC emphasized the use of audio-lingual material and pattern and structure practice (Lee, 2011). The number of new vocabulary items in textbooks was also controlled as it was in the previous NCs: 300–350 new words for 1st-year middle school students, 350–400 words for 2nd year, and 400–450 words for 3rd year. The length of sentences for each school year was also controlled. For example, the length of each sentence in a 1st year textbook had to be less than 10 words, 15 words for a 2nd-year textbook, and 20 words for a 3rd-year one.

The English curriculum in the Third NC did not show much qualitative difference compared with that of the Second NC. However, as Kwon and Kim (2011) emphasized, there exists a unique contribution in the former in that the English curriculum specified each year's learning objectives and divided English contents into language function and language materials; this distinction was maintained in the following decades until the Fifth NC—in particular, grammar items were highly refined and preserved as they were in the Third NC. Kwon and Kim (2011) noted that the sophisticated grammar items in the Third NC had both positive and negative aspects in English education in South Korea. The Third NC served as a reliable instructional guide for many English teachers and students; however, this positive side appears to have been overshadowed by the negative one. Because of the highly refined grammar items specified in the Third NC, English learning and teaching through GTM was consolidated and kept functioning as the main instructional method for the next 20 years until the introduction of the Sixth NC in 1992. In other words, the Third NC aggravated the stagnation of English education in Korea by overemphasizing grammatical aspects. Table 3.3 presents specific language functions and materials in middle school English specified in the Third NC as illustrated by Kwon and Kim (2011, p. 107).

Therefore, when discussing the situation surrounding English education in the 1970s, it should be noted that the essential characteristics emphasizing the GTM mainly for college entrance exam did not change. The continued use of GTM and English exams had been the subject of criticism by South Korean media in the 1970s.

The National Education Research Institute published a report that the middle school English education had a fundamental shortcoming, only resulting in the miscommunication even after the 10-year English learning at school. It was argued that English teachers need to teach English in English by using classroom English to strengthen students' ability of everyday English conversation. (Dong-A Ilbo, 1979, July 10)

On October 17, the Ministry of Education decided that middle and high school English textbooks will be revised next year [i.e., 1979] emphasizing speaking and listening in English teaching. The Ministry also designated 16 experimental schools across 11 cities and provinces. [...] This measure was taken to rectify the current practice, which only focuses on reading comprehension, resulting in the hindrance of going abroad even after

Table 3.3 Middle school English content structure in the Third NC

Middle school year	Language functions	Language materials

Year 1	1. Listening and speaking (4)
	2. Reading (4)
	3. Writing (5)
		1. Topic (3)
		2. Vocabulary (1)
		3. Sentence Structure
		  (a) Structure presentation (7)
		  (b) Structure components (3)
		4. Grammar Point
		  (a) Sentence type (4)
		  (b) Clause (1)
		  (c) Inversion (5)

Year 2	1. Listening and speaking (3)
	2. Reading (2)
	3. Writing (2)
		1. Topic (2)
		2. Vocabulary (1)
		3. Sentence Structure
		  (a) Structure presentation (11)
		  (b) Structure components (6)
		4. Grammar Point
		  (a) Sentence type (3)
		  (b) Clause (4)
		  (c) Sentence form (2)
		  (d) Direct/indirect speech (1)
		  (e) Comparison (2)

Year 3	1. Listening and speaking (2)
	2. Reading (3)
	3. Writing (3)
		1. Topic (4)
		2. Vocabulary (1)
		3. Sentence Structure
		  (a) Structure presentation (15)
		  (b) Structure components (2)
		4. Grammar Point
		  (a) Sentence type (3)
		  (b) Clause (1)
		  (c) Sentence form (2)
		  (d) Direct/indirect speech (1)
		  (e) Participial construction (2)
		  (f) Subjunctive mood (3)
		  (g) Comparison (2)
		  (h) Infinitive

Note: Parenthesis—number of specific items
Adapted from Kwon and Kim (2010), p. 107

learning English for six years in middle and high schools and for college graduation. (Kyunghyang Shinmun, 1978, October 17)

In addition, newspapers insisted that specialized in-service training in sub-fields such as conversation, pronunciation, composition, reading, and grammar needed to be provided to English teachers. The U.S.-bound in-service teacher training continued during the 1970s as the speaking and listening proficiency of the teachers was regarded as relatively low (Kim & Oh, 2019). As shown above, the 16 experimental schools endorsed by the ministry designed a specialized curriculum and focused on teaching English conversation.

While English learning in middle school and high school did not show a practical difference from that in the 1960s, a noticeable change in delivering English education was identified in the 1970s: the use of cassettes for speaking and listening. Private education companies rapidly introduced audiotapes for their supplementary study material in English conversation. As explained in Chap. 2, recordings of English lesson were used even in the 1930s—Inoue's English lesson, for example, was recorded and sold in Korea. In this sense, the use of technology in English education may not have been a novel innovation. Nonetheless, the introduction of audio-recording in a cassette format needs to be mentioned because of the Audio-lingual Method and language labs established in many universities in Korea.

As noted, language teaching methods influenced by American structuralism (Harris, 1951) and behaviorism (Skinner, 1957) endorsed the use of the Audio-lingual Method in English learning (Richards & Rodgers, 2014). Pattern drills and repetition of exemplary sentences were emphasized, and it was assumed that error-free sentences should be produced from the beginning as incorrect sentences containing errors may result in forming a bad habit that is difficult to correct later. Language labs were first established at Yonsei and Seoul National Universities in the 1960s and subsequently extended to most universities in South Korea in the 1970s. In academic journals specializing in English education, many papers endorsed effective English teaching in lab contexts (Pae, 1995). In these language labs, the central control desk was located where the instructors and teaching assistants managed the cassette tapes. Students were placed in a booth with a headphone and a microphone; while listening to the model sentences attentively, they were required to repeat, memorize, and internalize the speech pattern and sound system of English. The late Dr. Kim Jin-man (2007), an emeritus professor at Korea University who had actively been involved in English education from the 1960s to the 1980s, criticized the effectiveness of installing English labs in university by stating that "it was overly optimistic to expect dramatic results other than giving grade through labs" (p. 159).

The situation in English education in the 1970s, however, seemed favorable for the introduction of technological advancements. Besides the installation of language labs at the tertiary level, publishers launched audiovisual material for English learning. Using portable audio players, cassettes, and color slides, these publishers advertised that students could enhance their listening and speaking abilities in English. Below is an excerpt of a newspaper advertisement.

> In the package, there are 14 cassette tapes and textbooks including five popular movie scripts such as "For whom the bell tolls" and "Wuthering Heights" and the essential summary for the English conversation beginners. This package is designed to learn "live English" after listening repeatedly. (Dong-A Ilbo, 1980b, January 26)

It should be noted that the influence of these technological innovations was relatively limited; language labs were installed in colleges, and audiotapes were mainly intended for adult learners of English. This meant that for most English learners at the secondary level, learning methods did not change fundamentally. English was still considered one of the most crucial school subjects, as it had been for previous generations. As mentioned in the previous section, the intensifying competition resulted in the nationwide abrogation of middle school entrance exams from 1969. However, the competition for the best academic credentials, which were assumed to lead to a prosperous life in Korea, was not alleviated. To control the potential source of social unrest represented by the education fever, the government decided to abolish high school entrance exams from 1974; similarly to the case of middle school allotment, middle school graduates were assigned to a high school nearby. Because of the gradual abolishment of high school entrance exams, the difference in the students' academic ability between individual schools, particularly between the first-tier and second-tier high schools within the same district of education, was substantially minimized (Chung, 2013). For this reason, the 1974 policy was called the High School Equalization Policy (高校平準化政策).

Although the excessive competition for high school admission was gradually controlled by the introduction of the Equalization Policy, this was not the case for college entrance exams. Private tutoring and private cram schools became much more crowded with high school students. In addition, at the end of the 1970s, it was reported that a significant number of 1st-year college students had received private tutoring for their college entrance exam, which in turn intensified academic competition to get into top-tier universities through various means of private education.

> Despite the mounting criticisms and awareness in excessive private tutoring, upon the new academic year, private tutoring is causing havoc throughout the nation. In particular, it turns out that a large portion of first-year students in top universities like Seoul National had received private tutoring for this year's college entrance exam. [...] The fever of private tutoring gets heated and expands to the first school years of elementary schools. This phenomenon is making the nation obsessed with all students' private tutoring. (Dong-A Ilbo, 1980a, February 14)

However, not surprisingly, most students could not get into their dream universities because of the limited quota. While some of them decided to prepare for the college entrance exam again, retaking the test the following year at their own expenses, for students from the upper social class, studying abroad was a viable option. As the economy in South Korea improved due to the success of the government-initiated development plans, the number of high school graduates who went abroad to undertake their college study increased rapidly (Dong-A Ilbo, 1980c, November 5).

In summary, English education in 1970s' South Korea needs to be understood in the backdrop of President Park's economic development and educational contexts. As the October Yushin prolonged the military dictatorship in 1972, education in South Korea also reflected the heightened political tension. Anti-communism and patriotism were emphasized across school subjects; in this context, students' critical awareness of the social circumstances could not be encouraged. English education needs to be examined in a similar manner. As Kwon and Kim (2010) noted, the Third NC, similarly to the Second NC, emphasized speaking and listening practices influenced by the U.S.-based discipline-oriented curriculum and the Audio-lingual Method (Skinner, 1957). Many pattern drills and memorization of sample English sentences were provided in textbooks. Because the rapid economic development focused on foreign export, oral English proficiency became a matter of priority, and technological advancements such as the use of tapes and English labs contributed to Korea's speaking and listening ability in English. However, at the secondary school level, students were still exposed to severe peer competition for college entrance. The Korean government decided to abolish high school entrance exams from 1974 as it had done with middle school entrance exams from 1969 (Phee, 2011). Despite this measure, English education in secondary school remained for the most part similar to that of the 1960s. English teachers still adhered to teaching English grammar and reading mainly for their belief in the practical preparation toward the college entrance exam (Kim, 2009b), and students received both public English education and private instruction through *hagwons*, or cram schools, and tutoring. The widespread private education at the expense of the students and their parents became increasingly perceived as a social problem and was officially banned in the early 1980s by another dictatorial military regime led by Army General Chun Doo-hwan.

3.6 The Establishment of the Fifth Republic and English Education in the 1980s

Korea's political and economic circumstances of the three decades between 1960 and 1980 are not dissimilar. Military dictatorship was disguised as democracy and national security. Freedom of speech and anti-government rallies were almost always regarded as communist scheming instigated by North Korea. Protesters were oppressed and imprisoned; for example, eight anti-government activists were arrested, imprisoned, and executed within 18 h of the death sentence proclaimed by the court. This tragic judicial murder is named the People's Revolutionary Party Incident fabricated by the Korean Central Intelligence Agency (CIA) (Hankyoreh, 2011). While suppressing fundamental human rights, Park Chung-Hee's regime continued export-oriented economic development by implementing four terms of 5-year economic development plans from 1962 to 1981. Notably, after the October Yushin, the government transformed the economic structure from light to heavy industries. Under robust government support, Samsung Electronics, POSCO, Hyundai Heavy Industries, and Daewoo Shipbuilding could lay their business foundations. Chun et al. (2008) stated that the percentage of heavy industry products among Korean exports in 1970 was 12.8%, rapidly increasing to 41.5% in 1980 and to 65.9% in 1990.

After a short stint of democracy following the assassination of President Park by the chief of the Korean CIA, a new military clique led by Army Major General Chun Doo-hwan held political power in 1979. This military coup is officially called the Coup d'État of December Twelfth (12.12 軍事叛亂), and through the indirect election by its perpetrators, General Chun was proclaimed President in 1980, effectively commencing the Fifth Republic of Korea. Through his military coup, President Chun endeavored to gain recognition from the people in South Korea. He introduced policies of appeasement in many areas, with the so-called "3S" policy being one of them (the "3S" meant sports, sex, and screen). By introducing various measures based on this 3S policy, Chun's Fifth Republic aimed to divert the public's interest in politics to other unrelated areas—for instance, the bidding on and successful hosting of the 1988 Seoul Olympic Games in 1981. Chun also created professional baseball and soccer leagues while easing the censorship on sexually sensitive contents in TV dramas and movies. The nationwide broadcast of color TV started on December 1, 1980.

While advocating the 3S policy above, President Chun tried to introduce innovative measures in education. Korean students' overzealous attitude toward learning, often related to their hakbul orientation, was a deep-rooted social problem. As presented in the previous sections, the abolition of middle and high school entrance exams and the Equalization Policy were effective in alleviating the excessive competition among students. However, the desire to gain admission to prestigious universities did not virtually disappear. Thus, the end of the 1970s presented a fertile ground for an educational unrest. Responding to this phenomenon, President Chun announced the July 30 Educational Reform. For most Koreans, this reform policy represented a blitz move (Kang, 2009); on July 30, 1980, the National Security Emergency Countermeasure Committee organized by Chun announced the plan to "normalize" education and suppress excessive private tutoring, all of which were made headlines in all Korean newspapers. According to this plan, from August 1 (i.e., from the day following the announcement), all types of private tutoring had to be banned, and independent college entrance exams for student selection were prohibited. The National Academic Ability Test (大學入學 學力考查) was introduced.

As an additional measure for the July 30 Educational Reform, specific enforcement disciplines were publicized on August 7, 1980, which included the total prohibition of private and group tutoring, enrollment in *hagwons* or cram schools, and school learning after regular hours. To address the persisting need for learning outside of school, the government introduced "private tutoring through television media" (TV 課外) by establishing KBS TV3, which was later renamed Educational Broadcasting System (EBS). In this broadcast, more than 40% of the entire content focused on high school learning material (Kang, 2009). Since this broadcast was free of charge and resource books were reasonably priced, the educational measure was enthusiastically embraced by many parents of high school students.

Another critical move by the government was to ease university admission by increasing the admission quota and controlling degree conferring by limiting graduation quota. This measure was first regarded as an effective measure to alleviate the competition for being admitted to a university because the admission quota was 30% higher than the graduation quota. Therefore, the competition rate decreased, providing each student with a better chance of being admitted to the desired university. However, this policy soon caused vehement protests from college students and their parents as the assessment of students' GPA and expulsion from college, in principle, were conducted annually, and not at the time of graduation—if the students' cumulative GPAs belonged to the lower 30%, they could be expelled as early as during their 1st year. Kang (2009) pointed out that this measure reflected President Chun's intention to divert college students' participation in politics toward their learning; being too focused on competing against each other, college students were not able to grow critical awareness of Korean society and politics, which would, in turn, guarantee Chun's absolute political control over the nation. In the end, because of the high volume of protests regarding the graduation quota, most students with less competition at the time of admission could graduate from the university that they had been admitted to, regardless of their GPAs. For this reason, Kim et al. (2019) stated that the Korean youth who attended university in the early 1980s were the luckiest in Korean history.

Although admission and (eventually) graduation became relatively easy for this fortunate generation, it did not necessarily mean that they would be in luck even after graduating university. As the number of bachelor's degree holders increased, the job market requiring a college degree was soon inundated with candidates. Consequently, having a greater number of college graduates meant that the competition for a good job would intensify compared to previous decades.

In terms of English education, the changing international relationships and economic development necessitated emphasizing listening and speaking proficiency in English. The 1980s were the years of rapid economic development. The GDP per capita increased from $1704 in 1980 to $5737 in 1989 (Countryeconomy.com, 2019). Upon this economic development at its backdrop, three significant factors intervened in the gradual transition from English reading and grammar only to the addition of listening and speaking in English: (1) the introduction of the Test of English for International Communication (TOEIC) in 1982; (2) winning the bid for hosting the 1988 Summer Olympic Games; and (3) the liberalization policy for foreign travel.

In retrospect, the introduction of the TOEIC by the Educational Testing Service (ETS) should be noted as an innovation in English learning in Korea. First introduced in Japan in 1979, the TOEIC was intended to "assess the practical English proficiency required in everyday situations or international business with an emphasis on communicative functions" and was introduced in Korea in 1982 (YBM, 2019a). Gradually, the independent, in-house English tests administered by many Korean industries were replaced by the TOEIC. Spearheaded by Samsung in December 1982, LG (January 1984), POSCO (November 1984), and other major companies in South Korea adopted the TOEIC for either recruitment or promotion requirements (YBM, 2019b). Since the TOEIC score adopted a numeric system where a specific score is presented out of 990 points, employers could quickly compare and evaluate the applicants' English proficiency in English listening and reading. Notably, the listening components constituted half of the entire TOEIC test, and 495 points were allotted to the listening components out of 990 points. The priority given to listening comprehension was a revolutionary measure in the 1980s, when most English tests did not yet include listening comprehension as a testing element. For college graduates and office workers, the TOEIC score was perceived as one of the critical elements that would determine their success in the job. Although the TOEIC was criticized as not having a close correlation to the test takers' authentic English proficiency, it was groundbreaking that the TOEIC included listening comprehension as its main component. This fact exerted a positive washback effect in South Korea and could even be attributed to the inclusion of listening comprehension in the college entrance exam from 1993.

Another remarkable event that gained phenomenal interest among Koreans through the 1980s was the successful bidding, preparing for, and hosting of the 1988 Seoul Summer Olympic Games and Paralympics, which was decided on September 1981, followed by that of the 1986 Seoul Asian Games in November 1981. Both decisions were regarded as a lift of the nation's spirit by most South Koreans. Against this backdrop, early English education was introduced in October 1981 (Kang, 2014), and, starting from 4th year of elementary school, English instruction was gradually introduced using school hours for extracurricular activities or lunch recess. On October 14, 1981, Dong-A Ilbo illustrates an ambivalent opinion toward the introduction of early English education at elementary schools.

> The Ministry of Education decided to introduce English education for fourth-, fifth- and sixth-year elementary school students starting from next year to "teach live English." Considering the controversies surrounding early English education, the Ministry recommended teaching simple conversational English by using school hours for extracurricular activities and lunch hours upon each school's situations, without including English as a regular school subject. [. . .]
>
> Even though we do not entirely endorse all the decisions made by the Ministry, this time, in general, we agree with the idea of teaching English in elementary schools. However, we have a couple of concerns about the effectiveness of the Ministry's decision.
>
> First of all, we have doubts regarding how much children could learn with only an hour per week. Foreign language is the school subject that requires continuous practice. If we decide to teach them English, we need to teach at least two or three hours a week. It is also quite paradoxical to teach English using lunch hours. If English is so vital to teaching as to reduce lunch hours, it would be much better to increase teaching hours.
>
> Moreover, there are other problems with teachers and facilities. In fact, secondary schools have many concerns regarding a lack of sufficient number of teachers and facilities to teach English conversation effectively. Also, it deserves our careful consideration whether English conversation would be possible in a classroom of more than 70 students. [. . .]
>
> In short, although we acknowledge the necessity of teaching English at elementary schools, the current situation would only yield suspicious results. We were informed that, because the Ministry already admitted this practical difficulty, the decision of early English education has been recommended to each school, rather than to be mandated as a regular school subject.
>
> Therefore, we would like to make a recommendation to the Ministry that the ideal context should be organized to maximize the effectiveness of early English education, not making an impression with a hasty introduction of it. (Dong-A Ilbo, 1981, October 14)

As presented in the above editorial, early English education was a recommendation from the government, and the actual administration of it was upon the principal's decision. Thus, depending on the educational district, early English education showed remarkable variability. In limited areas where the socioeconomic status of the students was relatively high, the education continued, whereas in most areas, mainly because of the lack of teachers who could teach English conversation, the ministry's recommendation was largely neglected. However, although early English education was not mandated nationwide, it should be noted that oral proficiency in English was gradually prioritized among South Koreans.

The third noticeable trend in Korean society was the exponential increase in foreign travel. In a cover story commemorating the 25th anniversary of the liberalization of foreign travel in Korea, Son and Choi (2014) stated that before 1983 it was almost impossible for Koreans to travel abroad; only in the case of official duties, business purposes, or study, limited numbers of Koreans were allowed to leave the country. When the travel passport was first introduced in Korea, only Koreans aged over 50 were issued one after depositing 2 million Korean Won (i.e., $1700) into the national travel fund. This regulation gradually eased, and, from January 1, 1989, virtually all Koreans could request a passport and go abroad.

The gradual liberalization of foreign travel and the hosting of the 1988 Seoul Olympic Games resulted in a nationwide English fever among adult Koreans. Many reached a consensus that they needed to be able to speak English at least at a basic level. With this sentiment, English speaking and listening abilities were regarded as crucial to successfully hosting the Summer Olympic Games, the largest international event that Korea had ever held until the 1980s. Thus, from the early 1980s, many Koreans endorsed English learning. Newspaper articles illustrated the social atmosphere in the early to mid-1980s, further resulting in encouraging the English fever.

> Recently, a radio station launched an English conversation program for taxi drivers, in which not only taxi drivers, but also taxi users, showed great interest. In fact, the chances are getting higher for ordinary persons, not only for those whose occupation requires frequent personal contact, to converse with foreigners. It might be a common practice for taxi drivers uninterested in English thus far to learn English if more foreign travelers visit Korea in the future. [...]
>
> Three to four years ago, English learners made a copy of audiotapes imported from foreign countries to learn English conversation. Nowadays, however, they learn English effectively by using a new material which is tailormade for Koreans, who have a different first language than foreigners. In this material, annotations are also provided in Korean. For this convenience, English-learning materials such as "Jung Chul Cassette," "Min Byung Chul Everyday English," and "Joh Hwa Yoo English conversation" have an incomparably high record of sales volume. The companies publishing these materials are getting progressively and systematically commercialized. (Dong-A Ilbo, 1983, April 25)

As presented in the article above, private English institutions made extraordinary financial gains during the 1980s, and English conversation textbooks and supplementary audiovisual materials were sold in large volumes. In addition, most major radio stations in South Korea installed English conversation programs such as "3-minute everyday English" (MBC Radio), "English conversation I, II" (KBS TV2), and "English Bible" (CBS) (Kyunghyang Sinmum, 1981, September 21).

The above social phenomenon surrounding the mega sporting events, economic development, and the liberalization policy of foreign travel all resulted in an exceptionally high demand for English. This demand was geared toward increasing oral English proficiency. As explained in the previous section, the export-oriented national economic development under President Park's regime in the 1960s and 1970s also increased the demand for oral English. The situation in the 1980s, however, added diverse dimensions such as international events and travel abroad to the existing economic factors. All these changes propelled English education in Korea toward speaking and listening proficiency.

At the secondary school level, however, the progress in English education was slow. Most of the 1980s overlap with the Fourth NC, which lasted from December 1981 to February 1987. Given the central control of the NC, the political turbulence from the old military regime by Park Chung-hee to that of Chun Doo-hwan was the central motif for the revision of the NC. According to Kwon and Kim (2010), the Fourth NC did not have essential innovations compared with the Third NC. Although Pae (2000) highlighted that the former focused on a cognitive instructional method that prioritized deductive learning through internalizing grammatical rules, not much advancement was found in the latter, except for the optional elementary English education being mandated as the class of "Special Activity" (特活). The three guidelines for elementary English education were the following:

1. To instruct students to be able to read English pronunciation accurately
2. To encourage students to be interested in English and familiarize them with it
3. To make students lay a foundation of communicative competence (Kwon & Kim, 2010, p. 117)

The objective of middle school English education in the Fourth NC did not show a fundamental difference from that in the Third NC. The course objective was to enhance "students' ability to use English, make them contribute to the development of Korean culture through understanding the culture of the people in English-speaking nations," and specific goals were "1) to make students develop the ability to understand and use easy English related to everyday and general topics, and 2) to develop students' foundations for understanding the culture of the people in English-speaking nations" (Kwon & Kim, 2010, p. 118). In the objective specified in the Fourth NC, Kwon and Kim (2010) noted that the focus was on intra-national or domestic use of English, not international use for communication. As indicated, the objective was "to contribute to the development of Korean culture." In the previous NC, the focus was outward international orientation, such as "preparing students to be able to participate in international activities in the future," as it had been in the Second NC (Kwon & Kim, 2010, pp. 118–119).

Nonetheless, the Fourth NC turns its focus toward domestic use of English. Kwon and Kim (2010) interpreted this as an indication of self-awareness and self-confidence. While going through the rapid economic development of the 1970s and restoring the national pride that had been crushed by the Korean War, Koreans gradually developed the consensus that learning English was primarily not for adapting to the culture of other English speakers, but for Koreans themselves to develop their own culture through it.

Other than the objective of English, the Fourth NC does not show a fundamental difference from the Third one in terms of the language functions, grammar usage, language materials, and instructional methods presented in Table 3.3 in Sect. 3.5.

Thus, secondary school students in the 1980s learned English as one of the regular school subjects as others had done in the previous decades. Although the number of language labs increased in the 1980s (Kwon & Kim, 2010, p. 127), grammatical pattern practices and the GTM were still the major, if not the only, instructional method.

The abovementioned characteristics of the Fourth NC aggravated the discrepancy between public education and Koreans' heightened awareness of oral English. Even though Korean society, in general, had been rapidly transformed into an open one, accepting the necessity of enhancing English speaking and listening ability, public education at school, as well as the national curriculum, still followed outdated practices. As shown in various newspaper articles throughout the 1980s, Korean workforces were exposed to the pressure of the TOEIC. Moreover, the general public was pressurized to communicate in English in order to accommodate foreign travelers coming to international sporting events and to travel abroad. Unfortunately, education at primary and secondary schools could not reflect the social needs and essentially reiterated the previous teaching and learning methods. Teacher qualifications and facilities were not yet prepared to lead communication-oriented English classes, which gradually resolved in the following decade of the 1990s.

3.7 The Origin of *Hakbul* and Its Implications for English Education in South Korea Until the 1980s

As stated in Chap. 2, at the end of the Korean Empire and during the Japanese Colonization Period, having a high level of English proficiency equated to "climbing the social ladder" into the elite society. In this regard, English learning motivation was instrumental from the beginning, when English instruction began spreading after the Korea-U.S. Treaty of 1882. It was widely recognized, for instance, that any worker who could speak basic English in Jemulpo (now Incheon, vicinity of Seoul) Customs Office earned a monthly salary that was four or even five times higher. The instrumental nature of English learning faced fundamental changes during the Japanese Colonization Period. English learning did not serve the purpose of communicating with other English speakers or foreigners, which was only permitted to Japanese officers and merchants; deprived of the opportunity to communicate in English, Koreans, particularly school-aged ones, started to consume it for internal competition. It was essential to obtain a high score on the English test in college entrance exams. As mentioned in Chap. 2, Kyungsung (or Keijo) Imperial University (京城帝國大學) prioritized English to the extent that the weight of the English test score was greater than that of the national language (i.e., Japanese) test toward the total score of the admission test. The college entrance exam was extremely competitive during this period, with the Government-General of Korea preventing Koreans from receiving tertiary education by mandating the national language test for all applicants. For Koreans, whose first language was not Japanese but Korean, it was challenging to gain an excellent score in the national language test. Thus, only a few elite Koreans earned the opportunity to be admitted to Kyungsung Imperial University, which was the only comprehensive university in Korea (Park, 2003). Many others chose 2-year technical colleges or pursued tertiary education in Japan. The inclusion of the English test in college entrance exams and the deprivation of authentic communication with English speakers gradually turned the nature of English learning from instrumental and communicative to test-oriented, merely serving higher education.

However, despite this transition to tertiary education, it should be noted that Koreans' primary motivation for learning English before the liberation from Japan in 1945 was not significantly different from the instrumental motivation in the previous Korean Empire era before the 1910 annexation. Before the Japanese Colonization Period, those who had English-speaking skills could successfully secure a job regardless of their background or academic degree, as shown in the success story of Mr. Lee Ha-Young in Chap. 2. This had changed after Japan annexed the Korean Empire in 1910; in fact, the establishment of higher educational institutions across Korea had impacted the professional job market. The college diploma, and particularly that from Kyungsung Imperial University, had often been considered a guarantee of the degree-holders' ability and was regarded as the indicator of a person's maximal potential as human resource. Only a few chosen elites were offered high-salaried office jobs at Government-General of Korea or its related branches across the country. The inclusion of English in the college entrance exams had elevated its status as one of the crucial factors for success. This historical transition surrounding English shows that the primary motivation for learning the language in Korea was instrumental; tertiary education, by including English in college entrance exam, essentially provided a warranty for decent occupation after graduation. Therefore, the motivation to learn English in Korea had mostly remained the same: while before the Japanese annexation this was outright instrumental, after the annexation it became affiliated with college education.

During the Japanese Colonization Period, as shown in the following excerpt, Drake (1930) reported that English was widely believed as the "golden key" to be on track for a successful career path in Korea. He recounted his experience of teaching English to missionary candidates:

These students, presumably, were the pick of the Korean Christians, as they were definitely preparing for the native ministry. Their syllabus included some eight periods a week of English. It was suggested that this was a complete waste of time, as no village pastor in Korea would find any use for English, and accordingly it was proposed to abolish English from the syllabus. Promptly the students went on strike, threatening to leave in a body unless English were reinstated. The significance was unmistakable. To the Korean—to the Japanese too—English, rightly or wrongly, is the open sesame to any successful career. To such an extent that one is pestered everywhere, in trams, in trains, by progressive young men anxious to learn English. "Please will you teach me English?" they accost you, so that you feel inclined to answer, "Certainly; if you can spare a few minutes I'll teach you now." Though actually you put them off by mention of a fee. To counter this the more subtle ones will ask you to teach "Bible," assuming that religious instruction will gladly be given free. But you can unmask the motive quite simply by recommending them to some missionary, at which they will shake their heads and say, "But he teach [sic] Korean Bible. I wish to read Bible in English." You see the point. These theological students who threatened to leave the seminary if English teaching were denied them had no intention of remaining village pastors all their days. ... [T]he scholars didn't attend the missionary schools because they wanted to become Christians. It was absurd to suppose that they would. They saw in them merely the road to individual advancement, and they patronized them accordingly. (Drake, 1930, pp. 166–168)

The zeal toward social success via English learning did not change following the liberation from Imperial Japan in 1945, when the Japanese unconditionally surrendered to the U.S.-led allies. Particularly for Koreans living under the north 38th parallel, English was important because the USMG was stationed there for 3 years, from 1945 to 1948. As mentioned above, the official languages for public documents were both English and Korean, and in the case of difficulty in the interpretation of the document, English had the priority over Korean. After the USMG Period, because of the Korean War, which lasted over 3 years, the military and economic ties between the U.S. and South Korea became even stronger than before. Having acknowledged this, however, English learning motivation had not changed. Compared with the Japanese Colonization Period, the opportunity to have authentic communication in English with English speakers, particularly with the U.S. citizens, had evidently increased, but such communication was limited only to a few Koreans dealing with foreign affairs such as joint military operations and international trade. Still, most Koreans considered English an essential school subject needed for high school students to take college entrance exams and enter higher education.

Soon after the highly destructive Korean War, the Korean government led by President Rhee Syngman started the reconstruction of the nation, but this was critically hindered by the widespread inflation and corruption (Seth, 2017). The systematic reconstruction started after 1961, when Major General Park Chung-hee gained political power and was elected as President of South Korea. He spurred economic development, and the rate of economic development in Korea continued breaking the records set in previous years. During more than three decades of military-led governments which ended in 1993 (with Presidents Park Chung-hee, Chun Doo-hwan, and Roh Tae-woo), the Korean economy was "rapidly transformed in a process sometimes referred to as the South Korean 'economic miracle' or the 'miracle on the Han,' referring to the Han River that flows through Seoul" (Seth, 2017).

However, despite such rapid economic expansion, the role of English at schools did not change fundamentally. As illustrated in the English curriculum from the First to Fourth NC, schools did not have sufficient facilities to introduce communicative English lessons. Moreover, English teachers did not have speaking and listening proficiency. As a result, it was not until 1992 that the Sixth NC officially highlighted communicative competence as the focus of English education. Even after the new curriculum was introduced in 1992, the practice of English education did not experience a rapid change, and this was firmly related to college entrance exams. The inclusion of English in the college entrance exam continued and students, as well as English teachers, paid the utmost attention to the best method for obtaining a high score in it (Kang, 2014).

Korean students became accustomed to learning English while competing against each other in order to get a higher English test score than other students; the rationale for justifying the competition among classmates was a better chance to be admitted to a prestigious university. The social recognition of a university degree and the name of a university had consistently been consolidated in South Korea as the nation went through various stages: the Japanese Colonization Period, the USMG Period, the Korean War, and the Post-War Reconstruction Period. Koreans experienced the power of English (or more precisely the English test score) in the college entrance exams and came to aspire to earn a higher score than other test takers. To alleviate the competition among students, the Ministry of Education of Korea took various measures, including the abolishment of middle school entrance exam in the 1960s, the high school equalization policy in the 1970s, and the expansion of admission quota in university in the 1980s. However, the competition did not entirely disappear, and the aspiration toward a higher academic degree continued in South Korea.

Because of this academic environment, competitive motivation in English learning became increasingly popular. This type of motivation is distinctly found in a series of L2 motivation research conducted in South Korea (Kim, 2006, 2010; Kim & Kim, 2016). The findings of previous research in L2 motivation have reiterated that a considerable interface exists between this competitive motivation and instrumental motivation (e.g., Gardner & MacIntyre, 1991). Kim (2010, p. 215) distinguishes the difference between the two motivational components as follows.

> Instrumental motivation is defined as the desire to learn an L2 for anticipated rewards (e.g., promotion, [prestigious] university acceptance, and the use of the L2 in a foreign country), and competitive motivation is the desire to learn an L2 to keep pace with other L2 learners. These two factors share similarity because the source of motivation arises from external environments faced by each student. (. . .) However, the two constructs, instrumental motivation and competitive motivation, cannot be conceptually merged into one because competitive motivation is possibly more related to Korean students' aspiration to obtain higher English testing scores than their peers. (. . .) The presence of other people is always assumed; competition to occupy a better position in life is impossible without assuming that other people are competitors.

As stated above, it should be noted that competitive motivation was mainly connected to the negative washback effect (cf. Bachman & Palmer, 1996) of the nationwide high-stakes college entrance exam. Competitive motivation implies that students learn English because of their aspiration to occupy a better social status than their peers. This is because, at least in the Korean context, English is generally considered a tool to enter prestigious universities and "climb the social ladder"; this results in intense competition among Korean high school students.

It is often stated that the competitive motivation identified by Kim (2006, 2010) is linked to *hakbul* orientation in Korea (Kim, 1997, 2001; Lee, 1993; Oh, 2000). *Hakbul* (學閥), or academic credentialism, meaning the strict stratification of society based on one's university degree or college diploma, still affects Korean society. Although the influence of *hakbul* seems to have diminished, this works in Korea somewhat similarly to the Indian caste system (Kim, 2001). *The Korea Herald*, a major English newspaper in South Korea, defines *hakbul* and the society of credentials, reporting that *hakbul* still becomes a crucial factor in one's job selection, marriage, and social success.

> "What school did you graduate from?" This is one of the most frequently asked questions you hear after finishing college and launching a career. In a society which highly values an individual's educational credentials, the school you attended is regarded as the most important element in determining your future, as in your job, salary, and even marriage, regardless of what potential and capabilities you actually have.
>   "In Korean society, people are graded by the name value of the schools they come from," said Jung Tae-Hwa, senior researcher at the Korea Research Institute for Vocational Education and Training. "This is a society in which it is hard to breathe for those full of potential and ability." (Cho, 2010, April 5)

The *hakbul* orientation is expressed by the traditional catchphrase "Dragon Gate," which has gained widespread recognition in many Asian countries, including China, Japan, and Korea. Zeng (1995, p. 59) explains the term as follows:

> In East Asia, the "Dragon Gate" is one of the images in folk culture, visualising the dream of socio-academic rise. In this totemic metaphor, carp fish represent men from humble origins. As soon as a carp flips over the "Dragon Gate," he will turn into a dragon, the sacred creature of success and glory. The gate especially epitomises the high-stake examination system. Admittedly Chinese in its origin, it also mirrors "degreeocracy" . . . as related to the sine qua non examinations for gaining university admission.

Oh (2000) stated that the *hakbul* orientation had been severely strengthened during the economic development period from the late 1960s. In previous generations, the *hakbul* was mostly used for the employment of government office and public sectors. However, during the rapid expansion in domestic economy through the reconstruction and export-oriented economic policy under President Park's regime, *hakbul* functioned as a screening device to choose the best candidate among many job applicants. During the expansion cycle of domestic economy, the name of the university that the job applicants had graduated from was often regarded as the person's job potential. Thus, Korean universities were stratified, and those graduates from top-tier ones could enjoy the monopoly of the best employment opportunities; those from the second tier could be offered the second-best opportunities, and so forth.[8] While economic development had reached maturity in the 1980s, parents could provide better educational opportunities to their offspring, which resulted in the expansion of college education; Korea eventually became an "overeducated society" (Oh, 2000, p. 282). As Oh pointed out, the prime motive for a college education was the desire to succeed in life through securing a stable, highly paid job. In an overeducated society where most job-seekers have a college diploma, the degree itself does not offer much advantage. From this stage, the *hakbul* functioned as a stratification device that categorized—or in many cases discriminated—job applicants in the employment process.

---

[8]In the 2010s, the stratification became much worse, resulting in a new pejorative term, *jijapdae* (地雜大), denoting "schools outside of Seoul with excessively low quality of education" (Lim, 2015, p. 5).

Note that the tradition of holding *hakbul* through a single high-stakes test was still part of the Koreans' mindset. In the 1950s and 1960s, various types of college entrance exams existed in Korea, but the crucial element was the university main test (大學 本考查) administered by each university, sometimes accompanied by nation-wide preliminary academic tests (from 1969 to 1981). While addressing the criticism that these main university tests were too difficult for high school students to prepare for, the Fifth Republic led by President Chun Doo-hwan abolished the university main tests and initiated the National Academic Ability Test from 1981. After the 12-year administration, this test changed into the College Scholastic Ability Test (CSAT; 大學修學能力試驗) in 1993, functioning as the "Dragon Gate" among Korean students and their parents (see Chap. 4).

The CSAT has had a long-lasting impact on high school final-year students' social and academic lives for decades. The CSAT has a normative multiple-choice format and is administered once a year in November. The purpose of the test is "measuring students' higher order and analytical thinking skills (which are the main goals of high school education) so that colleges could screen students with the relevant academic capabilities for higher education" (Choi & Park, 2013, p. 112). The CSAT scores are a crucial determinant of university selection—that is, if students earn a better score than their peers, they will have a wider choice of colleges. High scores equate to being able to enter 4-year university undergraduate programs, whereas low scores mean entry into "less prestigious" but practical (as perceived by some Koreans), 2-year vocational colleges.

In the CSAT, English language is one of the six areas: Korean, Mathematics, Korean History, Science/Social Science/Vocational (choose one), Foreign Language (i.e., English), and optional Second Foreign Language (choose one from Arabic, Chinese, Classical Chinese, French, German, Japanese, Russian, Spanish, and Viet-namese). Moreover, although it is not currently implemented, for more than 10 years after the mid-1990s, students who could demonstrate high proficiency in English obtained extra credits for university admission. At that time, some high school students took the Test of English as a Foreign Language (TOEFL) or the Test of English for International Communication (TOEIC) in order to submit official scores from the Educational Testing Service to the university admission committee. In this social context, English was regarded as an essential "Dragon Gate" to ascend the social ladder to a better class by being admitted to a prestigious university.

The *hakbul* orientation in Korea has produced many negative side effects (Park & Kim, 2003). As mentioned above, the CSAT score obtained in one's graduating year of high school is a crucial determinant to the college entrance exam, and university prestige is highly stratified in Korea. Across the country, a total of 201 4-year universities are found (E-narajipyo, 2017), and these institutions are classified according to the undergraduate students' CSAT scores. Park and Kim (2003) stated that there exist a variety of factors consolidating such stratifications: the superiority of national universities to private universities; that of metropolitan universities to rural universities; and that of universities with a long-standing academic tradition to universities with a shorter or no academic tradition. These factors, combined with students' CSAT score ranges, result in highly stratified university rankings. It is widely believed that graduates from high-ranking universities control Korea's political and economic power. For this reason, students and their parents continue to make their best efforts to gain admission to high-ranking, prestigious universities. Because of this concept of academic credential, or *hakbul*, where society values the diploma from a high-ranking university, students tend to pay more attention to a university's name and reputation, not to their own academic interest (Park & Kim, 2003).

In analyzing the progress of English learning until the 1980s, the *hakbul* in Korea would be one of the vital factors to understand Koreans' high level of motivation and enthusiastic attitude toward learning English. The extreme competition among Korean students is based on the belief in the crucial importance of a degree obtained from a top-tier university. As illustrated in regard to the "skirt whirlwind" phenomenon, this competitiveness had often been associated with the family business resembling the characteristics of uterine familism by Wolf (1972) or amoral familism by Benfield (1958), where the immediate family composed of the offspring and their parents (mostly mothers) becomes the utmost priority, excluding other family members. This form of extreme familism reflects the strong desire among Korean parents to encourage their children to improve their social class and live a prosperous life. In many cases, *hakbul* results in unhealthy social problems in Korea, such as an excessive suicide rate among schoolchildren under academic pressure (Hong et al., 2017) and amotivation or demotivation in English learning (Kim, 2011; Kim & Seo, 2012). The competition surrounding English learning worsened in the following decades as it became a mandatory subject in elementary school; early study-abroad programs also became widespread among Koreans. Chapter 4 deals with the complex dynamics and issues in English learning from the 1990s to the 2010s.

3.8   Chapter Summary

This chapter summarizes the historical progression of English education in South Korea from 1945 to the 1980s. The vicissitudes of historical events during the latter half of the twentieth century invited rapid changes in English education and the subsequent motivation to learn it among Koreans. The inseparable political and economic ties with the U.S., particularly during the period of post-war reconstruction after the Korean War, increased the need to learn English in order to be employed in public sectors or private companies affiliated with the U.S. military troops in the 1950s. However, the need to learn English soon was associated with college entrance exams, and English continued to function as one of the three key school subjects (i.e., Korean, Math, and English) in the admission tests. Therefore, academic competition intensified in the 1960s and 1970s, while South Korea marked a rapid economic expansion due to the government-led economic development plans. During the period of economic expansion, the university diploma was regarded as an effective method to recruit competent workers for companies, and having obtained it from a prestigious university was often considered the symbol of the degree-holder's human potential. Therefore, English learning motivation in this particular period showed the characteristics of competitive motivation, and the orientation toward *hakbul*, or academic credentialism, intensified. It should be noted that the *hakbul* and competitive motivation did not appear for the first time after the Korean War. As explained in Sect. 3.7, the lack of opportunities for higher education during the Japanese Colonial Period from 1910 to 1945 had already fueled competition toward a better social position, and English served as the ladder toward the upper social class via the admission to and graduation from Kyungsung Imperial University or other technical colleges in Korea during the colonialization period. Thus, the nature of competitive motivation surrounding the learning of English was mainly about internal competition among Koreans in academic contexts. To obtain high exam scores in the English test, which was part of their college entrance exam, Korean students during both the Japanese Colonialization Period and the post-war reconstruction period spent their time and energy preparing for it.

The hosting of major international events including the 1988 Summer Olympic Games promoted further motivation for learning English: developing communicative competence. Moreover, in order to address the growing demand of economic exchange with foreign countries, proficiency in English speaking and listening was required, and these dimensions became part of English education and evaluation. The introduction of elementary school English, although optional, was also initiated during the 1980s, and the TOEIC and other speaking- and listening-oriented tests were introduced. However, the fundamental educational assumption of the effectiveness of a university degree remained unchanged, which aggravated *hakbul* in South Korea. Nonetheless, the nature of instrumentality in English learning seems differentiated among pre-university students and university ones. In the case of secondary school students, as the primary motive was represented by admission to top-tier universities, this often equated to stable job prospects; university students, however, needed to take the oral proficiency in English represented by the TOEIC score into their account. For university students in the 1980s, the competition toward *hakbul* had already finished, yet another level of competition to score high in the TOEIC or similar tests toward job selection lay ahead (see also Sect. 4.3 in Chap. 4 for the TOEIC fever).

References

An, Daechun, & Kim, Sanghoon. (2007). Relating Hofstede's masculinity dimension to gender role portrayals in advertising. *International Marketing Review, 24*(2), 181–207.
Bachman, L. F., & Palmer, A. S. (1996). *Language teaching in practice: Designing and developing useful language tests.* Oxford, England: Oxford University Press.
Benfield, E. C. (1958). *The moral basis of a backward society.* Glencoe, IL: The Free Press.
Bruner, J. S. (1960). *The process of education.* Cambridge, MA: Harvard University Press.
Cho, Gap-Je. (1998). *Nae mudeum'e chim'eul baeteora 3: Hyeukmyeongjeonya [Spit on my grave 3: Before the night of revolution].* Seoul, Korea: Chosun Ilbo.

Cho, Ji-Hyun. (2010, April 5). Education-based elitisms challenged in Korea. Retrieved August 13, 2018, from http://www.koreaherald.com/common/newsprint.php?ud=20070919000047.

Cho, Soon-Kyung, & Lee, Sook-Jin (1995). *Naengjeonchejewa saengsan'eui jeongchi: Migoonjeongki'eui nodongjeongchaekgwa nogongwoondong. [The Cold War system and politics of production: Labor policy and labor movement during the U.S. military government].* Seoul, Korea: Ewha Womans' University Press.

Choi, Hee Jun, & Park, Ji-Hye. (2013). Historical analysis of the policy on the college entrance system in South Korea. *International Education Studies, 6*(11), 106–121.

Chosun Ilbo. (1955, July 10). Jinbonya toebonya: Yeong'eo gyoyuk'e daehan jabgam [Progression or retrogression: Miscellaneous thoughts about English education]. Retrieved August 3, 2019, from http://proxy.cau.ac.kr/ac7d73d/_Lib_Proxy_Url/cdb.chosun.com/search/pdf/i_archive/read_pdf.jsp?PDF=19550710004&Y=1955&M=07 .

Chosun Ilbo. (1959a, January 26). Daehak'ipsireul apdugo: Yeong'eo [Ahead of college entrance exam: English]. Retrieved October 12, 2019, from http://proxy.cau.ac.kr/ac7d73d/_Lib_Proxy_Url/cdb.chosun.com/search/pdf/i_archive/read_pdf.jsp?PDF=19590126204&Y=1959&M=01.

Chosun Ilbo. (1959b, July 2). Yeong'eo gyoyuk'eui banseong [Reflection of English education]. Retrieved August 3, 2019, from http://proxy.cau.ac.kr/ac7d73d/_Lib_Proxy_Url/cdb.chosun.com/search/pdf/i_archive/read_pdf.jsp?PDF=19590702204&Y=1959&M=07.

Chosun Ilbo. (1962, December 14). Daehak iphakjagyeok kookga gosa moonje: Suhak, sahoe, kook'eo,yeong'eo [National test for university entrance qualification: Mathematics, society, Korean, English]. Retrieved August 3, 2019, from http://proxy.cau.ac.kr/ac7d73d/_Lib_Proxy_Url/cdb.chosun.com/search/pdf/i_archive/read_pdf.jsp?PDF=19621214005&Y=1962&M=12 .

Chun, Young-Jae, Hwang, In-Sung, Kim, Deuk-Kap, Chang, Sung-Won, Han, Chang-Soo, Chun, Hyo-Chan, Kang, Sung-Won, Im, Soo-Ho, Son, Min-Joong. (2008). *Daehanminkookgyeongje 60nyeon'eui daejangjeong [The 60 year's great advances in the economy of the Republic ok Korea]* (SERI CEO Information Vol. 667). Seoul, Korea: Samsung Economic Research Institute.

Chung, Moo-Yong. (2013). 1970nyeondae joong, godeunghakgyo pyeongjoonwha jeongchaek'eui sihaenggwa 'gyoyookgyeokcha' [Implementation of the middle-high school equalization policy and the 'educational gaps' in 1970s]. *Yeoksamunjeyeongu, 29*, 111–135.

Countryeconomy.com. (2019). South Korea GDP: Gross domestic product. Retrieved August 10, 2019, from https://countryeconomy.com/gdp/south-korea?year=1989

Critical Studies on Modern Korean History. (1998). *The selection and refraction of the South and North Koreas in the 1950s.* Seoul, Korea: Yeoksabipyeongsa.

DellaVigna, S., & Gentzkow, M. (2010). Persuasion: Empirical evidence *Annual Review of Economics. 2.* 643–669.

Dong-A Ilbo. (1945, December 28). Gunsa yeong'eo hakgyo seollip [Military English school established]. Retrieved September 10, 2019, from http://newslibrary.naver.com/viewer/index.nhn?articleId=1945122800209202018&editNo=1&print-Count=1&publishDate=1945-12-28&officeId=00020&pageNo=2&printNo=6847&publish-Type=00020.

Dong-A Ilbo. (1948, July 6). Yeong'eo gyojae baekeub. [English textbook distribution]. Retrieved September 10, 2019, from http://newslibrary.naver.com/viewer/index.nhn?articleId=1948070600209202014&editNo=1&printCount=1&publishDate=1948-07-06&officeId=00020&pageNo=2&printNo=7636&publishType=00020

Dong-A Ilbo. (1951, July 31). Michinseon chokjin gyeonggwan yeong'eo gangjwa gaechoe [Holding an police officers' English course for promoting friendly relations with the United States]. Retrieved August 4, 2019, from http://newslibrary.naver.com/viewer/index.nhn?articleId=1951073100209102009&editNo=1&print-Count=1&publishDate=1951-07-31&officeId=00020&pageNo=2&printNo=8588&publish-Type=00010.

Dong-A Ilbo. (1957, October 4). Hyeonheang oekook'eo gyoyook'eui sibi [Argument of current foreign language education]. Retrieved August 3, 2019, from http://newslibrary.naver.com/

viewer/index.nhn?articleId=1957100400209204001&edit-No=1&printCount=1&
publishDate=1957-10-04&of-ficeId=00020&pageNo=4&printNo=10775&
publishType=00020.

Dong-A Ilbo. (1966, September 1). Yeong'eogyoyook 20nyeon'eui banseong [Critical recollection
of the past 20 years of English education] Retrieved August 6, 2019, from https://newslibrary.
naver.com/viewer/index.nhn?articleId=1966090100209205003&editNo=2&printCount=1&
publishDate=1966-09-01&officeId=00020&pageNo=5&printNo=13806&
publishType=00020 .

Dong-A Ilbo. (1971, July 19). Yeong'eogyosa yeonsoosaenggyeoljeong [Decision made for
English teachers receiving in-service teacher training]. Retrieved August 6, 2019, from
https://newslibrary.naver.com/viewer/index.nhn?articleId=1971071900209205016&
editNo=2&printCount=1&publishDate=1971-07-19&officeId=00020&pageNo=5&
printNo=15317&publishType=00020 .

Dong-A Ilbo. (1979, July 10). Joonghak yeong'eogyoyook deutgi malhagi wijooro [Emphasizing
listening and speaking in middle school English education]. Retrieved August 8, 2019, from
https://newslibrary.naver.com/viewer/index.nhn?articleId=1979071000209204004&
editNo=2&printCount=1&publishDate=1979-07-10&officeId=00020&pageNo=4&
printNo=17771&publishType=00020.

Dong-A Ilbo. (1980a, February 14). Gwagwaoei galsoorok geukseong [Aggravating fever of
private tutoring]. Retrieved August 8, 2019, from https://newslibrary.naver.com/viewer/index.
nhn?articleId=1980021400209201006&editNo=2&printCount=1&publishDate=1980-02-
14&officeId=00020&pageNo=1&printNo=17956&publishType=00020.

Dong-A Ilbo. (1980b, January 26). Screen English. Retrieved August 9, 2019, from https://
newslibrary.naver.com/viewer/index.nhn?articleId=1980012600209205026&editNo=2&
printCount=1&publishDate=1980-01-26&officeId=00020&pageNo=5&printNo=17940&
publishType=00020.

Dong-A Ilbo. (1980c, November 5). Daehaksaengdeul yoohakboom jogeonwanwah dui heemangja
neul'eo [Increased number of college students aspiring study abroad after conditions lowered].
Retrieved August 9, 2019, from https://newslibrary.naver.com/viewer/index.nhn?
articleId=1980110500209205001&editNo=2&printCount=1&publishDate=1980-11-05&
officeId=00020&pageNo=5&printNo=18181&publishType=00020.

Dong-A Ilbo. (1981, October 14). Kookminhakgyo'eui yeong'eogyoyook [English education at
elementary school]. Retrieved August 10, 2019, from https://newslibrary.naver.com/viewer/
index.nhn?articleId=1981101400209202001&editNo=2&printCount=1&publishDate=1981-
10-14&officeId=00020&pageNo=2&printNo=18470&publishType=00020.

Dong-A Ilbo. (1983, April 25). Yeong'eohoihwareul paewooja: Galsoorok yeolgi [Let's learn
English conversation: Getting heated attention]. Retrieved August 11, 2019, from https://
newslibrary.naver.com/viewer/index.nhn?articleId=1983042500209206001&editNo=2&
printCount=1&publishDate=1983-04-25&officeId=00020&pageNo=6&printNo=18940&
publishType=00020.

Drake, H. B. (1930). *Korea of the Japanese.* London: John Lane the Bodley Head Limited.

E-narajipyo. (2017, November 1). Size of higher education in Korea. Retrieved September 4, 2018,
from http://www.index.go.kr/potal/main/EachDtlPageDetail.do?idx_cd=1548

Gardner, R. C., & MacIntyre, P. D. (1991). An instrumental motivation in language study: Who
says it isn't effective? *Studies in Second Language Acquisition, 13*, 57–72.

Han, Hong-Koo. (2001, May 8). Geudeul'eun oe malduk'eul an bak'at'eulkka [Why did not they
choose the army for their permanent job?] Retrieved August 4, 2019, from http://h21.hani.co.kr/
arti/culture/culture_general/2391.html.

Han, Hong-Koo. (2003). *Daehanminkooksa 1 [History of the Republic of Korea: Vol. 1].* Seoul,
Korea: Hankyoreh.

Hankyoreh. (2011, November 14). Segye choiak'eui sabeopsarin, jojakbooteo sahyeongkkaji Park
Chung-hee jakpoom [The worst judicial murder in the world: Park Chung-hee fabricated and

sentenced them to death]. Retrieved August 9, 2019, from http://www.hani.co.kr/arti/politics/politics_general/505417.html.

Harris, Z. S. (1951). *Structural linguistics*. Chicago: The University of Chicago Press.

Hofstede, G. (1991). *Cultures and organizations: Software of the mind*. London: McGraw-Hill.

Hong, M., Cho, H. N., Kim, A. R., Hong, H. J., & Kweon, Y.-S. (2017). Suicidal deaths in elementary school students in Korea. *Child and Adolescent Psychiatry and Mental Health, 11*: 53. DOI https://doi.org/10.1186/s13034-017-0190-3

Hwang, Youngsoon. (2014). The history of American English education in Korea: Reflection and new direction. *The Korean Journal of American History, 40*(2), 201–238.

Hyun, P. (1996). *Segyereul gooreumcheoreom tteodonun sanai [The guy wandering the world like a cloud]*. Seoul, Korea: Pooreunsoop.

Kang, In-Chul. (1996). *Hankookgidokgyohoiwa gookga siminsahoi 1945-1980 [Korean Christian church and the national, civil society 1945-1980]*. Seoul, Korea: Hankook Kidokgyoyeoksayeonguso.

Kang, Joon-Mann. (2009 *Ipsi jeonjaeng janhoksa [Atrocious history of school exam war]*. Seoul, Korea: Inmulgwa Sasangsa.

Kang, Joon-Mann. (2011). *Teukbyeolhan nara daehanminkook [Special country: The Republic of Korea]*. Seoul, Korea: Inmulgwa Sasangsa.

Kang, Joon-Mann. (2014). *Hankook'ingwa yeong'eo [Koreans and English]*. Seoul, Korea: Inmulgwasasangsa.

Kim, Boo-Tae. (1997). *Hankuk hakryeoksahoiron [Investigation of literati society in Korea]*. Seoul, Korea: Naeil'eulyeoneunchaek.

Kim, Dong-Hoon. (2001). *Hankook'eui hakbul, tto hanaeui caste inga [Korean hakbul: Is it another caste?]*. Seoul, Korea: Chaeksesang.

Kim, Jin-Man. (2007). Yeong'eo'eui munje [The problems in the English language]. In Ji-Kwan Yoon (Ed.), *Yeong'eo nae maeum'eui sikminjoo'eui [English: The colonialism in my mind]* (pp. 153–172). Seoul, Korea: Dangdae.

Kim, Jong-Chul. (2009a). Park Chung-hee coup d'etat badadeurin Kennedy [Kennedy who accepted the coup d'etat by Park Chung-hee]. Retrieved November 12, 2018, from http://www.mediatoday.co.kr/?mod=news&act=articleView&idxno=78173.

Kim, Jung-Hoon, Shim, Nari, & Kim, Hyanggi. (2019). *386 sedae yoogam [Resentment toward 386 generation]*. Seoul, Korea: Woongjinjisikhouse.

Kim, Kwan S. (1991). *The Korea miracle (1962-1980) revisited: Myths and realities in strategy and development (Working Paper #166)*. Working paper published at the Kellogg Institute for International Studies. Retrieved August 7, 2019, from https://kellogg.nd.edu/sites/default/files/old_files/documents/166_0.pdf.

Kim, Tae-Young. (2006). Motivation and attitudes toward foreign language learning as socio-politically mediated constructs: The case of Korean high school students. *The Journal of Asia TEFL, 3*(2), 165–192.

Kim, Tae-Young. (2010). Socio-political influences on EFL motivation and attitudes: Comparative surveys of Korean high school students. *Asia Pacific Education Review, 11*, 211 222.

Kim, Tae-Young. (2011). Korean elementary school students' English learning demotivation: A comparative survey study. *Asia Pacific Education Review, 12*, 1–11.

Kim, Tae-Young. (2016). An investigation of socio-educational aspects of English education during the Japanese colonial period: Focusing on Chosun Ilbo and Dong-A Ilbo articles. *Studies in English Education, 21*(1), 179–210.

Kim, Tae-Young, & Kim, Ji-Young. (2018). English education in South Korea during the U.S. military government occupation and the first national curriculum: Focus on newspaper article analysis. *Modern English Education, 19*(3), 22–34.

Kim, Tae-Young, & Kim, Yoon-Kyoung. (2016). A quasi-longitudinal study on English learning motivation and attitudes: The case of South Korean students. *The Journal of Asia TEFL, 13*(2), 138–155.

Kim, Tae-Young, & Oh, Shinyu. (2019). English education during the second and third National Curriculum period in South Korea: Focusing on the newspaper article analysis. *Foreign Language Education, 26*(2), 73–98.

Kim, Tae-Young, & Seo, Hyo-Sun. (2012). Elementary school students' foreign language learning demotivation: A mixed method study of Korean EFL students. *The Asia-Pacific Education Researcher, 21*(1), 160–171.

Kim, Young-Seo. (2009b). *Hankook'eui yeong'eogyoyooksa: 19segi ihoo han, yeong, il bigyoyeongoo [History of English education in Korea: A comparative analysis of Korea, Britain, and Japan after the 19th century]*. Seoul, Korea: Hankookmunwhasa.

Korea Herald. (2015, August 10). S. Korea's GDP surges 31,000-fold since 1953. Retrieved July 30, 2019, from http://www.koreaherald.com/view.php?ud=20150810000642.

Kwon, Oryang, & Kim, Jeong-Ryeol. (2010). *Hankook yeong'eogyoyooksa [History of English education in Korea]*. Seoul, Korea: Hankookmunwhasa.

Kyunghyang Shinmun. (1948, July 6). Yeong'eo jubo baegeub jungdeung'gyo gyogwayong'eulo [Distribution of English weekly bulletins to use secondary school textbooks]. Retrieved September 10, 2019, from http://newslibrary.naver.com/viewer/index.nhn?articleId=1948070600329202014&editNo=1&printCount=1&publishDate=1948-07-06&officeId=00032&pageNo=2&printNo=543&publishType=00020.

Kyunghyang Shinmun. (1969, December 8). Kookmingyoseo yeong'eosoo'eop [English education at elementary school]. Retrieved August 6, 2019, from https://newslibrary.naver.com/viewer/index.nhn?articleId=1969120800329207028&editNo=2&printCount=1&publishDate=1969-12-08&officeId=00032&pageNo=7&printNo=7439&publishType=00020.

Kyunghyang Shinmun. (1970, March 20). Hyeonsil'e matge gyoyook sikidorok: Daehaknawado kisool eopseo silup [Need to educate considering practicality: Without skills, falling into unemployment even after college graduation]. Retrieved August 6, 2019, from https://newslibrary.naver.com/viewer/index.nhn?articleId=1970032000329202009&editNo=2&printCount=1&publishDate=1970-03-20&officeId=00032&pageNo=2&printNo=7524&publishType=00020.

Kyunghyang Shinmun. (1978, October 17). Naenyeonbooteo joonggogyo yeong'eogyoyook gaeseon malhagiwa deutgi wijooro [Emphasizing speaking and listening in the next year's improved English education in the middle and high schools]. Retrieved August 8, 2019, from https://newslibrary.naver.com/viewer/index.nhn?articleId=1978101700329207014&editNo=2&printCount=1&publishDate=1978-10-17&officeId=00032&pageNo=7&printNo=10168&publishType=00020.

Kyunghyang Sinmun. (1981, September 21). TV, radio Eohakgangjwa poojjeok neul'eotda [Rapid increase in TV, radio language programs]. Retrieved August 11, 2019, from https://newslibrary.naver.com/viewer/index.nhn?articleId=1981092100329212001&editNo=2&printCount=1&publishDate=1981-09-21&officeId=00032&pageNo=12&printNo=11070&publishType=00020.

Lacina, B., & Gleditsch, N. P. (2005). Monitoring trends in global combat: A new database of battle deaths. *European Journal of Population, 21*, 145–166.

Lankov, A. (2011, January 23). Labor activist Chon Tae-il's death: A walk up call. Retrieved August 7, 2019, from http://www.koreatimes.co.kr/www/news/nation/2011/01/113_80158.html.

Lee, Chung Sup. (2017). The urbanization and migration in the period of the Japanese occupation. *The Korean Journal of Geography, 52*(1), 105–122.

Lee, Heung-Soo. (2011). *Segyewhasidae yeong'eoga gyeongjeda: Yeong'eo'eui gwageowa hyeonjae geurigo mirae [English is economy in the era of globalization: Past, present and past of the English language]*. Seoul, Korea: English MouMou.

Lee, Jung-Kyu. (2003). *Credentialism and academic factionalism in Korean society: Origins and development.* Seoul, Korea: Jibmundang.

Lee, Kyu-Hwan. (1993). *Hankookgyoyook'eui bipanjeok ihae [Critical understanding of education in Korea]*. Seoul, Korea: Hanol Academy.

Lim, Seungju Shawn. (2015). When did it all begin? How neoliberalism wrecked the ecology of Korean universities. *The SNU Quill, 54*, 4–5. Retrieved August 14, 2019, from http://snuquill.com/wp-content/uploads/2015/06/Volume54.pdf.

MacGreggor, G. (1951, June 8). Education pushed by South Koreans despite destruction of many schools. ProQuest Historical Newspapers. *The New York Times*, p. 3.

Mok, K. H., & Neubauer, D. (2015). Higher education governance in crisis: A critical reflection on the massification of higher education, graduate employment and social mobility. *Journal of Education and Work, 29*(1), 1–12.

Moon, Eun-Kyong. (2005). A historical research on English textbooks in the formation stage of the contemporary educational system in Korea. *Foreign Languages Education, 12*(3), 245–269.

Oh, Chun-Seok. (1964). *Hankook singyoyooksa [New educational history in Korea]*. Seoul, Korea: Hyundaegyoyookchongseo Choolpansa.

Oh, Wook-hwan. (2000). *Hankooksahoi'eui gyoyook'yeol: Kiwon'gwa simwha [Education fever in the Korean society: Its origin and aggravation]*. Seoul, Korea: Gyoyookgwahaksa.

Pae, Doo-Bon. (1995). Development of English language education as a science in Korea. *English Teaching, 50*(2), 7–45.

Pae, Doo-Bon. (2000). *Oikook'eo gyoyookgwajeongron: Irongwa gaebal [Study of foreign language curriculum: Theory and development]*. Seoul, Korea: Hanshinmunwhasa.

Park, Cheol-Hee. (2003). The rise of colonial education competition and preparatory education for entrance examinations. *Asian Journal of Education, 4*(1), 65–92.

Park, Hong-Ki, & Kim, Jae-Chun. (2003). *Hakbul report [The reports of academic clique]*. Seoul, Korea: The Book.

Park, Sang-yong. (2017, August 14). Iljegangjeomgi Seoul ingu 39manmyeong: Ilbon joongkuk deung oikook'in'i 3boon'eui 1 chaji [390,000 people lived in Seoul during the Japanese colonization period: 1/3 of them were foreigners including Japanese and Chinese]. Retrieved July 31, 2019, from https://www.hankyung.com/society/article/2017081458401

Phee, Jung-Man. (2011). *Hankookgyoyooksaihae [Understanding Korean educational history]*. Seoul, Korea: Hau.

Richards, J. C., & Rodgers, T. S. (2014). *Approaches and methods in language teaching* (3rd ed.). Cambridge, England: Cambridge University Press.

Seth, M. J. (2017). South Korea's economic development, 1948-1996. Oxford Research Encyclopedia of Asian History. Retrieved August 11, 2018, from http://asianhistory.oxfordre.com/view/10.1093/acrefore/9780190277727.001.0001/acrefore-9780190277727-e-271?print=pdf.

Skinner, B. F. (1957). *Verbal behavior*. Brattleboro, VT: Echo Print Books & Media.

Son, In-Soo. (1992). *The U.S. military government period and education policy*. Seoul, Korea: Minyoungsa.

Son, Min-Ho, & Choi, Seung-Pyo. (2014, January 3). Jayoowha 25nyeon: Haeoiyeohaeng eojewa oneul [25 year of liberalization: Past and present of foreign travel]. Retrieved August 10, 2019, from https://news.joins.com/article/13548604.

Song, Ho-Geun. (2006). *Hankook'eui pyeongdeungjoo'eui, geu maeum'eui seupgwan [Egalitarianism in Korea: Its functional habit]*. Seoul, Korea: Samsung Economic Research Institute.

The Korean Educational Development Institute. (1994). *Hankook'eui gyoyookjipyo 1994 [Educational index of 1994 in South Korea]*. Seoul, Korea: Korean Educational Development Institute.

The United States Department of States. (2019). Proclamation No. 1 by General of the Army Douglas MacArthur. Retrieved July 31, 2019, from https://history.state.gov/historicaldocuments/frus1945v06/d776.

Underwood, H. G. (2002). *Hankookjeonjaeng, hyeokmyeong geurigo pyeongwha [The Korean War, revolution and peace]*. Seoul, Korea: Yonsei University Press.

UNESCO. (2019). Republic of Korea: Education and literacy. Retrieved July 30, 2019, from http://uis.unesco.org/country/KR.

Wolf, M. (1972). *Women and the family in rural Taiwan*. Stanford, CA: Stanford University Press.

YBM. (2019a). Gaebalbaegyeong/gaebalgigwan [Background of test development/test developer]. Retrieved August 10, 2019, from http://exam.ybmnet.co.kr/toeic/info/since.asp.

YBM. (2019b). Yeonhyeok [Test history]. Retrieved August 10, 2019, from http://exam.ybmnet.co.kr/toeic/info/history.asp.

Zeng, K. (1995). Japan's Dragon Gate: The effects of university entrance examinations on the educational system and students. *Compare, 25*, 59–83.

Chapter 4
Historical Overview of English Learning in South Korea: An Era of Economic and Cultural Prosperity from the 1990s to the 2010s

This chapter investigates the changing role of English as a useful device for communication among South Koreans from the 1990s and 2010s. It also explores how such changes have influenced Korean students' and parents' attitudes toward learning and teaching English. Furthermore, it looks at how the multitude of socio-educational phenomena that occurred in South Korea, such as the introduction of elementary school English education and the TOEIC fever, changed Koreans' perceptions of English and eventually impacted the students' motivation to learn English.

English has been closely related to the modernization process enforced by neighboring imperialistic nations in nineteenth century Korea. As explicated in Chap. 2, in the late nineteenth century, English began to replace classical Chinese rapidly (Moon, 1976). After World War II and the Korean War, English became even more crucial because of the close political and economic alliance between the United States and South Korea (Kang, 2011; Seth, 2002). Furthermore, from the 1990s, the discourse of *segyehwa* (世界化) or *gookjehwa* (both mean globalization in Korean), similar to *kokusaika* (国際化) in Japan (Kubota, 2002), gradually gained political support. English proficiency was soon equated with South Korea's national competitiveness in the global market.

The desire to successfully host the 1988 Seoul Summer Olympic Games ushered in the need for English communication among Koreans. Moreover, the acquisition of the United Nations (UN) and the Organization for Economic Co-operation and Development (OECD) memberships status in 1991 and 1996, respectively, brought in an exponential increase in international English communication. Through most of the 1990s, South Korea was governed by its 14th President, Kim Young-sam, who held office from February 1993 to February 1998. He declared the establishment of a New Korea (新韓國) by enhancing "National Competitiveness" in the era of globalization and information (Yoon, 1999). Similar to previous governments in South Korea, the Kim Young-sam government regarded education as the key to national development and prosperity despite the intensifying international competition (Economic Planning Board, 1993).

© Springer Nature Singapore Pte Ltd. 2021
T.-Y. Kim, *Historical Development of English Learning Motivation Research*,
English Language Education 21, https://doi.org/10.1007/978-981-16-2514-5_4

As explained in Chap. 3, the English frenzy was harbored in the economic structure of South Korea. The traditional agricultural society was rapidly transformed into a modern industrial society under the strong (or even ironclad) leadership of the late President Park Chung-hee, who was a former Major General in the South Korean army. After the 1970s, foreign export was prioritized, and the Korean government, as well as industry, paid great attention to English language ability in order to export Korean goods abroad. Korean conglomerates and companies established in-house English education programs in the 1970s, and 80% of these companies conducted their own English test (Kang, 2011). Based on the English test scores, employees received a merit-based bonus at their workplace. For this early English fever, the Educational Testing Service in the U.S. launched the Test of English for International Communication (TOEIC) in Korea in 1982, after its initial launch in Japan in 1979 (McCrostie, 2009). Through the 1980s, English was increasingly highlighted as a priority in various industrial sectors across South Korea, and in some cases, native English speakers were invited for the hiring process in company job interviews to assess the English proficiency of Korean applicants (Kang, 2011). In middle and high schools in Korea, English continued to be instructed as one of the three major school subjects (i.e., Korean, English, and Math) in the 1980s. This meant that students were critically influenced by their English test scores at school and in the college entrance exams, as their parents' generations had been before. These emphases on English, however, did not gain full momentum yet until the 1990s when the motto of globalization inundated Korea.

4.1 Fundamental Changes in the 1990s and Their Impact on English Education in South Korea

In explaining the 1990s "English fever," it would be informative to illustrate the changing international diplomatic terrain surrounding South Korea first and then the domestic changes. The end of the Cold War and the dismantling of the communist bloc in Eastern Europe created a détente or peaceful atmosphere in the Korean Peninsula; both North and South Koreas obtained official membership from the UN in 1991. Continual economic development for several decades enabled South Korea to become a member nation of the OECD in 1996. The OECD is often regarded as a group of leading nations defining themselves as committed to democracy and the free market economy. Since most OECD member nations have attained a high level of economic prosperity and have a relatively high human development index, OECD membership is often considered the symbol of a developed country (OECD, 2002).

The acquisition of the OECD membership in 1996 brought permanent changes in South Korea. First, in order to retain its membership status, South Korea needed to maintain international standards in foreign exchanges and expand close international collaboration in terms of economic policy. The 1996 fiscal year statistics show that the Gross Domestic Product (GDP) of South Korea had already reached US$559.3 billion, ranking 11th place internationally. In order to maintain sustainable development in the future, the South Korean government needed to educate its young generations to keep the global standard, and for this reason, the participation in the OECD marked another cornerstone for the enhancement of South Korean economy and its overall quality of life.

These external changes in international trade compelled most Korean companies to test their employees' English proficiency. Samsung was proactive in embracing this change (Kang, 2011). In October 1993, they announced a recruitment plan for their applicants that adopted an English listening comprehension test instead of the traditional paper-and-pencil test, which primarily evaluated the applicants' knowledge in their undergraduate major and current affairs. The establishment of the World Trade Organization (WTO) facilitated Korean companies' adoption of various sets of English tests in their recruitment process. While preparing for the economic changes coming from the WTO, the Kim Young-sam government promulgated that the year 1995 marks the founding year of globalization of Korea, which was metaphorically equated with "the Second National Foundation." Under this social milieu, English was perceived as the most useful tool for globalization, and office workers in downtown Seoul began attending English classes at private English institutes to pass their company's in-house English tests. Thus, compared with the previous year, English institutes witnessed an increase of 30–40% of their student enrollment in 1995.

In some cases, companies signed commissioned education contracts with private English institutes, and a group of English instructors was dispatched to the company to teach a team of office workers. The employees' English performance was one of the crucial elements in their annual evaluation for promotion at work. Those who exhibited a high level of English proficiency received an English-merit bonus (Dong-A Ilbo, 1995).

The influence of TOEIC also needs to be noted. The TOEIC began exerting exponential influence when the top 30 companies in Korea, including Samsung and LG, decided to include this test in their job openings to measure their applicants' English proficiency from June 1995 (Kang, 2011). According to Kang (2011), the number of TOEIC test takers in Korea exceeded 420,000 in 1995, and more than 500 companies decided to take their job applicants' TOEIC scores into account. English also affected the lives of employees significantly. For example, LG group used English for their internal seminars; Samsung C & T Corporation announced English as their official language, and its employers had to use anglicized names instead of their ethnic Korean names (Nam, 1996). These changes would not be a problem if they were initiated gradually, voluntarily, and upward; however, in reality, they were implemented in a violent, top-down manner (see Sect. 4.3 for more discussion).

Although these English-only policies in Korean companies could not be maintained given the sheer absurdity of using English exclusively—and not Korean (their L1)—for communication among Koreans, it should be noted that English proficiency continued to function as a discriminatory device among the employees in the next decade. Kyunghyang Shinmun (2006), one of the major newspaper media in South Korea, reported that 79.2% of the managers in the Department of Human Resources in most companies reasoned that English proficiency affected their employees' promotion opportunities and their annual salary negotiations. Park and Kim (2007), in a special cover story of Hankook Ilbo (another major newspaper in Korea), reported a "Spartan-style" English institute or *hagwon* for middle-aged office workers, where even corporal punishment was allowed for those whose English test score was mediocre.

English fever in the Korean job market emerged from the neoliberal idea of globalization, following the acquisition of the UN and the OECD membership status in the 1990s, necessitating changes in English education as well. Among various educational efforts exerted during this period, the introduction of elementary English education would be the most notable one. Discussions on introducing elementary English education had been initiated in previous decades. For example, in the 1970s, elementary school students in urban areas, particularly in Seoul, invited private tutors to their homes. In private elementary schools, English education was intermittently conducted. However, the significant opposition toward early English education was raised for it was felt violating the shared egalitarianism in South Korea (see Sect. 3.4 in Chap. 3). Another opposition suggested a potential identity crisis of young students learning a different language other than Korean (L1) (Kim & Oh, 2019). This position indicates that given the developmental nature of the cultural, national, and ethnic identity of young learners, it would be inappropriate for young pre-adolescent students to be exposed to another language at the elementary level.

On the other hand, some L2 professionals supported the idea of learning English at the elementary level, pointing out that this was the optimal period before students reach a "critical period" in learning a foreign language (Birdsong, 2013). They argued that by using eclectic approaches at the elementary level, students could attain a relatively high level of English proficiency without sacrificing their cultural and national identities as Koreans. It was not until 1997, however, that the introduction of elementary English education was implemented at the national level across South Korea (see Sect. 4.5 for more discussion).

Along with the introduction of elementary school English education, the emphasis on English proficiency at the college level increased. From the 1990s, universities in Korea started to offer their undergraduate courses in English. Until the 1980s, except for English-related courses offered in the Department of English Education or English Linguistics and Literature, virtually no undergraduate courses were instructed in English in Korea. However, spearheaded by Korea University, an increasing number of South Korean universities started to offer courses in English. In the same period, short-term study abroad programs to learn English gained widespread popularity among college students. Applying for a year of study leave, university students went abroad, mostly to English-speaking countries, to learn English (Kang, 2011).

The study-abroad to learn English was accelerated in the 2000s when Korean universities promoted English-use policy on campus. For example, universities in

Seoul including Seoul National, Sungkyunkwan, and Kyunghee Universities announced that as one of their graduation requirements, all students must submit an official English test score such as the TOEIC or TOEFL score, or they must pass their in-house English test. English proficiency was preferred not only as a graduation requirement but also in the admission system. In 2001, in undergraduate admissions, a total of 72 universities including Korea, Sungkyunkwan, and Kyunghee Universities established special admission quota for students with an exceptionally high English test score. This growing trend of recruiting English-speaking students in the university is related to the annual international university assessment often conducted by recognized publishing groups such as QS and The Times. Since Korean universities concluded that the number of international students and the level of globalization, both critical factors in university rankings, are represented by English ability, they established special admission systems for international students and Koreans who had excellent proficiency levels of English-speaking skills. As a natural chain reaction, many high school students and parents shared the consensus that the high TOEIC or TOEFL score is the determining factor for admission to prestigious universities in Korea. For this reason, private English institutes specializing in high school students' TOEIC and TOEFL test preparation burgeoned in *Gangnam* (i.e., new downtown) or *Jongro* (i.e., old downtown) area in Seoul (Kang, 2014).

Kang (2007) criticized this spread of English courses in universities, as follows:

> The current situation in South Korean universities seems to overly emphasize education for English, by English, and of English. Even for professors who studied in an English-speaking country and can speak quite a high level of English, their English communication skills are often just half of those in Korean. Both professors and students in classes delivered in English confessed that the degree of lecture delivery and comprehensibility of the lecture was low. In this situation, it would be utterly unrealistic to expect top-quality, creative contents in lectures. It is not easy to understand undergraduate major courses even in Korean. Thus, English-medium major courses would be almost a meaningless waste of time between professors speaking a moderate level of English and students being able to understand English somehow. In short, English-medium courses miss "two rabbits" at the same time: English itself and lecture contents.

However, despite Kang's (2007) pertinent criticism, the English-medium courses in universities spread across Korea. In the mid-2000s, the administrators at colleges were more concerned with their external reputation and international standing in university ranking, and thus, the overall quality of education was sacrificed.

4.2   Changes in College Entrance Exams in 1993: The College Scholastic Ability Test

In Chap. 3, it was argued that Koreans' desire to secure a safe occupation and be promoted at their workplace had continuously functioned as one of the most significant motivators for them to learn English. After the rapid economic expansion during the 1970s and 1980s, for most Korean high school students and their parents, the college entrance exam was often considered the initial screening factor for success in life. In the era of rapid economic development, the face validity of a college diploma and the name of the college engraved in the diploma served as the most convenient criteria for employers to measure the degree holder's potential as a promising candidate for the job (Oh, 2000). In this social atmosphere, the college graduates who held the diploma from the most prestigious university were bestowed advantages in the labor market (Lee & Brinton, 1996). For this reason, so-called SKY institutions (a combination of the initials of Seoul National, Korea, and Yonsei Universities), the top three universities in South Korea, had monopolized the role of elite education (Hultberg et al., 2017). Thus, the college entrance exam has long been prioritized in South Korea. Seth (2002) describes the atmosphere on the day of national college entrance exam in South Korea as follows:

> A great air of tension hovered throughout South Korea on 17 November 1999. A special task force had spent months planning for that day. The night before, President [Kim] Dae Jung had appeared on television to announce that the nation was prepared for the event. All nonessential governmental workers would report to work only later in the morning, as would employees of major firms. Thousands of special duty police were on hand in many cities; thirteen thousand police had mobilized in Seoul alone. Flights at all the nation's airports had been restricted, and special efforts had been made to halt construction to avoid creating noise or commotion of any kind. It was the day of the national university entrance examinations. (Seth, 2002, p. 1)

In this social milieu, the exam format of college entrance exam was and still is the central focus of high school students and their parents. As mentioned in Chap. 2, English served as the crucial determiner in the college entrance exam of Kyungsung Imperial University during the Japanese Colonization Period. Even after the liberation from Japan and after a series of education reforms, the basic format of the English test in the college entrance exam did not show a fundamental change. Despite the minor revamp, most of the previous English tests were composed of reading comprehension, grammar, and vocabulary. In some cases, these subsections followed a fill-in-the-blank format or even essay or composition type questions; in other cases, they were designed as multiple-choice questions. In the National Academic Ability Test (大學入學 學力考查) administered from 1981 to 1992, pronunciation was also measured through a multiple-choice format. However, the tests administered until 1992 did not measure the test takers' listening or speaking ability.

From 1993, the Ministry of Education of Korea decided to introduce a new type of college entrance exam—the College Scholastic Ability Test (CSAT; 大學修學能力試驗) intended to "measure learner's knowledge and ability mainly in the areas of communicative competence, listening comprehension, reading comprehension, and grammar knowledge" in its English subtest (Min, 2007). The adoption of a new college entrance test was the first systematic effort to implement a listening test as the nationwide admission test. Students were first required to attentively listen to the listening script in either monologue or dialogue format depending on the genre of speaking, and then choose one out of five choices. Due to the nature of this passive multiple-choice format, the listening section included in the CSAT did not measure students' listening ability in a direct manner. Moreover, in the years after CSAT was first administered, almost the same pattern of the test was repeated, which cast serious doubt on the CSAT's construct validity in measuring the authentic listening ability.

Despite these drawbacks, the introduction of the listening section in the CSAT should be marked as a remarkable advance in the history of English education in South Korea. To date, 17 questions out of 40 in the English section in the CSAT are allotted for the listening subsection. Given the exponential influence of the college entrance exam, the inclusion of listening elements in the test resulted in a renewed interest in oral proficiency, particularly listening proficiency, encouraging students and teachers in Korea to prepare for the listening test. As a result, a positive washback effect occurred—South Korean students' English listening ability showed a significant increase compared with those in previous generations (Kwon, 2000).

4.3 The TOEIC Fever and Its Negative Ramification in South Korea

In twenty-first century South Korea, a variety of English tests were devised, and the English education market was inundated with private English tests. As mentioned in previous sections, the TOEIC, which was first administered in Japan, was introduced to the Korean job market in 1982. The rapid inclusion of special admission quota for college students who could speak a high level of English resulted in the "outburst" of TOEIC frenzy from the latter half of the 1990s. Many Korean students and parents alike devoted their time and financial means to acquire a high TOEIC score. Kang (2011) estimated that the number of TOEIC test takers in secondary schools in 1999 was 11,938, which outnumbered that in 1998 (2775) by four times. It is ironic that the TOEIC, initially made to assess the English communication skills of non-native English speakers at work, was utilized not by workers but by students who were much younger than the target population. The TOEIC fever was spread even to Korean elementary school students with the naïve belief that the earlier preparation begins, the better the TOEIC score. Due to this nationwide TOEIC boom, the number of TOEIC test takers in the first quarter of 2000 was 165,283 in Korea. This number was an increase of 55.5% in the same period in 1999. Given the exponential increase in the number of the TOEIC test takers, test-taking tips were shared by the test takers, and in some cases, illegal information sharing was identified. For example, as the ETS established a massive amount of item pools, and in most cases, the same question was reused next time, the test takers would share the exam questions that they have taken and restore the entire set of exam questions through collaborative online work. Additionally, TOEIC instructors focused on test-taking strategies while overemphasizing their practical random guessing skills tailor-made for the TOEIC (Kang, 2014).

In the twenty-first century, the number of young TOEIC test takers, including both elementary and secondary school students were noteworthy; it was only 1596 in 1999, but it skyrocketed into 44,145 in 2001, which is increased by 27 times within 3 years. The ETS was also quick to catch this new demand from young test takers in Korea. In 2001, they established *the TOEIC Bridge*, a mini set of TOEIC for the youth. The ETS (2019) states that this test "accurately assesses the English proficiency of beginning to intermediate learners with reliable, valid, and consistent test scores" (Para 1), and Korean students and parents welcomed this new English test. While closely monitoring this trend in TOEIC, private English institutes in Korea also quickly responded. The establishment of English institutes targeting young learners soon followed, and new weekly or monthly TOEIC study magazines were competitively published (Lee, 2011b).

The TOEIC frenzy in the first decade of the twenty-first century seems mostly attributable to the admission policy in high schools and universities. As mentioned above, South Korean universities concerned about their external ranking began recruiting students with high TOEIC test scores. High schools soon followed this educational trend. In the student selection process, foreign language high schools in Seoul including Daewon, Daeil, Ewha, and Hanyoung Foreign Language High Schools recruited the gifted students with language-talents solely considering the test scores of the TOEIC, TOEFL, or TEPS (i.e., Test of English Proficiency developed by Seoul National University). Additionally, while recruiting new students, 95 high schools across South Korea added extra points for those who submitted high TOEIC scores (Kang, 2011). Although professors in academia continued to warn against this deviant use of TOEIC (Yoon, 2014), initially established to assess the English proficiency of Japanese office workers, such concerns could not attenuate the TOEIC frenzy.

Not only the *TOEIC Bridge* but also other domestic English tests such as the Primary English Language Test (PELT) and the Test of Practical English Language (TOPEL) were launched, and many Korean elementary school students took one of these English tests in the 2000s. In the case of PELT, approximately 270,000 elementary school students were registered in 2003, and by October 2014, the accumulated test takers were over 400,000. Newspaper articles (e.g., Heo, 2004) reported that excessive competition among the students' mothers fueled the outbreak of the English test among elementary school students. Children's English test scores gradually functioned as the symbol of parental support for their children's English study. This support often includes the socioeconomic status of the parents, and the parents of students who achieved a higher TOEIC score than other students take pride in their high social ground. Heo (2004) reported an elementary school student's comment that the girl felt ashamed of herself because she failed in the exam and felt scared to see her mother's face because her mother is infuriated with her and said that she is not entitled to eat home-cooked meals.

The expansion cycle of the TOEIC did not meet any challenge until the mid-2010s when companies in Korea gradually realized that the TOEIC score did not represent the test takers' real English proficiency. However, before they reached this consensus, the TOEIC frenzy continued in Korea. For example, in 2008, the total number of TOEIC test takers exceeded 2,000,000 in a single year. This figure includes jobseekers, primary, secondary, and tertiary school students altogether. It was the most significant number of test takers since the TOEIC was introduced to South Korea in 1982 when only 1379 Koreans applied for the test (Kang, 2011). Moreover, the cumulative number of TOEIC test takers in South Korea from 1982 to 2008 was estimated 18 million, which meant that 3.8 persons out of 10 Koreans took this test.

However, this unprecedented power of the TOEIC in Korea showed a significant change in the 2010s. The primary motive to this downturn was the realization of the TOEIC as the test of passive English knowledge excluding English speaking and essay writing. In the conventional TOEIC test format, only English listening and reading proficiencies are assessed through various question formats. Thus, although companies in South Korea recruited those who gained the perfect score (i.e., 990 points) in TOEIC, in many cases, the new employees could not demonstrate the expected English proficiency, particularly in English communication with overseas commercial partners at work. Although the TOEIC Speaking section complements the traditional TOEIC, the test score shows a significant discrepancy with real-time English communication. In the cover story of Weekly Donga Magazine, Koo (2015) reported the interviews with new employees in a Korean company. For example, Mr. Jung, a 5th-year office worker in the department of corporate advertisement at a large-sized company in Korea stated that his TOEIC score was 950 (out of 990) and the TOEIC Speaking level was 7 (out of 8) when employed. However, he confessed that like other co-workers who also gained more than 900 in the TOEIC, he was not very confident during telephone conversations with international counterparts. Mr. Lee, another interviewee who was completing his 6th-year also confirmed this by stating that his English test score did not correctly reflect his English proficiency, and a high score in TOEIC and the real ability of English reading and speaking were different matters.

As the above perception toward the TOEIC and other English tests spread among HRD managers and recruiters in South Korea, the popularity of TOEIC gradually waned. Lee (2014) reported that Korean conglomerates such as LG changed their workforce recruitment policy, and the TOEIC was critically affected by the changing job market. The number of TOEIC test takers for the purpose of job preparation was 800,000 in 2009, and the number steadily increased, reaching more than 900,000 in 2012. However, starting from 2013 the number shows a downturn to 880,000. Moreover, in the university admission process, the special quota for foreign language specialists was abolished or significantly decreased (Choi, 2017). In this changing atmosphere in Korean universities, a consensus among university administrators seems to have been reached that students' English proficiency and their academic performance do not overlap, and in many cases, students admitted through the foreign language specialist quota underperformed in their academic disciplines. Additionally, the majority of Korean students and parents opposed to the specialist admission on the ground that it is only for the upper social classes with a "gold spoon in their mouth from birth" (Choi, 2017). The TOEIC or other English test-based university admissions are considered to provide an undue advantage to students from wealthy family backgrounds, whereas students from lower socioeconomic backgrounds can hardly succeed due to the exponential amount of money spent for the TOEIC test preparation.

In the 2020s, the demand for TOEIC is still high, but the demand by primary and secondary school students has significantly declined. English-test scores are still required by many universities for students' graduation requirements, but the undergraduate admission quota for recruiting English language specialists has been significantly reduced, if not discarded. The English-test frenzy represented by the TOEIC presents the devastating power of English when combined with occupational purpose or academic misuse. In the decades of TOEIC frenzy, Korean students of various ages from elementary schools and adult job seekers experienced unnecessary competition in the attempts to achieve a better English score than others. This social atmosphere seems to have intensified Korean English learners' competitive motivation toward English learning (Kim, 2006, 2010).

4.4   Bok Geo-il's Argument of English as an Official Language

In the discussion of English frenzy in the 1990s and the first decade of the twenty-first century, it is informative to understand novelist Mr. Bok Geo-il's argument on English as an official language (英語 公用語化論) in South Korea. Mainly based on economic principles, in his controversial book entitled "*National Language in the Age of Global Language*," Bok (1998) argued that Koreans need to adopt English as an official language given the fact that English is a de facto global language in and outside of South Korea. Bok (1998) argued that "given the current trend that various civilizations in the world are being merged into 'the Global Empire,' it is unreasonable and unrealistic to regard English merely as the language of the Anglo-Saxons. English is now the standard language of human beings. It would be of no use to disregard this fact" (p. 182). He continues:

> It is tremendous to think of the resources that the citizens of Korean society spend to learn English. A total of 530,000 elementary school students learn English in private English institutes, which resulted in the spending of 350 billion won [i.e., $300 million]. ... As we get old, the importance of English snowballs and the persons who invest in English are not merely limited to students. As we see middle-aged men who put earphones in their ears to learn English, we have spent an enormous amount of investment to learn English. However, to date, we have not started an official discussion of upgrading the efficacy of English investment. The surest way to upgrade it is to make English an official language [in South Korea]. (Bok, 2003, p. 180)

While explaining the former colonies of the U.K. and the U.S., Bok (1998) continues:

> The cases of India, the Philippines, and Singapore corroborate that it is not a hugely tricky matter to adopt English as the official language. In such nations, the preference toward English is evident, and the benefits coming from the use of English in their daily lives are

more than we roughly estimate. We have to pay attention to the fact that the reason why English had been firmly rooted in these nations was that they were former colonies of the U.K or the U.S. However, they do not think English as the 'vestige of colonization.' It should be noted that once English is adopted as an official language, the attitude toward English is fundamentally changed. (Bok, 1998, p. 181)

Bok's claim was groundbreaking at the end of the twentieth century. He made it clear that English is not used only by the traditional Anglo-Saxon countries such as the U.K and the U.S. As classical Chinese had functioned as the de facto lingua franca in East Asia before the period of modernization in the nineteenth century, Bok claimed that English is also used as a global language and no one can claim its ownership. Bok (1998, p. 183) continued that "it is time for us to embrace English, the global language, into ours. Moreover, we should proclaim that we will be willing to do our job in developing this global language."

Immediately after his argument was published in a book, vehement nationwide reactions erupted; some of them developed into a chain of heated debates, discussing the pros and cons, in Chosun Ilbo, the opinion-leading newspaper in Korea. For example, Nam (1998) criticized Bok saying that his argument was vulgar hyper-globalism, and it was groundless to expect that the status of Korea would be sublimed once Koreans used English as an official language. Similarly, Han (1998) criticized Bok for pursuing opportunistic economic logic. Han argued that in many cases, rationalism and economic principles could not explain the funda-mental development of the human race, and cultural identity as Koreans and Korea-ness should be taken into account seriously in Bok's argument. Chosun Ilbo (1998) also reported the result of a small-scale survey analysis conducted in Seoul Joongang Hospital with 114 medical doctors and the managerial staff. The result showed that 44.7% agreed with adopting English as an official language, whereas 55.3% disagreed with the idea.

A few adverse reactions were based on the ethnocentric stance—the importance of Korean identity and nationalism prioritizing the superiority of Korean language, culture, and even civilization to English counterparts without providing substantial evidence. As a consequence, to some, Bok Geo-il was considered a betrayer of Korean tradition and culture. However, not all criticisms were emotional ethnocen-trism. Perhaps the most logical counterargument leveled against Mr. Bok was initiated by Dr. Park Noja, a cultural critic and professor of Korean studies at the University of Oslo, Norway. Park (2006) argued that the cause and effect surround-ing English proficiency needs scrutiny. According to him, the superb English proficiency of Europeans is the result of intensive foreign language education coming from their high economic power, and English itself was not the cause or motive propelling economic development at all. Moreover, the learning of a foreign language is an individual citizen's decision at their own discretion. If the nation imposes it in the form of the English as official language policy, it is not an advancement of liberal education but only a retroactive, medieval labor system enforced to all commoners or slaves. Park (2006) also pointed out the disparity among the upper and lower classes in South Korea. Given the current situation in South Korea, if English becomes an official language, private English education will be regarded as a must to all South Koreans since public English education cannot make them achieve such a high level. Thus, South Korean youths from the upper class will be able to enjoy high-quality private education, but their inferior counterparts will not and will eventually become third-class citizens.

Interestingly, concerning the English divide between the upper and the lower classes that Park (2006) raised, Bok (2002) held an opposing opinion. Bok argued that the adoption of English as an official language is toward making an egalitarian society. He stated that because English functions as a linguistic and cultural capital, the current educational system only aggravates the unequal distribution of this capital between the haves and the have-nots. This systematic inequality will disappear when English becomes the official language in South Korea; with everybody using English, Koreans will relish equal opportunities. In a Dong-A Ilbo column, Bok (2002) stated:

> Once we officialize English, this will be able to contribute to the equality of opportunity. In other words, opposition to the officialization of English is to allow a specific social group to monopolize knowledge and information [in English]. It is the same as the medieval elites' monopolizing information written in either Latin or classical Chinese. Knowledge and information are power. Be English an official language or not, the upper class in our society will keep teaching English to their children, and their children having superior English command will rule those who are deprived of knowledge and information due to the lack of English ability. (Bok, 2002)

The debate on English as an official language continued throughout the first decade of the twenty-first century. With the English frenzy ignited by the TOEIC syndrome and the university admission system favoring students with superb English proficiency, Bok's provocative argument toward officializing English in Korea was maintained. Notably, after the inauguration of President Lee Myung-bak (tenure: 2008–2013), new English policy proposals such as English immersion and the National English Ability Test (NEAT) were produced and continued until the 2010s. In this context, it seems clear that Bok's (1998, 2002) proposal of adopting English as an official language provided fertile ground for the proponents of intensive English education.[1]

4.5 The Nationwide Implementation of Elementary English Education in South Korea

The Kim Young-sam government in Korea emphasized globalization in order to maintain competitiveness at the international level, and as mentioned above, the acquisition of membership to the UN and the OECD in the 1990s expedited the need

---

[1]Bok's (1998, 2002) argument of English as an official language in Korea seems to have striking similarity to Mori Arinori's proposal of English as the national language in Japan in the later nineteenth century. They both based their argument on the economic ground and could not realize their proposals in both nations (See Chap. 5).

to enhance overall English proficiency nationwide. In this backdrop, from 1997, public elementary school English was implemented across South Korea. Kwon (2000) regarded this education reform would be the most significant change in the history of South Korea's English education. According to the Ministry of Education (1995) of Korea, there were seven crucial features of the elementary school English curriculum:

1. The learning of oral language is the primary goal.
2. English is taught from the third grade.
3. Affective goals are more important than cognitive goals; thus, various techniques to improve learning motivation are encouraged.
4. Vocabulary is strictly controlled.
5. Sentence length is controlled to seven words for third and fourth grades and nine words for fifth and sixth grades.
6. A functional syllabus was employed with nine categories of functions.
7. Cognitive-oriented evaluation is not encouraged to test student progress.

In the Seventh National Curriculum period—from 1997 to 2008—the third and fourth-grade students received 1 class-hour (i.e., 40 min) English education per week, and fifth and sixth students 2 class-hours. The implementation of elementary school English education was made possible mainly through the strong educational drive from the presidential office. For this reason, sufficient systematic preparation was not made before the Spring semester of 1997. The lack of preparation resulted in serious confusions in elementary schools. For example, the emphasis on oral proficiency rather than written increased the difficulty for elementary school English teachers, most of whom did not have much hands-on experience of instructing listening and speaking activities in class. For teachers who were more familiar with traditional reading and writing-based English classes, class activities emphasizing oral proficiency felt alien (Min, 2007).

Moreover, elementary school English teachers were in urgent demand during the first several years of this nationwide, large-scale implementation. The number of elementary school English teachers who graduated from the Department of English Education at the University of Education could not meet the massive demand across South Korea. In order to address this imminent problem, the Ministry of Education offered various intensive in-service training sessions to homeroom teachers at elementary schools. However, considering the significant demand for English teachers, this administrative effort was insufficient. As a consequence, the Ministry of Education had to recruit graduates of the college of education who already had teacher licenses to teach English at secondary schools, not at elementary schools. With an only a short period of training, these secondary school certificate holders were granted elementary school teacher license and were allowed to work as elementary English teachers (Koo, 2018b).

Despite the benefits of elementary school English education, a couple of significant side effects have been reported. First, the competition toward English learning at the elementary level was re-ignited. In the 1960s and 1970s, early English education was conducted among students from affluent family backgrounds, and only a few private elementary schools endeavored to implement English education in their school curricula (Kim & Oh, 2019; see also Chap. 3). However, the nationwide implementation of elementary English education had expedited students' academic competition in English as a major school subject. In most cases, the competition was aggravated when combined with private English institutes or *hagwon*s. This *hagwon* marketing was based on so-called the-earlier-the-better position. In other words, although public English education starts from Grade 3 at elementary school, if the student did not learn English much in advance, he or she would be in a disadvantageous position because most (if not all) students had already acquired basic English skills. Therefore, compared with the previous generation who started to learn English once they are enrolled in secondary schools, the current generation learning English from Grade 3 elementary school has a relatively high level of stress and experiences demotivation in learning English due to the excessive competition among them and the high expectation from their parents and the society (Kim, 2011; Kim & Seo, 2012).

Other shortcoming of elementary school English education was the initiation of early childhood (or preschool) English education. The introduction of elementary school English education from Grade 3 resulted in the introduction of private English education at a lower level from Grade 1 in elementary school and eventually in teaching English to kindergarten students. After 6 years of implementing elementary school English education in South Korea, Lee (2003) published questionnaire survey results of the parents of kindergarten students asking about their preference for early childhood English education. A total of 18% of parents in Seoul, Cheonan, and Gwangyang "agreed strongly" with early childhood English education at kindergarten, and 66% of them "agreed" with it. In total, 84% of the parents responded positively to the idea of early childhood English education. Moreover, as of 2012, 72.5% of private kindergartens had already incorporated English education in their curriculum at least as a weekly extracurricular session (Jang, 2012).

In summary, the elementary school English education introduced in 1997 came from the top-down administrative decision from the Kim Young-sam government and its main motive was closely affiliated with the neo-liberal idea of national competitiveness driven by intensified globalization. At the initial stage of its implementation, owing to the lack of systematic preparation through teacher training, there was a great demand for elementary English teachers. Further, elementary English education provoked unnecessary competition among young students and eventually resulted in demotivation in learning English (see Chap. 6 for related research). However, in terms of communicative orientation, the elementary English education highlighted speaking and listening proficiency, which alleviated the traditional over-emphasis on reading and grammar. In terms of cognitive and affective development of South Korean students, elementary school English education seems to have a positive effect. In a large-scale comparative study, Kwon (2006) reported that Korean high school students' English development in their listening, reading, and writing skills and their affective development in the motivation and confidence level had significantly increased after the implementation of elementary school English instruction. He compared the questionnaire survey results of students attending high schools in 2006 with those of the 2003 cohorts who did not receive an elementary English education. Although such significant differences might not be solely attributable to the influence of elementary English education, Kwon (2006) speculated that the introduction of elementary English education in Korea had a positive impact on South Korean EFL learners.

4.6   The Invitation of Native English Teachers Through the EPIK

The rapid implementation of elementary English education resulted in a substantial shortage of English teachers. In 1995, the Ministry of Education of Korea decided to invite and place native speakers of English across South Korean elementary and secondary schools. The primary purpose of this move was to enhance the communicative skills of Korean students, to expedite international understanding, and above all, to reformulate teaching methodologies employed in South Korean schools. Thus, while referring to Japan Exchange and Teaching (JET) in Japan and the Native-speaking English Teachers (NET) in Hong Kong, the English Program in Korea (EPIK) was organized and sponsored by the Ministry of Education. The Ministry defined native English speakers as the citizens of seven English speaking countries, including the U.S., the U.K., and Canada. Immediately after its initiation in 1995, 660 native speakers of English were selected and hired after receiving orientation sessions for 60 h (Lee, 2015). Jeon (2009) summarized the eligibility requirements and duties of the EPIK teachers as follows:

> The EPIK program specifies the following eligibility requirements for prospective teachers: (1) citizenship in the following countries: Australia, Canada, Ireland, New Zealand, the United Kingdom, the USA, and South Africa; (2) a B.A. degree; (3) good mental and physical health; (4) good command of English; and (5) ability to adapt to Korean culture and living. Applicants must have studied from the junior high level (seventh grade) and resided for at least 10 years or more in the above-listed countries. An EPIK teacher's duties include: conducting English conversation classes for Korean teachers and students, preparing teaching materials for English language education, assisting in developing teaching materials, assisting with activities related with English classes and/or jointly conducting English classes, and performing other duties as specified by the host Provincial Office of Education (Jeon & Lee, 2006). Salaries range from US$1,900 to US$3,000 per month, depending on the candidate's eligibility, the location of the school, and the contract period. (Jeon, 2009, p. 236)

The number of EPIK-sponsored native speakers of English plummeted in 1997 while South Korea (as with other Southeastern Asian nations) faced the financial crisis, or the International Monetary Fund (IMF) trusteeship, but the number started to recuperate at the turn of the century and steadily increased until the mid-2010s. As

Table 4.1 Number of native speaking English teachers from 2000 to 2010

Year	2000	2001	2002	2003	2004	2005	2006	2007	2008	2009	2010
Number	146	139	131	541	866	1017	1909	2937	4332	7997	8546

From Lee (2015, p. 51)

shown in Table 4.1, the number of native-speaking English teachers showed a steady increase until the year 2010. In terms of regions, most of them worked in Seoul (1646 teachers as of 2010) or Gyeonggi-do (2256 as of 2010) vicinity of Seoul where more than 12 million people live.

As Jeon (2009) stated above, the hired EPIK-sponsored native-speaking English teachers worked as assistant teachers in South Korean schools. This means that Korean English teachers accompanied them, and in case of necessity such as speaking practice, group work, and student monitoring, they assisted Korean teachers. Thus, when an EPIK-sponsored native speaking teacher was allotted to a Korean school, it was expected to have a teaching team where a Korean English teacher and a native-speaking teacher divided their role in the class and showed a synergistic educational impact on students' English development.

The historical evaluation of EPIK-sponsored native-speaking English teachers does not reach a consensus. Previous research showed that native English-speaking teachers brought a positive impact in English classrooms in Korea in terms of students' attitudes and motivation toward learning about English culture (Lee & Kim, 2013). However, criticisms also emerged, particularly toward the lenient selection criteria and process of the EPIK-sponsored teachers. The main selection criterion was the homeland of the applicants. In other words, as long as the applicants were born and educated in the traditionally English-speaking countries aforementioned, the initial condition was met. The applicants' specific undergraduate major was not considered, and the applicants merely needed to prove their graduation from a 4-year university in English-speaking countries, regardless of their major. Given this leniency, many of the EPIK-sponsored teachers did not possess adequate knowledge about education, particularly for teaching primary and secondary school students in South Korea. The 60-hour orientation before embarking on their job in Korea was not sufficient for them to be familiarized with the South Korean education system and students (Lee, 2015).

Another criticism was on the lack of or mediocre collaboration between Korean English teachers and these EPIK-sponsored native English teachers (Heo & Mann, 2015). Although their collaboration was highly anticipated and encouraged at the governmental level, the lack of monitoring from the authorities soon made this program fall prey to a "laissez-faire" laxation of the two parties. Since the team teaching and collaboration between Korean English teachers and the EPIK teachers was not strictly enforced, the Korean English teachers' activism and enthusiasm primarily decided the quality and degree of collaboration between them. In other words, if a Korean English teacher's educational philosophy was on enhancing students' English communicative competence, the teacher could make the best of the native-speaking assistant teachers. However, if a Korean teacher was not very enthusiastic about team teaching, the EPIK-sponsored teachers could, in the worst case, end up with doing passive, menial works such as reading dialogue script aloud to students.

The third criticism was related to the first one: the EPIK teachers' lack of understanding of education. It was reported that some EPIK-sponsored native teachers did not have sufficient understanding of Korean culture and tried to argue for the supremacy of their homeland and English-speaking culture. Lee (2015) criticized: "some NS (i.e., native-speaking) teachers implicitly or explicitly expressed that their own culture and way of life represent the norm or are superior to the Korean culture and way of life" (p. 52).

In order to remedy such criticisms raised during the first decade of the twenty-first century, from 2015 onwards, the Ministry of Education decided to recruit EPIK-sponsored teachers only if they have completed TESOL certificate programs in their home countries (Lee, 2015). However, more recent statistics show that the number of EPIK native-speaking teachers shows a gradual decrease primarily due to the educational budget. For example, in 2016, the total number of 4962 EPIK teachers were hired in Korea, which represents a 41.8% decrease compared with 8520 teachers in 2012 (Yonhap News, 2016b, October 6). The EPIK-sponsored native-speaking English teachers still serve an essential role in various levels of Korean schools, but the selection and administration of the EPIK teachers are now more closely monitored.

Despite the above shortcomings, the positive impact of EPIK is not negligible. First, these EPIK teachers provided ample opportunity to speak in English to both Korean students and teachers. Before the implementation of this program, it was a rarity to meet English-speaking foreigners in classroom settings particularly in rural areas in Korea. In this regard, the daily interaction with native English speakers provided an authentic opportunity to have meaningful communication and alleviate the fear of English communication. Through this experience, Korean students and teachers could convince themselves of the importance of communicative competence. Second, Korean English teachers gradually formulated realistic expectations toward native English speakers. Before the implementation of EPIK, many Korean English teachers relied excessively on native English speakers' intuition and implicitly believed in the efficacy, if not superiority, of native English-speaking teachers in English instruction and classroom management (Jeon, 2009). However, as explained above, the EPIK-sponsored teachers' lack of experience and proper educational training resulted in various problems in their classroom management. Lee (2015) succinctly stated that "many ordinary Korean teachers realized that they could not solely rely on the native teachers in providing high-quality teaching . . . and began to take responsibility for their own English teaching" (p. 53).

4.7 The Introduction of Teaching English in English (TEE) Certification

With the EPIK, at the turn of the century, the Ministry of Education of Korea actively encouraged Korean English teachers to use English in their English classes. As discussed in previous chapters on the negative consequences of the Japanese Colonization on English education in Korea in Chaps. 2 and 3, for decades, the Grammar Translation Method was the most widely used in English classes in Korea. Thus, students have learned English for 6–10 years, but they did not have sufficient opportunities to use English for communicative purposes. Instead, they developed extensive but passive knowledge in English, particularly grammar and vocabulary. The EPIK policy illustrated in the above section was to change the current situation in English classes, and for more than a decade, native speakers of English have actively been invited and allocated to different levels of schools across South Korea.

However, the EPIK had its inherent limitation from the beginning because most of the assistant English teachers sponsored by the EPIK program did not have adequate teacher training including knowledge in linguistics, education, and other related subdisciplines required in schools (Lee, 2015). Therefore, a better viable alternative to the EPIK would be to enhance Korean English teachers' teaching skills, particularly skills of using English in their English classes. According to Lee (2011a), from 2009, starting with the Seoul Metropolitan Office of Education, Teaching English in English (TEE) Certificate Program was initiated, and other provincial offices of education soon followed.

The theoretical foundation of the TEE Certificate Program was based on modern linguistic theories. For the nature of EFL classrooms where authentic English input is limited, it is crucial to increase English input through English teachers' active role as authentic input providers. Through learners' English interaction in the form of L2 output, the L2 input would be meaningfully internalized into the learners' existing sets of L2 rules, transformed into intake, and contribute to the learners' L2 proficiency development (cf. Gass, 1997; Krashen, 1985; Long, 1996; Swain & Lapkin, 1995). Additionally, it is expected that while engaged in teaching English in English in their classes, English teachers can develop their teaching expertise and re-affirm their professional identity (Lee, 2017; Manh, 2012). Given this, it was considered crucial to have English teachers equipped with TEE certificates. When they provide a moderately challenging level of English input to their students, Korean students can develop English communicative competence in their classes.

For these policy initiatives, the Ministry of Education of Korea, in conjunction with the Office of Education in most cities and provinces across South Korea, encouraged Korean teachers to obtain TEE certification. For example, the Seoul Metropolitan Office of Education (2016) distinguished primary school and secondary school levels. In each level, there existed two types of certificates: TEE-Ace (A) and TEE-Master (M). To qualify for TEE-A, 3-year (elementary school teacher) or 1-year (secondary school teacher) teaching experience was required. Additionally, 12 credit hours (elementary teacher) or 4 credit hours (secondary teacher) of in-service English teacher training were required. For applicants meeting these preliminary requirements, the Office of Education provided intensive TEE training, and after completing this training, the applicants' TEE performance and English proficiency during a demo class was evaluated by assessors (mostly postgraduate-level teachers or professors in English education). Upon acquiring a satisfactory score, they were certified as TEE-A teachers. In the case of TEE-M certificate, the process was more robust. The TEE-M applicants should have 7 years (elementary teacher) or 10 years (secondary teacher) of teaching experience, and they should have completed 28 credit-hour in-service English teacher training. For those meeting the initial requirements, the Office of Education conducted English interviews and evaluated their teaching portfolios, including the activities related to TEE instruction submitted by the applicants. On completing these steps, the TEE-M applicants were required to complete extensive TEE training. After obtaining their TEE-M license, these teachers could function as TEE-A assessors, mentor teachers, and lecturers for in-service training (Seoul Metropolitan Office of Education, 2016). Since its official introduction in 2009, the TEE Certificate Program was developed into a systematic program, and TEE-A and TEE-M certificates had upgraded English teachers professional teaching skills.

Note that previous research investigating the effectiveness of TEE or English-medium-instruction (EMI) presents inconsistent attitudes toward it. In general, studies have reported that during the initial stage of introduction in the early 2000s, English teachers were pessimistic about using TEE in their classes for the following reasons: (1) too many students in a classroom, (2) widening gaps in English proficiency among students, (3) lack of teaching methods in TEE, and (4) lack of teacher confidence (Lee, 2017). After its official introduction in 2009, after various in-service training of TEE, an increasing number of English teachers in South Korea showed positive attitudes toward TEE because TEE is believed to have a beneficial impact on students' listening and speaking proficiency (Ahn, 2011). Park and Min (2014) reported mixed findings, though. English teachers in Korea refrained from using English in their classes, mainly due to the lack of students' understanding of English and the difficulty of delivering teaching contents within a limited class hour. Nonetheless, they believed that TEE is more effective than TEK (i.e., Teaching English in Korean) in developing students' listening and speaking skills and encouraging lively classroom activities.

More recent findings present that the TEE certificate program is not as rigorously mandated as in the previous decade. By using semi-structured interviews, Lee (2017) investigated 18 secondary English teachers who did not participate in the TEE Certificate Program. Contrary to the widespread perception that these teachers do not have sufficient English proficiency in conducting TEE instruction, the teachers used TEE in their English classes. The primary reason for not being TEE-certified was the excessively complicated assessment procedure in the TEE certification system. Secondly, the TEE certification prioritized teachers' (i.e., not students') English-speaking ability, which contradicted the teachers' teaching philosophies. Thirdly, the purpose of the TEE Certificate Program is only for obtaining a certificate, without leading to long-term teacher development.

Moreover, the lack of institutional monitoring after the TEE licensure is pointed out as a problem as well. In Daejeon Metropolitan Office of Education, in 2017, a total of 610 million won (the equivalent of $52,000) was spent for TEE in-service training, but none of TEE certified teachers fulfilled their occupational duty of working as designated English teachers at their school (News 1, 2018). Additionally, in Jeju Self-Governing Provincial Office of Education, it was reported that schools in Jeju Island do not take full advantage of TEE certified teachers and these teachers conduct the same instructions as other non-TEE certified teachers do (Jeju Shinbo, 2018).

4.8   Study Abroad and the Goose Father Syndrome in South Korea

The elementary school English education, the EPIK, and the TEE certification had a common thread: the emphasis on oral proficiency. Noticeably, in the twenty-first century, an increasing focus was placed on verbal or speaking and listening proficiency rather than literacy, reading, and writing proficiency in English. Until the 1980s, special authorization was required for average Koreans to go abroad for sightseeing or study. It was only in 1989 that Koreans could go abroad without any restrictions from the government. From that point on, Koreans gradually realized that prompt and hands-on ability in English speaking and listening was urgently needed (Kim, 2015). Those who were familiar with the traditional way of learning English, such as memorizing a vast vocabulary list and having an erudition of complex English grammar, could not communicate with the local people in English-speaking countries. Therefore, many Koreans, disappointed with their poor command of English and slow progress of public English education, began looking for alternatives. One way was to apply for English study-abroad.

As mentioned previously, the acquisition of UN and OECD member status appears to have been the catalyst for realizing the communicative function of English. Thus, in the 1990s, Korean youths started traveling overseas for backpacking trips (Kyunghyang Shinmun, 2010). However, the catastrophic turmoil of Asian financial crisis that struck Korea as well as other Asian nations negatively affected this trend, and it was only after 2000 that international study and travel were back on track. In fact, in the early 2000s, dissatisfied with public education in South Korea, particularly with English education, many Koreans tried to seek better educational opportunities abroad, leading to an "education exodus" (Chow, 2012). This twenty-first-century trend received scholarly attention because sending children in elementary, middle, and high schools for study-abroad was regarded as an unprecedented phenomenon. The destinations for learning English and study abroad were primarily the U.S., Canada, U.K., Australia, and New Zealand, where English is used daily. It was at the same period that the term "kirogi kajok" (기러기 가족) or goose families started to appear on the headline news coverage. Chow (2012) explains this phenomenon as follows:

> Sending children abroad to boarding schools and universities was once an option exclusive to a small group of elite families, but today, early study abroad is widespread among middle-class families: the children, often accompanied by their mothers, attend public schools in English speaking countries, while the fathers remain in Korea to support them. These families are known as "kirogi kajok" in Korea, or "goose families." The "goose" refers to the seasonal visits reuniting the separated families—the way geese migrate each year. This arrangement has become so widespread that in 2004, the phrase "goose family" was added to the Korean dictionary. (Chow, 2012, Para 3)

The rapid increase in the number of goose families in the mid-2000s was regarded as a social problem at that time in South Korea. For example, young children, separated from their parents, may not develop a secure sense of identity. The mothers often accompanied the children, experiencing hardships in a foreign country with different social customs, language, and culture. Further, the separated fathers suddenly lost their roles as fathers providing timely advice to their children (Chow, 2012).

Notably, in the case of fathers, depending on their financial capability, two jargons were widely circulated in South Korea: Eagle father and penguin father. In the former case, they are financially secure, and can visit their children in an English-speaking country at their will. However, in the latter case, they do not have such affluence and cannot visit overseas as often as eagle fathers do. In the mid-2000s, the goose father syndrome was featured even in the U.S. newspapers. For example, in the New York Times, Onishi (2008) explains these terms in a feature on Korean families in New Zealand.

> Wild geese fathers were initially relatively wealthy and tended to send their families to the United States. But in the last few years, more middle-class families have been heading to less expensive destinations like Canada, Australia, and New Zealand.
>
>   Now, there are also "eagle fathers," who visit their families several times a year because they have the time and money. Those with neither, who are stuck in South Korea, are known as "penguin fathers." (Para 10–11)

The English frenzy surrounding study abroad and the goose father syndrome can be explained as upward mobility among Koreans. According to Kang (2011), Koreans have long developed a strong sense of mutual comparison. As explained in Chap. 2, English has been regarded as the language of power and the symbol of secular affluence. Finding employment was relatively easier for those who could speak a moderate or higher level of English than for those who could not. Through the Japanese Colonization Period and the Korean War, the favoritism toward English had increased, and in the era of rapid economic development after the Korean War, English skills was prioritized in industries exporting goods to other nations.

Moreover, given the relatively dense population, particularly in major cities, including Seoul, the capital city, it gradually became the norm for South Koreans to maintain a constant sense of comparison. The comparison with neighbors became a source of joy and pride, or in some cases, sadness and inferiority (Kang, 2014). One's own, as well as one's children's proficiency in English has also been the object of comparison because English was regarded as the steppingstone to the upper social class.

Undoubtedly, this competitive atmosphere among Koreans had a positive effect in terms of enhancing their living conditions. Since the comparison was mostly geared toward achieving the best, or at least better than their previous living conditions, it functioned as the source of rapid development and improvement. The remarkable economic development in the 1970s and 1980s in South Korea could also be understood from this perspective. When we extend this comparison from the individual level to the macro, international level, the neighboring nations surrounding South Korea become the targets to surpass. In this case, the comparison and competition transformed from centripetal (i.e., competition among Koreans) to centrifugal (i.e., competition with other nations than with Koreans). Since South Korea attempts to be better than other neighboring nations such as Japan—the former colonizer— and particularly North Korea, South Koreans collaborated with each other and exerted their best efforts to boost their economy under the strong, dictatorial leadership of Presidents Park Chung-hee, Chun Doo-whan, and Roh Tae-woo for three decades from 1960 to 1993.

However, the same sense of comparison also intensified internal competition among Koreans. In this case, the directionality is reconfigured from centrifugal to centripetal. Given the relatively homogenous ethnic structure in Korea, the neighboring effect or "keeping up with the Jones" tendency among Koreans explains the pandemic of English frenzy in the 1990s and 2000s. Under this social milieu, the academic performance of children soon becomes the concern of family members', particularly when the parents notice their children do not outperform their friends. Lee (2016) investigated how the parents of South Korean early study-abroad students in the *Gangnam* district—the most affluent area in Seoul—thought about English and its relation to their children through in-depth interviews with 23 parents. The parents stated that English was a requisite for maintaining their high socioeconomic status, and for this reason, English functions as "a capitalistic instrument through which they could hand over their socioeconomic class to their children," and "English was perceived to help their children get high-paying jobs" (Lee, 2016, p. 35).

As presented in Chaps. 2 and 3, people with extraordinary English proficiency had easy access to social success through a monopoly over secure occupation and promotion opportunities. Korean parents endeavored to teach their children English through various instructional methods. While ensuring their children are equipped with English proficiency, most Korean parents strengthened the belief that family wealth could be maintained in their children's generation. In this regard, as Park and Abelman (2004) commented, English education in South Korea can be considered as an inter-generational project. The notion of the inter-generational project of English education or "alter-ego familism" will be elaborated in Chap. 7.

4.9   The Establishment of the English Village: Past and Present

The study-abroad syndrome and related social problems such as the goose fathers, evoked keen national interest in South Korea in the 2000s. On reaching family consensus, more than a few upper- and middle-class families sent their children to English-speaking countries. However, for those who could not risk such financial investment, they needed to find alternative ways for their children to learn English. The advantage of learning English abroad is the extent of exposure to classroom input as well as everyday English conversations. As Krashen (1985) argued, when surrounded by a massive amount of input, so-called "comprehensible input" or $i + 1$ will have a beneficial impact on students' learning an L2. In addition, study-abroad students experience the target language culture in a naturalistic manner for an extended period.

Developing this idea, the provincial government and Office of Education in Korea started to design artificial English Villages (영어마을) in suburban areas across South Korea. In less-populated areas, faux self-sustaining villages were constructed, imitating American or British townships. The purpose was clear: to have Korean students experience English-speaking culture in an authentic environment. In these English Villages, only English was to be spoken among students and between students and staffs. The staff members were either native English speakers or near-native speakers such as 1.5 generation immigrants to English-speaking countries or adult Koreans who had high English proficiency. The staff members were primarily part-time employees and conducted their assigned jobs in various places in the English Village. Thus, the students in the English Village could experience authentic English communication and enjoy the cultural experience at a reasonable price (see Chap. 7 for "Kitsch" English).

The first English Village opened in Gyeonggi Province in 2004, and soon, a total of 32 similar villages were competitively established across South Korea (Korea Times, 2012). Including private English Village or facilities bearing similar names (e.g., English experience center, international center, international education center), approximately 50 English Villages were operational (Yonhap News, 2016a, June 5). For a decade, these English Villages were enthusiastically welcomed to many Korean parents given the relatively inexpensive cost and authentic cultural experience that these facilities provide. The English programs were operated in either short-term periods (e.g., a weekend or a week-long program) or long-term ones using summer or winter vacations lasting 4–6 weeks. Throughout the program, students' Korean (L1) use was entirely prohibited, and the "English-only policy" was mandated. Those detected to have spoken Korean in the English Village were expelled from the village and did not receive the certificate of participation.

On students' motivation and attitudes towards English learning, the short-term English Village shows a relatively positive effect. According to Choi (2011), the short immersion program offered in the English Village was effective in increasing Grade 6 elementary school students' motivation and attitudes. In her research,

100 students were divided into three groups based on their English achievement test scores before their participation in the English Village. Her survey results show that in general students' attitudes toward English learning had changed positively after the experience. However, in students' changes in English learning motivation, only the middle-level group's motivation increased in a statistically significant manner, whereas the high and low-level group showed no significant increase. Choi's (2011) study presented that the middle-level Korean students are benefitted the most in the English Village experience, but the other groups were also positively affected in their attitudes toward learning English.

Note that most of the villages were government-subsidized, which meant that the operation and management were determined by the local government. Initially, the English Villages were established to provide alternative methods of English learning and experience at relatively low cost. For those who could afford study-abroad English education, they could send their offspring to English-speaking countries; those who could not, sought the English Village as a viable alternative. However, the establishment and management of an English Village required continuous expenditure from the local government. For example, Yonhap News (2016a, June 5) reported that the English Village in Incheon was operated by an Incheon government subsidy of 3 billion won (approximately $25 million) annually. During the economic downturn in 2016, the Incheon Metropolitan City decided to raise students' program fee to 50% of the total cost, which was estimated as 190,000 won ($150). Incheon citizens' responses to this decision were not favorable at all, and Yonhap News (2016a, June 5) presented survey results showing that 75% of the parents did not want to enroll their children in the English Village if the program fee increased unexpectedly. Additionally, Korea Times (2012) reported that the English Village in Paju, north of Gyeonggi Province, had recorded 10.4 billion won (approximately $9 million) of accumulated deficit in 3 years from 2009 to 2012.

Another problem with the English Village was the dubious qualification of its English instructors. Since the local governments established their English Villages competitively, in some cases, the hired English instructors did not have adequate educational qualifications to teach young children or adolescents. In the worst case, unqualified international students from the Philippines, Poland, and Romania were employed, and the government subsidy was spent on their salary, unconfirmed management, and ancillary fees in some private English Villages (YTN, 2009).

Primarily due to the cost of operation and the increasing dissatisfaction from the students and parents, many English Villages across South Korea now officially ceased to operate or changed the nature of the village from English institutes to camping sites, filming locations, or railbikes. For those still operational, the local governments are increasingly reducing the subsidy or yielding its management to private corporations. As a result, as of October 2018, among 28 government-funded English Villages, 11 of them either closed or are used for different purposes (Koo, 2018a).

4.10   The Debate on Implementing the National English Ability Test (NEAT)

Perhaps the most radical educational reform suggested during the first decade of the twenty-first century would be the National English Ability Test (NEAT). This proposal emerged from President Lee Myung-bak's intention to upgrade students' English proficiency, particularly speaking and writing ability. Immediately after he was elected as President in December 2007, the Presidential Transition Committee placed English as the most prioritized school subject, and English immersion education, which had been implemented successfully to a few private elementary schools in South Korea (e.g., Younghoon Elementary School located in Gangbuk-gu, Seoul), was proposed.

The NEAT (Levels 2 and 3) was geared toward replacing the current CSAT English section, and the NEAT (Level 1) aimed to replace official English tests such as the TOEIC and the TOEFL administered by the Educational Testing Service (ETS) in the U.S. The NEAT (Levels 2 and 3) was for high school students, whereas the NEAT (Level 1) was for adults. The NEAT Level 2 was mainly for the college-bound students focusing on academic English, and Level 3 was for the students aspiring to develop communication skills in English. All these tests intended to measure students' four skills in English (i.e., listening, speaking, reading, and writing) directly through an Internet-based testing format. Thus, the Ministry of Education of Korea (or officially the Ministry of Education, Science and Technology [MEST], active from 2008 to 2013) strived to introduce the NEAT to develop all four skills of English among students.

As mentioned above, the NEAT could be used for either high school students for university admission (Level 2) and general communication skills in English (Level 3) or for adults as a replacement of the TOEIC or the TOEFL. However, in terms of the number of test takers or the national interest, the NEAT was mainly proposed for high school students in order to replace the current CSAT English section. The administration of NEAT was expected to bring positive washback effect to English classrooms in South Korea (Jin et al., 2012). There was a consensus at the government level that the existing CSAT could not encourage speaking and writing instruction in schools in Korea, and thus adopting the NEAT, which includes all four subskills in English for Korean students, would fast-track the process. It was expected that each South Korean school actively instruct speaking and writing to the students (Lee, 2011b), and consequently, most students graduating from high school would be able to express their thoughts in verbal or written English (Jin et al., 2012).

The primary difference between the NEAT and the CSAT is that the NEAT aimed at assessing students' speaking and writing ability directly. The Internet-based testing infrastructure was expected to make this plan feasible. Besides, every high school test taker had two chances to take the NEAT annually, and they could submit a better score to qualify for the English requirement of the university where they were applying. Another difference lied in the testing format. In the CSAT, a norm-referenced testing format was used, which meant that students' relative rank among all test takers was the focus, and depending on their relative rank, students' level and score were decided. On the other hand, the NEAT adopted a criterion-referenced testing format. This significant difference meant that instead of comparing students' percentile in the normal distribution, their achievement level in four subsections was reported in four different grades—Grade A (highest) to D (lowest). Thus, initially, the NEAT only considered students' current achievement level in speaking, listening, reading, and writing without considering other test takers' performance (Jin et al., 2012).

According to Lee (2011b), the introduction of the NEAT had a couple of substantial benefits. First, a positive change in English classes across South Korea could be anticipated. Passive memorization of English grammar and vocabulary were discouraged, and the instruction of test-taking skills, particularly for multiple-test format would also be disfavored. Second, the NEAT would reduce the expenditure on private education to achieve high English test scores at the CSAT. In the criterion-referenced NEAT, students did not need to compete with each other and achieve higher scores than their peers. Additionally, this educational reform would impact private education as speaking and writing would be actively instructed. Third, the NEAT would remedy the shortcomings of the current CSAT, which does not measure students' speaking and writing ability. Fourth, since the NEAT adopted the Internet, online testing format, this would encourage the development of computer-assisted language learning (CALL) or e-learning. Finally, particularly for the NEAT (Level 1), this reform would prevent the overreliance on the externally imported English tests, reducing thus, the unnecessary expenditure of test-taking fees for the TOEIC or the TOEFL.

Although it is argued that the preparations for reform had started from 2006 (Jin et al., 2012), the active implementation of the NEAT was spearheaded by the political regime change in 2008 to President Lee Myung-bak, a self-claimed neoliberalist and the former CEO of Hyundai Construction (Lee, 2008). The feasibility of the NEAT began to be investigated from 2008, and in 2009, the NEAT for high school students were pilot tested to 4000 high school students in Seoul, Incheon, and Gyeonggi Province on May 28, 2009, to 5300 high school students in 15 cities and provinces across South Korea on September 10, 2009, to 10,000 students in 15 cities and provinces on December 21 and 22, 2009. Through these successive pilot tests, NEAT was initially expected to be fully implemented from 2012 in order to replace the CSAT. However, the full implementation, particularly for high school students, was delayed over several years, considering a few reasonable concerns.

Despite the cause of enhancing speaking and writing proficiency of the test takers, the NEAT was suspended and eventually canceled. The reliability of the Internet-based computer test could not be assured through the pilot testing, and 100% error-free administration could not be guaranteed. In 2013, two main NEATs (Levels 2 and 3) were administered on June 2 and July 28. During the June test, an Internet connection problem occurred. A couple of students' answers to some questions were not stored in the database, and these students had to re-mark the questions later. This incident exerted a substantially negative impact on universities where the NEAT score was expected to replace the CSAT English test, and only 36 colleges and universities (out of 347 across South Korea) adopted the NEAT. This possibility of experiencing technical problems in administering the Internet-based test format continued to evoke critical opposition to use the NEAT. Additionally, given the tight educational budget in the government, it was not practically useful to build NEAT centers where accurate Internet testing is guaranteed. These centers would be used only twice to accommodate more than 1 million NEAT test takers.

The second problem was the criterion-referenced format of the NEAT. In the pilot test administered in 2012, the number of NEAT test takers who scored the highest grade (i.e., Grade A) in all four subsections was 17.4% for Level 2 and 29.9% for Level 3 (Segye Ilbo, 2012). These high percentages were problematic for applications to universities, particularly to top-tier ones where the best high school students aspire to attend. The grades obtained from the NEAT could not provide sufficient information about the students' English proficiency, which the CSAT had provided for more than two decades. As a result, most highly ranked universities ended up excluding the NEAT from their admission requirements.

These shortcomings were the reason for the government's hesitation to implement the NEAT. However, the most severe problem of the NEAT was the increasing demand for private English education to prepare for this test adequately. Despite the government initiatives in implementing the NEAT, in reality, high schools in South Korea did not provide sufficient preparation for the NEAT. Despite the educational administrative efforts to provide systematic in-service teacher training through either offline or online media such as educational broadcasting (Jin et al., 2012), English education in the public school system did not change in a short period. In particular, high school English teachers had been accustomed to CSAT-style English test preparation. They did not have sufficient teaching experiences to fully implement speaking and writing instruction. Although the slogan that every English teacher should develop instructional skills in speaking and writing had resonated in the early 2010s (Joongang Ilbo, 2012), it was not easy to develop teachers' speaking and writing proficiency in English, not to mention their instructional skills.

Despite all these practical problems, in the Lee Myung-bak government, the Ministry of Education of Korea insisted on fully implementing the NEAT by the mid-2010s. Accordingly, most students (and their anxious parents) tried to find alternative methods to develop their speaking and writing skills in private education. While most English teachers at public schools did not have sufficient knowledge of the NEAT, private English institutes promptly published test prep kits and started to provide various courses for NEAT preparations (Cho, 2012). As a result, contrary to the initial expectation that the NEAT would alleviate the financial burden of private education as it measures basic communicative skills which can be covered by public English education at school, paradoxically, many private English institutes actively embraced this educational reform and reacted promptly. In the end, the Ministry of Education (2012) of Korea decided to introduce special monitoring of all private English institutes to ensure that the tuition fee for NEAT preparation is not overly expensive.

While going through such turmoil in educational policy, in February 2013, the new President Park Geun-hye (tenure: 2013–2017) was inaugurated, and the Ministry of Education, Science and Technology was reorganized and downsized into the Ministry of Education. According to Lee (2015), "the new Ministry of Education tried to suspend the NEAT, primarily because there was a concern that the NEAT would cause too much competition among young learners of English, and their parents would be compelled to rely on expensive private English education rather than on public education in order to get high scores on the NEAT for entrance to universities" (p. 60).

The overreliance on private English education worsened, particularly during this period. As mentioned above, since Korean students and parents shared the consensus that English teachers at school could not adequately prepare their students for the NEAT, most students began relying on *hagwon*s (學院) or cram schools for test preparation. For example, Yeon and Kim (2010) investigated South Korean middle and high school students' perceptions of English teachers in public and private education. They administered a questionnaire survey with 139 female students in Gyeonggi Province, vicinity of Seoul, asking about teachers in public and private sectors in five domains respectively: (1) expert knowledge in English, (2) teaching skills, (3) fairness of testing, (4) communication skills and class management, and (5) personality factors. It should be noted that their findings showed that the participants regarded private English instructors as more highly qualified than public English teachers in all five domains.

Moreover, the direct testing of speaking and writing had fueled a chain reaction at the lower school level. Since these productive skills require long-term investment in a foreign language, students and parents in elementary schools actively tried to find other ways to develop English speaking and writing proficiency. The public English education at elementary school allocated a 1-class hour (i.e., 40 min) for the third and fourth grades and 2-class hours (i.e., 80 min) for the fifth and sixth grades, and most students and parents alike felt that these time allocations were extremely limited for the students to develop a high level of English proficiency. Thus, they tried to find better English programs providing authentic English input domestically or even abroad. As a result, Statistics Korea (2014) reported that English was the most expensive school subject in private education. It was in this period that the term "English Divide" had become popularized in South Korean newspapers (e.g., Korea Herald, 2012). English divide denotes the widespread social phenomenon where families from affluent background have more access to English linguistic capital, which requires a monetary investment. In particular, English speaking and writing skills (as with other skills) require the instructor's careful attention, and for this reason, private tutoring or long-term exposure to authentic English input would be desirable. In this situation, the students' English proficiency gap widens owing to the different socioeconomic status of each family (Crookes, 2017); the more affluent a student's family is, the higher English test score the student achieves. In Kim's (2012) qualitative interview research, Korean elementary school students were keenly aware of the importance of English (or more accurately, the importance of English test scores); they showed a high level of competitive motivation to learn

English. For example, an elementary school student stated that even when an English-speaking foreign country conquers Korea, he would be all right as long as he commands a higher level of English than other Koreans. In sum, it can be stated that the educational policy to implement the NEAT to Korean high schools exerted an exponential impact on Korean elementary school students and parents and aggravated English divide in South Korea.

In the end, in the summer of 2014, the government plan to implement the NEAT to replace the CSAT or externally imported English tests such as the TOEIC or the TOEFL was rescinded officially. Despite the fact that a total of 46.5 billion won (equivalent of $40 million) had already been spent for the preparation of the NEAT (Ministry of Education, 2014), the combination of the inadequate in-service teacher training, incessant technical problems on the Internet connection, and the increasing cost of private education and its subsequent English divide had resulted in the catastrophic consequences surrounding the NEAT.

4.11   The Establishment of the Jeju Global Education City (JGEC)

In the first decade of the twenty-first century, study abroad in an English-speaking country was widespread in South Korea. As stated above, the introduction of elementary school English education and the focus on English speaking and listening proficiency had made many Korean students (and their parents) realize the importance of oral proficiency in English. Thus, the expenditure for study abroad including both short-term and long-term English-language study in and out of South Korea was in its apex in 2007, and more than $5 billion were spent only for this study abroad purpose (Yonhap News, 2017). This exponential expenditure had decreased in 2008 when the global financial crisis was aggravated, but in the 2010s, the annual average expenditure has surged around $3 billion.

Moreover, multiple free trade agreements among nations and the expediting globalization necessitate South Korean students' high level of English proficiency. For this reason, the Ministry of Education of Korea tried to initiate plans at the turn of the century such as "the 5-year Comprehensive Plan for Expediting English Education" in May 2005 and "Plan for Revolutionizing English Education" in November 2006. Despite these governmental efforts, however, the expenditure on study abroad did not decrease. Besides, expenses of private English education were on a steady increase up to $15 billion in 2011 (Lee, 2011b).

In this backdrop, the Korean government focused on reducing such expense for study-abroad English education. The government had estimated that $50 million were spent annually for approximately 9000 students' study abroad, and if these expenses had been spent domestically, they could revitalize the local economy and increase domestic employment up to 20,000 people. For this, the government announced an ambitious plan to construct the Jeju Global Education City (JGEC,

Table 4.2 Four zones in the Jeju Global Education City

Zone	Main characteristics
School Zone	International Schools: 9000 students in 7 schools (Four schools of North London Collegiate School [NLCS] Jeju, Korea International School [KIS] Jeju, St. Johnsbury Academy [SJA] Jeju, and Branksome Hall Asia [BHA] have been open.)
University Zone	Campus town to introduce the world's leading universities' degree curriculum and programs
Supporting Facilities	4660 households (531 detached houses, 4129 apartment units), commercial business facilities, community center, 119 emergency center and administrative support offices
Gotjawal Provincial Park	Eco park in *Gotjawal*, Jeju island's unique forestland (1,546,757 m^2), information center, trails, observatory

제주영어교육도시) on December 12, 2006.[2] The JGEC was initially planned to use English for everyday life purposes such as schooling, housing, cultural activities, sports, and extracurricular activities. In 2008, the Ministry of Education proposed the plan to host approximately 20,000 people (4550 households) including 12,000 students in the JGEC.

The city is still being constructed, and in Daejeong-eup, Seogwipo City, Jeju Self-Governing Province, it will take 3,792.049 m^2 with the total expense of construction of 1.9 trillion won (equivalent to $1.6 billion) (Kim, 2016). In the city space, four different zones are designed: School zone, University zone, Supporting facilities, and *Gotjawal* provincial park (see Table 4.2).

In general, JGEC seems to fulfill the purpose of providing English-medium education in South Korea. According to Kim (2016), as of 2015, $230 million were spent on the JGEC's three international schools (i.e., NLCS, KIS, BHA). For those who initially intended to study abroad, these schools would be viable choices. Kim (2016) stated that students attending these international schools could obtain both Korean and foreign (International Baccalaureate: IB) credits, and for this reason, they have the advantage of attending either Korean or English-medium foreign universities.

Despite the success of the JGEC, from a critical perspective, the establishment of the JGEC can be regarded as the official recognition from the Korean government that those who can afford a high cost of the tuition fee can escape the excessive competition for the pursuit of a domestic university degree. In fact, even before the establishment of the JGEC, affluent South Korean families would send their children to foreign schools, mostly in Seoul. The primary purpose of foreign schools is to

---

[2]Note that the English term (Jeju Global Education City) and the Korean term (제주영어교육도시) shows a subtle difference. In the Korean term, English (영어) replaces "Global" in JGEC. In the process of naming, globalization must have been equated with English proficiency. Ironically, the May 2019 Jeju Special Self-governing Province statistics (2019) show that the Chinese tourists were approximately 20 times more than the U.S. tourists (84,333 vs. 4337), casting doubts on the validity of JGEC's Korean term.

educate non-Korean children whose parents stay in Korea for occupational purposes. However, as of March 2008, for example, Seoul Academy International School, which has now rescinded its accreditation from the Ministry of Education of Korea for its legal violation, admitted 101 Korean students (60.8%) out of the total 166 students (Kang, 2011). In extreme cases, South Korean students were illegally adopted to American citizens and attended schools located in the U.S. military camps scattered in Yongsan in Seoul or Osan in Gyeonggi Province. According to Hankook Ilbo (2009), as of September 2008, 195 students from Asian heritage out of the total 656 students attended Seoul American School in Yongsan U.S.-base, and it is speculated that most of them were Korean students who went through "nationality laundering" through child adoption brokers; their parents paid approximately $150,000 in cases of no blood connection to the U.S. adoptees.

To most Koreans, all these cases conducted by a few upper-class Koreans were regarded as an illegal, or at best unjust, activities. However, the establishment of the JGEC was officially initiated at the governmental level. The students in international schools such as NLCS and BHA Jeju were accepted to world-leading universities including Cambridge, Imperial, Oxford, Stanford, Cornell, Toronto, New York, Seoul National, Yonsei, and Tokyo Universities (Kim, 2016, p. 28). While pointing out discriminatory practices in international schools, Jeong and Kwon (2018) high-light the stratification of education. According to them, given the nature of the International Baccalaureate (IB) curriculum that most international schools adhere to, the students are educated to become cosmopolitans, but the opportunity to receive this education is primarily based on the cultural and monetary capital. They argue that it would be a desirable direction to educate students having international understandings and global perspectives, but the point is that even those who cannot afford such expenses should be offered these opportunities at the JGEC. For example, most international schools in the JGEC are running their school based on the tuition fee combined with accommodation expenses (mostly student dormitory), which is around $25,000. This cost is more than ten times of the expenses for a private elementary school and three times of those for private special-purpose high schools (i.e., science high schools, foreign language high schools, and arts high schools) in South Korea. For this reason, the international schools in the JGEC are commonly criticized as noble private schools (Jeong & Kwon, 2018). From this viewpoint, international education through English-medium instructions at the schools in the JGEC widens English divide among social classes in South Korea. In other words, the access to and opportunity of international schooling is unequally distributed and provided only to upper social classes (cf. Igarashi & Saito, 2014).

From a historical perspective, the establishment and management of the JGEC is a radical movement going against the egalitarian educational effort in modern Korea. Ever since English was introduced to Korea in the late nineteenth century, English had been regarded as an effective means of employment and social success. During the Japanese Colonization Period, English began being included as a core school subject test for the admission to Kyungsung (or Keijo) Imperial University and other technical colleges across Korea. After the liberation from Japan and the outbreak of the Korean War, it was widely believed that with proper academic effort, students could attain high literacy level in English although it was mostly based on the passive knowledge of English grammar and vocabulary memorized through individual study. In this social atmosphere, all students "start on the same starting line" in that they learn English from the same teacher and the same textbook in the same classroom, regardless of each student's family background. Given this, the fundamental assumption in the educational system would be an equal opportunity to achieve academic success in the same educational affordances. The violation of equal opportunity in education was often subject to social punishment as shown in the case of elementary school English education in the 1960s in Chap. 3. From this underlying assumption, students' academic competition vying for excellence emerges, and this competition had long been regarded as fair and reliable; from this assumption, Korean students' instrumental and competitive motivations in learning English germinated (cf. Kim, 2006, 2010).

The international schools in the JGEC, however, are the "game-changer" in English education in South Korea. Combined with the massive amount of tuition fee and cultural capital only available in upper (middle) class in Korea, the international schools provide authentic English input from kindergarten to high school to their registered students. The Ministry of Education of Korea does not regulate the curriculum. In the case of "regular" schools in South Korea, their curriculum is strictly regulated by the Ministry, and their students need to take the CSAT to be admitted to Korean universities. A few students can prepare for the TOEFL and SAT for study abroad at their private expenses. In this case, in terms of English proficiency, the students attending regular schools in South Korea cannot usually surpass their counterparts attending international schools due to the sheer number of hours in English input and interaction. Given the vast amount of education conducted in English, the international school students in the JGEC are in an English-immersion environment.

As Lee (2011b) and Kim (2016) argued, the initial purpose of establishing the JGEC was to provide an environment for English-medium instruction in order to not spend an excessive amount of financial means overseas. This purpose seems to have been successfully achieved. However, the English divide between social classes in South Korea did not decrease, and in some cases, it widened after the establishment of the JGEC. The upper class can now enjoy more choices, either by studying abroad as they did before or attending the international schools established in the JGEC. The lower class still does not have such opportunities. In this regard, the success of the JGEC is only partial and incomplete; the upper class' monopoly of English opportunity seems to have been accelerated, and undesirable social gentrification is increasingly found in English education.

4.12   Controversies in Criterion-Referenced English Test: Negative Washback

The most recent trend in English education in Korea would be the implementation of a criterion-referenced test in the English section of the CSAT. In December 2014, the Ministry of Education of Korea announced that the English section in the CSAT would use the criterion-referenced format instead of a norm-referenced one. The current scoring system in the CSAT, except the English and Korean history sections, adopts a norm-referenced testing format where students' relative place in the entire test takers' score is considered. Among Level 1 (the highest level) to 9 (the lowest level), only 4% of the CSAT test takers each year will acquire Level 1, and the next 7% will get Level 2. The purpose of the CSAT is to assess student's scholastic ability objectively, and the CSAT score and levels are the crucial determiners in the college admission process. For example, in the rolling admission system through the admission officer, the combination of levels in each subject in the CSAT is used to screen applicants. In prestigious universities, unless the combined levels of Korean, math, English, and (social) science subtests reaches a particular score such as 4 or 5, the applicants cannot take essay-tests or be invited to admission interviews.[3] Only after they meet the minimum CSAT requirement, can they proceed to the next round of admission process.

In this admission system, all college-bound Grade 12 high school students make their best effort to meet the minimum combined levels in the CSAT, and on the day of taking the CSAT (i.e., usually every Thursday in the 2nd week of November), the testing centers, often secondary school classrooms, become "a fierce battleground." As all the applicants try their best to get a high score and the CSAT is held only once every year, the CSAT is an incomparably high-stakes test. The basic idea is that every CSAT test taker should perform better than their peers since the testing format is a norm-referenced one. As mentioned above, only the top 4% of the applicants of a section test can get Level 1. Even if a student scores almost a perfect score, if the other students perform equally well, the student cannot acquire a satisfactory level, leave aside Level 1.

In this educational context, all college-bound Grade 12 high school students competed against each other in English as well as other subjects included in the CSAT. Due to the nature of foreign language learning, raising the level of English has been regarded as the most difficult. Thus, the cost of private education in English was the highest. In 2016, the average monthly expenses for English private education were 79,000 won (i.e., $70), followed by math (76,000 won), Korean (16,000

---

[3]Depending on the university, the combination varies. For example, Chung-Ang University in Seoul requires the combination score should be at least 5 out of 3 sections of the applicant's choice. Korea University requires the score should be at least 6 (for humanities and social sciences stream) or 7 (for science stream) out of 3 sections. As the sections of the CSAT are Korean, Math, English, and (Social) Sciences, students have the freedom to exclude the weak section in the combination score calculation.

won), and (social) sciences (10,000 won) (Statistics Korea, 2018). As presented in the above sections, Koreans have spent a relatively high cost for their children's private English education. By studying abroad, sacrificing the family bond, living in the Jeju Global Education City, sending their children to the English Village, or having their children enrolled in English institutes to take the TOEIC or similar English tests, Koreans have competed with each other to gain better English proficiency. For these reasons, the cost of private education in English was the highest compared with other subjects in the CSAT.

The Ministry of Education, in this context, introduced a criterion-referenced test in the English section at the CSAT. They aimed to alleviate the cost for private education, to lessen the students' academic stress, to minimize the competition, and to escape from learning test-taking strategies. In this new testing format, the test takers only need to score 90% or higher in the English section to acquire Level 1. By introducing the new testing format where students do not need to compete with each other, the policymakers anticipated reducing students' stress about English and lowering the overly expensive tuition fee in English private education.

The new criterion-referenced test was applied from the academic year 2018 CSAT held on November 2017. Many educators, university admission officers, and media expressed grave concerns of introducing the criterion-reference test on English. Their concerns were based on the assumption that the English test would be easy, and students can easily acquire a high score in English. As a result, an unprecedentedly large number of students will acquire Level 1, which will make the discrimination power of the English section significantly reduced.

The result of 2018 CSAT English section was not different from these concerns. In 2018 CSAT, 10.8% of the test takers (52,983 students) acquired Level 1, which meant that they scored more than 90% in the English section. Additionally, 19.65% of them (103,756 students) scored more than 80% and acquired Level 2. These number of students were more than double compared with the previous English test results (Dong-A Ilbo, 2017). As expected, the number of students who acquired either Level 1 or Level 2 in the 2018 CSAT English section doubled, and the English test level and its score did not function as a critical determiner for the class of 2018 undergraduate students.

The massive increase in the percentage of students in the English section of the 2018 CSAT also yielded negative consequences. Since English was considered an easy section for many students and did not have a critical impact on the students' university admission, high school students started to invest more time and effort to other subjects such as Korean, math, and (social) sciences (Chosun Ilbo, 2018). Even in the easy English test questions, students were still relying on test-taking strategies in the CSAT. Academic associations related to English literature and education also raised their voice against the criterion-referenced English test in the CSAT (Yang, 2018). Dr. Yeo, President of Korea Association of English Linguistics and Literature, pointed out that the easy criterion-referenced test weakens English education in public schools. He stated that for the relative insignificance of English compared with other major school subjects, weekly hours of English instruction are being decreased, and students do not pay much attention to English at school. However, according to Dr. Yeo, as English is needed even after students are admitted to the university, they have to rely on private English education again at college because they have neglected the English education at secondary schools (Yang, 2018).

However, ironically, a complete reversal occurred in the next year's CSAT English section. In the CSAT for the class of 2019 undergraduate students, the difficulty level of the English test dramatically increased, and the number of students who acquired Level 1 shrank into 5.3%. This percentage was approximately half of the previous year. Thus, the students who did not study English much in the naïve hope of easy questions were in a disadvantageous position in the university admission process. Unless the difficulty level of the English section in the CSAT is stabilized, the confusion among the students and parents in South Korea may be repeated, and the preference for English, at least in the high school classrooms, will vacillate.

4.13   Chapter Summary

In this chapter, the changes in English education in South Korea after the 1990s were thematically analyzed. Compared with the previous generation, it seems clear that the economic situation in South Korea has remarkably improved, and by any standard, South Korea is now among the economically developed nations, with 11th place in the world in GDP (International Monetary Fund, 2018). In English education, innovation was extraordinary. With the acceleration of international trade, the need to develop oral proficiency in English rapidly increased, and most of the English frenzy in the 1990s and 2000s was a reaction to keep pace with this changing international trend. The first change was the renovation in the college entrance exam, and in the English section in the CSAT, for the first time in the history of educational assessment in Korea, listening comprehension was introduced. This had raised both students' and parents' awareness of the importance of listening comprehension. Additionally, the elementary school English education started in 1997, and in 1998, Mr. Bok Geo-il ignited the debate about using English as an official language in South Korea. The emphasis on English proficiency is also reflected in the TOEIC fever by the turn of the twenty-first century. As the TOEIC scores started to be included in the university admission system as well as the job application and screening process, many Korean students and parents actively responded to this change by taking the TOEIC or similar English tests. The emphasis on everyday English conversation had also resulted in government policies such as the invitation of native English speakers through the EPIK or the establishment of English Villages across South Korea. The Ministry of Education also tried to train in-service English teachers by encouraging them to be registered in the TEE certificate programs.

However, the educational changes toward hands-on communicative English proficiency were not as fast as the students and parents had expected. Thus, those who were not satisfied with the current public English education in South Korea tried to find alternatives such as studying abroad in English-speaking countries. Notably, the goose father syndrome hit hard in Korea in the mid-2000s. An alternative to study-abroad was the Jeju Global Education City, where international schools were established and offered English-immersion education to students from upper social class in South Korea. Those who could not afford such high expenses had their children enrolled in private English institutes (as known as *hagwons*) or once in a while sent their children to English Villages for short-term English immersion and cultural experience.

Responding to the widening English divide among Koreans, the Korean government first considered adopting the NEAT to replace the English section of the CSAT. The NEAT was innovative in that it adopted the Internet-based computerized testing format and included direct evaluation of the test takers' speaking and writing proficiency. However, due to the technical concerns and the political regime change, the NEAT was not implemented. The most recent changes in the English section in the CSAT also deserve our attention in that this test adopted a criterion-referenced format where the assessment of students' level is solely based on their performance, not compared with other CSAT test takers' relative performance. It remains to be seen whether this shift to a criterion-reference test will narrow the English gap among South Koreans.

Note that the above changes did not take place peacefully and gradually. For example, as shown in the nationwide introduction of the elementary school English education, the changes were top-down and mandated by the government. English learners in South Korea were also often overly sensitive to the test score, and those who were concerned about their children's English proficiency and test scores took another option: study-abroad. Many of them sacrificed the emotional and physical bond of being a family for the pursuit of their offspring's English proficiency development, as reflected in the goose father syndrome.

In general, the recent changes in English education positively impact English learning and teaching in South Korea. As Kwon (2006) reported, the introduction of elementary school English education is considered successful in increasing students' English proficiency. Additionally, as Lee (2015) argued, recent innovations in English education seem to have been recognized and accepted by most Koreans. Thus, the majority of Koreans now acknowledge the importance of developing all four subskills of English (i.e., speaking, listening, writing, and reading). Given the situations experienced a generation ago when English grammar and vocabulary knowledge were prioritized, these shifts in South Korean people's perceptions are remarkable.

However, as illustrated in this chapter, the changes also had negative consequences. For example, in terms of students' stress level and anxiety, the fierce academic competition in English (along with other school subjects) among English learners has negative ramifications. A tremendous level of demotivation and amotivation is found in students' approach to English learning. After the introduction of the elementary school English education, it was reported that most elementary school students suffered from gradual demotivation to learn English. In Kim's (2011) mixed methods research, elementary school students were demotivated due to the excessive competition among themselves and the high parental expectations placed upon them. As students advanced from Grade 3, when the public English education begins, to Grade 6, all the subcomponents of English learning motivation significantly decreased.

The excessive competition surrounding English education aggravates social inequality not only on the student level but also at the macro, societal level. The term English divide represents this aspect; based on parents' socioeconomic status, the children's opportunity to learn English, particularly to be exposed to authentic English input through extended study abroad is critically impacted. In Lee's (2016) study, English is widely perceived as a useful device to transfer the affluence and cultural capital of the parents' generation to the next generation. In modern Korea, after the nineteenth century, English had been functioning as a useful tool to have convenient access to limited information and expertise written in English. Despite a few notable exceptions such as the Jeju Global Education City, the Korean government has, in general, endeavoured to lessen the social discrepancy surrounding English learning by implementing educational reforms. Can the instinctive desire of becoming prosperous by learning English, strengthened by the lesson of the modern Korean history at the individual level, be suppressed by the top-down governmental efforts? Only the progression of time will tell.

References

Ahn, Byung-Kyu. (2011). The effect of an intensive in-service English teacher development program on teaching performance. *English Language Teaching, 23*(2), 1–23.

Birdsong, D. (Ed.). (2013). *Second language acquisition and the critical period hypothesis.* London: Routledge.

Bok, Geo-il. (1998). *Gookje'eo sidea'eui minjok'eo [National language in the age of global language].* Seoul, Korea: Moonji.

Bok, Geo-il. (2002, February 5). Yeong'eo yeolpoong ireoke bonda [I see English fever in. this way]. (Dong-A Ilbo Opnion column). Retrieved February 6, 2020, from http://www.donga.com/news/article/all/20020204/7785537/1.

Bok, Geo-il. (2003). *Yeong'eo'reul gongyong'eoro samja (Bok Geo-il'eul yeong'eo gongyongron) [Let's adopt English as the common language (Bok Geo-il's argument toward English as the common language)].* Seoul, Korea: Samsung Economic Research Institute.

Cho, Jin-joo. (2012, March 8). Yeong'eogyoyook'eopchedeul NEAT gyojae, program gyeongjaeng bongyeokhwa. [Fierce competition for the NEAT prep books and programs started among private English education institutes]. Retrieved July 16, 2019, from http://www.veritas-a.com/news/articleView.html?idxno=12315.

Choi, Seung-Hoo. (2017, April 25). Teukgija jeonhyeong: 'Gajinjadeul jeonhyeong' ohae beotna [Special student admission: Will it be disillusioned from the misunderstanding of the admission for the haves]. Retrieved July 8, 2019, from http://www.hani.co.kr/arti/society/schooling/792096.html.

Choi, Yoon-Hwa. (2011). The effect of a short immersion program at English Village on elementary school students' motivation at different English proficiency levels: A Gardner's AMTB based analysis. *English Language Teaching, 23*(2), 181–199.

Chosun Ilbo. (1998, July 10). Yeong'eogongyong'eohwa yeoronjosa chanseong 44-bandae 55 [Opinion poll regarding English as an official language: Agreed 44% - Disagreed 55%].

Retrieved July 9, 2019, from http://news.chosun.com/svc/content_view/content_view.html? contid=1998071070304.

Chosun Ilbo. (2018, April 4). Sooneungyeong'eo, pyeonggabangsikboda nanido jojeol yeonghyang deo keotda [English in the CSAT: Affected more by the adjustment of difficulty level than by testing format]. Retrieved July 12, 2019, from http://edu.chosun.com/site/data/html_dir/2019/ 04/04/2019040401124.html.

Chow, S. (2012, August 22). The Korean "goose family" phenomena: Educational migrants. Retrieved January 12, 2020, from https://globalprosperity.wordpress.com/2012/08/22/the-korean-goose-family-phenomenon-educational-migrants/.

Crookes, G. (2017). Critical language pedagogy given the English divide in Korea: A suite of practices, critique, and the role of the intellectual. *English Teaching, 72*(4), 3–21.

Dong-A Ilbo. (1995, February 16). Oegoogk'eoreul japara: Jikjang'in hagwonsoogang yeolgi/ daegiup uitakgyoyook 40% neul'eo [Seize the foreign language: Fever of officer workers' enrollment in private language school/An increase of 40% in large-scale company's commissioned education] A31.

Dong-A Ilbo. (2017, December 11). 2018 Sooneung deunggeup cut, yeong'eo 1,2deunggeup biyool 30%: Daehak eojjigana [CSAT level cut, the percentage of English section Levels 1 and 2 is 30%: How to go to college]. Retrieved July 12, 2019, from http://www.donga.com/ news/article/all/20171211/87673531/2.

Economic Planning Board. (1993). Outline of national budget of 1993. Retrieved June 27, 2019, from http://likms.assembly.go.kr/bill/nafs/nafsView.do?libDatId=LI00000076& tabMenuType=BudgLaw&strPage=1.

Gass, S. (1997). *Input, interaction, and the development of second languages*. Mahwah, NJ: Lawrence Erlbaum.

Han, Young-woo. (1998, July 9). Nonjaeng: "Jigoojegook"eun gangdaegook huimangsahang [Debate: "Global Empire" is the aspiration of world leading nations]. Retrieved July 9, 2019, from http://news.chosun.com/svc/content_view/content_view.html?contid=1998070970308.

Hankook Ilbo. (2009, February 12). Migoonhakgyo bonaeryeo: Maengmodo woolgogal ip'yangjigyo [To send American schools for US military personnel: Education through adoption making 'Mencius mom' agape]. Retrieved July 6, 2019, from http://sports.hankooki.com/lpage/ lifenjoy/200902/sp2009021207333894470.htm.

Heo, J., & Mann, S. (2015). Exploring team teaching and team teachers in Korean primary schools. *English Language Teacher Education and Development Journal, 17*, 13–21.

Heo, Yoon. (2004, October 21). Chodeungsaengdo yeong'eosiheom (PELT, EPAT, TOEIC) yeolpoong [English test (PELT, EPAT, TOEIC) fever even among elementary school kids]. In Kookmin Ilbo B09.

Hultberg, P., Calonge, D. S., & Kim, S.-H. (2017). Education policy in South Korea: A contemporary model of human capital accumulation? *Cogent Economics and Finances*, 5, 1–16.

Igarashi, H., & Saito, H. (2014). Cosmopolitanism as cultural capital: Exploring the intersection of globalization, education and stratification. *Cultural Sociology, 8*(3), 222–239.

International Monetary Fund. (2018, October). World economic outlook database. Retrieved July 13, 2019, from https://www.imf.org/external/pubs/ft/weo/2018/02/weodata/index.aspx.

Jang, Myung-rim. (2012). *Yooagyoyook senjinwha jeongcheak choojin hyeonhwang'gwa gwaje [Current status and future directions for the advancement policy of early childhood education]*. Seoul, Korea: Korean Educational Development Institute.

Jeju Shinbo. (2018, May 8). Yeong'eosueopneungryeok gatchumyeon moehana? hwalyongdo jeojo [What is the use of TEE ability? Less use of TEE teachers]. Retrieved July 3, 2019, from http:// www.jejunews.com/news/articleView.html?idxno=2112211.

Jeju Special Self-governing Province. (2019, July 11). 2019nyeon 5wol jeju'ipdo gwangwanggaek tonggye [Statistics on Jeju inbound tourists in May 2019]. Retrieved July 16, 2019, from https:// www.jeju.go.kr/open/open/iopenboard.htm?qType=title&q=%EA%B4%80%EA%B4%91% EA%B0%9D+%ED%86%B5%EA%B3%84&act=view&seq=1184531.

Jeon, M. (2009). Globalization and native English speakers in English programme in Korea (EPIK). *Language, Culture and Curriculum, 22*(3), 231–243.

Jeon, M., & Lee, J. (2006). Hiring native-speaking English teachers in East Asian countries. *English Today, 22*(4), 53–58.

Jeong, Seungmo, & Kwon, Sangcheol. (2018). Debates of global competitiveness and selective education over international school education: The case of Jeju Education City. *The Journal of Korean Urban Geographical Society, 21*(3), 17–33.

Jin, Kyung-Ae, Shin, Dongkwang, & Shi, Kija. (2012). *Gookgayeong'eoneungryeoksiheom'eui choojin hyeonhwanggwa baljeonbang'an [The current status of the National English Ability Test and plans for developing it]*. Seoul, Korea: Korean Educational Development Institute and Korea Institute for Curriculum and Evaluation.

Joongang Ilbo. (2012, October 5). NEAT neun yeong'eogyoyook hyeoksin sinhotan [NEAT is the harbinger of the revolution of English education]. Retrieved July 2, 2019, from https://news.joins.com/article/9497526.

Kang, Byung-Han. (2007, October 12). Yeong'eo soongbaeneun sinsadaeju'eui [Adoration of English: Neo-toadyism]. Retrieved March 29, 2021, from http://news.khan.co.kr/kh_news/khan_art_view.html?art_id=200710112324521.

Kang, Joon-Mann. (2011). *Teukbyeolhan nara daehanminkook [Special country: The Republic of Korea]*. Seoul, Korea: Inmulgwasasangsa.

Kang, Joon-Mann. (2014). *Hankook'ingwa yeong'eo [Koreans and English]*. Seoul, Korea: Inmulgwasasangsa.

Kim, Bok-Rae. (2015). The English fever in South Korea: Focusing on the problem of early English education. *Journal of Education and Social Policy, 2*(2), 117–124.

Kim, Tae Kyoung (2016). *Jeju yeong'eogyoyookdoshi'eui pageuphyogwa siljeung bunseok mit jeongchaekjeok sisajeom [Empirical analysis and political implication of the effect of Jeju Global Education City]*. Seoul, Korea: Korea Economic Research Institute (KERI).

Kim, Tae-Young. (2006). Motivation and attitudes toward foreign language learning as socio-politically mediated constructs: The case of Korean high school students. *The Journal of Asia TEFL, 3*(2), 165–192.

Kim, Tae-Young. (2010). Socio-political influence on EFL motivation and attitudes: Comparative surveys of Korean high school students. *Asia-Pacific Education Review, 11*, 211–222.

Kim, Tae-Young. (2011). Korean elementary school students' English learning demotivation: A comparative survey study. *Asia Pacific Education Review, 12*, 1–11.

Kim, Tae-Young. (2012). An analysis of Korean elementary and secondary school students' English learning motivation and their L2 selves: Qualitative interview approach. *Korean Journal of English Language and Linguistics, 12*(1), 67–99.

Kim, Tae-Young, & Oh, Shinyu. (2019). English education during the second and third National Curriculum period in South Korea: Focusing on the newspaper article analysis. *Foreign Languages Education, 26*(2), 73–98.

Kim, Tae-Young, & Seo, Hyo-Sun. (2012). Elementary school students' foreign language learning demotivation: A mixed methods study of Korean EFL context. *The Asia-Pacific Education Researcher, 21*(1), 160–171.

Koo, Eun-Seo. (2018a, October 22). Segeum nalrigo sarajineun yeong'eomaeul: 40%ga moon datgeona yongdo baggue [Dismantling English Villages after squandering government-subsidy: 40% of them closed or changed its use]. Retrieved July 11, 2019, from https://www.hankyung.com/news/article/2018101925161.

Koo, Heakyoung. (2018b). *A historical approach on the transition of elementary English education in Korea*. Unpublished Ph.D. dissertation. Incheon, Korea: Gyeongin National University of Education.

Koo, Hee-Eon. (2015, March 16). Yeong'eo gongbu heotbaljil'e jjideuneun cheongchun [Smothering youths in futile English learning] Retrieved July 8, 2019, from http://weekly.donga.com/List/3/all/11/99022/1.

Korea Herald. (2012, June 7). Editorial: English divide. Retrieved July 2, 2019, from http://www.koreaherald.com/view.php?ud=20120607000793.

Korea Times. (2012, September 6). Once-flourishing English Village struggle to survive. Retrieved July 11, 2019, from https://web.archive.org/web/20160531033935/http://koreatimes.co.kr/www/news/nation/2012/09/113_119289.html.

Krashen, S. D. (1985). *The input hypothesis: Issues and implications.* London: Addison-Wesley Longman.

Kubota, R. (2002). Impact of globalization on language teaching in Japan. In D. Block & D. Cameron (Eds.), *Globalization and language teaching* (pp. 13–28). London: Routledge.

Kwon, Oryang. (2000). Korea's English education policy changes in the 1990s: Innovations to gear the nation for the 21st century. *English Teaching, 55*(1), 47–91.

Kwon, Oryang. (2006). Impacts and effects of ten years of elementary school English education in Korea. *GTEC 2006 Report, 78–85.*

Kyunghyang Shinmun. (2006, May 18). Yeong'eo baewoogi yeolpoong: Heowa sil [English learning fever: The good and the bad]. Retrieved March 29, 2021, from http://news.khan.co.kr/kh_news/khan_art_view.html?art_id=200605171742281.

Kyunghyang Shinmun. (2010, June 22). 1990nyeondae, geurigo 2010nyeon: Dalrajin baenangyeohaeng poongsokdo [The 1990s and 2010: Changing trends in backpacking abroad]. Retrieved July 5, 2019, from http://news.khan.co.kr/kh_news/khan_art_view.html?art_id=201006221739175.

Lee, Byung-min. (2011a). *Seoul'yeongeogonggyoyookganghwageongchaek seongkwa boonseok mit baljeonbanghyang yeongu [Analysis of strengthening public English education policy in Seoul and study of developing this policy].* Seoul, Korea: Seoul Office of Education.

Lee, Da-Eun, & Kim, Tae-Young. (2013). A study of middle school students' perception toward English co-teaching of a native English teacher and a Korean English teacher: Focusing on affective factors. *The Journal of Modern British & American Language & Literature, 32*(2), 29–55.

Lee, Do-Hee. (2014, June 3). TOEIC Eungsi'inwon, choigeun 4hyeonman'e cheot gamso: Olhaedo harakse jisok [The applicants of TOEIC shows a decrease for the first time in recent 4 years: The downturn continues this year]. Retrieved July 8, 2019, from http://www.jobnjoy.com/portal/jobnews/foreign_company_view.jsp?nidx=8287&depth1=1&depth2=1&depth3=5.

Lee, Geun. (2008, March 18). Lee Myung-bak jeongbunun 'sinjayooju'eui inyeomjeongbu' [The Lee Myung-bak government is based on 'neoliberal ideology'] Retrieved July 16, 2019, from http://www.pressian.com/news/article/?no=55339#09T0.

Lee, Heung-Soo. (2011b). *Yeong-eoga gyeongjeda: Yeong'eo'eui gwageowa hyeonjae, geurigo mirae [English is economy: Past, present, and future of English].* Seoul, Korea: English Moumou.

Lee, Mun Woo. (2016). 'Gangnam style' English ideologies: Neoliberalism, class and parents of early study-abroad students. *International Journal of Bilingual Education and Bilingualism, 19* (1), 35–50.

Lee, Mun Woo. (2017). TEE uncertified teachers' perceptions regarding the TEE certificate program. *Studies in British and American Language and Literature, 126,* 195–214.

Lee, S., & Brinton, M. C. (1996). Elite education and social capital: The case of South Korea. *Sociology and Education, 69*(3), 177–192.

Lee, Yoon-Sook. (2003). Suggestions for preschool English education. *Modern English Education, 4*(2), 105–147.

Lee, Young Shik. (2015). Innovating secondary English education in Korea. In B. Spolsky & K. Sung (Eds.), *Secondary school English education in Asia* (pp. 47–64). London: Routledge.

Long, M. (1996). The role of the linguistic environment in second language acquisition. In W. Ritchie & T. Bhatia (Eds.), *Handbook of second language acquisition* (pp. 413–468). San Diego, CA: Academic Press.

Manh, L. D. (2012). English as a medium of instruction at tertiary education system in Vietnam. *The Journal of Asia TEFL, 9*(2), 97–122.

McCrostie, J. (2009, August 11). TOEIC no turkey at 30: Once-struggling test flying high in Japan as corporate partners take on larger role. Retrieved July 6, 2019, from https://www.japantimes.co.jp/community/2009/08/11/issues/toeic-no-turkey-at-30/#.XSDAa5NKh-U.

Min, Chan Kyoo. (2007). Innovative English education curricula and the strategies of implementation in Korea. In Y.-H. Choi & B. Spolsky (Eds.), *ELT curriculum innovation and implementation in Asia* (pp. 101–129). Seoul, Korea: Asia TEFL.

Ministry of Education. (1995). *The curricula of elementary school: General and the English subject.* Seoul, Korea: Ministry of Education.

Ministry of Education. (2012, October 22). Gookgayeong'eoneungryeoksiheom[NEAT] daebi yeong'eohagwon teukbyeol jido jeomgeum silsi [Launching special monitoring of English institutes for the National English Ability Test]. Retrieved July 2, 2019, from https://moe.go.kr/boardCnts/view.do?boardID=294&boardSeq=37731&lev=0&searchType=null&statusYN=W&page=285&s=moe&m=0503&opType=N.

Ministry of Education. (2014, August 28). Gookga'yeongeoneungryeokpyeonggasiheom [NEAT] sasilsang silpae gwanryeon seolmyeong [Explanation of the de facto failure of National English Ability Test]. Retrieved July 2, 2019, from https://www.moe.go.kr/boardCnts/view.do?boardID=295&boardSeq=56480&lev=0&searchType=null&statusYN=W&page=43&s=moe&m=0504&opType=N.

Moon, Yong. (1976). Hankook yeong'eogyoyooksa (1883-1945) [History of English education in Korea (1883-1945)]. *Sunggoknonchong, 7,* 618–654.

Nam, Dae-Hee. (1996, February 26). Yeong'eo jal mot hamyeon sapyo sseoyahalpan [Prepare for resignation letter if you cannot speak English well]. Retrieved March 29, 2021, from https://m.hankookilbo.com/News/Read/199602260034008272.

Nam, Young-sin. (1998, July 6). Banron: Nam Young-sin'ssi, Bok Geo-il'ssi'eui 'gookjehwa' bipan [Counterargument: Mr. Nam Young-sin criticizes Mr. Bok Geo-il's 'globalization']. Retrieved July 9, 2019, from http://news.chosun.com/svc/content_view/content_view.html?contid=1998070670317.

News 1. (2018, November 7). Daejeongyoyookcheong yeong'eogyosa simhwayeonsu yoomyeongmusil [Ineffective intensive in-service English teacher training at the Daejeon Metropolitan Office of Education]. Retrieved July 3, 2019, from http://news1.kr/articles/?3470966.

OECD. (2002). *Annual report 2002.* Paris: The Organization for Economic Co-operation and Development. Retrieved June 27, 2019, from https://www.oecd.org/about/2080175.pdf.

Oh, Wook-hwan. (2000). *Hankuksahoi'eui gyoyookyeol: Kiwongwa simwha [Education fever in the Korean society: Its origin and aggravation].* Seoul, Korea: Gyoyookgwahaksa.

Onishi, N. (2008, June 8). For English studies, Koreans say goodbye to dad. Retrieved July 10, 2019, from https://www.nytimes.com/2008/06/08/world/asia/08geese.html?_r=1&oref=slogin.

Park, Noja. (2006). *Dangsindeul'eui daehanmingook 1 [Your Rebublic of Korea 1].* Seoul, Korea: Hankyeore.

Park, S. J., & Abelman, N. (2004). Class and cosmopolitan striving: Mothers' management of English education in South Korea. *Anthropological Quarterly, 77*(4), 645–672.

Park, Sung Geun, & Min, Chan Kyoo. (2014). TEE certified teachers' perceptions and attitudes towards TEE/TEK. *English Language Teaching, 26*(1), 171–192.

Park, Won-Ki, & Kim, Hye-Kyoung. (2007, October 30). Mat'ado yeong'eoman neundamyeon [If only my English proficiency increase although being beaten]. Retrieved March 29, 2021, from https://www.hankookilbo.com/News/Read/200710300023750796.

Segye Ilbo. (2012, September 13). Suneung yeong'eo daeche NEAT, byeonbyeolryeok 'nonran' [NEAT replacing CSAT: Criticisms on discriminant power]. Retrieved July 2, 2019, from https://news.naver.com/main/read.nhn?mode=LSD&mid=sec&sid1=102&oid=022&aid=0002438916.

Seoul Metropolitan Office of Education. (2016). 2016 Yeong'eo(damdang)gyosa TEE injeungje sihaenggyehoik [Plan for English teacher TEE certificate program in the year of 2016].

Retrieved January 21, 2019, from http://buseo.sen.go.kr/view/jsp/bbsDownload.jsp?bbsCd=312&bbsSeq=84&orderNo=1.

Seth, J. (2002). *Education fever: Society, politics, and the pursuit of schooling in South Korea.* Honolulu, HI: University of Hawai'i Press.

Statistics Korea. (2014). 2013nyeon sagyoyookbi josa gyeolgwa [Survey result of private education expenditure in the year of 2013]. Retrieved July 2, 2019, from http://kostat.go.kr/portal/korea/kor_nw/1/1/index.board?bmode=read&aSeq=311886&pageNo=7&rowNum=10&amSeq=&sTarget=title&sTxt=%EC%82%B0%EC%97%85%ED%99%9C%EB%8F%99.

Statistics Korea. (2018). Chojoong'go sagyoyookbi josa [Investigating the cost of private education of primary and secondary school students]. Retrieved July 12, 2019, from http://kostat.go.kr/portal/korea/kor_nw/1/7/1/index.board?bmode=read&aSeq=366658&pageNo=&rowNum=10&amSeq=&sTarget=&sTxt=.

Swain, M., & Lapkin, S. (1995). Problems in output and the cognitive processes they generate: A step towards second language learning. *Applied Linguistics, 16,* 371–391.

The Educational Testing Service. (2019). TOEIC Bridge Test: Proven, reliable, trusted worldwide. Retrieved July 8, 2019, from https://www.ets.org/toeic/bridge.

Yang, Do-Woong. (2018, August 27). Yeong'eo jeoldaepyeonggaro yeong'eo gonggyoyook deo mooneojeotda [Due to the criterion-referenced English test, public English education is being collapsed]. Retrieved July 12, 2019, from http://www.kyosu.net/news/articleView.html?idxno=42522.

Yeon, Sang-Mi., & Kim, Tae-Young. (2010). The influence of secondary school students' perception about teacher in public and private education on their English learning motivation. *English Language Teaching, 22*(4), 107–131.

Yonhap News. (2016a, June 5). Jeongook yeong'eomaeul pyeswae'wigi: Jachidanchejangdeul seonsimgongyak'euro hyeolsenangbi [English Villages nationwide at the risk of closure: Heads of self-governing community squandered tax-payers' precious money for their political-patronage tactic]. Retrieved July 11, 2019, from https://www.yna.co.kr/view/AKR20160603136500061.

Yonhap News. (2016b, October 6). Hakgyoeseo sarajineun woneomin gyosa: 4nyeonmane 42% geupgam [Native-speaking English teachers disappearing at school: 42% decrease only within 4 years]. Retrieved June 29, 2019, from https://www.yna.co.kr/view/AKR20161006086100004.

Yonhap News. (2017, March 17). 'Joolgin jool'eotnunde ...' Jaknyeon'edo hae'oiyoohak yeonsoobi 4jowon neom'eotda ['Decreased, but...' Expenses for study abroad and learning abroad exceeded $3.5 billion]. Retrieved January 31, 2020, from https://www.yna.co.kr/view/AKR20170316170100002.

Yoon, Min-sik. (2014). [Eye on English] Test scores don't guarantee English skills. Retrieved February 8, 2020, from http://www.koreaherald.com/view.php?ud=20140205001246.

Yoon, Seok-Joo. (1999). *Gyoyookgaehyeok'eui jeongchijeok seonggyeok'e gwanhan bipanjeok gochal: Kim Young Sam jeongbu'eui gyoyookgaeheok'eul joongsim'eu ro [A critical investigation on the political nature of educational reform: Focusing on the educational reform of Kim Young Sam Government].* Unpublished master's thesis. Seoul, Korea: Korea University.

YTN. (2009, August, 6). Yeong'eomaeul gajja won'eomin gangsa chaeyong mool'eui [Scandal of hiring fake native English instructors in the English Village]. Retrieved July 11, 2019, from https://www.ytn.co.kr/_ln/0103_200908061049202323.

Chapter 5
History of English Learning and Its Motivation in Other East Asian Countries

This chapter compares L2 learning motivation among three East Asian countries (i.e., China, Japan, and North Korea). Beginning with China's Imperial Examination System originating in the Sui Dynasty, China's English education will be explained in the first section. Following significant sociopolitical events in China, the vicissitude of English education and Chinese people's perception of it are the primary foci in the first section of this chapter. In the second section, the case of English education in Japan will be explicated. U.S. influence during the nineteenth century and Meiji restoration revolutionized Japan's modernization, and the role of the English language has often been perceived as the symbol of industrialization and advanced technology. In the case of Japan, the changing role of English as Japan transformed from pre-modern feudal nation to advanced, world leader after World War II will be investigated. In the third section, the case of North Korea will be explained. Recently, Kim Jong-un, the supreme leader of North Korea, tried to improve its diplomatic relation with the USA and South Korea. This section will focus on recent changes of English education in North Korea and investigate the motivation of learning English there.

5.1 The Case of China

China is the top English-learning country in terms of the number of English learners. Wei and Su (2012) estimated that around 2000, 49% of students in China (i.e., 415.95 million) had learned one or more foreign languages, and 93.8% of them (i.e., 390.16 million) had learned English. In just 2000, 50,000 Chinese students went to the USA to learn English or to pursue higher education degrees, and this is the same as the total number of Chinese students in the USA from 1847 to 1953 (Bolton, 2002). More recently, Li (2017) stated that "English is taught in most colleges and universities as a compulsory course for a population of over 35.59 million students" (p. 6). Although the exact number of English learners in China differs depending on

© Springer Nature Singapore Pte Ltd. 2021

T.-Y. Kim, *Historical Development of English Learning Motivation Research*, English Language Education 21, https://doi.org/10.1007/978-981-16-2514-5_5

the statistics' source, the year of data collection, and the data collection methods, it seems likely that the sheer number of English learners in China exceeds that of other countries.

Following the significant sociohistorical events in China, English education in China and the reactions of Chinese students are the main focus of this section. This section starts with the discussion of China's traditional educational system centering on the issue of *keju* (科舉) or the Imperial Examination for government officials in the various pre-modern Chinese Dynasties. The Imperial Exam greatly influenced education in China as well as in neighboring countries, including Korea and Vietnam, that shared Confucian tradition. In the sixteenth century, communication between English speakers and the Chinese began to emerge. So-called "broken English" started to be used mainly for the exchange of commercial goods, particularly tea (Bolton, 2002). With increasing international trade and foreign intervention in China, the perception of English had undergone drastic changes. Although some regarded it as hampering the Chinese spirit, it was also enthusiastically embraced by a group of enlightenment scholars in the late Qing Dynasty established by the Manchus. The late nineteenth century was a slow but steady collapse of the Qing Dynasty for its internal and external turmoil, and finally in 1911, the Republic of China (ROC; 中華民國), a democratic nation, was founded as a result of the Xinhai Revolution espoused by Sun Yan-sen (孫逸仙, also known as Sun Wen [孫文]). However, ongoing warfare with the Japanese army and the reigning party's corruption invited fierce civil war. After ousting the Nationalist Party led by Chiang Kai-Shek (蔣介石) from mainland China, the People's Republic of China (PRC; 中华人民共和国) was established by Mao Zedong's (毛澤東) Chinese Communist Party (CCP) in 1949. While experiencing these major sociopolitical incidents, English education in China underwent significant changes. However, in general, after the 1978 Open Door Policy initiated by Deng Xiaoping (鄧小平), English has increasingly been instructed across China. The most recent trends reveal the widening gap in the social classes' wealth, and this gap affects the opportunity to learn English. The College English Test (CET), the nationwide English test for college students, had been implemented in China for decades and is now resulting in various side-effects.

5.1.1 Historical Background: Keju, or the Imperial Examination

When we discuss the educational system in China, it is necessary to analyze *keju* (科舉), or the Imperial Examination for appointing civil servants. Given the long history of China, the highly sophisticated officer appointment system to control the nation and aid the royal monarchy is unsurprising. The Han Dynasty is sometimes credited with developing an examination system to select the best candidates for government positions, but it is usually regarded that Emperor Wen of the Sui Dynasty (隋 文皇

帝, 541–604) first initiated the Imperial Examination in 587 to suppress local moguls and consolidate the emperor's direct control over the entire nation (Lee, 2008). The Tang and Song Dynasties also continued the same system to select government officials. During the Tang Dynasty, the exams were held regularly, and during the Song, the exam's authority was strengthened by introducing the final round of exam in front of the emperor in the main palace (Miyazaki, 1993). Although the Imperial Examination was discontinued in the Yuan Dynasty, which was the foreign Mongol monarchy, it was re-introduced in the Ming and Qing Dynasties until its official abolition in 1905 (Sutterby, 2012).

The Imperial Examination, which afforded considerable social recognition and authority to those who passed it and which lasted more than 1300 years, possessed the following characteristics:

> First, the Imperial Examination System carried the principle of open examination, fair competition, and selection according to excellence. Officials were selected no matter what one's family origin was and no nomination from high officials was required. The selection was made according to the result of the examinations. Second, the Imperial Examination System as a means of education and official selection at the end of education was part of and could not be separated from education. It promoted the development of education and society. Third, in the later stages of the system, the standards of talent selection were mainly one's understanding of Confucian classics, not one's actual ability nor the exploration of unknown fields. In another word, it focused on how well one learnt not how well one could perform, innovate or discover. Fourth, the aim of this examination was to obtain power, fame and wealth by serving the country, but it was actually serving the Emperor because the principle of conduct for the nominees was to do according to the Emperor's will. Fifth, it had built a bureaucratic society in which the officers were important, and other people were not important. Those who passed the examinations immediately became members of the nobility and the ruling class. (Gan, 2008, p. 126)

The Imperial Examination resulted in the overreliance on classical Confucius literature for imperial civil service (Gan, 2008). Although the processes varied by dynasty, usually seven processes were required to be fully appointed as an honorable capital government official who could work in the capital and the royal palace. As the main purpose of introducing the system was to suppress local moguls, the power of government officials appointed through this systematic Imperial Examination was steadily increased under the aegis of the emperor. Thus, with the introduction of the exam, the emperor's power was strengthened whereas that of local gentry rapidly waned (Miyazaki, 1993). As government officers often enjoyed authority and could accumulate decent wealth through their positions, the Imperial Examination was soon inundated with aspiring students across feudal China. The passing rate of accepted officers became extraordinarily severe in the exams' later stages, and consequently the fierce competition undoubtedly intensified. It is estimated that in its later administration, even at the local level, the passing rate was only 1–2% and most of those who did not pass waited for the next examination, usually held every 3 years in the Song Dynasty (Miyazaki, 1993).

Because the Imperial Examination did not restrict applicants based on their age, hometown, educational history, or family background, it was primarily regarded as fair. However, as the system continued for more than a thousand years, several major criticisms were leveled at its continued and unchanged administration. The first and most serious criticism was the vague assumption of the usefulness of Confucian knowledge gained from memorizing its literature. Although this assumption was anecdotally supported by the previous excellence of officers who passed the Imperial Examination, this evidence did not contradict the sharp criticism that the literary and practical, adroit administrative knowledge are entirely different skillsets (Miyazaki, 1993). A related criticism was the overemphasis on literary, archaic knowledge in Confucian schools of thought. Although the Imperial Examination for military officialdom was also administered, it was not the main focus on the Examination, and the officers who passed the military examination, in general, could not be promoted to the highest government rank (Gan, 2008). It was mainly due to the systematic limitation of the dynasty that the influential military officers could instigate military coups and be a potential threat to the empire (Miyazaki, 1993). The third criticism addressed the lack of national responsibility and educational accountability. As this exam system was consolidated, students with Confucian knowledge across China gathered in swarms to the exam center, but only 1–2% of the test takers could pass the initial local exam. The rest kept repeating the same examination until they passed it. Miyazaki (1993) stated that if the test taker passed the examination in his 20s, he was extremely fortunate, and it was not late if he passed it in his 30s. With no guarantee, the aspiring officers spent their financial means and enormous energy to pass the examination. While repeating the exam preparation, passing or failing was entirely attributed to the test takers' responsibility. The nation did not compensate for any expenses, and the test takers spent their own money for the test.

Historically, the Imperial Examination initiated in China also significantly affected other countries in Asia. For example, the same idea was adopted to select the government officers in the Korean Goryo (高麗) Dynasty in 954, and this system continued for almost a thousand years until 1894 by the Gabo Reform. As in China, students in Korea aspired to pass the Examination because it was clearly considered the ladder to success (Wagner, 1977). Ancient Japan also used this system. However, in Japan, the military power was highlighted throughout the Samurai shoguns (from approximately 794 to 1867), and for this reason, the appointment of local or metropolitan government officers was decided mainly by the powerful militias and their loyal retainers. In Vietnam, which shares a border with China, Confucian thought was widely spread. The Lý (李) Dynasty in Vietnam (1009–1225) adopted and administered the Imperial Examination in 1075, and the Examination was officially dissolved in 1919 (Ko, 2017).

The Imperial Examination system significantly affected western scholars, and some European nations started to administer similar exams in their educational system. Europeans regarded it as an advanced idea that anyone could take the test, and that solely based on test score, government officers were appointed regardless of one's kinship and academic background. In most European nations, appointing the government officers occurred mainly through the recommendation of other officers or sometimes through bribery (Knights, 2016). The Imperial Examination in China likely affected the administration of official tests for the government officer appointment system in the West (Miyazaki, 1993). For example, in the U.K., where the parliamentary democratic system had already been used, the officer appointment test was administered only after 1870. In the USA, the appointment test was first used in 1883. Ko (2017) states the influence of China's Imperial Examination on the West as follows:

> The imperial examination model also garnered the attention of Western thinkers (largely by means of missionaries and envoys), who would subsequently implement variations of the system in their own nations. For example, a modified version of the exam was adopted by the English East India Company, and later by the British government to select public servants (Higgins & Zhang, 2002). France, Germany, and the United States later adopted similar models to identify candidates for certain jobs. (Kaplan & Saccuzzo, 2012)

The historical influence of the Imperial Examination on China and its neighboring countries was exponential. First, its longevity consolidated the idea that literary knowledge was related to not only a learned human being's cultural erudition but also the crucial means to gain worldly social success (Ko, 2017; Miyazaki, 1993). Moreover, the idea of measuring one's knowledge in Confucian literature was developed into the stratification of the test takers into a hierarchy. It was widely believed that the highest score in the Imperial Examination proved intellectual excellence, and those who achieved top ranks could function better than the second-tier scorers.

As explained above, passing even the initial round of local exam was challenging, but upon passing it, the sitters' social and occupational status and related financial benefits were almost always guaranteed. Similar traditions have been witnessed in East Asian countries until recently. In Japan, lifetime employment at the same workplace was a tacit social norm, which meant that once people gained employment, they could hold that position or another within the company until retirement age unless they were involved in critical misconduct or criminal activities. A laborious competition cycle was created, with decent jobs for the top applicants (Miyazaki, 1993). To be employed at a large, prestigious company that practically guaranteed lifetime employment, students aspired to be admitted to the best universities with high rates of student employment.

The case of Japan was not an exception in Korea. In most cases, this employment record and the percentage of graduates' employment were in proportion to the university's social recognition (see Chaps. 3 and 4). If universities held recognized academic reputations, the graduates of the university were favorably positioned in the job market. To be qualified for admittance to the best universities, students needed to be admitted to the best high schools, which also had a positive reputation regarding students' admittance to prestigious universities. The same idea has been equally applied to junior high school, elementary school, and even kindergarten. Thus, academic competition has been justified in East Asia and was often regarded as the royal road to a financially affluent life working in a reputable company.

Academic competition is often closely related to academic credentialism. For example, as with China and Vietnam, in South Korea, it is widely believed that the students with higher college entrance exam scores deserve the best universities, and admission to such prestigious institutions is mostly regarded as being "a priority pass" to better employment opportunities and promotions (Kim, 2006, 2015). Accordingly, college entrance exams are excessively competitive, and students and parents alike do their best to earn high scores. Thus, in approaching East Asian exam-orientation and its related competitive motivation to excel beyond other test takers, understanding the long tradition of the Imperial Examination is essential.

5.1.2   First Encounters with English Speakers

The Chinese first encountered the English language in the sixteenth century. Chinese merchants learned some "broken English," or "pidgin English," for international trade of tea (or chai) in the district of Canton, or the south China seacoast. Chinese merchants were not enthusiastic about learning English and teaching Chinese to their western counterparts mainly due to the Chinese negative sentiment toward "teaching the language of the 'central flowery nation' [中華] to the outside barbarians" (Williams, 1836, p. 430, cited in Bolton, 2002, p. 185). Those who taught the Chinese language to foreigners were even regarded as traitors to the nation (Bolton, 2002).

For this reason, English education in China was informal, and for more than 200 years, English education was conducted at a hands-on level, focusing on merchant-related jargon English. The Chinese and British in the nineteenth century frequently needed to communicate about the exchange of goods. The British exported opium mostly illegally via the British East India Company, and a large amount of silver, which was initially used to pay for the silk export from China, was collected by Britain. This activity resulted in the drain of silver and the influx of opium addicts in China. The First Opium War (第一次鴉片戰爭) or the Anglo-Chinese War of 1839–1842 broke out in this politico-economic context. The British Royal Navy exercised its gunnery power and defeated the Qing armed forces. The Treaty of Nanking, the first of what were later called the unequal treaties, ceded Hong Kong Island to the British Empire and granted British indemnity and extra-territoriality of five treaty ports: Canton (Guangzhou), Amoy (Xiamen), Foochow (Fuzhou), Ningpo (Ningbo), and Shanghai. Derogatory views on jargon English prevailed and the "uncouth and ridiculous jargon was the almost exclusive medium of communication between natives and foreigners at the open ports" (Bolton, 2002, p. 186).

The British Empire was not satisfied with China's slow transition to open ports, and to expedite the opening policy of China, it initiated the Second Opium War or Anglo-Chinese War in 1856, resulting in the ratification of Treaty of Tientsin in 1862. Over 40 Chinese cities were opened to western missionaries, merchants, and colonial officers at the turn of the twentieth century (Bolton, 2002).

The opening of the nation in the late nineteenth century resulted in English-language instruction in missionary schools across China. Before the opening of China, it was mostly through the real-life, practical communication between the

Chinese and British merchants that the Chinese could learn English, and it was mostly jargon or broken English. However, by the early twentieth century, Chinese students received systematic English education in missionary schools. According to Green's (1934) recount, "hundreds of missionary schools have for years past been turning out thousands of Chinese who speak English at least as well as most non-English peoples; even among servants there are those who really resent being addressed in pidgin" (p. 331, cited in Bolton, 2002, p. 187).[1]

5.1.3   The Contributions of Missionary Schools in the Nineteenth Century in China

The role of missionary schools radically differed depending on the perspective: nationalist or modernist. In the former point of view, they were the vanguard of "disseminat[ing] values of the Judeo-Christian culture among the Chinese people" (Deng, 1997, p. 69) but in the latter's point of view, these school undeniably greatly contributed to China's modernization, encompassing various practical educational fields including "medicine, nursing, agriculture, sociology, economics, and law" (p. 69).

Between these opposing positions, the historical trajectory proved that the latter was dominant, at least in the nineteenth century, and thus more than a dozen missionary schools as well as universities were established across China. The "de-pidginization" of English was initiated in 1842 and facilitated after the 1860s (Bolton, 2002). Understandably, the first missionary schools were established in Macau, Hong Kong, and other parts in South China. Among these schools, the Morrison Educational Society School, which opened in 1839 and transferred to Hong Kong in 1842, and the Anglo-Chinese College, transferred from Malacca to Hong Kong in 1843, should be highlighted for their noteworthy Chinese modernist graduates. Tong King-sing (1828–1892), founder of the China Merchants' Steamship Navigation Company and the Kaiping Coal Mines, was one of the graduates. Yung Wing (1828–1912) and Wong Fung (1828–1878) were also presumably the first Chinese graduates of western universities (Yale and Edinburgh, respectively). Moreover, missionary schools contributed to girls' education in China: The Bridgman Girls' School was founded in Beijing in 1864, as well as the Shanghai Chinese-Western School for Girls in Shanghai in 1890. According to Bolton (2002, pp. 189–190), "by 1905, around 7000 girls were being taught at the primary level, and 2700 in secondary schools," which led to the subsequent establishment of women's colleges (e.g., Hwa Nan College [華南女子文理學院] in Fuzhou, Ginling College [金陵女子大学] in Nanjing).

---

[1]Pidgin English used in China, particularly in Canton, Hong Kong, and Macau rapidly decreased after the establishment of the People's Republic of China (PRC) in 1949 (Bolton, 2002).

American missionaries initiated tertiary education in China by establishing protestant missionary universities across China. Bolton (2002) emphasizes that "the 13 protestant 'Christian colleges' which were set up at the turn of the twentieth century had a profound influence on Chinese education" (p. 189). Although the foreign missionaries were expelled from China after the PRC's establishment in 1949, the contribution of these missionary universities was extensive, and by either merging or being renamed, these universities are still among the PRC's best performing universities.

However, at the turn of the century, the Chinese general public's sentiment toward the western missionaries and their culture gradually turned negative. As the Qing Dynasty continued to ratify unequal treaties with western nations and cede them its territories, the nationalist movement swept across the nation from 1899 to 1901, called the Boxer Rebellion (拳亂) or the Yihetuan Movement (義和團運動). The rebels supported traditional values motivated by pro-nationalism against Western colonialism, arguably represented by Christian missionaries. Yihetuan (義和團), meaning the Militia United in Righteousness, converged on Beijing, the Qing Dynasty capital, under the motto "Support the Qing and Exterminate the Western Foreigners (扶清滅洋)." The Qing Dynasty was divided into two positions for this movement. The pro-movement officials and generals were armed against the Eight-Nation Alliances (six European nations plus the USA and Japan) but were defeated. This movement hastened the dismantling of the Qing Dynasty by provisioning the foreign troops to be stationed in Beijing. Under this extreme social unrest, the official English education began by government initiatives.

5.1.4 Establishment of Tongwen Guan in Beijing and Its Implications

Chinese modernization through the introduction of Western civilization was gradual. The profoundly ingrained negative attitude toward the West prevented China from actively accepting the technology resulting from the industrial revolution, and the slow introduction of and rigidity toward advanced science eventually led to the Qing Dynasty's collapse due to repeated invasions by European countries, the USA, and Japan. The slow transition starkly contrasted with the case of Japan, which succeeded in transforming the entire nation from the feudal Shogunate system to the central imperial one through the Meiji Restoration (see Sect. 5.2).

Japan was quick to introduce English after the opening of the nation by American Admiral Matthew Perry in 1854. However, mainly due to Sino-centrism or the notion of China as the only "Central Flowery" (中華) nation in the world, China was slow in implementing English at the governmental level. It was only in 1862 after defeat in the Second Opium War or the Anglo-Chinese War (1856–1860) that English was instituted. This delay reflected the Self-Reliance Movement, which was the Chinese elite's attempt to revitalize the Qing Dynasty through political and economic reform in China. The defeat of the Second Opium War invited British and French armed forces into China, where they invaded Beijing, burned the Royal Palace, and forced the Xianfeng (咸豐) Emperor to escape.

Chinese scholars in this perilous period initially approached Western forces from two conflicting philosophies: Confucian conservatism versus practical self-reliance. However, despite their unwillingness, most accepted the need to learn Western knowledge and science to make China a robust nation capable of avoiding future humiliation (Adamson, 2004). This Self-Strengthening Movement during the second half of the nineteenth century intended to preserve their traditions and cultural heritage, and young Chinese needed to learn Western technology. In 1857, Feng Guofen (馮桂芬), the leading scholar for the Self-Strengthening Movement and active supporter of Western technology in the Qing Dynasty, proposed a fundamental reform requesting imperial permission to establish Western-style institutions for higher education. He emphasized the need to learn foreign languages as follows:

> If today we wish to select and use Western knowledge, we should establish official translation offices at Canton and Shanghai. Brilliant students up to fifteen years of age should be selected from these areas to live and study in these schools. . . . Westerners should be invited to teach them the spoken and written languages of the various nations, and famous Chinese teachers should be engaged to teach them classics, history, and other subjects. (translated by Teng & Fairbank, 1979, p. 51, cited in Adamson, 2004, p. 25)

The Qing monarchy accepted this proposal. The dynasty established Zongli Yamen (總理衙門) in 1861 to handle complicated foreign affairs. To support the translation of the Zongli Yamen, Tongwen Guan (同文館) or an Interpreter's College (Bolton, 2002) was founded in Beijing the next year.

In China's Ming Dynasty, a few translators were educated in Si Yi Guan (四夷馆) or the Office for the Languages of Nations of Four Directions, and they learned Mongol, Jurchen, Hui, and Burmese. However, at the governmental level, Tongwen Guan was the first institute that systematically taught English to select translator candidates. After its establishment in 1862, English-speaking faculty members were actively involved in the administration and education in Tongwen Guan. John S. Burdon, a British missionary, was the first head instructor from 1862 to 1866. In 1866, astronomy and mathematics were added to the curriculum. In 1869, William Alexander Parsons Martin, an American missionary and translator, took over the role until 1900. Tongwen Guan gradually diversified its curriculum, and by 1877, its foreign language offerings included not only English but also French, German, Russian, and Japanese. Additionally, various natural and social science subjects were included in the curriculum.

However, Tongwen Guan was not initially welcomed by most Chinese, particularly by the scholars and their families, who were concerned about their status. The instruction of Western languages, which many people still regarded as belonging to barbarians, faced fierce opposition from the literati class, resulting in Tongwen Guan's initial unpopularity. For almost a decade after its establishment in 1862, the status of Tongwen Guan graduates was not comparable with that of traditional officials who passed *keju* (科舉), or the Imperial Exam, which led them first to *shengyuan* (生員) and later to *jinshi* (進士), or the highest officer rank. The main work of the Tongwen Guan graduates was "to gain access to Western technology through the translation of scientific and technical books into Chinese" and sometimes "to pass on to the Zongli Yamen intelligence garnered from foreign newspapers produced in the treaty ports" (Adamson, 2004, p. 26). Nonetheless, public feelings toward Tongwen Guan improved by the late 1870s when the graduates started to be appointed in "the civil service or even diplomatic postings overseas and the status of the school, and therefore of studying English, rose accordingly" (Adamson, 2004, p. 26).

Tongwen Guan made a significant impact on English education and the instruction of Western technology in China. It lasted for approximately 40 years from 1862 to 1900, and other major cities such as Shanghai also invited foreign instructors to conduct similar training for potential translators and scholars at the provincial level. For example, the Shanghai Foreign Language School (*Waiguo Yuyan Wenzi Xueguan*, 外国语言文字学馆) offered a variety of courses such as foreign languages, history, and Chinese studies, all of which were related to the practical needs of the city's prosperous business community (Bolton, 2002). For English instruction, American missionary Young J. Allen (1836–1907) was recruited.

Tongwen Guan in Beijing and Shanghai Foreign Language School were both intended to train adult translators and scholars. Since the missionary schools actively disseminated Western values, particularly Christianity, the growing anti-Christian sentiment after the defeat in the Second Opium War resulted in the establishment of many Chinese-run modern schools, called *Xuetang* (学堂) across China. These modern schools emphasized the instruction of foreign languages as well as the Chinese language and mathematics (Bolton, 2002).

5.1.5   Chaos at the Turn of the Twentieth Century

Arguably, the common thread in English education in China is the anxiety about contaminating the Chinese spirit represented by Sino-centralism or the view of China as the Central Flowery Nation. In the nineteenth century, the slow introduction of foreign language education and Western civilization was also related to the emphasis of Sino-centralism and spite toward the "barbarian" nations. Such deep-rooted concerns regarding national contamination persist in modern China's English education system (Adamson & Morris, 1997).

At the turn of the twentieth century, the conflicting views of Western nations and their languages remained. Moreover, the Boxer Rebellion resulted in the intervention of various nations demanding territorial interests in China in exchange for suppressing the rebellion. Such ideological conflict and diplomatic impasse destabilized the Qing Dynasty and nullified the post-Tongwen Guan reforms.

Although China experienced extreme chaos in the first decade of the twentieth century, the status of English was consolidated for political reasons. Japan, which hastened its industrialization after the Meiji Restoration in 1868, was the first Asian nation to succeed in transforming a nation from a traditional feudal state into a modern Western-style one. For control of Korea, China and Japan were engaged in the First Sino-Japanese War from 1894 to 1895, and China experienced humiliating defeat from Japan, which affected educational reform in August 1902.[2] Emperor Guangxu announced an edict to abolish the existing Imperial Exam based on Confucian knowledge and to establish a Western-style educational system, and English was adopted as one of the mainstream curricula of senior secondary schools.

The previous section emphasized that with other scholars supporting the Self-Strengthening Movement, Feng Guifen (馮桂芬) proposed reforming China in 1857. Approximately half a century later, the old system was abolished, and a new Western education was introduced in the Qing Dynasty. In this sense, it was the eventual, but long overdue, victory of the reformers over the conservatives. For the second half of the nineteenth century, Tongwen Guan and other educational institutions, of both domestic and foreign origin, instructed Western languages, particularly English. However, reform was slow, staggering, and often met with significant challenges from conservative Confucians who emphasized the value of Sino-centrism. Successive Western invasions after the Opium Wars and internal conflicts also stagnated China's modernization and foreign language education. Thus, China's educational situation at the beginning of twentieth century was unsystematic due to the lack of finances and political stability. This turmoil ushered the new Republican era from 1911.

5.1.6   The Republican Era from 1911 to 1949

5.1.6.1   English as the Tool for Enlightenment and the Reaction from the Conservatives

English education from 1911 to 1949 is closely aligned with China's political situation during that period. Even after the establishment of the ROC led by modernizers including Dr. Sun Yat-sen (孫逸仙, also known as Sun Wen, 孫文), the political situation across China was consistently unstable. The ROC was founded on January 1, 1912, and after Dr. Sun Yat-sen's short provisional presidency, the political power was given to Yuan Shikai (袁世凱), who aspired to become an emperor, not an elected president. After Yuan's death in 1916, China was in extreme political turmoil. Warlords, or Junfa (軍閥), endeavored to hold power in different provinces in China, and only after 1928 when the Nationalist Party (or *Kuomintang*, 国民党) officially unified the entire mainland China did China enter a period of short-term peace (Waldron, 1991).

Dr. Sun Yat-sen, founder of modern China, argued for Three People's Principles: nationalism, democracy, and people's livelihood. Sun's ideas can be broadly

---

[2]This change is also attributed to the collapse of the Qing Dynasty after the Xinhai Revolution (辛亥革命) or the Chinese Revolution of 1911.

summarized as (1) the development of Chinese nationalism, (2) freedom from the rule of the Manchurian Qing Dynasty and all foreign powers, and (3) support for democracy. A group of patriotic scholars accepted these principles and became Sun's avid supporters. It is noteworthy that Dr. Sun and most of these young scholars studied abroad in the USA. According to Adamson (2004, p. 29), "the ideas of Thomas Huxley, John Dewey, Bertrand Russell, Paul Monroe, Adam Smith, and Charles Darwin" influenced these Chinese scholars and quickly replaced the role of traditional Confucianism. As these English scholars profoundly influenced these modernizers, the Republican government decided to emulate the U.S. education system across China in 1922.

The adoption of the U.S. education system in 1922 is also closely related to the so-called New Cultural Movement (新文化運動). Intellectuals and youths in metropolitan China increasingly began to challenge traditions such as arranged marriages and supported Western lifestyles and thoughts. These young intelligentsias enthusiastically supported individualism, societal liberation, and gender equality, and universities in China offered courses and lectures on Western-influenced subjects such as communism and anarchism. Writers including Lu Xun, Ba Jin, and Hu Shih published novels and essays promoting Western liberalism and criticizing the absurdity of traditional Chinese social customs. However, the New Cultural Movement is not thought to have directly influenced most working-class Chinese; only the metropolitan upper class was influenced.

During the Republican Era, the May Fourth Movement (五四運動) in 1919 is also worth mentioning because language was one of its central issues. The first debate addressed whether the classic or traditional form of the Chinese language should be used at school. The result was that instead of the traditional form or *wenyan* (文言), which lasted 2000 years, the natural, simplified, and vernacular Chinese language, or *baihua* (白話), should be instructed. The second debate considered the role of English in China. As was often conducted during the Qing Dynasty and in the following era of the communist People's Republic of China (PRC) in 1949, the role of foreign language, mainly English, in China was hotly debated. The U.S. education system was regarded as the model system for the government, and English (or in rare cases another foreign language) was one of the core three subjects (i.e., Chinese, math, and English) at secondary schools. However, despite this prevalence of English education, conservative scholars raised concerns about the "pernicious influence of English upon Chinese culture" (Adamson, 2004, p. 30). More radical conservatives argued for the abolition of English education, particularly at the elementary school level, because all education at that level should center on cultivating patriotic and efficient citizenship, and English education was regarded as unrelated to the cause.

5.1.6.2 English as a Symbol of Affluence: Instrumental Motivation

The New Cultural Movement in the late 1910s and early 1920s involved conservatives' anti-Western beliefs, which were related to the concerns about corrupting

Chinese culture and traditions. The Nationalist Party, which assumed political power under the leadership of Chiang Kai-shek, did not have a consistent policy in English education. Thus, due to the conservative criticisms leveled against English education after the May Fourth Movement, the American educational model was quickly discarded.

The latter half of the Republican era was represented by the Nationalist Party's conservative trends. The Nationalist Party, which assumed control of mainland China in 1928, soon embarked on educational reform but met with two grave challenges (Adamson, 2004). First, the tension between old and new was ongoing. Traditional ideas of Chinese spirit versus new Western philosophies and lifestyles acted like a pendulum. As shown in the New Cultural Movement, if the radical Western intellectuals were in control, the conservatives soon reacted vehemently to preserve old Chinese traditions often associated with the idea of self-cultivation and self-reliance. Second, the lack of educational investment was another hurdle in introducing educational reform under the Nationalist government of the 1920s and 1930s. Moreover, the remaining warlords in China, Imperial Japan's invasion of Manchuria in 1931, and the subsequent skirmishes and Second Sino-Japanese War (July 7, 1937–September 2, 1945) further complicated modern education in China. During this period of stagnation in modern education, the traditional Confucian schools remained operational in most remote areas.

However, by the second half of the Republican Era, English was increasingly regarded as a tool for affluence and cultural savviness among the Chinese general public at a time when the Nationalist Party prioritized U.S. diplomatic ties. Particularly, the aggravating military conflict with the Japanese army, which created Manchukuo (滿洲國), the de facto "puppet state" controlled by Japan, prompted the ROC to seek U.S. support. The three Soong sisters, educated in a girls' academy managed by Western missionaries, were instrumental to this diplomatic process. Two of them, Ailing and Meiling, married Chiang Kai-shek, the supreme leader of the Nationalist Party, and Chingling married Dr. Sung Yat-sen. Their active roles as first ladies during the Republican Era often garnered newspaper coverage. Their superb English proficiency was the envy of the Chinese public. As previously mentioned, China's Western-style schools established in the nineteenth and twentieth centuries functioned as windows to the industrialized nations, and the wealthy upper Chinese class often enrolled their children in these missionary schools to prepare them to study overseas. The Soong sisters exemplified Chinese attitudes toward English learning.

Therefore, two antithetical opinions existed toward English instruction: positive and negative, progressive and conservative, West-oriented and traditional China-oriented. These two opposing opinions were also reflected in the English education policy during the Republican Era. In the 1910s and 1920s, the Western structure, represented by the U.S. educational system, was embraced in the government policy. However, from the mid-1920s, the Republican government gradually turned conservative and emphasized patriotic, self-reliant education. The reasons for this change seemed complicated, but the retrospective trends upholding the pure Chinese spirit were at its core.

Nonetheless, in the latter half during the Republican Era, the general public's favorable attitudes toward English should not be ignored. Adamson (2004, p. 31) succinctly summarized the atmosphere surrounding English education during this era as follows:

> For some, knowledge of English offered social advancement as a mark of education, to the outrage of some members of the aristocracy (Borthwick, 1982). Lower down the social scale, a smattering of English still represented a passport to employment in the treaty ports, albeit in humble positions.

The emergence of the Chinese Communist Party (CCP, 中国共产党) and its ambivalent attitudes toward English learning are also worth mentioning. Soon after the Anti-Japanese War ignited by the Second Sino-Chinese War, particularly after the end of World War II in Asia and after imperial Japan's unconditional surrender to the Allied Forces, the CCP and the Nationalist Party started the Chinese Civil War. Both the CCP led by Mao Zedong and the Nationalist Party by Chiang Kai-shek actively endeavored to gain support from the USA. The CCP needed official U.S. recognition that it was the Chinese people's legitimate regime. The Nationalist Party needed practical military help from the USA, which was a continuation of the U.S. implicit support for the Anti-Japanese War. U.S. President Roosevelt did not opt for either political party but was "generally even-handed when the two political groups first emerged as potential governors of postwar China" (Adamson, 2004, p. 31). Both Zhou Enlai of the CCP and Chiang Kai-shek of the Nationalist Party could communicate with U.S. officials in English to vie for political hegemony.

U.S. ambivalence toward the antithetical political regimes gradually declined and after the Yalta meeting in 1945, the USA made a strategic decision to support Chiang Kai-shek's Nationalist Party. This decision became the source of the 1950s anti-English movement after the establishment of the PRC.

5.1.7 Political Hegemony in English Education in the Reign of Mao Zedong: From 1949 to 1976

The introduction of English in the previous era drastically changed after the PRC's establishment in October 1949. Even after the communist government was established, the focus of education for several years after 1949 was first language and literacy education for the public (Adamson, 2004). Notably, in the early 1950s, the popularity of English rapidly declined for complicated political reasons. First, the relationship with the USA was not amicable because of the ideological disparity between the PRC and the USA. The decamped Nationalist Party maintained robust diplomatic ties with the USA, which prompted the USA's economic sanction toward the PRC in the early 1950s. In this political turmoil, it was regarded as "unpatriotic" to learn the language of an enemy (Adamson, 2004). Instead, Russian replaced English with governmental support in the early 1950s.

The active promotion of the Russian language was apparently due to the Soviet Union and PRC's ideological similarities. In 1954, the PRC ordered that only Russian be instructed in secondary schools nationwide (Bolton & Graddol, 2012). However, due to the need to translate and interpret English into Chinese and to support the PRC's nation-building process, English education could not be entirely banned. Even immediately after the establishment of the PRC in 1949, the Chinese government was still aware of the practicality of English, including as the medium to gain international recognition for the PRC. At the individual level, foreign scholars and journalists sympathetic to the communist regime persisted in China. Thus, at the official, surface level, English instruction was banned as the language of U.S. imperialism, but at the practical level, English education was not and could not be banned. By 1957, the Ministry of Education in China announced that "junior secondary schools would teach either English or Russian," and "the target ratio of schools offering Russian to those offering English would be 1:1" (Adamson, 2004, p. 37). The political tension did not allow any importation of English-language books or other written materials from Western nations. Thus, in English education during the 1950s, teachers mostly relied on the old English textbooks from the Nationalist Party regime of the 1940s (Adamson, 2004). Thus, systematic English education during the 1950s had practical difficulties, making Russian education the preferred option.

The emphasis on the Russian language continued for almost a decade, and in the 25 years of Russian instruction from 1945 to 1969, it took the place of first foreign language for 7.8% of secondary school foreign language instruction worldwide (Lo Bianco, 2009). The surge of Russian reflected the influence of the Cold War. Lo Bianco (2009, p. 3) states as follows:

> The appearance of Russian reflects Soviet hegemony in Eastern Europe and the communist countries of Asia, especially China (Wen & Hu, 2007) but also Cambodia, Laos, North Korean, and Vietnam.

However, as the Soviet Union and PRC's political conflict escalated in the early 1960s, the foreign language situation reversed. Teachers of Russian were re-trained as English teachers. The pedagogical doctrines influenced by the Soviet Union rapidly disappeared and grassroots indigenous methodology in foreign language instruction gradually replaced Soviet pedagogy. Furthermore, the political situation in China presented a different educational atmosphere. The early 1960s could be regarded as a renaissance period in Chinese politics; political radicals including Mao Zedong were under tremendous pressure to prioritize economic development (Adamson, 2004).

Reflecting the changing Chinese political situation, innovations in English textbooks and instruction emerged. First, to determine the appropriate length of schooling and curricular content, a National Cultural and Educational Conference was held in the summer of 1960 (Adamson, 2004). The conference revised English education including the 5-year English curriculum (i.e., 3 years' junior secondary and 2 years' senior secondary school) during China's 10-year schooling system.

The aim of English education during this era was twofold: (1) the use of colloquial English, and (2) the ability to read professional English-language publications (Adamson, 2004). Additionally, the political agenda contained in the previous decade's reading passages were remarkably reduced after criticism for sacrificing language content for political propaganda.

Although innovative, the 10-year schooling curriculum soon faced numerous challenges across China. The old 12-year system was still appreciated in rural areas, and the new 10-year schooling system could only be implemented in Beijing and limited areas where students' educational standards could cope with such changes. Thus, in the subsequent 1963 curriculum that reverted to the 12-year system, university scholars convened to collect international trends in language education. The Ministry of Education in China reviewed Japanese, U.S., and U.K. educational systems, and it was decided that "oracy as well as literacy should be stressed, and that the syllabus and teaching materials should be carefully graded according to linguistic complexity" (Adamson, 2004, p. 92).

The slow but gradual progress in English education was severely hindered by Mao Zedong's 1966 Cultural Revolution. Understandably, public education was affected by the nation's political decision, but the English education during the Cultural Revolution was the most severely affected by political propaganda (Adamson, 2004). When the political tension between the CCP's hardcore ideologists and the utilitarian economists came to the fore, Mao supported the former. Lasting over a decade, the Cultural Revolution was the longest-lasting political movement in China's history, and its impact on academia, particularly on English education, was catastrophic. Mao ordered the formation of *hong weibing* (紅衛兵), or the Red Guards out of vanguard students to purify the negative capitalist influences and remaining feudal traditions in Chinese society. Mao defined the role of the Red Guards as follows:

> While the students' main task is to study, they should also learn other things, that is to say, they should not only learn book knowledge, they should also learn industrial production, agricultural production, and military affairs. They should also criticize and repudiate the bourgeoisie. The length of schooling should be shortened, education should be revolutionized, and the domination of our schools and colleges by bourgeoisie intellectuals should not be tolerated any longer. (Löfstedt, 1980, p. 124 cited in Adamson, 2004, p. 108)

The side effects were disastrous, especially from 1966 to 1968. During this initial period of the revolution, anyone who supposedly supported capitalism or Western ideas could be punished and were forcibly remove to remote rural areas for hard labor as an opportunity to learn the value of communist virtue and the proletarian way of life. In particular, English teachers were the primary target for this movement because they were seen as the symbol of capitalist vice smothering the human mind. Thus, they were severely criticized, eradicated, and persecuted across mainland China for the initial 3 years.

In this atmosphere, English education could not be properly conducted. Moreover, the plan for educational reform directed by the Central Committee of the CCP in 1967 ordered a total curriculum reconstruction. All current foreign language textbooks were banned and were required to be rewritten to include Mao Zedong's anti-capitalistic ideas. People's Education Press (PEP), which is under the direct leadership of the Ministry of Education in China, was shut down during this period. Not only English but all school subjects faced grave changes to their assessment and educational standards. As the most important criteria for evaluation and advancement in school was not the students' knowledge in the subject but their ideological suitability, students' actual knowledge was never assessed. Based on students' ideological loyalty, they were assigned to the university. No entrance exam or academic interviews were conducted.

The atmosphere of fear and persecution, however, suddenly changed when Mao expressed favorable attitude toward learning English in his public speech directed toward Red Guard leaders at Beijing University in 1968. Given the top-down state-controlled system in China, Mao's view was quickly spread over China, and accordingly, English education was gradually reinstated at the turn of the 1970s.

The rediscovered value of English was also supported by the detente between the PRC and the USA in the early 1970s. The USA finally recognized the PRC as an official member of the United Nations, and this meant that the PRC replaced Taiwan's position (Lam, 2002). While having diplomatic relations with Western countries, the PRC had so-called "ping-pong diplomacy" with the USA, which led to U.S. President Richard Nixon's state visit to China in 1972. Such a changing atmosphere benefitted English education in China, as did Premier Zhou Enlai's directive in 1972. Due to Zhou's directive, school exams, particularly university-entrance exams, were reinstated, which meant that students' English proficiency, not ideological loyalty, became the criteria for school assessment and the university selection process. In this renaissance period, PEP remained shut down, and local curriculum and textbook developers initiated producing English textbooks.

However, unfortunately, the educational renaissance during the Cultural Revolution was short-lived. Instead of the aging Mao, the so-called Gang of Four (四人帮), a new group of radical ideological conservatives, gained control of the communist party in 1973, sparking the Great Education Debate in 1974–1976. The debate demonstrated the victory of the conservative ideologists over practical pragmatists in the CCP. Under this drastic social change, English education was suppressed again.

Throughout the decade-long Cultural Revolution, English education was in great peril; in most cases, its instruction and instructors were severely persecuted, and in rare cases, particularly during the detente between the PRC and the USA, it was promoted, albeit not to the same degree of enthusiasm as before the Cultural Revolution. The death of Mao Zedong in September 1976 and the arrest and execution of the Gang of Four officially ended the Cultural Revolution. English education in the next generation began with more practical but still had a centralized focus.

5.1.8   Inauguration of Deng Xiaoping and the Open Door Policy from 1978 to the 1980s

Even after Mao's death and the execution of the Gang of Four, there was not an immediate change in English education in China. First, in 1977, the university entrance exam and enrollment for higher education were reinstated. However, the tragic aftermath of the Cultural Revolution remained even after the English language curriculum was published in 1978 and continued until 1982. The re-established PEP created new English textbooks, but due to the uncertainty of curriculum directives, systematic implementation of the 1978 new English curriculum was delayed. In January 1978, the Ministry of Education in China finally announced that the instruction of English and other foreign languages was to be reinstated in September. The new PEP textbooks were geared toward propagating economic modernization after the Cultural Revolution. Compared with the previous curriculum, the 1978 English curriculum emphasized political agenda less (e.g., the eulogy for Chairman Hua Guofeng, the successor of Mao Zedong) and instead, focused on moral messages (Adamson, 2004).

In 1978, Deng Xiaoping announced the Policy of Four Modernizations: to modernize agriculture, industry, science and technology, and defense. This policy is regarded as a predecessor of China's Open Door Policy (Lam, 2002). Cordial U.S. diplomatic relations were further expedited during this period. For example, in December 1978, the exchange of ambassadors was announced, and Deng visited the USA (Adamson, 2004).

After Deng's reign, English, as well as other foreign languages, was consistently emphasized, for it was considered crucial supporting the foreign trade and tourism (Lam, 2002). For example, English was officially recognized as the dominant foreign language in secondary school in 1982, and the first international conference on English language teaching was held in Guangzhou in 1985 (Lam, 2002). Since the Open Door Policy resulted in economic prosperity, particularly in major cities and coastal cities designated as Special Economic Zones, the need for English had skyrocketed. Translators and interpreters were in high demand in the Chinese economy. Mass media, such as TV and radio, also significantly contributed to the widespread boom for English education. English fever in China in the late 1970s and the early 1980s was conspicuous. In Tang Lixing's written recollection, he wrote:

> English learning has become a mania for the nation. Television courses, radio lessons, part-time or night schools have offered an almost unlimited variety of educational opportunities for people to learn English or further their education. The CCTV [China Central Television], for example, has been running a series of English programmes for beginners, intermediate learners, English teachers, ESP [English for specific purposes] learners, and even children, Three most popular TV programmes nowadays are "Sunday English", "Follow Me (BBC)", and "Ying Ying Learns English" (for children). (Tang, 1983, p. 45, cited in Adamson, 2004, p. 131)

As the above excerpt shows, the English learning situation in 1980 was remarkable. The economic reform experienced steady growth with the influx of foreign funds. The political stability in the 1980s also contributed to the exponential interest in English learning. Deng Xiaoping, who assumed political power after Hua Guofeng, Mao's de facto successor, continued the Open Door Policy, which further brought economic prosperity from major cities into even remote areas in China. In response to China's changing political and economic prospects, the PEP revised the previous English curriculum in 1982. Compared with previous generations, the 1982 curriculum was designed and tested for a relatively long time. Experts from the Beijing Foreign Languages Institute were invited as consultants, and competent textbook writers who were trained in the U.K. participated in the textbook design. Political themes were removed, and more listening and speaking activities were included. Considering this, the 1982 English textbook advanced toward diverse teaching methods and learning content. A new educational reform for the 1982 curriculum was the development of multi-track education, particularly the establishment of key secondary schools for elite education. Thus, the 1982 English textbooks were made considering different educational gaps between average and key secondary schools. Adamson (2004) summarized the English curriculum during this period as follows:

> New features of this phase include the amalgamation of a range of pedagogical approaches, and a gradual depoliticization of contents, marked by a defrosting in the portrayal of Western societies. These changes can be attributed to two factors: to the role of the outside agencies, the specialists in top institutions in China, who had knowledge of different approaches to English Language teaching around the world; and to the less stringent political restraints of the Dengist era, which made it acceptable to appropriate pedagogical ideas from Western countries and economically desirable to promote cross-cultural understandings. (p. 168)

However, it should be noted that at the tertiary level, the primary focus of English education was not oral skills but still grammar and translation. After the Open Door Policy was implemented, the Ministry of Education issued two national syllabi for college English courses in 1985 for students of science and engineering and in 1986 for students of social sciences and humanities (Li, 2017). Both syllabi placed significant focus on reading skills and vocabulary development. Given the practical use of English, it was assumed that the most necessary skills for the Chinese college students were receptive reading proficiency with accurate knowledge in English vocabulary. Notably, for students in science and engineering, translation skills were also emphasized. Thus, although listening and speaking skills were emphasized in the 1980s, these had limited impact on Chinese students who were learning English and instead accurate understanding of English passage and translation skills were the primary objectives at the collegiate level.

5.1.9 The Liberation Policy in the 1990s

Despite internal struggles such as the June Fourth Incident in Beijing in 1989, Deng Xiaoping's Open Door Policy continued in the 1990s. China successfully hosted major international events, including the 1990s Asian Games and the 1995

International Women's Conference. Additionally, their efforts to host the Summer Olympic Games began, which finally succeeded with the 2008 Beijing Olympics. Through the increased international economic collaboration, China also entered the World Trade Organization (WTO) in November 2001. To expedite hosting these international major events, the government encouraged English instruction (Bolton & Graddol, 2012).

The liberation policy spearheaded in the 1990s resulted in three significant educational changes in China (Bolton, 2002). First, the official recognition of English as the most important foreign, if not second, language to learn in China was widespread, which was in accordance with the educational policy agenda expressed in the 1993 national syllabus. This 1993 syllabus, although not explicitly stating the role of the English language, acknowledged that a foreign language was an essential tool for interacting with other countries and emphasized that many people should "acquire command of one or more foreign languages" to "accelerate socialist modernization" (Adamson & Morris, 1997, p. 21). Following this national direction, English consolidated its status as a de facto first foreign language. Second, the liberalization and Open Door Policy resulted in the so-called English fever in China. A growing number of private English institutions were burgeoning in major cities. Li Yang, a national celebrity for his innovative English learning method called "Crazy English," also contributed to the rapid spread of English education in China (Bolton, 2002). Additionally, English-language media including small publication companies, newspapers, magazines, and the China Central Television Station (CCTV) were established and thrived. Third, overseas study in English-speaking countries increased. *The People's Daily* (人民日報), an official newspaper of the Central Committee of the Communist Party of China, estimated that between 1978 and 2000 approximately 400,000 Chinese students went overseas to pursue a higher academic degree, and 110,000 of them returned to China (Bolton, 2002; Yan, 2001). It is a noticeable increase compared to the study abroad population from 1847 to 1953; for more than a century, it was estimated that only 50,000 Chinese students had studied in the USA. However, according to *The New York Times*, in the year of 2000 alone, 50,000 Chinese students were in the USA.

The comprehensive English instruction was not always appreciated by many learners in China. As presented in Chaps. 3 and 4, in the development of instrumental and competitive motivation surrounding English learning in South Korea, in China, students increasingly perceived that English was not mainly used for international communication but only for internal competition. In many cases, English tests were used to select the best students or job candidates, and English was accordingly perceived as serving for "social and economic mobility" (Zhao & Campbell, 1995, p. 385).

In some cases, the conservative movement, which prioritized "Chinese spirit," criticized the extraordinary influence of English in China. They often see the influence of foreign language as a contamination of the pure Chinese spirit and identity. Regarding such conservatism, Li (2015) stated the following:

Meanwhile, some Chinese scholars have expressed concerns over the 'contamination' of the Chinese language by foreign languages and 'net language.' When the 6th edition of the authoritative *Modern Chinese Dictionary* was published in 2012, there was a public outcry over the inclusion of the so-called 'alphabetic words,' words that contain abbreviations of English phrases such as MP4, GDP, and FTA. Some threatened to sue the compilers of the dictionary and the publisher for violating the law that gives the Chinese language special protection. Yet, the media seem to be happily embracing such terms and the new net language... (Li, 2015, Para 6)

Given the past history of English education in China, it is unsurprising to find such a conservative movement to purify the Chinese spirit. For example, in the 1980s, soon after Deng Xiaoping expedited the Open Door Policy, the Campaign against Spiritual Pollution was initiated, targeting "vices such as pornography, gambling, prostitution and even disco dancing, which were portrayed as slipping into China through the open door of international trade" (Adamson, 2004).

The widening gap between the rich and the poor in the socialist nation fueled the purification movement in China. The influence of elite private schools in China has been exponential (Deng, 1997). English education has primarily been the focus of this attention. Although the government discouraged employing native English-speaking teachers for the general public education, private sector language institutes could successfully invite such foreign teachers. In some cases, private primary or secondary schools affiliated with foreign investors provided excellent English education while charging an extraordinarily high tuition fees to students and parents of the wealthy upper class in China. As of 1997, "Jinghua Primary School in Beijing . . . charged each new student 14,000-yuan tuition plus a one-time capitalization fee of 30,000 yuan. . . . Zhonghua Yinghao School in Guangzhou asked for an entrance fee of 300,000 yuan, which was refundable upon graduation" (Deng, 1997, p. 132). To the average Chinese, such tuition was infeasible, but to the wealthy social class who benefitted from the 1970s Open Door Policy, private education was not regarded as a severe problem.

5.1.10   The Implementation of the College English Test (CET) in China

English education's current situation in China seems similar to that in South Korea. The total hours of public English education in elementary, junior high, and high schools are 1098 (Park, 2017). Each semester is composed of 21 weeks, and one academic year has 42 weeks. Similar to South Korea, a class is 40 min for elementary school, 45 for junior high school, and 50 for high school. Public English education starts in grade 3 elementary schools and lasts for 10 years.

The most distinctive feature of public education in China is the administration of the College English Test (CET) for most university graduates. Although the Ministry of Education of Korea strictly controls English education in South Korea, such control from the nation does not regulate the university admission and graduation process. English test and English requirements are not established by the South Korean government. Instead, individual universities and employers set a minimum level of English proficiency for graduation or employment requirements.

Conversely, the CET is a large-scale, nationwide high-stakes test administered by the Ministry of Education in China twice annually (June and December). The purpose of CET is to "examine the English proficiency of undergraduate students in China and ensure that Chinese undergraduates reach the required English levels" (Zheng & Cheng, 2008, p. 408). In 2017 alone, approximately 10 million university students took the CET level 4 or 6 (Gu, 2018). Since the CET is recognized across virtually all Chinese higher institutions and companies, it is increasingly perceived as a crucial requirement for graduation and employment in China. The CET has two standards: CET 4 and CET 6. Most universities require students to acquire the CET 4 level, which is considered general level, but depending on academic major or for graduate students, the higher standard of CET 6 level is required (Gu, 2018). Gu (2018, para 4) succinctly summarized the major modifications in the CET as follows:

> In the 31 years since its introduction in 1987, the CET has gone through several revisions. In 1999, the spoken English test (CET-SET) was added. In 2006, the proportion of the listening test was increased to 35 percent from 20 percent. During the reforms of 2012, the spoken test was given by computer for the first time. The structures of CET 4 and CET 6 have been completely aligned since December 2013. These changes aimed at emphasizing the test's speaking and listening components and strengthening the practical application of the English language in learning and professional environments.

Although the CET has sometimes been criticized because test takers can acquire a higher score after learning test-taking skills, in general, this government-initiated English test has contributed to improving Chinese students' English proficiency. Moreover, due to the competition among the provinces and major cities across China, a higher score in the CET is increasingly required for bachelor's degree's graduation requirement. However, misuse or arbitrary use of the CET has also been reported. In residential permit applications, the CET score has reportedly been required. Additionally, in some school districts where the quality of education is higher than others, the CET score is sometimes required even prior to students' starting their tertiary education (Gu, 2018).

The use of CET in China emphasizes the use of the exam for internal stratification. To select the best candidate for tertiary education and employment, stakeholders often use English tests including CET, and in this regard, English learning in China does not seem to serve the purpose of communication with English as lingua franca. Regarding this, Bolton and Graddol (2012) stated that we should be cautious in investigating the number of English learners in China because it may oversimplify the situation to say that 416 million Chinese people studied English around 2000 (Wei & Su, 2012). They criticized this view as follows:

> However, one important finding derived from the survey is that the numbers of people who actually find a significant use for English in their daily lives is a small fraction of the total that had studied the language, with a mere 7% reporting that they 'often' use the language, compared with 23% for 'sometimes', and 69% for 'seldom.' In contrast to such Outer Circle, English-using societies in Asia as India, Malaysia, Singapore, and the Philippines, it seems

that the use of English in China is restricted to a small number of domains. (Bolton & Graddol, 2012, p. 7)

5.1.11   Newest Trends in English Learning in China

In a featured article in the *South China Morning Post*, Bermingham and Wang (2019) reported that the returnee students who were educated mostly in English-speaking countries are not welcomed as they were in previous years. As the Chinese economy slows, *haigui* (海龜, literally "sea turtle") overseas-trained youth are no longer seen as holding a significant advantage over locally educated employees. As indicated by the prevalence of CET above, for decades, CET is mandated for many Chinese university graduates, and their English proficiency skills have increased compared with previous generations. Recent statistics showed that in the 40 years since the Open Door Policy was implemented in 1978, a total of 3.13 million or 83.73% of the overseas-trained Chinese students have returned to China. In 2017 alone, according to the Ministry of Education in China, 480,900 Chinese overseas-trained students returned to their homeland, an 11.19% increase from the previous year. Moreover, nearly half of them had a master's and doctoral degree, which is a 14.9% increase from the previous year.

These statistics indicate that English proficiency only does not place *haigui* students in the top spot in their employment market. As the Chinese economy and science technology have nearly or already caught up to Western competitors such as the U.S. and the U.K., the *haiguis* also face fierce competition to be employed. For more than 40 years, in general, the term, *haigui*, has been synonymous with social elites. It is because, after the initiation of the Open Door Policy, Deng Xiaoping decided to send Chinese students overseas to acquire new science and technology. Deng's strategy was successful in that many *haiguis* significantly contributed to shaping modern China. Talented returnees' pioneering endeavors established many IT companies including *Sohu, Baidu*, and *Sina* (Bermingham & Wang, 2019). However, as the science technology and social structure within China rapidly sophisticated and modernized, the merit of employing these *haiguis* has declined. Further, potential employers in China have concerns about recruiting *haiguis* because they do not have secure Chinese networks despite their expert knowledge in their field. Thus, given the same skills in local students, Chinese companies, whether local or international, do not see benefits to hiring such returnees graduated from overseas, mostly English-speaking, universities.

Recent returnees to China become more selective in their university major in English-speaking countries (Zweig & Ge, 2018). When students selected the right major and their engagement in cooperative scholastic efforts was appropriate, their actual salary and satisfaction level increased. Nonetheless, this is not universal for undergraduate returnees, and therefore, economists at the Southwest University of Finance and Economics in Chengdu found that these returned undergrads' salary is not different from domestic students, and a master's degree increase salaries by merely 20% (Zweig & Ge, 2018).

As emphasized in the previous sections, learning English in China had often been linked to instrumental orientation (Gardner, 1985). The influence of the Imperial Examination, officially dismantled in 1905, appears to have continued, and it is now inherited in the learning of the English language. Both the Imperial Examination and English learning have been motivated by the practical worldly desire to achieve social recognition, wealth, power, and authority through language literacy and oracy. Because the English boom in mainland China was motivated by increased job opportunity, if it is not regarded as useful to this utilitarian purpose, the high demand for learning English in China may not endure. English had long been regarded as the language of the West where modern technology and science flourished after the industrial revolution. In the case of nineteenth century China, the continual defeat of the Qing Dynasty by Western nations resulted in China's humiliation in chartering its territory to these external nations. Even with intermittent resistance from traditional conservatives, the establishment of Tongwen Guan in the 1860s and its gradual replacement of the traditional Confucian test awakened the Chinese recognition of the importance of foreign language education, mainly English, as a means of self-strengthening. Similar perception of the English language as the essential tool for learning advanced technology and sciences continued even after the Open Door Policy had been fully enacted in the 1980s.

However, as illustrated by Bermingham and Wang (2019), if the value of acquiring advanced knowledge through this useful foreign language is now being outweighed by the domestic connections in technology and science fields, the need for English instruction may not continue. Moreover, rapid advancements of China as a world-leading nation vying for its ideological and economic hegemony with the USA, particularly after the COVID-19 pandemic, facilitated the need to learn the Chinese language from other nations. The Chinese government is also active in dispatching Chinese language teachers to other nations (Moore, 2001). All these new trends found in English education recently will present different prospects in China in the 2020s and beyond. The motivation to learn English as an instrument for academic and employment success may not remain the same given the current rise of China as the potential world leader.

5.2   The Case of Japan

5.2.1   The Transition from Old Education System in Japan from 1858 to 1945

In the traditional Japanese system, the nationwide examination for officer appointment was not held except for a very short period in the seventh century (Sujimoto & Okita, 2011). For approximately 700 years, the Japanese society had been ruled by a series of dominant *Samurai* clans, or shogunate, including the Minamoto (and Kamakura) shogunate (1192–1333), the Ashikaga shogunate (1336–1565), and the Tokugawa shogunate (1603–1867). Situating the emperor at the apex, de facto political power was placed on these shogunates. Particularly, the Sengoku Period (戦国時代), or Warring States Period, which lasted for more than a hundred years in the sixteenth century, strengthened the power of armed Samurai. Tokugawa Ieyasu (徳川 家康), the successor of Toyotomi Hideyoshi (豊臣 秀吉), who unified the Japanese islands and ended the Sengoku Period, had the total control of Japan under the aegis of the Japanese emperor and stabilized the Japanese islands.

The Tokugawa shogunate lasted more than 250 years when the role of Samurai has gradually changed. In the Sengoku Period, they practiced sophisticated martial finesse preparing for fierce battle, but in the time of peace, they rather focused on administration for the society. The Samurai class inherited and monopolized their social status and developed into rural barons. In every prefecture, a *Daimyo*, or feudal lord, was appointed by the Shogun in Edo (now Tokyo) and controlled the area. Thus, education in Tokugawa shogunate was conducted for the Samurai class while for other lower peasant, technician, and merchant classes, literacy education was not the Shogunate's primary concern. Sons of the Samurai class were educated in literacy related to the prefectural administration as well as basic martial arts such as fencing and archery.

It was Tokugawa Yoshinobu (徳川 吉宗, 1684–1751), the eighth shogun of the Tokugawa shogunate, who introduced literacy education to both the Samurai class and the other common classes (Sujimoto & Okita, 2011). To strengthen the traditional value and loyalty to the nation and shogunate, he focused on educating ethics and moral lessons to children and ordered all *Teranai* (手習), or feudal school, teachers to emphasize correcting customs, keeping social etiquettes, and bearing the value of loyalty and filial duty on children's mind, as well as teach literacy skills in March 1723. In the middle and late eighteenth century, the traditional, feudal education was widespread across many Japanese prefectures through the efforts of Confucian scholars (e.g., Bato Jishu, Koga Seiri, Shibano Ritsujan, Rai Shunjui) based in Osaka. The ethics education and basic literacy skills expanded to other social classes in the shogunate feudal Japan, but the education was mostly limited to spreading the state-controlled values related to neo-Confucianism, and in this regard, the education in Japan in the eighteenth century shares similarities with that of China and Korea. Another noteworthy point would be the strict classification of the social class. The ruling class was almost always the Samurai and the ruled classes were composed of farmers, merchants, and manufacturers. The literacy education with basic martial arts instruction mainly targeted the Samurai class, and the lower common people did not have sufficient, if any, educational opportunities.

Like the Joseon Dynasty in Korea, Japan, under the control of Tokugawa shogunate, closed their ports and did not exchange goods with nations other than China and the Netherlands. However, with the industrial revolution and the development of navigation skills, in 1808, a British battleship appeared in Nagasaki and threatened to open fire to the city. In the following year, the Tokugawa shogunate ordered Japanese officials who used Dutch for diplomatic and trading purposes to learn English to be ready for their future threats, and this is regarded as the first English education in Japan (Sasaki, 2008). Note, however, that this order in 1809 was neither related to systematic instruction at school nor focused on the youth in general.

Traditional feudal Japan started to be shaken by Commodore Matthew C. Perry (1795–1858) in 1853. For the U.S. government, the Japanese islands were the ideal location to open the Eastern trade market. Perry sailed to Tokyo Bay with a squadron of four U.S. *kurofune* (黒船), or black vessels, and requested the opening of the port and foreign exchange with the USA. Since the Tokugawa shogunate government maintained their alienation policy since 1683, Japan first vehemently refused that offer, but later accepted the diplomatic letter of the U.S. President Millard Fillmore. The USA and Japan co-signed the treaty in 1854 and opened the diplomatic relations in 1858.

Under this rapid social transition, the Tokugawa shogunate established the *Bansho Shirabesho* (蕃書調所), or the Public Institute for the Study of Barbarian Books, in 1858, which was renamed as *Yosho Sinrabesho* (洋書調所), the Institute for the Study of Western Books. In this institute, English was instructed as a school subject in 1860 for the first time in Japan (Sasaki, 2008). In the history of Japanese modernization, this institute held a unique status in that this was renamed *Kaiseisho* (開成所) in 1863, and under the Meiji Restoration in 1868, this became one of the predecessors which were later merged into the University of Tokyo. At the private level, Fukuzawa Yukichi (福澤 諭吉, 1835–1901), a Japanese writer, author, teacher, translator, entrepreneur, and educator, established a school for the western studies in October 1858, and this school became the predecessor of now Keio University (慶應義塾大学). Fujuzawa's school is considered the first private English school in Japan (Kim, 2009).

It is noteworthy that the English education conducted during this period was not provided to all Japanese youths. Only children from the traditional Samurai class or upper middle (or above) class had the chance to learn English at *Bansho Shirabesho*, a situation which continued until 1872 when the Meiji government, established after the Meiji Restoration which restored the political power from the Tokugawa shogunate to the Japanese emperor, promulgated the Education System Order (Sasaki, 2008). This order was revolutionary in that the Meiji government endeavored to establish eight national universities, 256 middle schools, and 53,760 elementary schools across the Japanese islands. Although English was taught to none of the elementary school students, in 1886, the law mandated that all Japanese children receive at least 4 years of elementary school education, and the duration of the elementary school education extended into 6 years in 1911. English instruction started at the secondary school level (i.e., middle school), and only 20% of Japanese elementary students could advance to the 5-year-long middle school before 1945 (Yamamoto, 2004).

The main characteristic of English education, as well as the learning of so-called Western studies, was utilitarianism. The Japanese Ministry of Education founded in 1871 established 6 years of elementary school education, which were mandatory, 5 years of boys' middle school or technical school, and 4 or 5 years of girls' middle school. After middle school education, various 2-year technical colleges and 4-year comprehensive universities followed. The education system placed the 4-year comprehensive national universities atop, and at the bottom, various mandatory elementary schools were located. This means that at the time of modernization in Japan in the late nineteenth century, most university graduates were employed in government positions or offered high-ranking occupations immediately after their graduation with the assumption that they have learned necessary skills for the reformation of the traditional Japanese society (Sujimoto & Okita, 2011).

In understanding Japan's English education policy, it is important that the fundamental attitude of the Japanese government was to maximize the effectiveness of Japan's accelerated modernization under the slogan of "Enrich the country, strengthen the military" (富国強兵). English education, in this case, became the most essential tool to import the advanced technology of the west. The establishment of the *Yosho Shirabesho*, the Institute for the Study of Western Books, can be understood from this point of view. The fundamental assumptions of the establishment of a private English school by Fukuzawa Yukichi in 1858 and the public English education at the *Yosho Shirabesho* in 1860 would be that the rapid dissemination of Western knowledge was of utmost importance and for this purpose, translation from English to Japanese would be prerequisite. Thus, intensive English instruction targeting selected few elites resulted in training English-Japanese translators. Additionally, given the limited opportunities for average people to travel abroad, communication-focused English education was not the priority.

In this sociocultural milieu, the introduction of the Grammar-Translation Method (GTM) must have been the natural consequence (Sasaki, 2008). To translate the original English texts in Japanese precisely, it would be necessary to have proficiency in reading comprehension with the extensive vocabulary and grammatical knowledge. Therefore, the GTM was particularly favored in Japan, and this love of grammar and vocabulary without oral and aural skills in English was also transmitted into the colonized Korea in the early twentieth century.

The GTM practiced in Japan has its cultural lineage of teaching Chinese as a written form ever since the eighth century (Sasaki, 2008). Practice and memorization of classical Chinese Confucian scriptures were widely thought to develop or "cultivate" young students' minds, which was the same in the instruction of Latin and classical Greek through the GTM across Europe (Howatt, 2004). Most Japanese people believed that the GTM was effective "forcing [children] to analyze the differences between Chinese and their mother tongue" (Sasaki, 2008, p. 66). Given this, the dominance of the GTM in English education after Japan opened its society to the western world in the mid-nineteenth century would be attributable to both the zeal toward modernization through rapid dissemination of western knowledge originally written in English and the cultural heritage of cultivating young minds. Also, as early as the Meiji Period, the entrance examinations to advanced schools in Japan adopted translation questions from English to Japanese (Koike & Tanaka, 1995).

However, a few modernists strongly supported the use of English in Japan. For example, Mori Arinori (森 有礼, 1847–1889), a social reformer and the first

Japanese minister of education was the open advocate of English use. He was born to the son of samurai in Kagoshima prefecture, studied abroad in London in 1865, and moved to the States in 1867 where he became Christian. After working as the ambassador to the U.K., he was appointed as the minister of education in 1885. Based on his western experience, he advocated adopting English as the national language in Japan. His arguments were based on two factors. First, it is imperative to adopt English and abolish Chinese to develop civilization. Second, given the limited natural resources in Japan, it is important for Japan to become the hub nation of international trades, and for this, it is important to adopt English which is the main language of foreign exchange (Kim, 2009). Although Mori's proposal did not come to realization due to his assassination in 1889 by an ultranationalist on the same day of promulgation of the Japanese Constitution by the Meiji Government, his English-only proposal represents the desire to use English as the prime tool for expediting the modernization and enlightenment in Japan.

Compared with Mori's radical proposal, a more moderate method to teach English to Japanese was tried in the 1920s. It was to invite British scholars to Japan and have them teach English through English. Kojiro Matsukata, an entrepreneur who "were educated in America and France and considered a working knowledge of English to be an asset" (Yamamoto, 1978, p. 151), persuaded the minister of education and provided financial support from 1922. Thus, with the form of the Japanese government's invitation, a group of British scholars visited Japan. For example, Dr. Harold Palmer, a lecturer on spoken English at University College London, was invited as an advisor to the Japanese Ministry of Education and stayed in Japan from 1922 to 1936 (Smith, 2013). He established the Institute for Research in English Teaching (IRET) in Tokyo in 1923 and endeavored to enhance Japanese students' pronunciation and oral skills in English. According to Yamamoto (1978), "the aim of IRET were as follows: (1) to compile materials for English-language courses, (2) to encourage reforms in language-teaching methods, (3) to start research and experimental work in linguistic subjects, and (4) to train teachers of English by means of lectures and demonstration classes" (pp. 152–153).

With Dr. Palmer's continuous efforts, Japanese teachers of English showed the willingness to use different innovative methods while "engaging in innovative demonstrative lessons at the annual Institute Conventions" (Smith, 2013, p. 2). IRET was a pioneering institute for English education in Japan given that the proposal to establish a similar institute in the U.K. was rejected by the U.K. government in the 1920s and 1930s. Palmer's teaching method called "oral method" made a remarkable contribution to language education in Japan. For example, Rinshiro Ishikawa, a Japanese professor and scholar, adopted Palmer's method at the Tokyo Higher Normal School (東京高等師範学校) and spread his method throughout Japan (Yamamoto, 1978). Additionally, Naganuma Naoe (長沼 直兄, 1894–1973), influenced by Palmer's oral method, established the Institute for Research in Linguistic Culture in 1947 and the Tokyo School of Japanese Language (東京日本語学校) or simply known as "The Naganuma School" in 1948.

Another remarkable contribution of the IRET in Japan is the work of A. S. Hornby. Palmer's successor at the Institute, Hornby published an English dictionary, entitled *Advanced Learners' Dictionary*, initially conceived and developed as the IRET's research project. The dictionary was published in Tokyo in 1941 and reprinted while renaming its titles into *A Learner's Dictionary of Current English* (1948) and *An Advanced Learner's Dictionary of Current English* (1952) (Kim, 2009). In the English education in Japan, the two British scholars made a remarkable contribution, and in particular, Hornby's English dictionary gradually gained scholastic popularity and was also imported to South Korea and other parts around the world in the mid-twentieth century.

It should be re-emphasized that the strenuous effort to invite English-speaking foreign scholars and the establishment of *Bansho Shirabesho*, English school or Keio University, and the IRET were all directed toward making Japan, as a nation, stronger and expedite the process of modern industrialization.

5.2.2 Resistance to the English Boom in the Early Twentieth Century

As mentioned in previous sections, it was imperative for the Japanese to learn English and import the knowledge of the Western world to Japan to strengthen the nation. The central reform ignited by the Meiji Restoration succeeded, and the consecutive victories in the Sino-Japanese War (1894–1895) and the Russo-Japanese War (1904–1905) were regarded as proof of success in the national reform toward industrialization. However, unfortunately, the result of successful reformation of the nation as a modern developed country was to follow the same step as the Western imperialism where European and American nations colonized "less-developed" Asian and African nations. Japan, as a rising new world power, held total control over Taiwan in 1895 and of Korea in 1910 and started to colonize these neighboring Asian countries (Okano, 2011).

Historically, Japan had been greatly influenced by her neighboring countries such as China and Korea (Koike & Tanaka, 1995). The ancient civilization, initiated from China, was transmitted to Japan via Korea (McKenzie, 2010). The unidirectional flow of oriental civilization from China, then Korea, and to Japan lasted more than a thousand years, and it was a typical attitude to learn the Chinese way but adapting it creatively to the situation in Japan. This is epitomized as the phrase as Wakon-Kansai (和魂漢才: Japanese spirit and Chinese scholarship). This traditional motto was also succeeded as Wakon-Yosai (和魂洋才: Japanese spirit and western scholarship) in process of modernization in the nineteenth century, and even as Wakon-Beisai (和魂米才: Japanese spirit and American scholarship) (Ota, 2011).

The above practical orientation toward new advanced civilization or technology was equally applied to English instruction in the nineteenth century. Their basic stance was that it would be best to learn the language of the advanced Western world to directly import their technology and cultural heritage. Once it was completed, then it would be better to focus on the uniqueness of Japan with the support of the West.

As the Meiji Restoration made Japan as a modern nation at a relatively fast pace, this stance was also reflected in English education in Japan. The teaching of English by using English as the medium of instruction was increasingly regarded as the primitive, less-developed educational status, and the instruction of English through Japanese became popular. After the trade treaty with the USA and other Western nations, Japan sent a group of students abroad to learn advanced technology and scholarship. After their return, they played a pivotal role in various social venues, including education. Furthermore, the rapid and meticulous translation of the western book from English to Japanese continued and was accumulated. Thus, at the latter half of Meiji Period, Inoue Kowashi (井上 毅), the minister of education from 1893 to 1895, even launched a campaign of education in Japan in Japanese (Koike & Tanaka, 1995).

The first decade of the twentieth century marked the last period of Emperor Meiji, and in 1912 the Taisho (大正) Period continued until 1926, which coincided with the reign of Emperor Taisho. For these two periods, English had been replaced with Japanese as the medium of instruction across Japan, and the instruction of English was still limited to the secondary school context which was not mandatory education. However, this should not be misunderstood as a decrease or lack of the power of English in Japan. In fact, in the first decades in the twentieth century, the spread of English education was particularly for the purpose of the entrance examination to higher educational institutes. English gradually became the essential subject for the entrance examinations, and the study of English passages by analyzing their grammatical structures and vocabulary items gain popularity in Japan. In the entrance examinations, test takers' English listening and speaking abilities were not measured at all and their reading comprehension with grammar and vocabulary knowledge was measured. As mentioned above, the translation of the passages written in a foreign language has a long cultural heritage in Japan (as well as Korea which has traditionally shared Chinese characters), and most Japanese nationals regarded this as the only and natural method for the learning of a foreign language and for the purpose of moral training of the youths. The GTM was regarded as the effective method for the exam English or *Juken-Eigo* (受験英語). Dr. Harold Palmer's oral method practiced in the 1920s and 1930s was a notable exception in this regard, but the major trend in English education in Japan was the exam English strongly affiliated with the GTM.

It is noteworthy that during the first half of the twentieth century, competition toward higher education was fierce in Japan, and English at the secondary school level was also intended toward preparing for the college entrance exams. Yamamoto (2004) emphasizes that the origin of academic credentialism in Japan started to be created as early as 1900:

> In the mid-Meiji era (circa 1900), popular perceptions of the university solidified. The middle and upper classes came to think that expensive university education, especially at the Imperial Universities, would guarantee prestigious jobs and social status. As a result, a near-universal examination system developed throughout the entire school and post-secondary system. Entrance examinations extended from elementary schools to middle schools then to higher education. ... Because of the extraordinary effort to get admitted to

a prestigious university, the status of graduates flowed from the university attended, not from the students' actual academic record within that institution. (pp. 108–109)

As presented in the case of Korea in Chaps. 2, 3, and 4, the concept of hakbul, or academic credentialism, is equally identified in the early twentieth century Japan. Japan needed to allocate college graduates to various vacancies in expanding industries, and in this process, the convenient selection criteria must have been the name of the university that the job applicant had attended. In the case of South Korea, a similar situation was found after the Korean War restoration period.

5.2.3 The Twentieth Century Post-War Period in Japan

Japan's engagement with World War II by attacking the Pearl Harbor in 1941 and her surrender in August 1945 to the Allied Forces completely revised the nature and characteristics of education in Japan. Since the nation was "occupied by the General Head Quarters (GHQ) of the Allied Powers until 1952" (Sasaki, 2008), educational upheaval occurred from totalitarian to democratic system. The education system in Japan also adopted a similar one to that of the USA: Six years of elementary school, 3 years of junior high school, 3 years of (senior) high school, and tertiary education such as 2 years of college or 4 years of university. According to Sasaki (2008), in April 1947, mandatory education expanded from 6 years (only covering elementary school education) to 9 years (extended to junior high school). English education was not conducted in the elementary level and was, in fact, one of elective foreign languages in the late 1940s and the 1950s. However, English soon became "the only" foreign language taught virtually every junior high school. This role of English as the de facto foreign language in Japan also affected the Japanese in general because the English instruction at the junior high school level meant "the mass popularization of EFL education in Japan" (Sasaki, 2008). In the prewar era such as the 1930s and 1940s, various socio-political factors limited widespread instruction of the English language, and after the second Sino-Japanese War and the active warfare with the USA in the first half of the 1940s, English was officially banned in Japan. Thus, the adoption of the 9-year mandatory education system in Japan meant that English was instructed at the national level across Japan for the first time in Japanese education history. Undoubtedly, this status change in English in Japan resulted in a shortage of English teachers at the junior high school level and as a temporary remedy, teachers in other subjects with minimum in-service training in EFL were forced to be appointed as English teachers in the 1950s and 1960s.

The 1950s and 1960s overlap with the prevalence of the Audio-lingual Method. This method highlighted error-free sentence making through numerous repetitions. Dialogue memorization and various forms of drill such as repetition, pattern, and substitution drills were highly encouraged (Larsen-Freeman & Anderson, 2011). In this scholarly trend worldwide, both Palmer's Oral Method and Fries' Oral Approach were welcomed by the Japanese ministry of education and advised to be instructed at secondary school. However, unfortunately, in the 1950s and 1960s, the lack of verbal communication skills among English teachers at secondary schools precluded the adoption of such communication-focused English teaching methods.

Perhaps, the most significant factor preventing the use of oral approaches in Japan was the negative washback of college entrance examination and the high school teachers' adamant attitude toward English instruction at the high school level. Sasaki (2008) stated that the only difference between prewar and postwar English education in Japan was the length of texts appearing on the college entrance exam sheets. The postwar exams used much longer (300–500 words) texts and diversification of question types. Thus, the grammar-translation method used for more than 100 years still was favored in Japanese teachers of English at the high school.

English learning motivation among students in Japan in this period was dominated by the desire toward egalitarian upward mobility. Before the expansion of mandatory education into 9 years, most students did not have the opportunity to learn a foreign language since their education stops at the elementary level. However, after the 1947 educational reform, virtually all students at least at the junior high school level had the chance to learn English although it was mostly taught in the GTM. The learning of English was required for the students to attend high school and 2 or 4-year college or university (McKenzie, 2010). Attending at and graduating from one of the top-tier senior high schools and universities was mostly equated with the royal road to social success, and in this regard, English learning for the 20 years after 1945 was characterized by the effective tool for internal competition among Japanese students for the higher academic diploma.

The spread of English education to virtually all secondary school students became the topic of occasional heated debate. In 1974, there was a fierce debate between Hiraizumi and Watanabe regarding the teaching of English to all students (Fujimoto-Adamson, 2006). Hiraizumi Wataru, a politician of Liberal Democratic Party, the ruling party, proposed an action plan for future foreign language education in Japan where English needs to be only taught to elite students who will need it for their future. Hiraizumi's assumption was that not all Japanese need to learn English and only a few elite translator and interpreters need to translate English information into Japanese. Undoubtedly, Hiraizumi's claim largely ignored the fact that more and more Japanese were going abroad with their increasing financial means. Thus, Hiraizumi's proposal to abolish general English education met strong opposition, but it would be noteworthy to cite the claim of Watanabe Shoichi, an English linguist. He argued that "English education for examination is valuable to train Japanese students' intelligence" (Imura, 2003, p. 284, cited in Fujimoto-Adamson, 2006). As Fujimoto-Adamson (2006) stated, "[a]lthough this counter-argument to Hiraizumi was necessary to avoid the creation of an English-speaking elite, the rationale supporting it still failed to consider the ever-growing practical needs of the population" (p. 276). As mentioned above, in the nineteenth century, English education was oriented toward elite students, and it was also a long tradition to equate the learning of a foreign language (mostly classical Chinese) with the cultivation of young minds. It is intriguing to find that these traditional thoughts came into its fore of public debate in the 1970s in Japan. The former which focused on elite education was outdated in the fast-growing economic and cultural exchanges in the 1970 Japan, and the latter which highlighted the classic maxim of mental cultivation was simply atheoretical although widely practiced in the East (i.e., the instruction of classical Chinese) and the West (i.e., the instruction of Latin or classical Greek).

In the 1970s, English education in Japan faces new challenges. The economic prosperity in the 1960s after the Tokyo Summer Olympic Games in 1964 made the Japanese public reach a new understanding that English is actually used as a real language around the world. Mass production of industrial goods and the need for exporting the items required oral fluency among Japanese students and workers. In addition, the economic affluence allowed many Japanese families to travel abroad and experience the English-medium communication. This need of English in speaking and listening was reflected in the Course of Study, or the national curriculum in Japan, and the Council for Improvement of English Teaching established in 1960 announced four recommendations:

1. One-month intensive in-service training for leading English teachers,
2. Two-month overseas training of selected English teachers,
3. Installing language laboratories in senior high schools across the nations, and
4. Expansion and establishment of specialized English courses or programs in senior high schools. (Koike & Tanaka, 1995, p. 18)

However, despite the governmental efforts and educational recommendations from the Council, English education in the 1970s did not change much, mainly due to the negative washback effect from senior high school and university entrance exams measuring knowledge in grammar, vocabulary, and reading comprehension. Taking such negative effect of exam into a serious potential problem, the Ministry of Education decided to decrease the class hour for English from 4 to 3 h/week in 1977. At the prefectural level, to alleviate the extreme competition among junior high school students, many prefectures in the 1970s recommended that "public high schools give their applicants multiple opportunities to take tests and consider the 3-year junior high school grades and the conduct of the students in the selection process" (Sasaki, 2008, p. 70). At the university level, the Ministry of Education in 1970 endeavored to adjust the difficulty level of the college entrance exams. Through a series of public hearings and university's initiatives in test reform, the Association of National Universities in Japan started to plan and develop the "Common Test" and established the National Center for University Entrance Examination in 1972. The first Common Test was taken in 1979, and approximately 320,000 students took the test for applying for any national or municipal universities. English, one of the three foreign languages (i.e., English, German, or French), was one of the five subjects in Common Test. Albeit the contribution of Common Test, more than 75% of all applicants did not take this test, and they intended to apply for private universities. Thus, the test reform aiming at alleviating students' study load and developing oral skills in English did not solve all the problems in English learning in Japan.

The high level of competition in college entrance exam was related to the public beliefs that the name of the university determines the graduates' future success in the society (Yamamoto, 2004). As mentioned above, this has a long tradition in Japan: for instance, at the end of the nineteenth century, for university graduates, they were appointed as government officials without taking any exams, or in the case of taking exams, the first round of exams was excepted. The latent sentiment toward upward mobility was ignited by the rapid economic development after the Korean War (1950–1953) and the Tokyo Summer Olympic Games in 1964. The public English education at junior high school consolidated the status of English as one of the key subjects for the entrance exams in senior high schools and universities.

However, the economic development also positively affected English education in that many Japanese had the medium level of affluence to go abroad, particularly to English-speaking countries. Their international experience evoked in many Japanese a sense of suspicion toward the effectiveness of the GTM, in which they felt enormous comfort in learning English. This collective sentiment necessitated the Ministry of Education to embark on the next phase of curriculum renovation. In the same period, in Europe, the concept of Wilkins' (1976) notional-functional syllabus became popular and English textbooks internationally made significant reorganization taking this notional-functional syllabus into their account. Japan also started to use such textbooks and assessment materials in the 1980s (Sasaki, 2008). Another benefit of economic growth in Japan was the systematic hiring of English-speaking teachers from abroad. The Japan Exchange and Training (JET) program was established in 1987 (General Information Handbook for the JET Programme, 2018). The Japanese government in the first year hired 848 English teachers from English-speaking "inner-circle" countries such as the U.S., the U.K., and Australia (and later French and German speakers were added in the JET program). The hiring of foreign English teachers gradually increased to reach approximately 8400 as of 2002 (Sasaki, 2008).

In sum, the 1970s and the 1980s marked the escalating tensions in English education. For the exam's purposes, English was mostly utilized as the tool of advancing the applicants' admission to a higher level of educational institution, and in this regard, the motivation to learn English was instrumental or in Kim's (2006, 2011) terms, competitive motivation which supposes other comparison groups imbuing the spirit of competition toward a better test score. Nonetheless, the global use of English and the mass transportation of Japanese people toward English-speaking countries simultaneously enhanced their sense of English as an international communication. The JET program fueled this social atmosphere and the Japanese people in general encountered many English-speaking teachers and travelers than ever before. Such rapid social change increased a different type of motivation: cultural exchange motivation or even international posture, defined as "a tendency to relate oneself to the international community rather than any specific L2 group" (Yashima, 2009, p. 145). For instance, in the previous era, English had long been regarded as the language of British and American, which was the reason why the imperial Japanese government officially banned the instruction of the English language during World War II. However, given the worldwide use of English as an international language, not simply as the language of British and American, "it has become increasingly difficult for Japanese EFL learners to identify a clear target group or culture" (Yashima, 2009, p. 145).

5.2.4   Japan's Dynamic Change in English Education in the Early Twenty-First Century

The last decade in the twentieth century could be characterized as an era of depression in Japan. The long-term bearish stock market and the declining real estate market loomed over the economic situation in Japan for more than a decade. This situation also exerted a significant impact on education. The educational reform toward alleviating students' study load in public education continued in the 1990s which period overlaps with the economic depression. For example, *Yutori* education emphasizing "further advancement of liberal, flexible, and comfortable school life" was highlighted across all school subjects (Sasaki, 2008, p. 75). In addition, Japanese educators endeavored to redefine the concept of learning and to enhance students' motivation for learning and grow their autonomy in responding rapid social changes (Kariya, 2002, cited in Sasaki, 2008).

The first decade in the twenty-first century still reflected the economic downturn and lethargic atmosphere in Japan. In this period, systematic national welfare and pension plans somewhat paradoxically prevented young students from seeking job positions. In the case of unemployment, the youth will be receiving unemployment relief fund from the government. Thus, before the second Abe Administration effective from 2012, the widespread educational atmosphere was so called the prominence of *Satori* generation or the generation of resignation. Whatever efforts they are making, the lion's share of the economy was only offered to the modicum of elite society, and the gap between the elite and the commoners was increasingly regarded as an unbridgeable one. New terminologies reflecting such lethargic young generation were coined at the turn of the century. For example, *hikikomori*, or the person staying in his or her place with no social contact, and *freeter* (フリーター), the compound noun combining free and *Arbeiter* (a German word for laborer), gained popular usage during this period (Honda, 2005; Kim, 2015).

Under this social atmosphere, Japanese students' English learning motivation at the turn of the century seemed to have been gravely changed. In fact, a great number of EFL research conducted in Japan dealt with the students' demotivation or the lack of motivation in learning English (e.g., Falout et al., 2009; Taguchi, 2015; Yashima, 2013). This new research trend of EFL learning demotivation may involve a variety of reasons. First, as mentioned above, learning English has traditionally been equated with the importation of the advanced Western technology represented by the U.S. and the U.K. (Koike & Tanaka, 1995; Sasaki, 2008). However, going through the rapid post-war reconstruction and economic boom for more than three decades from the 1960s to 1980s, Japan's role model to follow or exceed has largely disappeared and Japan itself became the role model for the fast following nations such as Singapore, South Korea, or Taiwan. Their economic growth also prompted many foreigners learn Japanese. This meant that most Japanese people did not need to learn English for foreign travel, particularly pre-arranged tours accompanied by tour guides. The domestic market size in Japan also needs to be considered. The economic development in the latter half of the twentieth century resulted in the expansion of domestic market. This meant that the industrial goods produced in Japan could be consumed in Japan without necessarily exporting them.

These socioeconomic changes seem to be somehow contradictory to the educational goal of learning and teaching English as a foreign language. As stated above, communication skills had consistently been emphasized in the Japanese Ministry of Education after the 1970s. Reflecting Wilkins' (1976) notional-functional syllabus in the 1970s and the communicative competence argued by Canale and Swain (1980), the national curriculum has consistently emphasized the communicative focus in English learning. The emphasis on communication in English has resulted in the changes in test format for college entrance exams in Japan. For example, in the year of 2006, the English test including listening comprehension for the first time in Japanese history was administered to approximately 500,000 high school graduates (about 40% of the high school graduates of that year; Sasaki, 2008). Direct testing of students' listening ability was a totally new renovation in English test in Japan because before this year, students' listening ability was only indirectly measured by multiple-choice written test items asking accent-location and correct pronunciation of an English word.

However, it should also be noted that despite the national curriculum mandating the use of English as a means of communication, in reality, most Japanese did not need English communication in their daily lives or for occupational purposes. Similar to the previous era, a few selected professional translators rapidly translated new information written in English into Japanese, and most Japanese people consumed such translated information. Accordingly, at the turn of the twentieth century, it was unsurprising to find demotivated students in English classrooms in Japan, and English instructors were not very successful in persuading them to continue English learning. Without having communicative competence in English, these students might not experience significant difficulties in making their living. For foreign travel, they may use Japanese pre-arranged tours, and for employment, they may simply focus on domestic market. Such an inward-looking tendency found among young Japanese students has often been regarded as a negative factor for English learning. Yashima (2013, p. 37) defines such an inward-looking tendency as *uchimuki* (内向き) and this is attributed to the expediting factor for Japanese students' demotivation to learn English.

Despite the above psychological consideration, it is remarkable to note that English instruction has been introduced to 5th- and 6th-year elementary school students as of April 2011. In fact, in the name of this school subject, it is not English "language" instruction but foreign language and culture. This means that linguistic features are not instructed to elementary school students. Only the novel features in English-speaking countries are explained to facilitate the students' interest in overseas countries and to enhance their motivation to learn English at the upper school level. Another remarkable trend is the use of assistant language teachers (ALTs). The JET program, started in 1987, gradually invited young English-speaking native speakers, and they worked as assistants to the Japanese teachers of English language in most middle and high schools. The existence of ALTs at school had a beneficial impact on Japanese students' motivation; for those students especially in rural areas where their encounter with native speakers of English is relatively limited, the existence of native English speaker in their classroom boosted their intrinsic type of English learning motivation. Although several problems in the administration and use of ALTs in Japan has been pointed out (e.g., Ohtani, 2010), the number of ALTs who participated in the JET program has steadily increased, and as of 2017, a total of 5163 participants from 40 different countries participated in the JET programs (General Information Handbook for the JET Programme, 2018). It should also be noted that the introduction of ALTs did not only perform in public sectors. Many private companies operate a similar process of hiring native English speakers and provide ALTs in their educational institutions.

However, the use of ALTs and the inclusion of listening comprehension in college entrance exam did not result in revolutionary changes in English education. Still dissatisfied with the lack of oral communication in the school system, many *eikaiwa* (英会話, English conversation) school attracts the college or adult students, and in *juken eigo* (受験英語, English for college entrance), GTM is still preferred.

The recent introduction of English education to 3rd- and 4th-year elementary school students also needs to be highlighted as an example of Japan's innovative educational endeavors. To address the communicative needs resulting from the upcoming Tokyo Olympics and Paralympics initially scheduled in the summer of 2020, the Ministry of Education (or officially the MEXT) proposed a new curriculum for primary English education across Japan. In this new proposal, from April 2020, a total of 35 hours (i.e., one class hour [45 min] a week) of "Foreign Language Activities" (外國語 活動) were allotted to 3rd- and 4th-year elementary school students, and 70 hours to Grades 5 and 6 students. The primary purpose of these activities was to "gradually develop intercultural understanding and to introduce achievable English listening and speaking abilities through materials and activities appropriate to the pupils' developmental stage" (Nemoto, 2018, p. 34). As this proposal focused on oral and aural proficiency development among Japanese elementary school students, it was regarded as an innovative move. Compared with the 2011 primary English education, this recent change made primary English education compulsory to Grades 3 and 4.

Regarding this educational reform, a couple of opposing opinions are also addressed. For example, the decision to lower the student age would make most students end up going to so-called cram schools to have higher English proficiency (The Japan Times, 2016), and it may result in lowering Grade 3 and 4 students' overall academic achievements as the addition of English education to these students will reduce the class hours allocated for other subjects (Sawa, 2020). As in the cases of South Korea and China, the full implementation of primary English education may involve educational ramifications for many years to come. Thus, while introducing the new communicative language teaching method at the elementary school level, English education in Japan now witnesses slow (but steady) educational innovation preparing for challenges and changes in the twenty-first century.

5.3 The Case of North Korea

5.3.1 Background Information About the North Korean Society and Education

Recently, the changing sociopolitical situation in North and South Koreas has renewed attention to English education in North Korea, officially the Democratic People's Republic of Korea (DPRK). Chapters 3 and 4 explained in detail the English education system and the historical progression of English learning motivation in South Korea. Compared with South Korea, North Korea is still regarded as a "hermit kingdom" to many outsiders, and education, especially English education, has not been well researched until recently (Oh & Kim, 2020). The main purpose of this section is to provide background information on North Korean education and the primary motivation for learning English in one of the most isolated nations worldwide.

After the Korean War (1950–1953), the Demilitarized Zone, located between North and South Korea, functioned as their de facto national border (Cho et al., 2013). Due to the ideological and social differences between North and South Korea, it is necessary to briefly introduce the educational system in North Korea before providing detailed explanations about its English education. The goal of education in North Korea differs remarkably from most nations. Article 43 of the North Korean Socialist Constitution states that the goal of socialist pedagogy is "to nurture future generations of strong revolutionaries, able to fight as champions of society and the people" and train "a new breed of communist, equipped with 'Intelligence, Morals, Integrity, and Physical Strength'" (Cho et al., 2013, pp. 194–195). Thus, members of society are educated not to pursue their happiness or wellbeing but to become strong revolutionaries for society, and education provides human capital to the nation. Cho et al. (2013) summarized the essentials of educational theory and practice in North Korea into four points:

> First, both the nature of the party [Workers' Party of Korea, 朝鮮勞動黨] and the essence of the working class should be realized through education. The "Monolithic Ideological System" of the party is therefore considered a core element of this. Second, and importantly, the notion of *Juche* ("self-reliance") should be firmly established in education, which means in practical terms that students should be trained in their country's history and the history of the Korean people. Third, education and revolutionary practices should be combined. Revolutionary practices refer not only to political practices but also the daily activities of communistic social life. Therefore, polytechnic education works as a critical principle in socialist education, reflecting the combination of student and worker. Fourth, the nation alone is responsible for all aspects of education and is therefore the sole source of direction and leadership in educational policy. (p. 195)

The fourth point has long been evidenced in propaganda boasting the superiority of the North Korean educational system to that of South Korea. In theory, North Korea fully supports public education, and private education, for which parents would have to pay, does not exist.[3] North Korea was also the first Asian country to implement an 11-year compulsory public education (Cho et al., 2013). Besides the compulsory education, elite and selected education also exist. For example, foreign education institutes are specialist secondary schools for students talented in foreign languages. Before 2012, schools providing rudimentary education adopted a 4-year system, but after the 2012 reform, these schools were renamed primary schools and extended to a 5-year system. Secondary schools last for 6 years and are called middle schools. The first 3-year span is allotted for lower middle school education, and the later 3-year span is for higher middle school. Since the education system in South Korea adopts the American system, elementary schools have a 6-year duration, and middle (i.e., junior high) and high schools each last 3 years in South Korea. This difference means that North Korean students begin college 1 year before their South Korean counterparts.

In a comprehensive review of North Korea's Year 2012 School Reform and Year 2013 Curriculum Charter (敎育綱領), Kim (2016) reported that for the North Korean population (i.e., 24,895,000), there were 4800 primary schools, which is on par with South Korean schools. Additionally, annual school days numbered approximately 266 days, including Saturday classes. North Korean students spend more hours at school compared with South Koreans, and this tendency is notable for school subjects such as national language (i.e., Korean), English, math, and science. In particular, the recent curriculum changes in North Korea reflected international education standards regarding learning objectives and content, teaching methods, and evaluation (Kim, 2015). English instruction was prioritized in the new curriculum, with more emphasis on communicative skills (see Sect. 5.3.5).

Based on the above information on the education system in North Korea, Sect. 5.3.2 will describe the historical progression of English education in North Korea. After brief explanations of remarkable political changes, the educational reforms and English curriculum will follow. In particular, the concept of *Juche*, or self-reliance, will be explained, highlighting how this unique North Korean philosophy infiltrated English instruction and textbooks in North Korea. Section 5.3.3 will illustrate the contents and characteristics of English textbooks in North Korea. Given the deep-rooted animosity toward the USA and South Korea adopting capitalism, the textbooks before the reign of Kim Jong-un, the current leader, focused on ideological propaganda highlighting the supremacy of communism over capitalism. Section 5.3.4 will describe the tragic situation called "the Arduous March" in the mid-1990s and early 2000s while explaining how this unprecedented turmoil resulted in lasting changes in the mindset of the North Korean people. Against this socioeconomic backdrop, Sect. 5.3.5 will elaborate the 2010s changes in English

---

[3]However, there has recently been a drastic increase in private tutoring, as will be discussed later in this section.

education, particularly after December 2011 when Kim Jong-un gained his political power after the demise of his father, Kim Jong-il. Kim Jong-un, having experienced a study abroad program in Switzerland in his teens, has emphasized the role of foreign languages, mainly English, and until the COVID-19 outbreak in 2020, the British Council at Pyongyang apparently introduced systematic communication-oriented authentic English education at some tertiary institutions, including Pyong-yang University of Science and Technology. In Sects. 5.3.6 and 5.3.7, the superficial and hidden motivations for learning English will be investigated while focusing on North Korean *Juche* ideology initiated by the former Supreme Leader Kim Il-sung and inherited by his son, Kim Jong-il, and grandson, Kim Jong-un.

5.3.2   English Education in North Korea: Its History and the Juche *Ideology*

As for all school subjects' instruction, English education in North Korea is deeply associated with the above-stated socialist educational purpose. English teaching and learning, textbooks, and class activities are all tightly aligned with the socialist paradigm. In analyzing English education in North Korea, the strongly communist political dimension, often associated with the *Juche* ideology initiated by Kim Il-sung, the late founder and premier of North Korea, should be scrutinized. It is particularly pertinent considering the living legacy of the Korean War (1950–1953), an atrocious civil war between the South and North. Since English was the language of "western enemies" represented by the USA, teaching and learning the English language was entirely banned for almost a decade after the July 1953 Armistice Agreement.

In retrospect, Japan's defeat in World War II resulted in a series of chain reactions on the Korean Peninsula. The Soviet Union officially declared war against Japan on August 9, 1945, and Japan announced unconditional surrender 6 days later on August 15. As part of Japanese disarmament on the Korean Peninsula, the Soviet Union was stationed north of the 38th parallel in Korea, and the U.S. Army to the south. In North Korea, the effort to eradicate the remaining educational system from Japanese colonization began before the foundation of the Democratic People's Republic of Korea on September 9, 1948, and the Soviet educational system replaced the old Japanese one. Before the outbreak of the Korean War on June 25, 1950, Russian and English were instructed in the North, but gradually English was overshadowed by Russian due to the political affinity between the Soviet Union and North Korea. English textbooks were published only in 1946, 1947, and 1948 in North Korea but not found after 1950 (Kim, 1990). This means that the Korean War was the catalyst that prevented English instruction because of the political animosity toward the USA, "the enemy nation."

However, the North Korean Workers' Party government gradually realized that English education was inevitable if they wished to keep pace with the modern technology and science in the West (Song, 2002). Thus, the motivation to learn

English, often considered instrumental and patriotic, was engendered in a top-down manner in North Korea. They needed their enemy's language to learn the USA and U.K.'s advanced technology. Additionally, the economic competition with South Korea under the aegis of the USA ignited the practical need for scientific and technical knowledge through learning English.

In the discussion of North Korean English education, as well as education in general, the concept of *Juche* requires further scrutiny. The literal meaning of *Juche* (主體) is "self-reliance," and originally, this word was first used in Japanese (*shutai*) after translating the concept of *Subjekt* in German philosophy, particularly Marxism (Myers, 2015). However, the widespread usage of *Juche* can be traced back to Kim Il-sung, when he was engaged in the Anti-Imperialist Youth League in the 1930s against the Japanese occupation of the Korean Peninsula (Cumings, 2005). The self-reliance idea was gradually developed and influenced by Marxist-Leninism, given the emphasis on the individual, the nation-state, and its sovereignty. Soon after Kim Il-sung consolidated his supreme leadership in the 1950s, the concept of *Juche* served as his dictatorial regime's theoretical foundation and was used to justify his (and the Workers' Party's) political decisions. The *Juche* ideology was further refined combining sub-principles: moving the nation toward claimed *jaju* (自主, meaning: political independence), through the construction of *jarip* (自立, meaning: economic sustenance) and an emphasis upon *jawi* (自衛, meaning: self-reliance in defense) to establish socialism.

In North Korea, the *Juche* ideology is eulogized because its fundamental idea was initiated and theorized by their leader Kim Il-sung. It is regarded as Kim's major contribution to make North Korea self-sustainable despite the constant and imminent military threat from the USA and the economic blockade from the U.S.-led United Nations. The *Juche* idea was and still is repeatedly taught to all North Koreans literally "from the cradle to the grave" under the portraits of the Kim family (i.e., Kim Il-sung, Kim Jong-il, and Kim Jong-un).

The *Juche* ideology has been criticized for deviating from the original Marxist-Leninism. For example, Kim Jong-il, son of Kim Il-sung, had criticized the communists and nationalists in the 1920s for their elitist posture separating themselves from the mass public. Thus, the *Juche* ideology is no longer an application of Marxist-Leninism but is a new theory in human history (Kwak & Joo, 2009). North Korea has endeavored to utilize the *Juche* ideology in their diplomacy while disseminating it to member nations of the Non-Aligned Movement (非同盟 運動) (Song, 2002). In the 1960s and 1970s, North Korea dispatched experts in agriculture, irrigation, physical education, culture, and civil engineering to developing countries in Asia and Africa (Hong, 1996). While providing various supports, North Korea tried to present itself as a model for developing nations, and the *Juche* ideology was regarded as a unique philosophy supporting the North Korean hegemony (Armstrong, 2009).

North Korean efforts to disseminate the *Juche* ideology to these countries was not successful in its diplomatic relations. However, the theory itself was adroitly used to justify the dictatorial Kim family's regime. The tenet "a human being is the master of his or her destiny and decides his or her fate" has been reinterpreted as the mass of an agentic human being represented by the Workers' Party; the sole leader of the

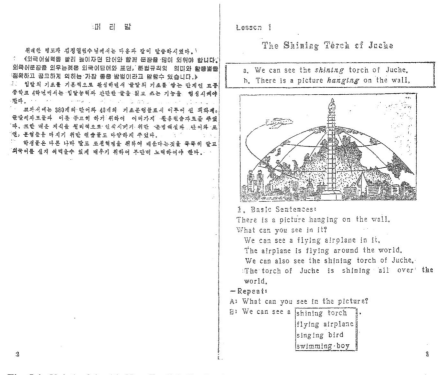

Fig. 5.1 Unit 1 of the 4th-Year English Textbook

Workers' Party was the supreme leader, Kim Il-sung (and then his son and grandson). Thus, the decision of Kim Il-sung was the decision of the Workers' Party, and that of the Party is not different from every individual human being in North Korea. As a result, the *Juche* ideology serves as a powerful ideological tool for idolizing the Kim family to the level now called Kim Ilsung-ism (or Kimilsungism) and Kim Jongil-ism (or Kimjongilism) (Ford, 2018; Isozaki, 2019). An exemplary case of personal idolization of the *Juche* ideology is the use of *Juche* for the name of an era, which means that Kim Il-sung's birth year (i.e., AD 1912) marks the 1st Year of *Juche*. Before Kim Il-sung's birth year, North Korea uses the Western chronicle (i.e., AD), but after his birth year, they use the Year of *Juche* (主體曆). The year 2022 thus becomes the 111th Year of *Juche*.

North Korea's efforts to disseminate the *Juche* ideology to the Non-Aligned Nations have led them to realize the importance of English as an international language (Song, 2002). It is not coincidental that North Korea reinstated English education in the 1960s and 1970s, which overlaps with that of establishing the *Juche* ideology and disseminating this occult philosophy to developing nations through diplomacy (Song, 2002).

Since the *Juche* ideology had been seamlessly aligned with the idolization of the Kim family in North Korea, it is repeatedly inculcated in North Korean youths. For example, the 4th year of secondary school's English textbook, Unit 1, which immediately follows the preface, begins with "The Shining Torch of *Juche*" (Fig. 5.1).

The *Juche* Tower was built to commemorate Kim Il-sung's 70th birthday on the east bank of the Taedong River in Pyongyang.[4]

5.3.3 The Contents and Characteristics of English Textbooks in North Korea

This section discusses the main characteristics of English textbooks before the Kim Jong-un era (i.e., prior to December 2011), and the newest trends in English education and its textbooks will be extrapolated in the following section. Note that English textbooks in North Korea may not differ from those used in different nations in that the contents also promote desirable social values and humanitarian goodwill to the benefit of the community members. Thus, this section succinctly summarizes the notably different characteristics.

As with other school subjects, the main argument in Article 43 of the North Korean Socialist Constitution presented above was explicitly reflected in the English textbooks. Socialist ideals and values were inculcated in various reading contents. Often these intentions were connected with hostile contents; U.S. atrocities and capitalism's inhumane characteristics were featured with provocative English vocabulary and idioms not often found in other countries' ESL/EFL coursebooks. The units for beginner students, due to their lack of English proficiency, did not (and could not) include much about these abstract, ideological contents.

However, for the upper years, particularly 5th- or 6th-year middle school students, anticipating their graduation from North Korea's 11-year compulsory education, ideological content and the animosity toward the USA were reflected in the textbooks. For example, Figs. 5.2 and 5.3 are from the 6th-year middle school English textbook used for first middle school (第一中學校) students (i.e., elite special school students) in North Korea at the turn of the century.

In this passage, the intended message is clear: the cruelty of the U.S. Army and deaths of innocent North Korean civilians. The *Sinchon* Massacre is regarded as one of the most tragic incidents during the Korean War; Pablo Picasso dedicated a picture in commemoration of the victims. To instill animosity toward the USA or the "Yankees" in the students, the text ingenuously uses emotion-laden, metaphorical words and phrases such as "the sworn enemy of the Korean people," "the US beasts," "hanged our people to death and buried them alive," and "we cannot live with them under the same sky."

Furthermore, since the English curriculum was aligned with the idolization of the Kim family, high-frequency words in English textbooks in North Korea show a remarkable difference from other ESL/EFL textbooks used in most other nations of the world. Park et al. (2001) presented the following 23 high-frequency word/phrase

---

[4]The *Juche* Tower is 1-meter taller than Washington Monument in Washington, D.C., which seems to reflect the desire to win over the USA (McCormack, 2004).

9. Writing

1) Composition : Which Sport Do You Like Best?
   Write a story about the sport you like best. Use the notes below if you want to.
   - Which sport you like best.
   - Why ?
   - How long you have been training it.
   - Whether you lost or won the game.
   - What you are going to do with it in the future.

2) Put into English.
   ① 모든 청소년학생들은 정성옥선수가 발휘한 위대한 장군님에 대한 무한한 충성심과 투쟁정신을 따라 배워야 한다.
   ② 제26차 올림픽경기대회 녀자유술경기에서 우리 나라 선수가 1등을 하여 조국의 영예를 떨치었다.
   ③ 우리가 어제 이야기하면 그 경기가 제일 진행되다.
   ④ 내가 다니던 과외체육학교는 그리 크지 않지만 그곳에서 많은 우수한 선수들이 자라났다.
   ⑤ 룡무가 자주 말하면 그 축구선수는 언제부터 선수가 되였니?

Summary of Grammar

Relative Pronouns and Prepositions (관계대명사와 전치사)
관계대명사는 전치사와 함께 쓰이며 규정분문에서 보여나 상황어로 된다.

1) 전치사는 관계대명사의 앞에 혹은 규정분문의 뒤에 놓인다.
   I know the man about whom you spoke.
   I know the man whom you spoke about.
   (네가 이야기한 그 사람을 나는 알고 있다.)
   This is the school at which we learnt.
   This is the school which we learnt at.
   (이것이 우리가 공부한 학교이다.)

2) 다음의 경우에는 전치사가 관계대명사앞에 놓인다.
   ① 《명사 혹은 미정대명사(all, one, none, some, both, each) + of + which (whom)》의 표현이 쓰인 경우
   I met several boys, all of whom I recognized.

94

(나는 여러 소년들을 만났는데 그들을 모두 알아 보았다.)
② who, which 가 전치사와 함께 다른 전치사구를 수식하는 경우와 whose가 전치사와 함께 쓰이는 경우
   This is the house at the door of which I saw him.
   (=This is the house at whose door I saw him.)
   (이것이 내가 문앞에서 그 사람을 만났던 그 집이다.)
   - 다음의 경우에는 전치사가 규정분문의 뒤에 놓인다.
③ 전치사가 동사 또는 다른 표현과 밀접히 결합되어 있는 경우 ·
   Football is a sport which I am fond of.
   (축구는 내가 좋아하는 경기이다.)
   (※ of which I am fond 라고는 하지 않는다.)
④ 전치사가 관계대명사 that 로 이어진 부문과 관계대명사가 빠진 문장에 쓰는 경우
   This is the man that I spoke of yesterday.
   (이 분이 내가 어제 이야기한 그 사람이다.)
   This is the house we live in.
   (이것이 우리가 살고 있는 집이다.)

Unit 12

The Sinchon Museum

Read

The US imperialists, the sworn enemy of the Korean people, have been trying to invade our country for more than a century since the invasion of the "General Sherman".

During the Fatherland Liberation War, they dropped 18 bombs per square kilometre upon the northern half of the Republic. They bombed schools, hospitals, cinemas, theatres and even

95

Fig. 5.2 Sixth-Year English Textbook (2000, pp. 94–95)

populated areas. During the temporary retreat, the Yankees shot or beat or hanged our people to death and buried them alive.

Sinchon is one of the places where the US imperialist wolves did the most barbarous atrocities. During the 52 days of their occupation of Sinchon County, they killed 35,383 people or one- fourth of its population. The Sinchon Museum lays bare all the atrocities committed by the Yankees: a bomb-shelter where 900 patriots were burnt to death ; the mass graves of 5,605 people. There are two powder magazines in which many people including 102 children and 400 mothers were confined. One day the US beasts rushed upon the mothers to tear their children away from them, saying that it was too happy for them to be together. So they were confined separately, the children in the upper magazine and the mothers in the lower one. The valley was filled with the hungry children's cry for their mothers and the screams of the mothers calling for their children. To the children crying for food, the Yankees gave gasoline and burnt them to death.

The US imperialists are wolves in human shape. As a wolf cannot change into a sheep, so the aggressive and brutal nature of the US imperialists cannot change. We cannot live with them under the same sky.

The Korean people are sure to wipe the Yankees off the face of the earth for good and reunify our fatherland under the wise leadership of the great leader Marshal Kim Jong Il.

96

Words and Expressions

imperialist (impɛ́rəiəlist) n. 제국주의자 ɑ. 제국주의의
sworn (swɔːn) swear(맹세하다)의 과거분사
   sworn enemy 철천지원쑤, 불구대천의 원쑤
invade (invéid) v. 침입하다, 침략하다
invasion (invéiʒən) n. 침입, 침략
"General Sherman" 《셔먼》 호
drop (drɔp) v. 떨어 뜨리다, 떨구다
bomb (bɔm) n. 폭탄 v. 폭탄을 투하하다, 폭격하다
per square kilometre 평방키로메터당
half (hɑːf) n. 절반, 반 ʌ. 절반의
the northern half of the Republic 공화국북반부
populate (pɔ́pjuleit) v. 거주하다, 거주시키다
area (éariə) n. 지역, 지방, 공지
   populated area 주민지대
temporary (témpərəri) ɑ. 일시의, 림시의, 잠정적인
retreat (ritríːt) n. 후퇴, 회피
Yankee (jǽnki) n. 양키(멸시하는 말)
shot (ʃɔt) shoot (쏘다)의 과거
   shoot sb to death …를 쏘아 죽이다
beat (biːt) beat (때리다, 치다)의 과거
   beat sb to death …를 때려 죽이다
hang sb to death …를 목 매달아 죽이다
bury (béri) v. 파묻다, 매장하다
   bury sb alive 생매장하다

barbarous (bɑːbərəs) n. 야만의, 잔인한
atrocity (ətrɔ́siti) n. 만행, 폭행
occupation (ɔ̀kjupéiʃən) n. 점령, 점거, 강점
population (pɔ̀pjuléiʃən) n. 인구, 주민수
bare (bɛə) ɑ. 벌거벗은, 노출된 lay bare 들어 놓다, 폭로하다, 로시키다
commit (kəmít) v. (죄, 과오 등을) 범하다
bomb-shelter (bɔmʃéltə) n. 방공호
patriot (péitriət) n. 애국자
grave (greiv) n. 무덤, 묘
   the mass graves 공동묘지
magazine (mæ̀gəzíːn) n. (무기, 탄약 등의) 창고, 탄약고
   powder magazine 화약창고
confine (kənfáin) v. 가두다, 감금하다
rush upon …에게 달려 들다
tear (tɛə) v. 억지로 잡아 떼다
   tear sb away from ~ …로부터 을 떼내다
separately (sépəritli) ad. 따로따로 하나하나
upper (ʌ́pə) ɑ. 더 우에 있는, 상은 부의
valley (vǽli) n. 골짜기, 계곡
scream (skriːm) n. 비명, 빠지는 한 소리
gasoline (gǽsəliːn) n. 휘발유
   in human shape 사람(인간)의 탈을

97

Fig. 5.3 Sixth-Year English Textbook (2000, pp. 96–97)

group from the English textbook used in the 1990s. These words related to the North Korean social system or the idolization of the Kim family, which shows that English education was utilized to benefit the regime.

> worker, workday, labour, leader, republic, work team, generalissimo, labour party, social-ism, DPRK, beloved, respected, socialist, capitalist, communism, imperialism, war, battle, fight, defeat, the Korean Revolution Museum, the Grand People's Study House, the People's Palace of Culture (Park et al., 2001, p. 126)

While analyzing the English textbooks published in the 1990s, Park et al. (2001) summarized six characteristics of North Korean English textbooks: (1) idolizing the Kim family, (2) teaching the *Juche* ideology, (3) maliciously slandering South Korea and the West, (4) teaching communist ethics, (5) emphasizing science technology, and (6) focusing on physical strength and personal hygiene. The first and second characteristics are interconnected for the *Juche* ideology and had long been used for the theoretical foundation justifying the Kim family's political monopoly. Every English textbook included what Kim Il-sung or Kim Jong-il stated about English learning, and their quotations were highlighted in boldface and enjoyed a different font size in the preface. After Kim's quotation, brief paragraphs annotated the quotation. The Kim family's quotation reflected commonsense ideas on learning and teaching a foreign language. In the preface, Kim Jong-il was quoted as "it is important for each student to lay a firm ground stone to be a good language learner" (2nd year middle school), or "we must teach our students a foreign language to be able to use it in real life" (3rd year middle school). Additionally, as stated above, from the 1st year of middle school, the archaic word "generalissimo" was introduced to eulogize Kim Il-sung. An ingenious integration of the Confucian concept of the One Bodiness or trinity of king, teacher, and father (君師父一體) is integrated into the learning contents. For example, the first unit of middle school 1st-year textbook began with "Thank you, the respected father Generalissimo Kim Il Sung." In the upper years' textbook, the idolization of the Kim family was intensified. For example, the 6th-year textbook for the first middle schools published in 2001 devoted two separate chapters for the Analects of Kim Il-sung and Kim Jong-il. Unit 13 introduced Kim Il-sung's writing (Unit Title: "With the Century": Reminiscences of the Great Leader Generalissimo Kim Il Sung). Unit 14 presented excerpts of Kim Jong-il's work with an eccentrically elongated title (Unit Title: "Let Us Exalt the Brilliance of Comrade Kim Il Sung's Idea of the Youth Movement and the Achievements Made under His Leadership": An Immortal Classic Work of the Great Leader Marshal Kim Jong-il). Considering the above textbook was used among the 6th-year students who were about to complete their mandatory education, the last two units might have been intended as ideological armament for the students.

The primary purpose of the malicious slandering of South Korea and the West would be to maintain their political system by indoctrinating students in the ideological superiority of communism to capitalism symbolized by South Korea and the West (particularly the USA). Since the intentional slandering required students' basic English literacy, these vilifications start to appear in 4th-year middle school texts. For example, the miserable living conditions of the unemployed, often adapted from classic western literature written by Charles Dickens or William Shakespeare, were covered. If deemed convenient or due to inexperience, in some cases, the reading source was misinformed; "The Little Match Girl," an internationally recognized short story written by Danish author, Hans Christian Andersen, was misrepresented as occurring in England. Additionally, racial dehumanization and enslavement before the American Civil War were repeatedly introduced as if an ongoing social problem, with outdated vocabulary, such as "the negro." This content reflected the principle of "hatred education" in North Korea, where wealthy employers, bourgeois, and imperialists are set as the target of vented anger (Kim, 1990; Park et al., 2001). The public was united through their anger, and it became easy to imbue socialistic cause to the public.

Communist ethics, the fourth element outlined in the introduction, also showed a qualitative difference from that of South Korea. In each nation, people's collaboration is typically prioritized, and for North Korea, the value of mutual support and collaboration are often integrated with traditional values such as diligence, integrity, and respect for the elderly or with humanitarian causes. However, communist ethics are geared toward the social revolution, subverting the bourgeois class and promoting the value of labor. For example, Aesop's fable, "The Ant and Grasshopper," was included in 4th year, and a unit entitled "No Food for a Lazy Boy" dealt with a reading content focusing on the value of labor. Interestingly, reading passages on the U.S. unemployment strike and the Swiss struggle toward independence against Austria were included, alluding the strength of collaborative power of the proletariats toward *Ancien Régime* or oppressors (Park et al., 2001).

North Korean English textbooks reflected recent advances in science and technology. This socialist education prioritized hands-on and practical scientific ideas, and various topics on science and its related theories were accordingly introduced with examples. The emphasis on science and technology had long been emphasized by Kim Il-sung and Kim Jong-il for the development of the nation (Lee et al., 2005). Science topics such as air circulation, the solar system, procedure of chemical experiments, bird habitats, and gravity were included. The dominance of science topics is corroborated in the content analysis of English textbooks. For example, in the 6th-year textbook used in the first middle school published in 2001, 3 out of 14 chapters focused on science topics (i.e., Unit 2: Sailing Ships of the Future; Unit 4: Computers; Unit 5: Fire—Friend or Enemy), and all four supplementary reading materials also dealt with science (i.e., Readings 1: Food Preservation, 2: What Caused the Fire?, 3: Life in the Future, and 4: Satellites). Recent textbooks after Kim Jong-un's reign increased the percentage of science topics. The same school year textbook of the first middle school published in 2015 had 8 out of 11 chapters featuring science topics (i.e., Unit 1: Medical Services; Unit 2: Sleep and Dreams; Unit 4: For a Better Environment; Unit 5: Human Intelligence; Unit 6: Animals and Plants; Unit 8: Food; Unit 10: Secrets of Universe; and Unit 11: Natural Disasters). Park et al. (2001) stated that this content could be regarded as a prototype of content-based instruction. This meant that the learning content introduced information written in English that would be useful for their reading of English-language science books as part of their university education in the future.

Physical education and personal hygiene were also emphasized in North Korean textbooks; for a collectivistic society where every individual's labor counts, physical health and hygiene become essential. From early years in English education, contents on physical exercise, sports, and bodily movement were frequently found, and the cause of these activities was explicated as "[t]hrough such exercise and sports, he builds up his body for labour and national defence" (English textbook published in 2001, 6th-year, Unit 2).

5.3.4   The Arduous March of the 1990s and North Koreans' Capitalistic Minds in the Twenty-First Century

Arguably, the most tragic incident in North Korea would be the period of the Arduous March (고난의 행군) in the mid-1990s (Ford, 2018). Due to the collapse of the former Soviet Union in 1991 and the Open Door Policy in China expedited in the 1990s, Kim Il-sung and his son Kim Jong-il were at an impasse in the 1990s. Further, due to devastating famine, the crop harvest in 1993 (and the following years) caused a critical situation, and the great flood in 1995 nullified North Korea's food ration system. On New Year's Day 1996, *Rodong Shinmun* (勞動新聞), the official daily newspaper in North Korea, argued that the nation must overcome the hardship through the spirit of "the Arduous March," which Kim Il-sung had presented during his partisan combat with the imperial Japanese army before the 1945 liberation. However, nationwide destructive famine and massive starvation were a cold reality. Depending on the source of information, the exact death toll from starvation varies from 330,000 (Joongang Ilbo, 2010) to 3,000,000 (Ryo, 2011).

The tragic collapse of North Korea's economic foundation in the 1990s resulted in the people's emotional detachment from their government. The number of North Korean refugees skyrocketed after the period; it was reported that the bodies of those who starved to death were frequently discovered in rural areas where the Worker's Party had lost its control. North Korean homeless children, called *kotjebi* (꽃제비, literally "fluttering swallow") were found on the street, and some of them, mainly in the border between North Korea and China, snuck into China through the porous border[5] and eventually flooded into South Korea with the aid of humanitarian agencies or Christian civil groups (McPhee, 2014). The majority of those who remained in North Korea also held an escalating but logical doubt about the legitimacy of the nation. In a newspaper article reporting the life of North Korean youths, North Korean millennials did not have a firm belief about the nation, which presented a stark comparison with their (grand)parents' generations (Fifield, 2017). In previous generations, the food ration system and the economic plans functioned effectively, and despite insufficient amounts, various types of food were distributed

---

[5]Although it is difficult to estimate the accurate number of North Korean *kotjebi* children, figures ranged from 50,000 to 100,000 as of 2014 (McPhee, 2014).

to all North Koreans. However, the Arduous March in the mid-1990s was the turning point, and the socialist government lost control of the food ration system, and each family sought a means to make a living.

Jangmadang (장마당, literally "market ground"), or a black market, was gradually founded by the commoners and functioned as the place to exchange goods and information. Due to the de facto defunct socialistic ration system, North Koreans were increasingly dependent on *Jangmadang*, where virtually all life goods could be exchanged. North Koreans joked that they could buy "everything but a cat's horn" in *Jangmadang* (Fifield, 2017). The orthodox hardliners in the North Korean government, unwillingly acknowledging the failure of the national economic system, became more lenient about the *Jangmadang* system, and now it is common to find customers and illegal merchants across North Korea, which can be regarded as the initial grass-root level of capitalism.

The *Jangmadang* generation, who spent their early teens in the 1990s and 2000s, are audacious in finding not only food but also information of the outside world (Fifield, 2017). The young generation's curiosity toward the new world is often associated with the interest in South Korean pop culture or K-pop. Contained in CDs/DVDs and later in USBs, various dramas, movies, and pop music from South Korea and the USA have illegally spread in North Korea. Watching this media is an open secret among many North Koreans, who might sacrifice their lives by detainment in a police station, or in some cases, in a concentration camp.

Such a transition from the old socialist regime to an actual grass-root capitalist but ostensibly rigid socialist regime seemed to evoke subtle chain reactions in various fields in North Korea. The young leader Kim Jong-un, who had a study-abroad experience in Bern, Switzerland, from 1998 to 2000 (Higgins, 2009), also took advantage of this homegrown *Jangmadang* and tried to incorporate elements of capitalistic lifestyle into the traditional socialist country. The famine in the late 1990s resulted in North Korea becoming a malformed market economy (Ford, 2018). Despite the escalating nuclear tensions with the USA and South Korea, Kim Jong-un is reported to introduce social reform emulating the Vietnamese or Chinese model (Ford, 2018). Although still recovering from the aftermath of the devastating famine and the Arduous March, North Korea currently has a better economic situation, and the signs of economic recovery are found in various areas including public and private English education in North Korea (Lankov, 2016).

5.3.5 Recent Changes in English Education in Kim Jong-un's Reign (from December 2011)

After Kim Jong-un's tenure began in 2011, English education witnessed varying degrees of progress in North Korea. These English textbooks differed from their predecessors in terms of their content and curriculum design (Kim, 2016). When analyzing recent changes in English education in North Korea, the contributions of

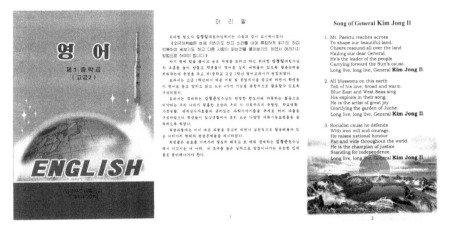

Fig. 5.4 Cover page and front matter of North Korean English Textbook

the British Council must be acknowledged. Until the suspension of the English language teaching program in Pyongyang in September 2017 due to the escalating concerns regarding North Korea's nuclear missile development, the British Council had dispatched four to 11 teacher trainers and English-language teaching advisors to Pyongyang since May 2000. For those 18 years, the British instructors were actively involved in training English teachers while staying in Pyongyang. Brian Stott, English project manager of the British Council, mentioned that the British Foreign and Commonwealth Office-funded project helped developing English teaching capacity in North Korea (cited in Lamers, 2010). Groups of North Korean English teachers in higher and secondary education systems in and out of Pyongyang participated in the program. The British Council program enabled these teachers to have more access to educational resources and opportunities to communicate effectively with native English speakers. According to Nick Shaw, an English teacher trainer at a university in Pyongyang for 2 years, the British Council supported three universities in Pyongyang to design and use modern English-language teaching materials; but at secondary school, old textbooks were used, and the exposure to authentic English materials was limited (Lamers, 2010).

The most recent 2015 English textbooks published in North Korea present remarkable progress in terms of its content and topics. Presumably, British Council's close collaboration must have been involved in these innovations. Compared with the textbooks of the previous era of leader Kim Jong-il until his sudden demise in 2011, the new English textbooks significantly reduced their ideological content and idolization of the Kim family.

Figure 5.4 depicts an English textbook published in 2015 and used by Grade 10 in the first middle schools across North Korea.[6] Students attending a first middle school

---

[6]Recent English textbooks in North Korea can be found in the Unification Ministry Resource Center, fifth floor of the National Library of Korea (located in Seocho-gu, Seoul).

are considered academically talented and belong to the elite social class; these graduates have priority admittance to prestigious North Korean universities including Kim Il-sung University, Kim Chaek University of Technology, and Kim Hyung-Jik University of Education. Due to the students' academic achievement, the textbooks used in first middle schools reportedly differ from those used in "ordinary" middle schools.

The design and ideological content found in the front matter does not differ much from previous English textbooks published in the early 2000s. The cover page depicts launching an intercontinental ballistic missile (ICBM) with the globe in the background. The second and third pages do not show any difference, in that the preface on page 2 introduces their late leader Kim Jong-il's didactic comment on the proper way to learn a foreign language, and page 3 includes the "Song of General Kim Jong Il," which idolizes the Kim family.

However, regarding the organization of the units and the contents, the recent English textbooks present remarkable improvements. First, the unit organization starts with oral skills, listening and speaking practices, and reading and writing sections. At the end of the writing section, grammar is introduced with close reference to its actual use. This innovation shows that the direct use of grammatical metalanguages (e.g., subject, verb, and relative pronoun) is generally avoided, and the textbook authors endeavor to incorporate theoretical advances in TESOL. Particularly noteworthy is the introduction of focus on form by encouraging students to notice errors in written dialogues or passages used in meaningful contexts. These organizational changes show qualitative differences compared with the textbooks used in the first decade of the twenty-first century.

Regarding content, the ideological content emphasizing the superiority of the socialist regime and the *Juche* ideology disappeared in the obtained English textbooks used in the first middle schools. Additionally, anti-American contents such as the *Sinchon* Massacre that provoke students' hatred toward the USA are omitted, except one simple translation task in the Year 6 English textbook (p. 52). However, it does not mean that emphasis on national pride also disappeared from the textbook. For example, a North Korean weightlifter's outstanding performance in the summer Olympic games is included with the conventional eulogy of their leader Kim Jong-un. This is illustrated by the following excerpt: "In the 21st century our sportspeople have made great successes in many events under the wise leadership of the respected Marshal Kim Jong-un who encourages them to successfully implement the plan of building a sports power" (English textbook, Grade 5, published in 2015, p. 59).

Although the contents and organization reflect recent advances in ELT, it is unclear how this renovation was possible within a decade. The British teacher trainers were likely involved in the textbooks' design. The British trainers who stayed in Pyongyang seem to have planned and designed the overall contents and even drafted a significant portion of the contents. First, the contents are carefully selected from British ones (e.g., *Jane Eyre* by Charlotte Brontë, from English textbook, Grade 6, p. 44), and British words and expressions, not American ones, are used throughout the textbooks. For example, the word "flat" is used instead of "apartment," and "lavatory" instead of "bathroom." Spelling conventions are also

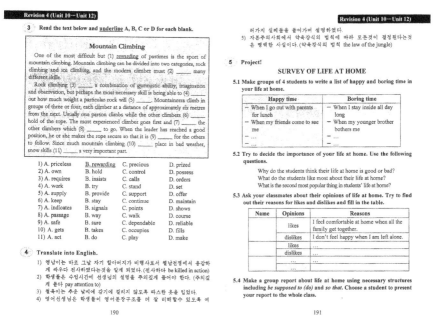

Fig. 5.5 Korean-English Translation Tasks (pp. 190–191)

British (e.g., favourite, labour, theatre). In geographical locations (e.g., Dover, London, Fullham, Yorkshire), tourist attractions (e.g., Wimbledon), and topics, U.S.-related content is not introduced but is replaced with other English-speaking nations' contents. The only exception was found in Unit 11 on natural disaster for Grade 6 textbook where the volcanic eruption in Mount Kilauea in the Hawaiian Islands is explained in the form of first-person narratives. However, even in this case, any mention of Hawaii or the USA is intentionally deleted.

Second, more direct evidence is found in the content organization. In some cases, the content seems to have modified or inserted at the authority's disposal. Abrupt political sentences or clauses, which lack coherency given the overall message, are often found in the textbook. For example, on page 98, Section 4 of the 5th-year English textbook contains a Korean sentence "조선의 어린이들은 경애하는 김정은원수님의 따뜻한 품속에서 세상에 부럼없이 행복한 생활을 누리고 있다" meaning "North Korean children live happy lives having nothing to envy in the world, under the warm arms of Respected Generalissimo Kim Jong-un."

Figure 5.5 presents pages 190 and 191 of the 5th-year English textbook, where immediately below a descriptive passage on mountain climbing, the translation task is presented. As indicated in the parenthetical tip, the first Korean sentence is related to a grandfather's death in the Vietnam War. The fifth Korean sentence also provides a statement about capitalism, translating as "It is an outright fact that everything is decided based on the law of the jungle in the capitalist society." However, the

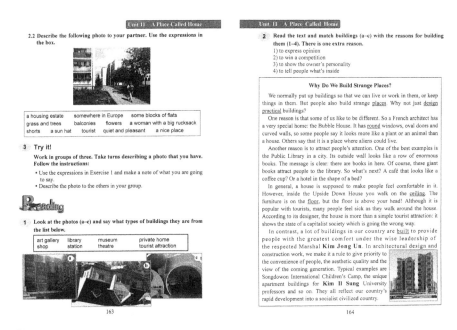

Fig. 5.6 Why do we build strange places? (5th-year English textbook, pp. 163–164)

content before and after this translation section does not contain ideological incul-cation. Throughout the main text in this 5th-year English textbook, the use of Korean language and translation were found only on pages 52, 98, 144, 190–191, and the remaining parts are all presented in English for both directions and content. In the case of a 6th-year textbook, similar translation tasks appear on pages 52, 99, 145, 176. It is speculated that in authorizing the textbook, these sections of Korean translation, which strengthen socialist ideology and can be utilized for idolizing the Kim family, were hastily inserted.

Another trace of inserting ideological or idolizing content is provided in Fig. 5.6 from page 164, Unit 11 of the 5th-year first middle school English textbook, where a strange building structure is described. The line and letter spacing in the fifth paragraph which emphasizes "the wise leadership" of the leader shows a visible difference compared to the preceding and following sentences. In textbooks in North Korea, it is often found that the boldface and bigger font size are used to highlight the leader's name. However, the line and letter spacing in these lines are visibly sparse, whereas the remaining parts are consistent in content and outline density.

5.3.6   English Learning Motivation in North Korea: Superficial Reasons

In discussing English learning motivation in North Korea, it is unsurprising that the integrative motivation often stated in the Gardnerian tradition in L2 motivation research does not seem to be an adequate concept in this case. Learning English in North Korea raises a fundamental, lingering question: Why do they need to learn English in an isolated country where the total number of expats (i.e., non-North Korean citizens) numbered less than 500 in 2010 (Lamers, 2010)? The opportunity to meet foreign language speakers in North Korea is limited, if not nonexistent, and only those who have graduated from universities focusing on foreign languages (e.g., Pyongyang Foreign Language University, International Relations University) are selected to work as diplomats and have reason to use a foreign language (Park, 1993). Thus, it would not be hyperbolic to state that North Korean learners of English lack the motivation to have authentic communication with other English-language users.

The first clue to explain North Koreans' motivation to learn English is the antithetical diplomatic and military relations with the USA. Kim Il-sung emphasized that North Koreans needed to be ready to use essential English expressions such as "hands up" and "surrender, or you will be shot to death" to U.S. soldiers or POWs. This militarist stance is the main difference from most of the world's motivation to learn English.

Ostensibly, foreign language education in North Korea was heavily influenced by geopolitical considerations. From the 1950s after the outbreak of the Korean War until the 1964 Central Committee of the North Korean Workers' Party's edict on the promotion of foreign-language education, English education was entirely eradicated from North Korea, while the Russian language was instructed as the primary foreign language. Moreover, even after the educational reform in 1964, Russian and English were instructed on a 50/50 basis, which meant that half of the North Korean students learned Russian as their first foreign language, and only the remaining half learned English (Song, 2002). It was not until by the mid-1970s that English became the primary foreign language in North Korean secondary school curriculum (Baik, 1994).

This slow historical progression from the preference of Russian to English reflects the deep-rooted animosity toward the USA and South Korea, which represented capitalism. During the Korean War, Pyongyang, the capital city of North Korea, faced air raid destruction by the U.S. jet bombers, and the Korean War, which lasted for more than 3 years, resulted in an estimated 3 million casualties and 2.5 million refugees (Yang, 1994). Having witnessed the massive destruction resulting from the enemy, although North Korea initiated the war under Kim Il-sung's careful preparation, it must not have been easy to embrace the instruction of the enemy's language.

However, ironically, Kim Il-sung, who started the Korean War (a.k.a. the Fatherland Liberation War in North Korea) and spread the seed of deep animosity toward the USA, emphasized the instruction of foreign language, specifically English, in the 1964 edict of the Central Committee of the Workers' Party of Korea. Moreover, in 1980, he declared that the development of North Korean science and technology depended on strengthening foreign language education (Kim, 1990, pp. 275–276). Kim Il-sung, a former communist partisan leader in his 20s and 30s, frequently communicated with communist party members in China and Russia and must have recognized the importance of foreign language skills. Thus, he ordered the establishment of Pyongyang Foreign Language University in November 1949 and that of Pyongyang Foreign Language Institute (i.e., elite high school) in September 1958 (Hong, 1996). The North Korean government had apparently realized the importance of learning a foreign language as early as the 1950s, but the instruction of English to the general public was much delayed due to political reasons. Only elite members of North Korea were chosen as interpreters or diplomats during the same period. However, after the 1970s, teaching English to North Korean students as their primary foreign language became imperative. What prompted this educational change in North Korea from elitist to mass education of English?

Song (2002) provided three convincing reasons for teaching English in North Korea: (1) strengthening the nation by incorporating advanced knowledge in science and technology, (2) propagating and brainwashing the *Juche* ideology, and (3) vying for the ultimate victory with the U.S. imperialism. The first reason to learn English was instrumental to develop their nation because most science and technology books and knowledge were written in English. Since the North Korean government could not ignore the phenomenon of English as an international language anymore, they needed to officialize the status of English as their primary foreign language. Having witnessed the South Korea's rapid economic development in the 1960s and 1970s under U.S. economic and military support, North Korea "may have come to the unavoidable conclusion that scientific and technical knowledge would be more easily obtained through the medium of English rather than any other foreign language" (Song, 2002, p. 49).

The second prominent reason would be the propagation of the *Juche* ideology worldwide. As mentioned above, North Korea invested various human and financial resources to developing countries, mainly in Asia and Africa, with the primary purpose of disseminating the *Juche* ideology to these nations. By winning their diplomatic support, North Korea endeavored to export the *Juche* ideology and eventually take a leadership role among the Non-Aligned Movement Nations. At elite tertiary level education, North Korea emphasized French language education during the 1950s and 1960s to support African nations' independence movement, and in Pyongyang, it was not difficult to find North Koreans highly proficient in French even in the 1990s (Hong, 1996). However, French instruction was limited only to special, elite education, particularly for the students in Pyongyang Foreign Language University, and English is instructed to the general public in order to first brainwash students with the *Juche* ideology so that they can disseminate this ideology to the rest of the world in English.

The third reason resonates with North Korea's still-prevalent anti-American sentiment. Kim Il-sung argued for the necessity of learning English while stating that "we should be ready to fight against the American and Japanese imperialists. If our youths do not know a word of English or Japanese, they will be at a loss in the case of capturing POWs. Every youth needs to speak simple foreign language expressions such as 'hands up' or 'surrender and throw your weapon away, and you won't be shot'" (Park, 1993). For this reason, as early as 1965, North Korea resumed teaching English as well as Russian. The acknowledged reason for reinstating English education was to know the enemy and eventually win the ultimate victory over the U.S. imperialists (Song, 2002).

5.3.7   English Learning Motivation in North Korea: Urgent Need for Endocentric Consolidation

As discussed above, English is taught for three reasons: (1) to increase scientific knowledge, (2) to disseminate the *Juche* ideology, (3) to win the ultimate victory over the USA (Song, 2002). However, it is dubious, if not entirely impossible, that most North Koreans would have the opportunity to learn new scientific knowledge directly from an English book (Baik, 1994). In addition, there is an extremely slim chance for them to explain the *Juche* ideology and discuss it with English speakers considering North Korean isolationism. It was recently estimated that merely 4000 to 6000 foreign nationals visit North Korea annually before the COVID-19 pandemic (Borowiec, 2014), and given this limited number, it is not easy for North Koreans to meet any expatriates, let alone English speakers. The third reason, for winning the ultimate victory over the USA, is also unlikely as civilians do not usually meet with or confront U.S. military personnel. Moreover, the third reason for learning English cannot explain the situation immediately after the Korean War in the 1950s when English education in North Korea was entirely banned. The necessity of using simple English expressions with U.S. hostages or POWs must have been imminent in the 1950s during and after the Korean War, but ironically English was completely banned until 1964.

Therefore, the three so-called likely reasons for learning English in North Korea do not seem logical, which necessitates investigating another implicit agendum underlying English education for the general public. The first pragmatic function of widespread English education would be the internal ideological consolidation among the students. English is supposedly learned to disseminate the *Juche* ideology to other nations (Song, 2002). However, although this external dissemination may be an unattainable goal, English instruction still fulfills the ideological consolidation among domestic students. Often with the idolization of the Kim family, the *Juche* ideology is effectively combined with communist ethics, and the hatred education mostly leveled against the USA, as illustrated in the above example pages (i.e., the *Sinchon* Massacre). With regurgitative readings of various contents imbuing the socialist system's superiority and the Kim family's justification in English, students take the established system for granted and grow autonomous self-censorship among themselves, which results in refuting anything related to the capitalist system. Thus, the emphasis of English education functions as internal consolidation, and this process does not allow different perspectives to potentially dismantle the foundations of the Kim family idolization and socialist thesis.

Another practical consideration is linked to university admission purpose and the role of English in the preliminary entrance examination for university admission in North Korea. It is reported that the North Korean education system differs from South Korea's (as well as other countries) in that the students' family background is critically considered in the first round of university admission. According to Thae (2018), former North Korean Deputy Ambassador to the U.K., if North Korean students have a relative or family member classified as a *bandong*, or nonconformist to the regime, the students cannot receive any recommendation letter from their high school teachers and are disqualified to apply for university. In this case, they are denied the opportunity to take a university entrance exam and are assigned to a job, temporarily deprived of higher education opportunities.

Those whose family background qualifies and are considered loyal to the North Korean regime can receive a letter of recommendation and apply for a university. In the second round of the application process, students first take a preliminary qualification test for two consecutive days on six different subjects: revolutionary history, literature, English, chemistry, physics, and math. Depending on the subjects, students answer three to five essay-type questions. In the English subject test, students perform English composition and translation (NK Chosun, 2013). This preliminary test has recently changed its format from an essay-type to multiple-choice computerized test, reflecting the technological advances in North Korea. The test results are instantly made public, and students can learn their score immediately after they take the test (Thae, 2018).

Following the preliminary test, another assigned by the Worker's Party is administered. Students' personal choice in university selection is usually considered, but the Party makes the application; only one university is assigned to the student. The main test is usually administered in February by each assigned university. The test is composed of three core elements: department subject test, physical test, and interviews. One out of two applicants are usually selected, and the students not selected by the university are required to take a job or serve in the Korean People's Army (朝鮮人民軍) for 10 years. This situation means that students are not allowed to apply for university the next year but does not mean that students who failed to enter university have no opportunities to reapply at all. After working for 3 (for women) or 5 years (for men), they can apply for university with the recommendation of their supervisor at work. Men who completed the 10-year mandatory military service are in an advantageous position to be admitted to university because every university has a quota for discharged military personnel (NK Chosun, 2013). Due to this priority admission system for former soldiers or current workers, the competition among *jiktongsaeng* (直通生), or young high school graduates, is becoming intense (Thae, 2018).

The initial screening of the applicants based on their family background demonstrates that North Korean education is the principal means of ideological control and sustaining the political regime (Joongang Ilbo, 2018). Despite individual students' academic excellence, their university admission is not guaranteed because of the initial screening. Thae (2018) testified that family background functions as a crucial factor for university admission. If a family member was involved with South Korea before or after the Korean War, students cannot major in diplomacy or any major related to foreign exchange. Although Thae's testimony was mainly about the 1980s, other recent North Korean defectors have also corroborated that family heritage still functions as the initial screening. The nonconforming "misconduct" of close family members such as parents and siblings, not remote family members (i.e., grandparents, uncles, or aunts), seems to be the factor preventing students from applying to university.

When selecting their university major, students highly prefer to major in English for its practical economic values. Graduates of Pyongyang Foreign Language University earn considerably higher salaries than others, and for this reason, in the early 1990s, only one out of every 10 university applicants was selected annually (Park, 1993). In addition to the monetary reward, students enrolled in this university were prioritized for study-abroad, foreign exchange students, and work at the International Bureau of Worker's Party of Korea or the Department of International Affairs at the Political Cabinet.

To summarize the university admission system, English is regarded as important for the preliminary university test. For this reason, current in-service teachers are employed by wealthy families to teach their children English, which is illegal in the North Korean education system (Thae, 2018). Public education is the only kind in North Korea, but after enduring the Arduous March in the mid-1990s and early 2000s, the *gajeong gaebyeol gyosa* (家庭 個別 教師), or private home tutor, is widespread. Some, if not most, in-service teachers who aspire to earn additional money aside from their official salary work as private home tutors.

Note that the emphasis on English education for university admission and extensive private tutoring consolidate the current North Korean regime. While students strive to be admitted to the university, the education system is justified unquestioningly. The idolization of the Kim family and the *Juche* ideology included in the reading passages in their English textbooks are instructed and engraved into young minds. Thus, both the ideological concretization and the university admission process surrounding English education fulfill the function of endocentric consolidation among the students. The external motivations to learn English, such as increasing scientific knowledge and disseminating the *Juche* ideology, are a façade. As presented in the above investigation, the implicit motivation to introduce English education to the public is to establish a permanent political system represented by the Kim family. In this regard, despite the lack of English speakers to have authentic communication in North Korea, English provides practical benefits to learners in the form of university admission. English also provides a positive influence on the political regime as it contributes to the stabilization of the system while strengthening the ideological armament of the youth.

5.3.8 Summary and Future Directions of English Education in North Korea

At the moment of drafting this book chapter, it would be premature to speculate on the future of English education in North Korea. Since 2018, while having a series of summit meetings with South Korean President Moon Jae-in and the U.S. President Donald Trump, Kim Jong-un has endeavored to boost the North Korean economy at the risk of negotiating their nuclear power with the USA. It is still unclear whether Chairman Kim's efforts to enervate his nation's economy will be successful. In the analysis of the recent changes in the English textbook, however, we identified several critical educational advances. First, their previous ideology-laden reading material were replaced with more science-related topics. Despite the remnants of the idolization of the Kim family still identified (particularly in the preface and front matter), most of the content is ideologically neutral and even can be utilized in other nations' ESL/EFL textbooks.

This recent, qualitative change is remarkable considering the previous textbooks published in Kim Jong-il's era, which were based on the principle of hatred education, vilifying the U.S. capitalist system and emphasizing their cruelty. The current English textbooks are more neutral in ideology and show striking similarities to ESL textbooks published by international publishing companies. The British teacher trainers and textbook writers from the British Council were likely deeply involved in the new textbooks, but the political decisions regarding textbooks is entirely dependent on the North Korean Ministry of Education. In this regard, the reform in the English textbook in North Korea may present the practical stance of the current regime.

Whether the change in English education qualifies as reform will require the test of time regarding the sustainability of the North Korean regime or even the Worker's Party of Korea. As China has proven, the Open Door Policy after the Cultural Revolution during Mao's era resulted in the transformation of English textbooks. Similar to the case of North Korea in the 1950s and 1960s, English education in China was eradicated but soon reinstated. After Deng Xiaoping's reign, English education was actively conducted. For example, at the initial stage during the Cultural Revolution in the 1960s, English instruction was entirely banned and was derided as the language of the Western imperialists. However, from 1978, English instruction was enthusiastically welcomed by the Chinese public. China's English textbook closely reflected the changing social atmosphere. In Mao's era, textbooks included ideological content justifying the Chinese socialist cause, but in Deng's era, such political slogans gradually disappeared. In this regard, the practical stance in Kim Jong-un's regime is similar to that in Deng's in the late 1970s, but as stated above, the progress of English education in North Korea will require test of time.

It is not easy to evaluate the current status of English education in North Korea. However, while analyzing recent English textbooks and summarizing the anecdotal reports from recent defectors from North Korea, most North Koreans take it for granted that their system may not be superior to that of other nations and have adopted utilitarian attitudes toward their southern compatriots and even the USA. While confronted with the USA at the national, political, ideological levels, such confrontation may have already ceased at the level of everyday lives of North Korean people. Such resigned and acquiescing attitudes seem to be reflected in recent English textbooks. Unlike their parents' generation, the teenaged students learning through these English textbooks may not be as ideologically rigid but rather more practical and utilitarian in their political orientations. While reciting the firm pledge toward the Kim family at school, they may listen to Korean pop (K-pop) music and watch Hollywood blockbusters at home. Thus, this masquerade may last for a considerable period, but the recent reform of English education in North Korea may function as a catalyst subverting the status quo. The future of English education in North Korea and the North Korean regime remains to be determined.

References

Adamson, B. (2004). *China's English: A history of English in Chinese education.* Hong Kong, China: University of Hong Kong Press.

Adamson, B., & Morris, P. (1997). The English curriculum in the People's Republic of China. *Comparative Education Review, 41*(1), 3–26.

Armstrong, C. K. (2009, April). *Juche and North Korea's global aspirations* (Working paper #1 of North Korea International Documentation Project). Washington, DC: Woodrow Wilson International Center for Scholars.

Baik, Jonghak Martin. (1994). *Language, ideology, and power: English textbooks of two Koreas.* Unpublished doctoral dissertation. University of Illinois at Urbana-Champaign.

Bermingham, F., & Wang, O. (2019, February 12). China's crowded labour market is making life tough for foreign workers and new graduate 'sea turtles'. Retrieved February 13, 2019, from https://www.scmp.com/economy/china-economy/article/2185133/chinas-crowded-labour-mar ket-making-life-tough-foreign-workers.

Bolton, K. (2002). Chinese Englishes: From Canton jargon to global English. *World Englishes, 21* (2), 181–199.

Bolton, K., & Graddol, D. (2012). English in China today. *English Today, 28*(3), 3–9.

Borowiec, S. (2014, September 14). Despite warnings, more western tourists are traveling to North Korea. Retrieved March 28, 2019, from https://www.latimes.com/world/asia/la-fg-north-korea-tourists-20140912-story.html.

Borthwick, S. (1982). *Education and social change in China: The beginnings of the modern era.* Stanford, CA: Hoover Press.

Canale, M., & Swain, M. (1980). Theoretical bases of communicative approaches to second language teaching and testing. *Applied Linguistics, 1*, 1–47.

Cho, J.-a., Lee, H.-k., & Kim, K.-s. (2013). North Korea: An overview. In P. J. Hsieh (Ed.), *Education in East Asia* (pp. 193–213). London: Bloomsbury.

Cumings, B. (2005). *Korea's place in the sun: A modern history.* New York: W. W. Norton.

Deng, P. (1997). *Private education in modern China.* London: Praeger.

Falout, J., Elwood, J., & Hood, M. (2009). Demotivation: Affective states and learning outcomes. *System, 37*(3), 403–417.

Fifield, A. (2017, December 15). A new film captures North Korea's 'bold and audacious' millennials. Retrieved March 20, 2019, from https://www.washingtonpost.com/news/world views/wp/2017/12/15/the-jangmadang-generation-new-film-shows-how-millennials-are-chang ing-north-korea/?noredirect=on&utm_term=.84195d811f13.

Ford, G. (2018). *Talking to North Korea: Ending the nuclear standoff.* London: Pluto Press.

Fujimoto-Adamson, N. (2006). Globalization and history of English education in Japan. *The Asia EFL Journal Quarterly, 8*(3), 259–282.

Gan, H. (2008). Chinese education tradition: The imperial examination system in feudal China. *Journal of Management and Social Sciences, 4*(2), 115–133.

Gardner, R. C. (1985). *Social psychology and second language learning: The role of attitudes and motivation.* London: Edward Arnold.

General Information Handbook for the JET Programme. (2018). Retrieved October 23, 2018, from http://jetprogramme.org/wp-content/MAIN-PAGE/COMMON/publications/2018_GIH_e.pdf.

Green, O. N. (1934). Pidgin English. *Fortnightly, 142,* 331–339.

Gu, M. (2018, August 14). An introduction to China's College English Test (CET). Retrieved February 7, 2019, from https://wenr.wes.org/2018/08/an-introduction-to-chinas-college-english-test-cet.

Higgins, A. (2009, July 16). Who will succeed Kim Jong Il? Retrieved March 21, 2019, from http://www.washingtonpost.com/wp-dyn/content/article/2009/07/15/AR2009071503930.html?tid=a_inl_manual.

Higgins, L. T., & Zhang, M. (2002). An introduction to Chinese psychology: Its historical roots until the present day. *The Journal of Psychology, 136*(2), 225–239.

Honda, Y. (2005). Freeters: Young atypical workers in Japan. *Japan Labor Review, 2*(3), 5–25

Hong, Jung Ja. (1996). Jamggodaedo yeong'eoro haneun Pyongyang oegook'eodae haksaengdeul [Students at Pyongyang Foreign Language University talk in English even in their sleep]. *Wolgan Mal, 118,* 110–114.

Howatt, A. P. R. (2004). *A history of English language teaching* (2nd ed.). Oxford, England: Oxford University Press.

Imura, M. (2003). *Nihon no eigo kyoiku nihyakunen [English education in Japan for the past 200 years].* Tokyo: Taishukan Shoten.

Isozaki, A. (2019, August 26). North Korea revamps its constitution: An end to juche is just one of the major changes made in the latest amendment. Retrieved January 31, 2020, from https://thediplomat.com/2019/08/north-korea-revamps-its-constitution/.

Joongang Ilbo. (2010, November 23). Bookhan 'gonan'eui haenggoon' 5nyeondong'an joomin 33man myeong geulmeojook'eo [330,000 civilians starved to death during the period of 5-year 'Arduous March']. Retrieved March 19, 2019, from https://news.joins.com/article/4695274.

Joongang Ilbo. (2018, December 23). 'Geumsujeo'nun daehak hapgyekjeung'eul moonda! [Those who are born with gold spoon grabs university admission certificate in their mouth!]. Retrieved March 13, 2019, from https://news.joins.com/article/23231742.

Kaplan, R., & Saccuzzo, D. (2012). *Psychological testing: Principles, applications, and issues.* Belmont, CA: Wadsworth.

Kariya, T. (2002). *Kyouiku kaikaku no gensou [Disillusion of educational reforms].* Tokyo: Chikumashobou.

Kim, Hyung-Chan. (1990). Joongdeung gyoyook [secondary education]. In Hyung-Chan Kim (Ed.). *Pukhan'eui gyogook [Education in North Korea]* (pp. 256–278). Seoul, Korea: Ulyumunhwasa.

Kim, Jin-Sook. (2016). Bukhan'eui 'jeonbanjeok 12nyeonje euimoogyoyook'e tareun hakjewa gyoyookgwajeong gaejeong donghyang [Recent trends in the revision of schooling system and curriculum in North Korea based on 'general 12-year compulsory education']. *KDI Bukhan Gyeongje Review, 2016*(6), 3–16.

Kim, Tae-Young. (2006). Motivation and attitudes toward foreign language learning as socio-politically mediated constructs: The case of Korean high school students. *The Journal of Asia TEFL, 3*(2), 165–192.

Kim, Tae-Young. (2011). Korean elementary school students' English learning demotivation: A comparative survey study. *Asia Pacific Education Review, 12*(1), 1–11.

Kim, Tae-Young. (2015). *Hankook'eui yeong'eohakseup donggi yeongu [Study of English learning motivation research in South Korea].* Seoul, Korea: Hankookmunhwasa.

Kim, Yeongseo. (2009). *Hankook'ei yeong'eogyoyooksa [History of English education in Korea]*. Seoul, Korea: Hankookmunhwasa.

Knights, M. (2016). *Old corruption: What British history can tell us about corruption today*. London: Transparency International.

Ko, Kwang Hyun. (2017). A brief history of imperial examination and its influences. *Society, 54*, 272–278.

Koike, I., & Tanaka, H. (1995). English in foreign language education policy in Japan: Toward the twenty-first century. *World Englishes, 14*(1), 13–25.

Kwak, Tae-Hwan, & Joo, Seung-Ho. (Eds.). (2009). *North Korea's foreign policy under Kim Jong Il: New perspectives*. London: Routledge.

Lam, A. (2002). English education in China: Policy changes and learners' experiences. *World Englishes, 21*(2), 245–256.

Lamers, M. (2010, April 4). Teaching English in North Korea. Retrieved March 2, 2019, from http://www.koreaherald.com/view.php?ud=20081007000032.

Lankov, A. (2016). *The resurgence of a market economy in North Korea*. Moscow: Carnegie Endowment for International Peace. Retrieved February 11, 2020, from https://carnegieendowment.org/files/CP_Lankov_Eng_web_final.pdf.

Larsen-Freeman, D., & Anderson, M. (2011). *Techniques and principles in language teaching* (3rd ed.). Oxford, England: Oxford University Press.

Lee, Byungmin., Yang, Hyun-Kwon, & Kwon, Oh-Hyun. (2005). The current state of English education in North Korea. *Foreign Languages Education, 12*(4), 267–297.

Lee, Nam-Hee. (2008). The state examination system: Its lights and shadows. *Oneul'eui Dongyangsasang, 18*, 117–136.

Li, W. (2015). China's language policies. Retrieved February 10, 2019, from https://ioelondonblog.wordpress.com/2015/06/12/chinas-language-policies/.

Li, X. (2017). ELT at tertiary institutions in China: A developmental perspective. In E.-S. Park & B. Spolsky (Eds.), *English education at the tertiary level in Asia: From Policy to practice* (pp. 6–26). Abingdon, England: Routledge.

Lo Bianco, J. (2009). English at home in China: How far does the bond extend? In J. Lo Bianco, J. Orton & Y. Gao (Eds.), *Critical language and literacy studies: China and English: Globalisation and the dilemmas of identity* (pp. 192–210). Bristol, England: Multilingual Matters.

Löfstedt, J.-I. (1980). *Chinese educational policy: Changes and contradictions 1949-79*. Stockholm: Amqvist and Wiksell.

McCormack, G. (2004). *Target North Korea: Pushing North Korea to the brink of nuclear catastrophe*. New York: Nation Books.

McKenzie, R. (2010). *The social psychology of English as a global language: Attitudes, awareness and identity in the Japanese context*. Dordrecht, Germany: Springer.

McPhee, S. (2014). Kotjebi: North Korean children in China. *Asian Affairs, 45*(3), 484–489.

Miyazaki, I. (1993). *Joongguk'eui siheomjiok: Gwageo [China's exam hell: The imperial examination]* (Joogguksa Yeonguhoi Trans.). Seoul, Korea: Cheonghyeonsa.

Moore, M. (2001, September 20). The rise and rise of Mandarin—but how many will end up in speaking it? Retrieved February 21, 2019, from https://www.telegraph.co.uk/news/worldnews/asia/china/8776515/The-rise-and-rise-of-Mandarin-but-how-many-will-end-up-speaking-it.html.

Myers, B. R. (2015). *North Korea's Juche myth*. Busan, Korea: Sthele Press.

Nemoto, A. K. (2018). Getting ready for 2020: Changes and challeges for English education in public primary school in Japan. *The Language Teacher, 42*(4), 33–35.

NK Chosun. (2013). Bukhan'eui daehakiphaksiheom'eun namhan'gwa eoteotke dareulkayo? [How does the university entrance exam in North Korea differ from that in South Korea?]. Retrieved March 13, 2019, from http://nk.chosun.com/news/articleView.html?idxno=151962.

Oh, Shinyu, & Kim, Tae-Young. (2020). A comparison of high school English textbooks between pre and post-2013 Revised Curriculum in North Korea. *Modern English Education, 20*(1), 43–55.

Ohtani, C. (2010). Problems in the assistant language teacher system and English activity at Japanese public elementary schools. *Educational Perspectives, 43*(1/2), 38–45.

Okano, K. H. (2011). A cultural overview of education in Japanese civilization: Adaptive learning at the global periphery. In Y. Zhao (Ed.), *Handbook of Asian education: A cultural perspective* (pp. 184–198). New York: Routledge.

Ota, N. (2011). Yakon-Yosai and globalization. In C. Holroyd & K. Coates (Eds.), *Japan in the age of globalization* (pp. 148–157). London: Routledge.

Park, Min Je. (1993). Bukhan'eui oikook'eogyoyook: Russia'eo'eseo yeong'eowuijuro [Foreign language education in North Korea: from Russian to English]. *Tongil Hankook, 112*, 102–105.

Park, Sunok. (2017). English education and learners' affective factors in Korea and China: A case study. *The Journal of Linguistic Science, 80*, 99–122.

Park, Yak-Woo, Park, Ki-Hwa, Kim, Jin-Chul, Ko, Kyung-Seok, & Chung, Kuk-Jin. (2001). *Bukhan yeong'eo gyogwaseo bunseok [An analysis of English textbook in North Korea].* Seoul, Korea: Hankookmunhwasa.

Ryo, Hashiwara. (2011). *Kim Jong Il'eui soomgyeojin jeonjaeng: Kim Il Sung'eui jookeumgwa daeryang asa'eui susukeki'reul poonda [Kim Jong Il's hidden war: Solving the riddles of Kim Il Sung's death and mass starvation]* (trans. Changsik Yang). Seoul, Korea: Jayoo Media.

Sasaki, M. (2008). The 150-year history of English language assessment in Japanese education. *Language Teaching, 25*(1), 63–83.

Sawa, T. (2020, January 21). Japan going the wrong way in English-education reform. Retrieved March 20, 2021, from https://www.japantimes.co.jp/opinion/2020/01/21/commentary/japan-commentary/japan-going-wrong-way-english-education-reform/#:~:text=%E2%80%93% 20Beginning%20in%20the%202020%20academic,the%20basics%20of%20English% 20language.

Smith, R. (2013). Harold E. Palmer, IRLT and 'historical sense' in ELT. *IRLT Journal, 12*, 1.8. Retrieved October 10, 2018, from https://warwick.ac.uk/fac/soc/al/people/smith/smith_r/ harold_e__palmer_irlt_and_historical_sense_in_elt.pdf.

Song, Jae Jung. (2002). The *Juche* ideology: English in North Korea. *English Today, 18*(1), 47–52.

Sujimoto, M., & Okita, Y. (2011). *Ilbon'gyoyook'eu sahoisa [Social history of education in Japan]* (Trans: Kiwon Lee & Sungchul Oh). Seoul, Korea: Kyunginmunhwasa.

Sutterby, J. A. (2012). *Early education in a global context.* Bingley, England: Emerald Group Publishing.

Taguchi, K. (2015). *Demotivation in second language acquisition: Insights from Japan.* Bristol, England: Multilingual Matters.

Tang, L. (1983). *TEFL in China: Methods and techniques.* Shanghai, China: Shanghai Foreign Languages Press.

Teng, S.-Y., & Fairbank, J. K. (1979). *China's response to the West: A documentary survey, 1939-1923.* Cambridge, MA: Harvard University Press.

Thae, Yongho. (2018, February 27). Namgwa buk'eui daehakgyoyook bigyo [The comparison of educational system between South and North Korea]. Retrieved March 19, 2019, from https:// thaeyongho.com/2018/02/27/%EB%82%A8%EA%B3%BC-%EB%B6%81%EC%9D%98-% EB%8C%80%ED%95%99-%EA%B5%90%EC%9C%A1%EC%9D%98-%EB%B9%84%EA %B5%90-1%ED%9A%8C/.

The Japan Times. (2016, September 5). English heads for elementary school in 2020 but hurdles abound. Retrieved March 20, 2021, from https://www.japantimes.co.jp/news/2016/09/05/ reference/english-heads-elementary-school-2020-hurdles-abound/#.VFgpiLTcc.

Wagner, E. W. (1977). The civil examination process as social leaven: The case of the Northern provinces in the Yi Dynasty. *Korea Journal, 17*(1), 22–27.

Waldron, A. (1991). The warlord: Twentieth-century Chinese understandings of violence, militarism, and imperialism. *The American Historical Review, 96*(4), 1073–1100.

Wei, R., & Su, J. (2012). The statistics of English in China. *English Today, 28*(3), 10–19.

Wen, Q., & Hu, W. (2007). History and policy of English education in mainland China. In Y. H. Choi & B. Spolsky (Eds.), *English education in Asia: History and policies* (p. 1–32). Seoul, Korea: Asia TEFL.

Wilkins, D. A. (1976). *Notional syllabuses*. Oxford, England: Oxford University Press.

Williams, S. W. (1836). Jargon spoken at Canton. *Chinese Repository, 4 (January)*, 428–435.

Yamamoto, N. Y. (1978). The oral method: Harold E. Palmer and the reformation of the teaching of the English language in Japan. *ELT Journal, 32*(2), 151–158.

Yamamoto, S. (2004). Universities and government in post-war Japan. *The Canadian Journal of Higher Education, 34*(3), 105–126.

Yan, L. (2001). Some 110,000 overseas students returned home for careers. *People's Daily*. Retrieved March 29, 2021, from http://english.peopledaily.com.cn/200102/13/eng20010213_62241.html.

Yang, Seung Chul. (1994). *The North and South Korean political system*. Boulder, CO: Westview.

Yashima, T. (2009). International posture and the ideal L2 self in the Japanese EFL context. In Z. Dörnyei & E. Ushioda (Eds.), *Motivation, language identity and the L2 self* (pp. 144–163). Bristol, England: Multilingual Matters.

Yashima, T. (2013). Imagined L2 selves and motivation for intercultural communication. In M. T. Apple, D. Da Silva & T. Fellner (Eds.), *Language learning motivation in Japan* (pp. 35–53). Bristol, England: Multilingual Matters.

Zhao, Y., & Campbell, K. P. (1995). English in China. *World Englishes, 14*(3), 377–390.

Zheng, Y., & Cheng, L. (2008). College English test (CET) in China. *Language Testing, 25*, 408–417.

Zweig, D., & Ge, Z. (2018, July 27). How Chinese students who return home after studying abroad succeed—and why they don't. Retrieved February 12, 2019, from https://www.scmp.com/comment/insight-opinion/asia/article/2157081/how-chinese-students-who-return-home-after-studying.

Chapter 6
Recent Advances in EFL (De)Motivation Theory

Since Gardner and Lambert (1959) published their pioneering work, L2 motivation research has enjoyed academic prominence in second language acquisition (SLA). Among individual difference factors in L2 studies, L2 motivation has been the primary area of investigation (Dörnyei, 2005, 2009; Dörnyei & Ushioda, 2021). According to Dörnyei and Ryan (2015), from 2009 to 2015, at least seven anthologies on L2 motivation have been published, which reflects "a wider interest in the topic" (p. 73). It is indeed beyond the scope of this book to provide a coherent summary of all L2 motivation theories and related research. The above anthologies have already accomplished this task. Moreover, innovative ideas were actively added by systematic endeavors, often from Dörnyei and his colleagues. For example, various novel approaches in L2 motivation from the complexity theory and dynamic systems theory (DST) perspectives were extensively introduced in an edited volume by Dörnyei et al. (2015b). In addition, directed motivational currents (DMC) defined as "a motivational drive which energises long-term, sustained behaviour" (Muir & Dörnyei, 2013, p. 357) have been explained by Dörnyei et al. (2015a). Moreover, the intricacies of self-determination theory (SDT), often understood as the combination of amotivation and intrinsic/extrinsic motivation, and its influence on L2 learners' motivated engagement have actively been investigated by Noels and her Canadian colleagues (Noels et al., 1999, 2001, 2019). Two excellent L2-teacher resource books to motivate L2 students in the classroom or remotivate teachers' low level of teaching motivation are also on the market (Dörnyei & Hadfield, 2013; Dörnyei & Kubanyiova, 2014).

Therefore, in this chapter, only research relevant to East Asian contexts, mainly Korean, will be concisely introduced. First, while surveying dominant L2 motivation theories after the 1950s, this chapter succinctly summarizes the recent advances in L2 motivation theories including Dörnyei's (2005) L2 motivational self-system and its three subcomponents: the ideal L2 self, the ought-to L2 self, and the L2 learning experience. Demotivation, teacher motivation, and L2 teachers' emotional labor will also be introduced while considering East Asian EFL educational contexts. After that, exemplary macro, nationwide, and cross-national studies in L2 motivation will

© Springer Nature Singapore Pte Ltd. 2021
T.-Y. Kim, *Historical Development of English Learning Motivation Research*,
English Language Education 21, https://doi.org/10.1007/978-981-16-2514-5_6

be introduced. Competitive motivation (see Chaps. 3 and 4) and attitudes reflecting sociopolitical changes will be explained with specific reference to Kim and his colleagues' previous research (Kim, 2006a, 2010a; Kim & Kim, 2016b). In the latter half of this chapter, a recent trend of L2 learning/teaching (de)motivation studies influenced by activity theory (Engeström, 1987, 1999a, 1999b; Leont'ev, 1978) will be presented. This chapter concludes by introducing motivational languaging activity (MLA) as an education-friendly teaching tool that can enhance students' low level of L2 learning motivation.

6.1   A Brief History of Previous L2 Motivation Research

As Larsen-Freeman and Long (1991) and Block (2003) state, SLA is a relatively recent academic discipline. Studies on L2 learning/teaching motivation have been strongly influenced by related academic disciplines, especially educational psychology. In this regard, this section briefly outlines Gardner's (1985) psychological model of L2 motivation and other advancements in this field.

For more than three decades (around 1959–1988), Gardner and his colleagues' (Gardner, 1985, 1988; Gardner & Lambert, 1959, 1972; Gardner & Smyth, 1975) research gained academic prominence in the field of L2 learning motivation. In understanding the historical background of Gardner's research on L2 motivation, it may be informative to understand a deep-rooted antagonism between anglophone and francophone Canadians. Historically, the initial settlement in Canada was made by French descendants. Jacques Cartier erected a cross in the Gaspé Peninsula in 1534 to claim Canada the land of the French King Francis I. Gradually the French fishing fleet visited Saint Lawrence River and started to exchange goods with First Nations. French settlement was expedited in 1608 when Samuel de Champlain landed in the Saint John Harbor in 1604 and founded the city of Quebec. However, the British also claimed possession of the territory after the expedition by Humphrey Gilbert in St. John's and Newfoundland in 1583. Although French settlers thrived around the shores of the Saint Lawrence River and Nova Scotia in the early eighteenth century, French immigrants stopped coming, and the British settlers endeavored to take total control of the territory (including Quebec). After a series of fierce battles including the Battle of the Plains of Abraham and Battle of Fort Niagara in 1759, and the Battle of the Thousand Islands and the Battle of Sainte-Foy in 1760, the British gained control across the colony.

Even today, the population of francophone Canadians is relatively small: approximately 6.5 million, which comprises 24% of the population (The Canadian Encyclopedia, 2019). Population statistics show a decline of 6% since 1900. However, the population of francophone Canadians in Quebec province is estimated at 6.2 million, which constitutes 82% of the entire French population across Canada. These statistics present a stark contrast between anglophones' and francophones' geographical topology. Most francophone Canadians live in and around Quebec; the remaining majority English-speaking Canadians are spread over other provinces.

Due to the historically suppressed ethnic anti-Anglo sentiment, the province of Quebec conducted referenda in 1980 and 1995 inquiring about the sovereignty of Quebec separating from other provinces. The 1995 referendum was narrowly denied, by 50.58%. Under this sociopolitical context, it has always been the national priority to unite all the provinces of Canada into one nation. Gardner's L2 motivation research may need to be considered with this historical backdrop.

Among the extensive bibliography by Gardner and his associates, his 1985 book entitled "*Social Psychology and Second Language Learning: The Role of Attitudes and Motivation*" is often considered the major work for his theory, termed the socio-educational model (Gardner, 1985, 1988). The model can be summarized as follows: (1) there exist two types of distinctive language learning orientation: integrative and instrumental, (2) a crucial factor of L2 learners' proficiency is not instrumental but integrative orientation, and (3) the attitudes toward the target language community and L2 native speakers are incorporated into the overarching concept of motivation. Gardner (1985) stated that integrative orientation is "willingness to be like valued members of the language community" (Gardner & Lambert, 1959, p. 271) and instrumental orientation focuses on "the practical value and advantage of learning a new language" (Gardner, 1985, p. 133). For example, if a language learner wishes to integrate himself/herself into the culture and traditions of the target language group, the learner is motivated by integrative orientation. However, as identified in many EFL contexts in Asia, if the learner wishes to be admitted to a university having an academic reputation after earning a high score in English tests such as the TOEFL or the IELTS, this learner has instrumental orientation.

It should be noted that Gardner and his associates refuted a simple dichotomous understanding of the socio-educational model (Gardner & MacIntyre, 1991), particularly in understanding the concept of integrative and instrumental orientations or motivations. It would be more accurate to understand that Gardner explained the complex relationships among the many factors internal to the learner (e.g., Skehan, 1989, 1992). His primary concerns were integrativeness and L2 learning outcomes. He used refined quantitative methods such as factor analysis and structural equational modeling employing LISREL statistical software. Gardner's insights into L2 learning motivation exerted a significant influence on the research of the next generation.

However, as Oxford and Shearin (1994) criticized, Gardner et al.'s research had been overly emphasized for more than 30 years, and as a result, other types of studies on motivation with different epistemological stances were overshadowed (e.g., Sivan, 1986; Ushioda, 2003). Additionally, the importance of culture-embedded and situation-sensitive motivation (such as competitive motivation) uniquely identified in Korea was generally not investigated in the twentieth century. As Dörnyei and Csizér (2002) and Dörnyei and Skehan (2003) stated, various types of situation-specific motivations may be operative when a learner faces a new learning context, and this must have been investigated further.

Despite Gardner's (1985) terminology, "socio-educational model," L2 motivation is still operationalized as an individual phenomenon occurring in a learner's mind. The main focus was on an individual's L2 learning motivation or attitudes, and equal importance was not placed on the social contexts. For example, little attention was paid to the learner's social interaction with other L2 users, his or her host family, school system, and local communities (including family influence), or to the influences of the culture and norms of L2 communities. In this research tradition, for example, the significant parental pressure on Korean EFL students to pass the college entrance exam in order to build a prosperous family, which was described as the characteristics of uterine family in Chap. 3, was not adequately investigated. Other than an objective, if not superficial, description of the loose interconnectedness between individual L2 learners and their respective social contexts, the multi-layered dynamics of the L2 motivation process were not properly addressed in Gardner's model (cf. Dörnyei, 2001a, 2003, 2005).

As a natural consequence, after the early 1990s, there was a series of studies that urged a new theoretical framework (Crookes & Schmidt, 1991; Dörnyei, 1990, 1994; Oxford & Shearin, 1994) that did not rely on the conventional distinctions of integrative and instrumental motivations. Responding to the increasing demands for modification of the socio-educational model, Tremblay and Gardner (1995) also tried to incorporate recent advances in social psychology. They hypothesized two unique motivational constructs: observable *motivational behaviors* and unobservable *motivational antecedents*. In addition, they combined Goal Setting Theory (Locke & Latham, 1990), Attribution Theory (Weiner, 1992), and Self-Efficacy Theory (Bandura, 1993, 1997).

Undoubtedly, it would have been a valuable academic endeavor to incorporate theoretical advances from neighboring schools of educational psychology into L2 motivation research. However, it is not clear why social contexts, which were considered in the previous version of the socio-educational model in 1985, were not included in the modified version in 1995. In the 1985 model, four broad conceptual areas (social milieu, individual differences, language acquisition contexts, and outcomes) were covered (Gardner, 1985). Gardner's 1995 model did not consider them (Tremblay & Gardner, 1995).

Among the many proposals in L2 motivation made since the 1990s, Dörnyei's (1994, 1996, 1998, 2001a, 2001b, 2003) studies deserve our academic attention due to his efforts to establish an education-friendly and comprehensive model for L2 motivation. For instance, Dörnyei (1996) hinged on three levels of motivation: the language level, the learner level, and the learning situation level. What he considered crucial was situation-specific motivation, which encompasses various learning contexts. His proposal was presented as the Motivation-Learning Outcome Chain (Dörnyei, 1996), wherein L2 motivation affected the learners' learning behavioral patterns, and with the cognitive learning process, the learning behavior constituted L2 learning strategies.

In the following several years, the Motivation-Learning Outcome Chain was theoretically refined in Dörnyei and Ottó (1998) and Dörnyei's (2001a, 2001b, 2003, 2005) more recent model: the Process Model of L2 Motivation. Inspired by two German psychologists, Heckhausen (1991) and Kuhl (1987) (see also Heckhausen & Kuhl, 1985), Dörnyei and Ottó (1998) hypothesized three distinct stages: preactional, actional, and postactional stages, each of which was also divided into two sequences: motivational influences and action sequence. The process model, compared to previous models, is an advanced systematic schema because it attempts to capture a chronological timeline of L2 learning motivation, and incorporates actual language learning strategies in an action sequence L2 learners can readily put to use.

However, in comparison to the theoretical clarity of Dörnyei and Ottó's (1998) process model, its applicability for actual L2 classrooms needed much elaboration. Considering its theoretical aspects, L2 teachers do not have much means to enhance students' L2 motivation despite their knowledge in the longitudinally changing aspects of L2 learning motivation illustrated in the process model. Moreover, individual L2 learners' multiple motivations and goals in learning the L2 were not adequately addressed in the model. Different types of motivation have different origins, and their duration may belong to different stages among the three preactional, actional, and postactional stages. For instance, an L2 learner may create multiple motivations in order to obtain external rewards, and to be assimilated into the L2 community. In this case, the two motivations might belong to distinctive motivational stages. This potential shortcoming was acknowledged later by Dörnyei (2005, pp. 86–87) himself. Moreover, considering the nature of L2 learning and use, which "happens through and over time" (Ortega & Iberri-Shea, 2005) beyond the L2 classroom, a more longitudinal approach in analyzing learners' L2 learning and use motivation would be required. Given the time-consuming nature of EFL learning and use, different types of L2 motivation can be generated, maintained, or terminated depending on a learner's diverse L2 learning experiences throughout his or her lifespan.

Furthermore, this conceptual vagueness does not seem to be resolved even when trying to understand an individual L2 learner's motivational changes; the three stages posed cannot always be uni-directional, or from preactional to postactional. Failure to maintain L2 motivation in the execution stage might induce L2 learners' demotivation, which is defined as "specific external forces that reduce or diminish the motivational basis of behavioral intention or an ongoing action" (Dörnyei, 2001a, p. 143). In this case, motivation needs to be regenerated in the preactional stage. In other words, Dörnyei's (1998, 2001a, 2001b, 2003, 2005) process model seems to explain the case of successfully executed L2 motivation.

Despite the abovementioned potential weaknesses in the process model, it is a remarkable academic advancement. Motivation is systematically explained as a sequential longitudinal process, and accordingly regarded as a dynamically evolving concept. With a few exceptions (e.g., Dörnyei & Csizér, 2002; Gardner et al., 2004; Inbar et al., 2001; Kim, 2009a, 2009b, 2009c, 2009d, 2011a; Ushioda, 2001; Williams & Burden, 1997), longitudinal investigations in L2 motivation still deserve academic attention. As Ortega and Iberri-Shea (2005, p. 42) emphasize, "ultimately, longitudinal findings can have a central place in advancing our SLA theories and research programs." L2 motivation research will be no exception. The inherent shortcoming in the cross-sectional, single research design is our inability to adequately address the evolving nature of L2 motivation. Learners who are initially amotivated or showing an extreme lack of motivation might later become highly motivated students in L2 learning (or vice versa).

Ushioda's (2001) study, in this regard, is worth mentioning. Using open-ended and semi-structured interviews, she conducted a 3-year longitudinal study in Dublin, Ireland. The participants were undergraduate students majoring in French language. As the participants' French proficiency increased, their motivational constructs also showed a gradual change: from motivation deriving from experience (e.g., positive L2-learning experience, intrinsic-affective rewards, and positive L2-related experience) to motivation directed toward future goals (e.g., personal goals, short-term goals/incentives, and language-intrinsic goals). Ushioda's (2001) qualitative research explores the possibility of using longitudinal interview data to address the longitudinally changing nature of L2 motivation.

Another new trend in the field of L2 motivation will be the integration of macro-sociological perspectives. Norton [Peirce]'s (1993, 1995, 2013) works are exemplary. Her research shows the influence of Bourdieu's (1977, 1991) social-economics metaphor, *investment*. Investigating five female ESL immigrants in Toronto, Canada, Norton focuses on the invisible social barriers between the non-immigrant, native English-speaking population and the recent immigrant, non-native English-speaking population. Norton argues that English learning is an essential personal investment which is the key to social success and entry into mainstream (target-language speaking) society. The term "investment" deserves scholarly attention: by using the term, the domain in L2 motivation research can be expanded to include sociopolitical aspects in L2 learning.

It would be noteworthy to state the changing nature of integrativeness stated by Gardner and his associates. Given the historical background of the formulation of this concept, it would be relatively easy to conceptualize integration into the target community for L2 learners. Notably, in the research context in which Gardner (1985) was involved, French learners of English mostly lived in the province of Quebec and are of French ancestry, and they wanted to be integrated into the English-speaking majority in Canada. Thus, the socio-educational model argued by Gardner was based on the concept of the distinctly different population, region, and cultural heritage of the target language community. As defined by Gardner (2001, p. 5), integrativeness is the learners' "genuine interest in learning the second language in order to come closer to the other language community." However, the changing climate in English (particularly EFL) learning requires a critical reexamination of this concept. As Dörnyei (2009, p. 23) states, "it is not quite clear what the target of the integration is." Integrativeness in L2 learning motivation may not clearly explain current L2 learners, as they may not have a clear image of the specific target group to be integrated into the globalized world (Lamb, 2007). L2 learners may initially be motivated to learn English to obtain a stable or prestigious job in South Korea. English itself functions as the language of global networking among workers having different languages and nationalities in many international companies (cf. Block & Cameron, 2002). Given this, it seems logical to argue that L2 learners' L2 (particularly EFL) learning motivation may not be adequately explained by Gardner's (1985, 2001) concept of integrativeness.

It is not the intention of this book to state that the concept of integrativeness is no longer essential when creating and maintaining L2-learning motivation (Dörnyei, 2009). Recent studies (e.g., Al-Khalil, 2011; Oh & Kong, 2000) have verified that integrativeness is a significant determinant of successful L2 learning in languages that are less-commonly taught. For example, Oh and Kong (2000) found that students learning Arabic as a foreign language in South Korea with integrative motivation exhibited more positive attitudes toward Arab people, Arab culture, and Arabic language classes than those with instrumental motivation, who only showed more positive attitudes toward Arabic language classes.

However, it should be emphasized that the changing status of English as a global language has highlighted an urgent need for its conceptual reconstruction. English has served as a means of global communication for commerce, transportation, and immigration, and therefore the conventional demarcation between English as a foreign language (EFL) and as a second language (ESL) has become increasingly porous. Besides, it is difficult to imagine one or two communities or language groups in which English is used on a frequent or daily basis. Given this rapid transition in the function and role of English at the international level, it has become increasingly difficult, if not impossible, for English learners to create integrativeness in either the extreme or moderate form suggested by Gardner (2010).

To overcome the emerging shortcomings of Gardner's (1985, 2001) integrativeness, based on Hungarian nationwide, longitudinal data, Dörnyei (2005, 2009) proposed three main concepts in his L2 Motivational Self System (L2MSS): *Ideal L2 self, Ought-to L2 self,* and *L2 learning experience.* The ideal L2 self reflects desirable future images after attaining L2 proficiency. L2 learners may dream of a prosperous future regarding their job stability, financial situation, and respect from others. The ideal L2 self is a broad concept that incorporates both integrativeness and instrumentality. The reason is that the positive L2 self-images created by learners can be related either to their aspirations to be assimilated into L2 communities or to their realistic expectations to be successful in their schools or workplaces. Given this, the focus on the ideal L2 self is how L2 learners internalize reasons for L2 learning and make these reasons serve for the learners' learning goal. As long as they understand the reasons and see prosperous future images after acquiring L2 proficiency, those images function as the ideal L2 self.

The ought-to L2 self, on the contrary, is related to negative consequences from not achieving sufficient L2 proficiency. For example, young Korean EFL learners are compelled to learn English in order not to fail in the College Scholastic Ability Test, or become unemployed (Kim, 2006a, 2007). In this case, Korean EFL learners' L2 learning motivation can be attributed to external causes rather than their intrinsic interest in learning the L2; EFL learners feel that they ought to have at least a minimum level of English proficiency.

It seems important to note that not all instrumentality is related to the ought-to L2 self. Dörnyei (2009, p. 28) mentions that "when our idealized image is associated with being professionally successful, instrumental motives with a promotion focus. . .are related to the ideal self," while "instrumental motives with a prevention focus–for example, to study in order not to fail an exam or not to disappoint one's parents–are part of the ought self." Similarly, Higgins (1987, 1998) stated that an ideal self is *promotion* based because learners can foresee desirable future images, whereas an ought-to self is slanted toward *prevention* focused, which comes from social pressure or the desire to fulfill the wishes of significant others such as parents or teachers. Therefore, we should not equate integrativeness with the ideal L2 self or instrumentality with the ought-to L2 self. The criteria seem to be located instead in the promotion/prevention focus of the future image.

The third component in Dörnyei's (2005, 2009) L2MSS is the L2 learning experience. Since L2 learning motivation involves creating and maintaining L2 learning, the role of a learning experience is related to "executive" motives. Even though an L2 learner may create an ideal L2 self or an ought-to L2 self in the initial stage of L2 learning, his or her self-image might not be maintained unless appropriate L2 learning experiences are recognized. For example, as Lantolf and Genung (2002) report, when L2 lessons are based on rote memorization of grammar rules and vocabulary, there is a possibility of losing the ideal L2 self (e.g., a competent L2 user) before the semester is over.

Dörnyei's (2005, 2009) fundamental concepts were influenced by Markus and Nurius' (1986) possible self theory and Higgins' (1987) self-discrepancy theory. According to Markus and Nurius (1986, p. 964), possible selves "represent an individual's idea of what they might become, what they would like to become, and what they are afraid of becoming." Higgins' self-discrepancy theory states that we are motivated by the desire to reduce the discrepancy between our actual and ideal or ought-to selves. If the learner sees the gap between his or her ideal L2 learning and use situation and the current situation is not too narrow or too wide, the learner will be motivated to reduce the gap. If the gap is perceived to be too wide, this can lead to amotivation.

Because the L2MSS is a relatively new theoretical model in L2 motivation research, researchers have attempted to refine the concept through a series of sophisticated statistical analyses. For instance, by using structural equation modeling (SEM), Taguchi et al. (2009) investigated the ideal L2 self, ought-to L2 self, and other psychological subcomponents of 1300 Chinese, Japanese, and Iranian English learners. They found that Gardner's integrativeness and instrumentality can be subsumed into the concepts of the ideal and ought-to L2 selves. Using questionnaire methods, they measured L2 learners' attitudes and motivational variables. Variables included the ideal L2 self, the ought-to L2 self, the influence of family, instrumentality promotion, instrumentality prevention, attitudes toward learning English, cultural interest, attitudes toward the L2 community, and integrativeness. They distinguished instrumentality into two subtypes: instrumentality promotion and instrumentality prevention. The former is concerned with hopes, aspirations, advancements, and growth, whereas the latter concerns the presence or absence of outcomes and is related to the learners' safety, responsibilities, and obligations (cf. Dörnyei, 2009, p. 28). Taguchi et al.'s findings confirmed that Dörnyei's (2005) L2MSS and the concepts of the ideal L2 self and the ought-to L2 self are not country-specific findings but universally found phenomena; they found similar results in the three participating countries. In addition, they found that the ideal L2 self was correlated positively with integrativeness, but the ideal L2 self had a higher correlation with the learners' intended efforts toward learning English (the criterion measure) than did integrativeness. This finding shows evidence that the ideal L2 self has better construct validity than integrativeness and may possibly replace this concept. Furthermore, Papi (2010) analyzed the L2 anxiety construct from the perspective of L2MSS. He found that while the ideal L2 self and the L2 learning experience reduced learners' English anxiety, the ought-to L2 self significantly increased their anxiety.

The abovementioned studies empirically validate the legitimacy of the L2MSS. Nevertheless, future research should be expanded to include various L2 learning environments, because learners' future selves can be created, maintained, or even abandoned by the L2 learning experiences (Dörnyei, 2019, 2020).

In South Korea, Kim and Kim (2012) investigated the conceptual compatibility between Gardner's (1985) socio-educational model and Dörnyei's (2005, 2009) L2MSS. Using a questionnaire survey that included the ideal L2 self, the ought-to L2 self, integrativeness, and instrumentality (both promotion and prevention), they collected data from 495 Korean secondary school students. Their research findings also corroborated the validity of L2MSS, that it is possible to replace integrativeness with the ideal L2 self. It was also found that instrumentality (promotion) correlates strongly with both the ideal and ought-to L2 selves, whereas instrumentality (prevention) correlates only with the ought-to L2 self. In sum, Kim and Kim's (2012) research confirmed that Dörnyei's (2005, 2009) ideal L2 self explains Korean secondary school students' motivated behavior (the criterion measure) better than the instrumentality or integrativeness of Gardner's (1985) socio-educational model.

6.2   Recent Advances in L2 Motivation Research

Gardner and his colleagues made an extraordinary academic contribution to L2 motivation, and Dörnyei and his associates vigorously investigated the various aspects of L2 motivation. The sub-topics in the study of L2 motivation have since significantly diversified. A greater number of researchers are investigating various geographical, educational, and linguistic contexts (cf. Lamb et al., 2019). In this section, three recent trends in L2 learning and teaching (de)motivation will be highlighted: (1) Context-specific L2 motivation research (including demotivation and remotivation studies in East Asia), (2) L2 teacher motivation studies, and (3) macro or mega-level study in L2 motivation.

6.2.1   Context-Specific L2 Learning Demotivation in Asia

One noticeable trend in L2 motivation is the emphasis on context. As Dörnyei and Ushioda (2021) emphasized, understanding contextual factors is essential when investigating motivation. Similarly, Ushioda (2003) conceptualized L2 motivation as a socially mediated phenomenon, emphasizing that the study of L2 motivation should focus on broader society. Recently, highlighting the beneficial role of narrative inquiry, Benson (2014) noted that L2 learners' perception of societal influences is one of the main foci of motivation research. Identification of contextual factors of students' L2 learning (de)motivation has been spearheaded by the adoption of the complex dynamic systems theory (Dörnyei et al., 2015b).

Researchers in East Asia have actively published research findings on EFL learning motivation. In Japan, Ryan (2009) defines the Japanese EFL university context as "a motivation wasteland" (p. 407) for its rigid, teacher-centered traditional EFL instruction often linked to the university entrance exams. Moreover, the increasing number of demotivation studies in East Asian countries (e.g., Kikuchi, 2015; Kim, 2011a; Wang & Malderez, 2006) reflects the dominant role of English in regulating students' learning behavior related to university admission and initial job placement.

A related trend in contextual concerns is a series of studies examining motivation across different school grades. These cross-grade studies have indicated that in Asian contexts, students' motivation to learn English decreases as they advance to higher grade levels (e.g., Alavinia & Sehat, 2012; Hamada, 2008; Kikuchi, 2013; Kim, 2012a; Kim & Seo, 2012). These studies attributed demotivational phenomena to the influence of unique contextual factors. In Iran, Alavinia and Sehat (2012) investigated 165 students' demotivation; they found that along with learners' simultaneous learning of other languages and cumulative experience of failure, a negative learning environment was the prime cause of demotivation. In Japan, Hamada (2008) found that the perceived difficulty of English coursebooks was the strongest demotivator for high school students, and English grammar was the strongest demotivator for junior high school students. In Korea, Kim and Seo (2012) identified three prime factors in elementary school students' demotivation: negative impacts from their English teacher, unreasonable social expectations of EFL proficiency, and a widening proficiency gap among students. Accordingly, L2 researchers have argued that learners' motivation is a socially mediated phenomenon influenced by unique sociocultural contexts (Ushioda, 2003, 2013).

As Falout et al. (2009) and Kim and Kim (2013a, 2013b) stated, demotivation research in L2 learning is centering around the issue of English as a foreign language. Due to the mandatory nature of EFL learning in many countries for international communication, students experience varying degrees of demotivation. Kim and Kim (2013b) reviewed demotivation research in EFL contexts based on two criteria: research method and conceptualization of demotivation. First, previous EFL demotivation research adopted either quantitative or qualitative methods. For the quantitative research, the questionnaire survey with Likert-type questions has typically been used. For example, Falout et al. (2009) used a closed-item questionnaire to investigate demotivating factors for 900 Japanese university students. Participants were requested to recollect their past demotivating experiences in EFL learning. Results showed three macro aspects of demotivation: external factors (teacher immediacy, grammar-translation, and course level); internal factors (self-denigration, value, and self-confidence); and reactive factors (help-seeking, enjoyment-seeking, and avoidance). After Falout et al.'s (2009) study, similar studies soon followed (e.g., Ghadirzadeh et al., 2012, Kim, 2009a, 2009b; Sakai & Kikuchi, 2009). From these studies, the following common factors in demotivation were identified: teacher-related factors, difficult learning contents, inappropriate school facilities, and lack of students' intrinsic motivation and interest. Some researchers utilized pre-classified demotivating factors without conducting factor analysis (e.g., Alavinia & Sehat, 2012; Hamada, 2008; Warrington & Jeffrey, 2005). For example, Warrington and Jeffrey (2005) collected quantitative data from 188 Japanese university students. Participants were asked to choose five out of 15 possible demotivating factors. Based on the frequency of selected items, results were divided into significant and less significant factors in demotivation.

The studies mentioned above showed various demotivating factors but did not present decreasing trends in motivation. Kim (2011a) and Jung (2011) focused on the changing nature of (de)motivation. Jung adopted a closed-ended questionnaire to investigate Korean college students' demotivation and remotivation. All participants were requested to draw a graph on which they expressed their motivational changes from primary school to college. The graphs were aggregated into an average line which was presented as the average change of Korean EFL students (de)motivation.

Interestingly, the participants showed a definite increase in their EFL learning motivation until Grade 8 (second grade in junior high school or middle school), but after that their motivation showed a constant decrease until college admission. Similarly, Kim (2011a) examined 6301 Korean elementary school students and compared their EFL learning motivation from third to sixth grade. Among the various results reported, the participants showed a consistent decrease in all subtypes of motivation in a statistically significant manner.

Another trend in demotivation research in EFL learning is qualitative direction. An increasing number of researchers used interviews, open-ended questionnaires, and reflective essays. By using these methods, L2 learners' own words reflecting their previous L2 learning experiences and demotivation were collected and analyzed. For example, Kikuchi (2009) invited Japanese university students to express their previous experiences in English learning to investigate their EFL learning demotivation when attending secondary schools in Japan. He found five demotivating factors: (1) individual teacher behavior in the classroom, (2) the grammar-translation methods used in the classroom, (3) in-house tests and university entrance exams, (4) the memorization of vocabulary items, and (5) textbook/reference book-related issues.

Similarly, Keblawi (2005) conducted interviews as well as an open-ended questionnaire to investigate EFL demotivating factors in Arabian secondary school students. Semi-structured interviews were conducted with 25 students and 10 teachers. Keblawi found that proximal learning contexts such as instructors, learning groups, and English textbooks demotivated EFL learners when perceived negatively.

Compared with Kikuchi's (2009) and Keblawi's (2005) research which used oral interviews for their main research instruments, other qualitative research on EFL demotivation used written reflective essays for their primary analysis. Trang and Baldauf (2007) investigated 100 Vietnamese college students' demotivation by analyzing their stimulated recall essays, which were comprised of three parts: (1) the existence of demotivation and its sources; (2) how they had overcome demotivation; and (3) how they can minimize the effects of demotivation. Hamada (2008) asked 36 Japanese junior high school students to respond to an open-ended questionnaire. Students were asked eight short essay questions about various sources of EFL demotivation, such as teachers, learning environments, and study methods. Hamada found that grammar and confidence issues were the strongest demotivators.

Similar reflective essay methods were adopted among South Korean university students. Based on the grounded theory approach (Corbin & Strauss, 2008) and Shoaib and Dornyei's (2005) previous qualitative research, Kim and Lee (2013a, 2013b) focused on the changes in students' motivational and demotivational factors from kindergarten to undergraduate university programs. Kim and Lee (2013a) collected essay data from 75 college students who were asked to recollect their experiences learning English for the past 10 years, from kindergarten to university. The most important finding showed that participants' motivational factors and their demotivational counterparts were not antithetical or opposite concepts. In other words, the lack of a motivational factor did not mean the ample existence of the same factor in demotivation. For example, learning methods, school exams, grades, and competition sometimes functioned as motivational factors, but could also play significant roles in the same participant's demotivation. This result implies that motivation and demotivation are not "the other side of a coin," but instead should be understood as unique and independent psychological constructs. Kim and Lee (2013b) expanded the scope of their investigation by collecting similar data from 30 graduate students majoring in English education. The results showed four demotivating factors: instruction methods, teachers, colleagues, and tests. These results were not different from Sakai and Kikuchi's (2009). Remotivation factors were different from demotivation factors; they were methods befitting the students' learning styles and the teachers' attention and encouraging words.

In sum, the above qualitative studies adopting reflective essays demonstrate the complex relationship between motivation, demotivation, and remotivation. Although conceptually related, these constructs may function independently, and within an L2 learner's psyche, the same external factor may function as a (re)-motivating or demotivating factor depending on the learner's perception and his or her educational contexts.

Kim's (2018) research investigated both motivation and demotivation among 455 Korean high school students. Her research is unique in that she adopted a mixed-methods analysis which combined a Likert-type questionnaire and individual inter-views with 12 selected students by using stratified random sampling. She found that the primary motivating factors were instrumental motivation (both prevention and promotion) and the ought-to L2 self. In contrast, the major demotivating factors were difficulty in learning English and the lack of self-competence due to accumulated learning failures. These factors presented differently depending on the students' English proficiency. Specifically, with regard to demotivating factors, those with

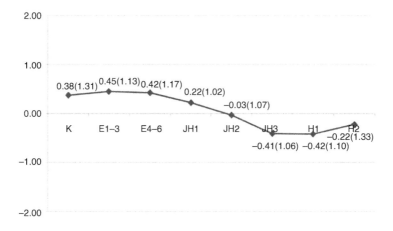

Fig. 6.1 Averaged pattern across all participants ($N = 64$)

low English proficiency showed a statistically high level of demotivation in the factors linked to difficulty in learning English and the lack of self-competence due to learning failures. However, those with high English proficiency had high motivation in teacher-related factors. Kim also noted that low-level EFL students tended to become demotivated after experiencing repeated failure in English, which led to further amotivation.

Though they did not utilize mixed-methods research, Song and Kim (2017) identified general trends in EFL students' demotivation and remotivation by using an amalgamated graph mapping Korean high school students' motivational changes. Sixty-four Grade 11 students were asked to draw a graph indicating their motivational intensity from kindergarten to their current grade (grade 11, or second-year high school). Among the 64 participants, 28 showed noticeable motivational changes, divided into two groups: a demotivation group (15 students) and a remotivation group (13 students). The reasons for demotivation and remotivation were further investigated by follow-up interviews with 23 out of the 28 participants. Figure 6.1 presents the averaged pattern across all participants, and Fig. 6.2 shows the averaged pattern across the remotivation group ($+2 =$ very interesting, $+1 =$ interesting, $0 =$ neither interesting nor boring, $-1 =$ boring, $-2 =$ very boring. Note that the numbers above the line indicate the average score of motivation for each period, and those in parenthesis show its standard deviation) (Song & Kim, 2017, pp. 95–96).

As indicated in Fig. 6.1, most of the participants became increasingly demotivated in junior high school, or middle school in South Korea. In their third year of junior high school and first year of high school, they were the most demotivated. After attending high school, they gradually regained their motivation, though not to a full degree. Follow-up interviews found that most participants experienced a decline in motivation during their junior high school days "mainly due to external factors, such as the need for memorization, the nature of the teaching

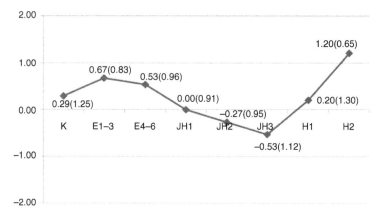

Fig. 6.2 Averaged pattern across the remotivation group ($n = 13$)

and learning, the difficulty of the learning content, and their declining test scores."
(Song & Kim, 2017, p. 101). They also experienced demotivation when they
"perceived the social pressure to learn English negatively and did not realize the
necessity of EFL learning" (p. 101). However, for the remotivation group, as shown
in Fig. 6.2, their motivational intensity increased in their first and second years of
high school. Song and Kim (2017) attributed the increase in the remotivation group
to both external and internal factors. External remotivation factors included changes
in their learning methods and inspiration from their classmates; internal factors
included increased awareness of the necessity of English for their future, experiences
of success, and interest in English culture.

6.2.2 L2 Teacher Motivation and Emotional Labor

It was not until 1995 that L2 researchers paid attention to L2 teacher motivation, thus
research is still at a developing stage. Note that the first systematic research on L2
teacher motivation was not from the field of L2 motivation but the extension of L2
teacher research. In 1995, Pennington (1995) presented the results of her study of
ESL teachers' job satisfaction and motivation. Due to the lack of advancement
opportunities in their career structure, ESL teachers in Hong Kong were gradually
demotivated. Pennington suggested enhancing work conditions with the aim of
fulfilling ESL teachers' ideal teacher selves.

Another initial research in this area is that of Kassabgy et al. (2001), who
investigated teacher values, teaching rewards, and job satisfaction of 107 in-service
teachers in the USA. ESL context and also in the Egyptian EFL context. They found
that the teachers were motivated mainly by intrinsic reasons and prioritized intrinsic
rewards over extrinsic rewards. Survey results analyzed through factor analysis
presented five unique factors in teacher values (i.e., what teachers think is essential

for their career): (1) a relationship orientation, (2) extrinsic motivation, (3) autonomy needs, (4) a self-realization factor, and (5) institutional support needs. Results also showed four factors in teaching rewards (i.e., what teachers think makes teaching a good job): (1) good management, (2) a professional position, (3) one's students, and (4) a challenging job.

Specific factors constituting L2 teacher motivation were gradually investigated in the twenty-first century. At the initial stage, research efforts centered on early career motives. In other words, researchers investigated the "why" part of becoming an L2 teacher. For example, Igawa (2009) examined English teachers' initial career motivation by surveying EFL teachers in Japan and Cambodia, and ESL teachers in the USA. First, 27 EFL teachers in Japan were asked to make a list of possible reasons they chose to become an English teacher. From their responses, 13 categories were established, and from these categories, 49 Cambodian EFL teachers and 34 U.S. ESL teachers were asked to select the three most appealing reasons for choosing the English teaching profession. Results showed that for both Japanese and Cambodian EFL teachers, their enthusiasm toward English and intrinsic motives in teaching and English were the major reasons for becoming English teachers. However, results from the U.S. ESL teachers showed a striking difference: the most common answer to what caused their initial career motivation was "other" reasons. The U.S. teachers' responses to this open-ended question included "to travel abroad," "to live abroad," "interests in foreign culture and people," "free time," "money," and "talented as a teacher." As Kim and Kim (2016a, p. 32) stated: "the discrepancy between ESL and EFL teachers' career choice motives may imply that EFL teachers' career choice should be analyzed with different categories of measurement."

Another EFL teacher motivation study conducted in Iraq shows insight into the initial career motives in Asian EFL teachers. Koran (2015) conducted a study in Iraqi secondary schools and universities by collecting data from 37 EFL teachers. Intrinsic rewards and altruistic reasons to teach English to children and to contribute to society were identified as the most popular reasons for becoming EFL teachers in Iraq. Interestingly, social recognition and job security were also identified as an initial career choice. Especially in the case of female EFL teachers, parents' recommendation to choose the teaching profession was also stated. Social recognition, job security, and parental recommendation all seem to reflect the educational context in Iraq (and possibly other countries as well). Teachers in public schools have a government officer position, so their employment is more secure than other professions. Moreover, guaranteed maternity leave and the tradition of childcare in school contribute to the idea that teaching is a female-friendly profession, which explains parents' recommendation for female EFL teachers.

Similar findings were found in South Korea. Kim and Kim (2015) reported the initial career motives of 94 in-service EFL teachers at elementary and secondary schools. The survey results showed four constructs in initial career motives: global orientation, job security, altruism, and ought-to self. Regarding job security and altruism, Koran's (2015) study showed similarities. However, two unique factors were identified by Kim and Kim (2015): *Global orientation* reflects Korean EFL teachers' aspirations to be fluent English speakers; and professional goal to teach

English competently in this era of globalization. *Ought-to L2 self* reflects the recommendation from the teachers' parents. Extending the notion of ought-to L2 self, L2 teachers may feel a psychological burden to choose language teaching as their career due to their parents. As indicated by Dörnyei (2005, 2009), this L2 self is developed by responsibilities or duties, and L2 teachers may feel that they choose this profession in order not to disappoint their parents. In research conducted by both Koran (2015) and Kim and Kim (2015), parental suggestions and job security were identified as the common factors, and this might be due to the secure job status that comes from a government officer position.

Material or monetary rewards, including pension plans for teachers, were identified as strong motives for choosing the profession (Gao & Xu, 2014; Hayes, 2008). Moreover, in less-developed regions where the opportunity for tertiary education is relatively limited (particularly for women), becoming teachers after attending a college of education is often regarded as the only viable option for young high school students (Erten, 2014).

However, in many cases, particularly in the East Asian contexts, EFL teachers suffer from various levels of demotivation. For example, Sugino (2010) investigated the demotivating factors for 97 EFL instructors at universities in Japan. Using questionnaires, he extracted four subcomponents in teacher demotivation: students' attitudes, students' abilities related to school facilities, working conditions, and human relations. In this study, students' negative attitudes and behaviors toward the teacher were identified as the most demotivating factors among these components.

Recent research conducted in South Korea presented similar findings. Lee and Kim (2018) conducted a questionnaire survey to 63 novice English teachers across Korea, investigating both their initial career motives and demotivating factors. Regarding the initial motives, six factors were identified: ideal L2 self, ideal L2 teacher self, job security, fear of having other careers, ought-to L2 self, and altruism. Regarding demotivation, the administrative overload other than the activity of teaching English, and students' disinterested and indifferent attitudes in English classes were extracted as the most demotivating factors. Kim and Kim (2015) also reported three negative factors on EFL teacher motivation: obstacles to communicative language teaching, inadequate administrative support, and lack of social recognition. Among these factors, obstacles to communicative language teaching were the strongest demotivator.

Qualitative studies which have investigated L2 teacher demotivation present a much more complicated picture of L2 teacher demotivation. Kumazawa (2013) used interviews with four novice EFL teachers in Japan. A narrative analysis showed that teachers experienced varying degrees of self-discrepancy between their initially imagined possible selves and their reality in education. An overly large gap between their initial ideal selves and their actual selves can lead to teacher demotivation. Through constructing their new self-concept as English teachers, which "is negotiated and reconstructed through interacting with the environment as well as through exercising the teachers' own sense of reflectivity" (p. 53), the novice teachers gradually overcame EFL teaching demotivation. By utilizing activity theory, Song and Kim (2016) showed that in-service EFL teachers' motivation fluctuates dynamically and has individual variations. Two experienced EFL teachers in South Korea were recruited and interviewed. Despite their similarities in age, years of teaching, and teaching contexts, the teachers "demonstrated different but equally dynamic motivational changes in relation to teaching English" (p. 142). In addition, teacher agency and teaching beliefs were shown to mediate teaching motivation. The above qualitative studies in L2 teacher demotivation systematically present how the longitudinally changing nature of teacher (de)motivation and the unique socio-educational factors surrounding each EFL teacher can result in different levels of teaching (de)motivation.

More recently, L2 teachers' emotional labor has started to be investigated as one of the related factors in L2 teacher (de)motivation. Recently the function of emotion in learning and teaching of L2 has been explored (Dewaele, 2005; MacIntyre et al., 2016). Because teaching is not just conveying specific learning contents to learners (Hargreaves, 1998), it always involves both cognitive and emotional aspects. For this reason, in the twenty-first century, researchers have started to pay academic attention to the emotional challenges each L2 teacher experiences in their daily teaching routines (King, 2015; Zembylas, 2002). Excessive job-related stress and burnout are often shown to have negative influences on L2 teachers' job satisfaction.

Moreover, communicative language teaching requires L2 teachers to teach effective communication skills, which necessarily involve emotional aspects. Thus, L2 teachers' emotional labor can be aggravated. Hochschild (1983) is one of the most influential figures in this area. He has noted that emotional labor is executed when there exists a conflict between a person's expected emotions in a particular situation and his or her actual feelings. Therefore, emotional labor can be defined as "displaying required emotion or at least projecting situationally appropriate emotions in job-related situations" (Kim & Kim, 2018, p. 23). Since teaching is essentially an interactive job requiring constant interpersonal interaction with students, parents, other teachers, and administrators, the emotional aspect of teaching has been explored by researchers in education in general (e.g., Schutz & Pekrun, 2007). In the field of EFL/ESL teacher education, students' low motivational level often requires L2 teachers' enhanced level of classroom involvement: they need to lighten up the class participation, introduce stimulating class activities, and make tailor-made suggestions to individual students. As King (2015) states, L2 teachers often need to perform their role as class "cheerleaders" while suppressing their own negative feelings.

The emotional labor in EFL/ESL teachers takes a more serious dimension in the case of private EFL/ESL education, particularly in East Asian countries. For example, as presented in Chap. 4, in South Korea, private English education is widespread, and even before attending elementary schools, young children (or in some cases infants) attend English kindergarten or day nursery (Joongang Ilbo, 2018). Since a large sum of money is often spent in these private sectors, it is challenging for each English instructor to ignore the opinion of the children's parents. If they are dissatisfied with the instruction or the instructor, the parents will pull their children out of the private kindergarten, which will directly relate to a decrease in the kindergarten's finances.

In this educational context, Kim and Kim (2018) conducted exploratory qualitative research on EFL teachers' emotional experiences in class and the emotional labor they perform. Three EFL teachers were invited for semi-structured interviews. Results presented two different levels in teachers' emotional labor: interpersonal and intergroup. As for the interpersonal dimension, they showed that the participants conducted varying degrees of emotional labor by suppressing negative emotions and maintaining an extended level of patience in the face of students' problematic classroom behavior. By contrast, they exaggerated their positive emotions to encourage their students' English conversation. The teachers also regulated their emotions when interacting with the children's parents. Regarding intergroup level, emotional challenges escalated when there was a conflict between the institutes' demands and the teachers' teaching philosophies.

Influenced by Dörnyei's (2005, 2009) notion of L2 motivational selves, Kubanyiova (2007, 2009) developed the concept of possible language teacher self. Possible language self includes personalized "language teachers' cognitive representations of their ideal, ought-to and feared selves in relation to their work as language teachers" (Kubanyiova, 2009, p. 315). She distinguished the ideal language teacher self and the ought-to language teacher self. The former "constitutes identity goals and aspirations of the language teachers, that is, involves the self which they would ideally like to attain" (p. 315). Language teachers are motivated when they make an effort to reduce the gap between their actual and ideal teaching selves. The latter refers to "the language teachers' cognitive representations of their responsibilities and obligations with regard to their work," and "this may involve latent expectations of colleagues, parents, and students as well as the normative pressures of the school rules and norms" (p. 316). According to Kubanyiova, the major difference between the ideal language teacher self and the ought-to language teacher self is that in the former case, the teachers' attempt to reduce the gap between the actual and the ideal teacher selves would be related to the teachers' vision of positive consequences. In the latter, their effort to reduce the gap between the actual and the ought-to teacher selves would be related to the teachers' visions of negative consequences. She also developed another type of teacher self: feared language teacher self, which refers to "someone that the teacher could become if either the ideals or perceived obligations and responsibilities are not lived up to" (p. 316).

In Kubanyiova's (2009) study, L2 teachers in Slovakia who participated in in-service teacher training were investigated for 10 months. Results showed that L2 teachers were influenced by various contextual factors and experienced a gap between their ideal teacher self and their actual realities. Kubanyiova (2009) highlighted the positive role of ideal language teacher self in that it contributed to the teachers' perceived sense of teacher development. In another related research conducted by White and Ding (2009), the ideal teacher self and the ought-to teacher self were investigated by collecting data from 23 L2 instructors in China, the U.K., and Ireland who participated in an E-learning Autonomy Group (ELAG). In this study, teachers' possible teacher self exerted a powerful influence on L2 teacher motivation, and their possible teacher self was the social concept that was created and reshaped by constant interaction with others. The above research by Kubanyiova (2009) and White and Ding (2009) presented the possibility of applying the concept of teacher self to the field of teacher development; the concept of possible teacher self shed light on understanding language teachers' teaching motivation.

In South Korea, Lee and Kim (2016) endeavored to incorporate Kubanyiova's concepts of language teacher self to the field of L2 teacher motivation. By using semi-structured interviews with two in-service EFL teachers with more than 15-year teaching experience, they investigated L2 teacher motivation, demotivation, teaching experience, and their possible language teacher self. The participants were also required to draw a graph delineating the changes in their teaching motivation for the past decades. The results showed that the participants had different language teacher selves reflecting their unique EFL learning experiences in past years, their L2 self, and social contexts. To be specific, the participants' positive EFL learning experiences and the ideal L2 self as a language learner contributed to creating the ideal language teacher self. By contrast, the ought-to L2 self which was created when they learned EFL as language learners also affected the creation of the ought-to language teacher self. Moreover, their EFL teacher self played a significant role in enacting their motivated teaching behavior: the teacher with an ideal language teacher self made various efforts to enhance her teaching motivation. However, the other teacher who mostly created the ought-to language teacher self was often affected by external factors, which had a negative impact on teacher motivation.

6.2.3   The Rise of Large-Scale, Cross-National Studies in L2 Motivation

The third noticeable trend in L2 motivation research is the initiation of large-scale, meta-analytic studies. In educational research, except for some longitudinal statistical data at a national level (e.g., Korean Educational Development Institute, 2020), it is rare to find large-scale studies involving participants in various school levels and grades. It is also true that due to the research timeline and the lack of financial support and systematic effort from the research team, it is not easy to collect large-scale data. However, in order to present overall trends convincingly and to capture the most salient aspects of a research phenomenon, it is highly desirable to conduct large-scale research.

In the case of motivation research, such large-scale survey data are not usually found, but since the millennium, the number and variety of samples seem to have increased. For example, Schmidt and Watanabe (2001) reported the result of a survey of motivation, strategy use, and learner preferences for different types of classroom activities with 2089 ESL learners with five different mother tongues. Dörnyei et al. (2006) presented longitudinal changes in foreign language choice in three successive years (1993, 1999, and 2004), involving 13,391 Hungarian participants. This book-length study systematically analyzed the young Hungarian teenagers' changing preferences among five foreign languages (i.e., English, German, French, Italian, and Russian) for 12 years. The participants increasingly preferred the English language to the Russian language, which reflected the socio-political changes in Hungary—from restrained, formerly communist Eastern Europe Soviet bloc to a more pro-American nation opening its borders to broader Western European nations.

Moreover, their research paved the way for the L2MSS replacing Gardner's (1985) socio-educational model. Dörnyei et al. (2006, p. 10) criticized Gardner's definition of integrativeness as ambiguous, in that "it has no obvious parallels in any area of mainstream motivational psychology and its exact nature is difficult to define." Of course, the disregard of Gardner's concept of integrativeness in mainstream psychology might not be the sole reason to refute its theoretical legitimacy. However, their second criticism, the difficulty of defining integrativeness, is still viable. Thus, by analyzing questionnaire results from the quantitative data across the nation, they compared the theoretical robustness between Gardner's socio-educational model and their L2MSS, and argued that the latter had better predictive power to reflect the changing nature of English as lingua franca and the outdated construct validity of integrativeness, at least for the English language.

Recently, You and Dörnyei (2016) illustrated geographical, school-level, and gender differences in English learning motivation involving over 10,000 Chinese students. They adopted a six-point Likert scale questionnaire survey to two different L2 learner populations: secondary and university students. Since it was a large-scale nationwide survey, participants were divided into three main regions in China: Eastern, Central, and Western. You and Dörnyei found that L2MSS could adequately explain the Chinese L2 learners' motivation. In other words, L2MSS has universal applicability to various geographical contexts, including mainland China.

Interestingly, they found that Chinese L2 students had positive ideal self-images using and learning English, which was somehow contradictory to the widespread belief that Chinese learners are mainly instrumentally motivated. Although both promotion- and prevention-focused instrumentality played essential roles in Chinese students' L2 learning motivation, their motivation was better explained by Dörnyei's (2005, 2009) L2MSS. Regarding gender difference, the level of female students' subcomponents of L2 learning motivational scales exceeded their male counterparts, but in the ought-to L2 self, the gender difference was not clear. The ought-to L2 self also showed no geographical difference.

Another nationwide mega-study is found in Kim and Seo's (2012) research. Their research is unique in that they incorporated a large-scale quantitative study with 17 individual interviews with EFL teachers in South Korea. In most large-scale research, typically a quantitative research method (particularly the Likert scale questionnaire) is used. It is a rarity to find a mixed-methods approach in the field of L2 learning motivation. Kim and Seo first conducted a questionnaire survey of 6301 elementary school students from Grades 3 to 6 in Incheon Metropolitan City, vicinity of Seoul, South Korea. For the questionnaire items, Gardner's (1985, 2001) concepts of instrumentality and integrativeness and Ryan and Deci's (2000) intrinsic and extrinsic motivations were included. The questionnaire data showed that all of the subcomponents in motivation consistently decreased in a statistically significant manner as participants' grades increased from Grade 3 to the upper grades. To identify potential reasons for this continual decrease in students' EFL learning motivation, Kim and Seo (2012) further conducted follow-up interviews with in-service EFL teachers. The teachers attributed the decreasing trends to three potential factors: (1) the negative effect of the English teachers who do not provide lessons matching students' needs, their impatience while teaching, and their disinterest in teaching and their pupils; (2) excessive social expectations toward English proficiency; and (3) the widening English proficiency gap among students, which reflects the phenomenon of English divide (i.e., the impact of students' socioeconomic class on their English proficiency and test score; see also Chap. 4). Despite the limitation of not including students' interview data, Kim and Seo's (2012) mixed-methods research provided convincing data that the decrease of EFL learning motivation starts at a relatively young age (from elementary school years). This study also showed the possibility of using mixed-methods research in the field of L2 learning (de)motivation.

Taguchi et al.'s (2009) cross-national comparison study, although not meta-analytic, is worth mentioning. They investigated various factors including the ideal L2 self and the ought-to L2 self in L2MSS of 1300 Chinese, Japanese, and Iranian English learners. The questionnaire data presented various cross-national differences. For example, it was identified that compared to Chinese and Iranian students, Japanese students showed a relative lack of interest in learning English. According to Taguchi et al., "English proficiency is not as strongly related to successful job-hunting in Japan as it is in China" (p. 84). Thus, the utilitarian motivation to learn English in Japan is not as high as that in other developing countries (see Sect. 5.2 in Chap. 5 for Japanese students' inward tendency and demotivation). Moreover, Taguchi et al. (2009) found that Gardner's (1985) critical concepts of integrativeness and instrumentality can be subsumed into the concepts of the ideal and ought-to L2 selves, which is another supporting evidence of the theoretical robustness of L2MSS over Gardner's socio-educational model.

Similarly, Yang and Kim (2011) conducted a cross-national comparison study on L2MSS and perceptual learning styles. They investigated the ideal L2 self, motivated L2 behavior, and the perceptual learning styles of Chinese, Japanese, Korean, and Swedish high school students. The statistical findings indicated that the Swedish students showed a significantly higher level of the ideal L2 self than the others, whereas the Japanese students showed the lowest level of the ideal L2 self. However, the Chinese high school students were most likely to be motivated to learn English. Yang and Kim attributed the reason for Chinese students' high level of L2 learning motivation to the social discourse excessively emphasizing the instrumental use of English (particularly for the college entrance exam purpose). It was also found that learners' ideal L2 self and motivated L2 behavior correlated significantly with their visual and auditory learning styles.

Although the above mega-studies provide a wealth of conclusive findings, these studies did not investigate EFL students' motivational differences in three different school-aged groups: elementary, junior high, and high school. Schmidt and Watanabe's (2001) participants were adult ESL students; Dörnyei et al. (2006) focused on Grade 8 students; and You and Dörnyei (2016) focused on secondary schools and universities. South Korea, like many other EFL countries, starts English education in elementary schools (Grade 3) and continues until high school graduation (Grade 12). This continuity of English language learning strongly indicates the necessity of investigating the 10-year longitudinal changes in students' EFL learning motivation.

6.3 Sociopolitical Impact on L2 Learning Motivation: Competitive Motivation in South Korea

As reported in Chaps. 2, 3, and 4, South Korean students experience an extremely high level of academic stress while they are attending secondary schools. As English is instructed as a mandatory school subject, English learning and teaching cannot ignore this sociopolitical aspect. Both students and teachers are aware of the high level of stress, which has been attributed to competitive motivation in EFL learning in South Korea (Kim, 2006a, 2010a; Kim & Kim, 2016b). As the emergence of competitive motivation was explained with the concept of *hakbul* in Sect. 3.7 in Chap. 3, the theoretical aspect of competitive motivation will be elaborated in this section.

Kim (2006a) investigated how Korea-specific sociopolitical factors influenced high school students' EFL learning motivation and attitudes. Questionnaire data and English test scores were collected from 364 high school students in Grade 11 (183 male, 181 female) in a metropolitan city in 2002. Based on the pilot study results and Lee's (1996) previous study conducted in South Korea, 55 EFL motivation questionnaire items with Cronbach alpha index of 0.91 were selected. Additionally, referring to Gardner's (1985) Attitudes/Motivation Test Battery, 20 questionnaire items were added asking about attitudes toward Americans and English learning. A factor analysis of the motivational questionnaire revealed seven motivational factors: (1) instrumental motivation, (2) competitive motivation, (3) intrinsic motivation, (4) self-development motivation, (5) cultural-exchange motivation, (6) heuristic motivation, and (7) integrative motivation. According to Kim (2006a), the second factor, competitive motivation, takes a crucial position in Korean students' EFL learning motivation in that:

> This factor is similar to the first factor, instrumental motivation, in the sense that learners are motivated by external sources. However, the competitive motivation seems more related to the participants' aspiration to occupy a superior position in life and to be evaluated positively by others. (Kim, 2006a, p. 175)

Connecting the above-stated competitive motivation to the exam-oriented Korean tradition, Kim (2006a) highlighted the role of the College Scholastic Ability Test (CSAT) in determining the students' admission to a university. Despite the diversification of university admission, the CSAT score is still one of the crucial determinants of post-secondary academic study. In the subtest of CSAT, English is one of the four areas (the others are Korean, math, and [social] science or vocational inquiry). In order to earn a high score in the English subsection in CSAT, students needed to perform better than "others," until recently before the adoption of a criterion-referenced grading system from 2017 (see Sect. 4.12 in Chap. 4 for the adoption of criterion-referenced testing in the CSAT). Thus, it was of utmost importance to occupy a superior position to other classmates or potential competitors. Competitive motivation, as a psychological construct, shares substantial similarities with Ames' (1992) performance goals or Nicholls' (1984a) ego orientation. According to Ames (1992, p. 262), the nature of performance goals is as follows:

> Central to a performance goal is a focus on one's ability and sense of self-worth (e.g., Covington, 1984; Dweck, 1986; Nicholls, 1984b), and ability is evidenced by doing better than others, by surpassing normative-based standards, or by achieving success with little effort (Ames, 1984; Covington, 1984). Especially important to a performance orientation is a public recognition that one has done better than others or performed in a superior manner (Covington & Beery, 1976; Meece et al., 1988). As a result, learning itself is viewed only as a way to achieve the desired goal (Nicholls, 1979, 1989), and attention is directed toward achieving normatively defined success.

Indeed, the high test score in CSAT was the public recognition that one has done better than the other students who took the same test nationwide in the same year. Therefore, the concepts of competitive motivation and performance goal share a significant portion of similarities. However, a main difference is the existence of constant competition. The competition to enter university does not end even after successful admission to one's desired university. To be employed at a large-sized company, college graduates need to take an English proficiency test, such as the Test of English for International Communication (TOEIC). Even after they are employed, they must take similar English tests on a regular basis in order to be promoted. In all of these exam-focused social structures, it is crucial to gain a better and higher score than other potential competitors. Given this, it is a chronic phenomenon to find competitive motivation in EFL learning among students in South Korea (and also in other countries with rigid, exam-oriented social structures).

In Kim's (2006a) research, most of the above seven motivational factors were significantly correlated with the English test score. Intrinsic motivation showed the strongest correlation ($r = 0.28$), instrumental motivation was the second strongest ($r = 0.24$), and integrative motivation was the third strongest ($r = 0.24$). However, narrowing down participants to only the high English proficiency group (the upper 25%) presented different results. The correlation of intrinsic motivation ($r = 0.27$) and integrative motivation ($r = 0.21$) with the test score was stronger than the other motivational factors. All of the correlation results were significant at the level of $p < 0.01$.

Note that the correlation between competitive motivation and the test score was negative in the high proficiency group ($r = -0.26$). This result is in sharp contrast to the result of the entire population, which did not yield a statistically significant correlation. These comparative results indicate that the role of competitive motivation, though extracted as one of the major motivational subfactors among Korean high school students, is minimal. Among the high English proficiency group, the existence of competitive motivation was detrimental to their academic achievement. In other words, the role of competitive motivation was very limited at best—and even detrimental for the high proficiency group.

Another significant finding in Kim's (2006a) study was the existence of so-called "Machiavellian motivation" coming from anti-American attitudes among Koreans. The questionnaire results about students' attitudes toward Americans and English learning showed a negative correlation between negative attitudes toward English learning and the English test scores ($r = -0.34$, $p < 0.01$), which would be an expected result. However, there was a statistically significant, positive correlation between negative attitudes toward Americans and their English test scores ($r = 0.25$, $p < 0.01$). It is an unexpected result, as most of the previous research indicated that if students have positive attitudes toward the target language speakers, they have higher L2 proficiency. The correlation result explained above, however, was contradictory to these previous studies.

Regarding this unexpected result, Oller et al.'s (1977) argument is worth mentioning. They present the possibility of achieving a high level of second language proficiency even in the case of the learners' extreme detest of the target language speakers and communities. They contended that the existence of negative attitudes toward the target language group could cause the L2 learners to exert more effort in order to excel in the target language. This specific type of motivation is known as Machiavellian motivation (Oller et al., 1977).

An interesting contrast is identified between attitudes toward English learning and attitudes toward Americans. In the case of the former, the correlation was not unexpected: there was a negative correlation between students' negative attitudes toward English learning and their English test scores. In other words, if they had a strongly negative sentiment toward English learning, they presented a low English test score, and vice versa. However, as stated above, there was a positive correlation between students' negative attitudes toward Americans and their English scores. In other words, if they had a profoundly negative sentiment toward Americans, their English test score was high, and vice versa. The contrast between the two types of attitudes showed that the high school students in this study did not link English language only to English speakers in the USA. Instead, as Kim (2006a, pp. 184-185) stated, "[t]hey seem to be disillusioned from naïve view of equating English learning with positive evaluation of Americans." They take a pragmatic stance such as "English learning is one thing and linking the U.S. to it is another thing" (p. 185).

Four years later, Kim (2010a) conducted a replication of his previous research (Kim, 2006a).[1] Again, the participants were Korean high school students, and questionnaire data were obtained from 673 students in a metropolitan city in South Korea. Kim (2010a) compared their data with what he published in 2006 (Kim,

---

[1]Note that Kim's (2006a, 2010a) data were collected in 2002 and 2006, respectively, and there exists a four-year interval between the data collection and the publication year.

2006a), and thus the total number of subjects was 1037. The primary purpose of this study was to compare longitudinal changes in motivation and attitudes in the 4 years between the studies. Notably, the Machiavellian motivation found in the positive correlation between negative attitudes toward Americans and English test score was reanalyzed in the new data set.

The results obtained from the factor analysis presented similar results in the subcomponents of EFL learning motivation. Competitive motivation was also identified in this study. Seven motivational factors were identified: competitive, instrumental, intrinsic, cultural-exchange, travel, integrative, and amusement motivations. Among the seven factors, five had also been identified in Kim's (2006a) previous study. In sum, regarding motivational subcomponents, there were considerable similarities between Kim's (2006a) previous participants and his new participants, and competitive motivation was consistently identified in both studies.

However, in the analysis of attitudinal factors, the Machiavellian motivation was not found. Unlike Kim's (2006a) previous data which showed a statistically significant positive correlation between negative attitudes toward Americans and English test scores, in Kim's (2010a) data, no statistically significant correlation was identified between negative attitudes toward Americans and English test scores. Instead, there was a positive correlation between positive attitudes toward Americans and English test scores ($r = 0.17$) at the level of $p < 0.01$.

Kim's (2010a) study also presented the regression analysis results; the factors predicting English test scores were calculated. In Kim's (2006a) study, 16% of the total variance of English test scores was explained by three factors: (1) negative attitudes toward English learning, (2) integrative motivation, and (3) cultural exchange motivation. However, Kim's (2010a) study showed that only 9% of test scores were explained by two factors: (1) instrumental motivation and (2) positive attitudes toward English learning.

The comparison of Kim's (2006a, 2010a) two studies yields the following theoretical implications. First, the consistent existence of competitive motivation reflects Korea-specific exam orientation, which reflects the influence of *hakbul*, or academic credentialism, explained in Chaps. 2 and 3. Nonetheless, it is noteworthy that the role of competitive motivation in English test scores was very limited. Second, L2 learners' attitudes toward the target language speakers show flexibility.

Regarding the existence of Machiavellian motivation found in Kim's (2006a) research, a specific sociopolitical incident significantly affected the high school students' attitudes toward Americans: In the early summer of 2002 (i.e., the same time period as Kim's, 2006a data collection), it was reported that two female junior high school students were killed by a U.S. army armored vehicle. To protect South Korean national defense, the U.S. army was stationed there after the Korean War (1950–1953). However, the death of the two young girls ignited violent political rallies, and in the summer and fall of 2002, according to Kim (2010a), the positive correlation between negative attitudes toward Americans and English test scores must have reflected this sociopolitical incident. By contrast, 4 years later in 2006 (i.e., the data collection year of Kim's, 2010a study), the impact of this tragic incident is no longer shown, and the negative attitudes toward Americans did not show any statistical correlation with the participants' English test scores.

Among the various findings in Kim's (2010a) research, the regression results surrounding the factors influencing English test scores would require further investigation. The explanatory power of both motivation and attitudes in the English test score decreased from 16% to 9% in the 4-year interval. Follow-up research was conducted by Kim and Kim (2016b), and this research compared data collected in three different periods: 2002, 2006, and 2010. By recruiting 434 high school students in 2010, Kim and Kim (2016b) reported the results of changing motivational trends by comparing data in three different academic years. By utilizing basically the same questionnaire items, they reported the changes in EFL motivational factors first and attitudinal factors second. Compared with seven motivational factors in the data collected in 2002 and 2006, Kim and Kim's (2016b) supplementary data collected in 2010 showed six motivational factors: competitive ($M = 3.44$), instrumental ($M = 3.26$), international posture ($M = 2.83$), heuristic ($M = 2.81$), cultural exchange ($M = 2.31$), and intrinsic motivation ($M = 2.25$). Note that competitive motivation ranked first regarding the mean score of the motivation factors extracted ($M = 3.44$ on a five-point Likert scale). The correlation between competitive motivation and English test scores became stronger: from $r = 0.11$ in 2006 to $r = 0.19$ in 2010, both of which were statistically significant at the level of $p = 0.01$.

In Kim and Kim's (2016b) study, the attitudes toward Americans were also compared. As mentioned above, due to the sociopolitical influence in 2002 ignited by the tragic accident which sacrificed two young junior high school girls in South Korea, a statistically significant positive correlation between the negative attitudes toward Americans and English proficiency ($r = 0.25$, $p < 0.01$) was identified in 2002. However, the 2006 and 2010 data did not show such Machiavellian attitudes. In 2006 data published in Kim (2010a), the correlation between negative attitudes toward Americans and English test score was negative but statistically non-significant ($r = -0.09$, $p = 0.070$). Moreover, the 2010 data published in Kim and Kim (2016b) also showed that the correlation was statistically non-significant ($r = 0.07$, $p = 0.187$).

Since Kim and Kim's (2016b) study was quasi-longitudinal, comparing the data collected in 2002, 2006, and 2010, the predictability of motivation and attitudes on English test scores was also investigated. It would be noteworthy that the predictability of motivation and attitudes was decreasing over the years from 16% in 2002, to 9% in 2006, and eventually to 8% in 2010. To be specific, 16% of the participants' English test scores in the 2002 data were explained by three factors: negative attitudes toward English learning, integrative motivation, and cultural exchange motivation. However, in the 2006 data, 9% of the variance in English test scores was predicted by the two variables of instrumental motivation and positive attitudes toward English learning. In the case of the 2010 data, merely 8% of the participants' English test scores was explained by only one variable: negative attitudes toward

English learning. Regarding this decreasing influence of EFL learning motivation and attitudes in English test scores, Kim and Kim (2016b) commented as follows:

> [I]t is possible that the English learning of Korean high school students can progress regardless of their level of motivation and attitudes. Kim (2012b) found amotivated but incessant learning to be a putatively unique phenomenon in Korea. Korean society and schools circulate and elaborate on the strong need for students to learn English; this may compel students to compete to acquire higher English test scores. In this sense, learning English is regarded as a requisite, not an option, for Korean high school students. The fierce competition appears to stimulate students to achieve a certain level of English achievement without them necessarily being motivated to do so. (p. 150)

In other words, in Kim and Kim's (2016b) view, the exam-oriented Korean society nudges students to be engaged in a fierce "exam war," competing with each other to acquire a higher score. In this intense competition, students are put in the position of exerting their best to outperform their ability regardless of their current level of motivation and the nature of attitudes toward English speakers or English learning per se. The decreasing trends identified in Kim and Kim (2016b) illustrated the possibility of amotivated EFL learning in the educational context in South Korea and other countries where academic credentialism exists. More detailed explanations of amotivated EFL learning will continue in Sect. 7.5, Chap. 7.

6.4   The Emergence of Activity Theory in L2 Learning Motivation

Language learning is by nature a longitudinal process, and L2 learners go through various changes in their L2-learning motivation. Even highly motivated L2 learners may experience demotivation (i.e., a noticeably reduced level of interest). Besides, the changing global status of the English language highlights the need to approach various phenomena related to L2 learning through a different theoretical lens sensitive to motivational changes that each learner may experience while learning English as a lingua franca.

In this regard, Vygotsky's (1978, 1987) sociocultural theory (SCT), specifically Activity Theory (AT), has the potential to function as an epistemologically useful tool for understanding and analyzing L2-learning motivation by paying particular attention to the interaction between the language, learner, and learning environment. According to Lantolf and Thorne (2006), SCT is a theory that explains the mind prioritizing the role of language as a tool that mediates humans' relationships with the world. Through physical and psychological mediational tools such as language, humans can direct and control their own and others' behavior, influence their environment, and change it (Lantolf, 2000; Lantolf & Appel, 1994). In recent years, inspired by Vygotsky's (1978, 1987) SCT and the mediational potential of human language, Swain (2006, 2010) and her colleagues (Knouzi et al., 2010; Swain

& Lapkin, 2011; Swain et al., 2009) have developed the concept of languaging, or "the activity of mediating cognitively complex ideas using language" (Swain & Lapkin, 2011, p. 105), and applied languaging in enhancing cognitive and emotional functions. (These characteristics of languaging will be elaborated in the following section.)

Often considered a sub-discipline of SCT, AT (Engeström, 1987, 1999a; Leont'ev, 1978), by centralizing the volitional aspects of SCT and focusing on the motivational dimension of human activity, provides a useful lens for analyzing L2-learning motivation (Kim, 2005, 2010b; Lantolf & Genung, 2002; Ushioda, 2007). Activity is defined as a system, where only purposive human behavior that brings recognizable changes will function (Davydov, 1999). According to Leont'ev (1978), activity is explained as follows:

> Activity is a molar, not an additive unit of the life of the physical, material subject… [A]t the psychological level, it is a unit of life, mediated by psychic reflection, the real function of which is that it orients the subject in the objective world. In other words, activity is not a reaction and not a totality of reactions but a system that has structure, its own internal transitions and transformations, its own development. (p. 50)

The AT framework focuses on the dialectic relationship between humans as active agents engaging in purposeful behavior motivated by specific biological or culturally constructed needs and their external sociocultural milieus. Leont'ev (1978), a colleague of Vygotsky, perceived human activity to be *object*-directed and argued that in human activity, a dual function of the object is simultaneously realized. That is, the object, or ultimately the desirable state, represents both the power to pursue the object (the means) and the product (the end). For instance, a learner's imagination of his or her successful mastery of L2 proficiency as an object provides one with the energy to sustain L2 learning (the means), and through an arduous process, the learner completes L2 learning (the end). In this regard, Engeström (1999b) stated that objects "are generators and foci of attention, motivation, effort, and meaning" (p. 304).

Engeström (1999a) further developed a sophisticated model of an activity system as shown in Fig. 6.3. This model incorporates the crucial components of human activity: subject, object, instruments (often mediational tools or artifacts), rules, community, and division of labor. For example, in an L2 classroom, learners can become the subject, and the intended L2 proficiency would be the object. To achieve the object, L2 learners can utilize a variety of mediational tools that can facilitate their learning. Notebooks, pen and paper, and laptop or tablet computers are physical artifacts, and language learning strategies such as mnemonics and metacognitive strategies would be mental artifacts. L2 teachers, too, can function as mediational tools as long as they facilitate students' L2 learning, and in this case, are human artifacts. Regarding rules, for example, in a traditional, teacher-centered L2 class, students need to pay attention to their teachers' lectures. An example of division of labor is the case where students work in pairs; a student in the pair can initiate a model dialogue and the other can be a conversational partner. To fulfill an assigned

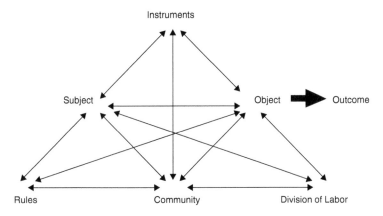

Fig. 6.3 A complex model of an activity system (Engeström, 1999a, p. 31)

task, each member of the pair can divide their role in this work. Community, in this case, can be the whole class or the assigned pair.

The complex model (Fig. 6.3) is not static but depends on the changes in neighboring components included in the system. For example, if an L2 learner, as the subject, has moved to another school, the community, as well as other components in the model, will also change. Thus, it is inevitable to have a qualitatively different activity system in this case. Regarding such a changing nature, Cole (1996) considered the AT model as a relational view.

It is noteworthy that for more than two decades, a group of SCT scholars (e.g., Kaptelinin, 2005; Leont'ev, 1978; Markova, 1990; Wertsch, 1985) have refined AT notions of motivation by distinguishing between the concepts of *motives*, *needs,* and *motivation.* According to Markova, a need is transformed into a motive or some "guiding or integrating force" (Wertsch, 1985, p. 212) once it is directed at an object, that is, the activity's focus or orientation (Kaptelinin). Motives, which can explain why someone engages in an activity, are inherently unstable, gaining or losing power depending on the condition, content, and course of the activity (Gillette, 1994; Lantolf & Genung, 2002; Lantolf & Thorne, 2006). Activities are manifested concretely as goal-oriented actions, and goals, in contrast to motives, have clear starting and ending points and are related to specific actions (Engeström, 1999b; Kim, 2007). Like motives, goals have a regulatory function in any activity and are unstable when they are modified, postponed, or abandoned (Lantolf & Appel, 1994).

Kim (2007, 2010b) developed a model of L2 motivational development based on SCT and AT. As shown in Fig. 6.4, when a need integrates with an object, which provides the general orientation for some behavior, it transforms into a motive. However, a motive does not gain full momentum until it is incorporated with a specific goal and a sense of participation in an L2 community. The relevance of this distinction between motive and motivation is in surveys conducted in the L2 classroom, where it is commonly found that because of bias or self-deception, students responding positively to survey items asking about their motivation levels

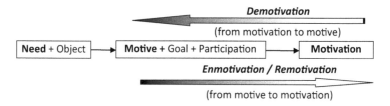

Fig. 6.4 Relationships between learners' needs, motives, and motivation

may, in reality, not provide evidence to support their behavior reflecting L2-learning motivation (Dörnyei, 2003). To capture this distinction, one must consider the role of learners' specific and concrete goals and participation in actual or imagined communities of practice (Wenger, 1998). Therefore, motivation can be understood as "the realization of motives" (Markova, 1990, p. 28).

In Fig. 6.4, the process from motive to motivation is termed enmotivation, and the reverse process from motivation to motive is termed demotivation. Figure 6.4 highlights the dynamic changes between motive and motivation. When a learner does not participate in a community of L2 use or learning, or does not see concrete goals anymore, such an L2 learner may lose his or her initial motivation. In this case, the close link between motive, goal, and participation is dissolved, and the learner becomes demotivated. If the learner creates a viable goal and begins to participate in new L2 communities, the link among motive, goal, and participation becomes reconnected. In this case, a demotivated learner may reignite the endeavor to learn the L2, and thus become remotivated.

Kim (2010b) has schematically depicted the relationship between motive and motivation by using Engeström's (1987, 1999a) complex model of an activity system (see Fig. 6.5). In this schematization, motive functions only in the upper, fundamental triangle including subject, object, and instruments. However, motivation is conceptualized as functioning in the expanded triangle where all the elements belonging to rules, community, and division of labor are involved. It is because the transformation from motive to motivation requires either actual or imaginary participation in a variety of communities, rules, and division of labor related to L2 use or learning in an activity system.

In this conceptualization, we can understand that the conflicts between elements in the upper fundamental triangle including subject, object, and instruments and elements in the lower expanded triangle including rules, community, and division of labor may prevent the transformation from a motive to a motivation. As a result, an L2 learner may fall prey to demotivation. Conversely, although a learner may not be very enthusiastic to learn an L2 initially, if the tension between the upper triangle and the lower one disappears, the learner can be remotivated. For example, an L2 learner may adjust his or her learning objective in the upper triangle (cf. Lantolf & Genung, 2002), or the community in the lower triangle may be changed as the learner advances to a new semester. In this regard, both Figs. 6.4 and 6.5 visualize the

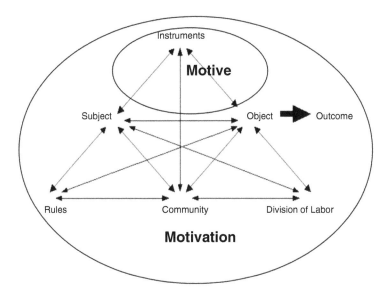

Fig. 6.5 Motive and motivation in Engeström's (1999a) model

dynamic changes in L2 learning motive/motivation and illustrate the complex relationships among motive, motivation, demotivation, and remotivation.

Extending the above notion of AT-based motivation theory, Kim (2010b) also explicated the concept of amotivation. Miettinen (2005) reiterates that the object plays a crucial role in AT. Since activity is an object-oriented human endeavor, if there is no object, an activity system cannot sustain it. For example, although a learner may set up an object in L2 learning such as "communicating with native speakers of the L2," the activity system will collapse if the same learner does not see the merit of retaining the learning object. Specifically, if the learner thinks that there is no point in learning the L2 any more, the object will dissolve, and the entire activity system illustrated by Engeström (1987, 1999a) will collapse. The outcome will be amotivation (see Sect. 6.4.2 and Kim, 2011b for cases of amotivation).

6.4.1   Activity Theory and L2 Motivational Self-System

To date, few studies have provided theoretical analyses of the relationship between AT and Dörnyei's (2005, 2009, 2019) L2 Motivational Self-system (L2MSS). A clue to investigate the relationship may lie in the similarity between the ideal L2 self in the L2MSS and the object in AT. Both involve the L2 learners' imagination. Dörnyei (2005, 2009) and Higgins (1987) suggest that L2 learners' awareness of the gap between their current self and future desired self is the initial step for their motivation because without realizing this perceptual gap, they may think the lengthy process of L2 learning only as a difficult and worthless external ordeal. In this sense,

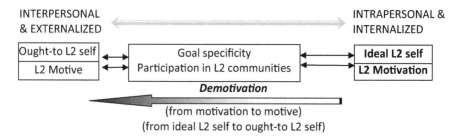

Fig. 6.6 Relationship between the L2 motivational self-system and AT-based L2 motivation theory

creating a future self is not different from the object in Engeström's (1987, 1999a) AT model in that this orients the learner to make efforts to learn the L2. The object, however, needs to be manageable and within the reach of L2 learners, which implies that the ideal L2 self should not be too abstract but visualized lucidly. Kim (2009a) suggested that L2 learners' visual learning style has a significant positive relationship with their ideal L2 self. They suggest that the learners' ability to create a detailed future image is linked to their ideal L2 self. From an AT perspective, the object needs to be operationalized into a series of concrete and manageable goals as shown in Fig. 6.4 where goals and participation are integrated into motive, resulting in motivation. By creating goals with clear starting and ending points (Engeström, 1999b), L2 learners can consolidate their future vision or ideal L2 self.

As shown in Fig. 6.4, when the distal need to learn an L2 is integrated with the object, a learning motive is created. In this regard, the ought-to L2 self in the L2MSS is the motive stage in Fig. 6.4 because the learner is yet to attach a personal meaning of his or her learning to the motive, although he or she may perceive the importance of L2 learning. Through various means such as media, school contexts, and the influence of significant others (e.g., parents or teachers), L2 learners may remotely understand the necessity of learning an L2 in the motive stage or ought-to L2 self. However, they may not visualize a competent future self at the personal level. In other words, learners with an ought-to L2 self may not fully internalize their personalized L2 self yet (Dörnyei, 2009). Once the ought-to L2 self with external origins is integrated with specific L2 learning goals and participation in such communities through the learner's alignment or imagination (Wenger, 1998),[2] the ideal L2 self is activated. Figure 6.6 shows the relationship between the L2MSS and AT (Kim, 2009b, 2010b).

---

[2]Wenger's (1998) notion of reification is relevant in explaining participation. Reification is defined as "the process of giving form to our experience by producing objects that congeal this experience into 'thingness'" (p. 58). As long as learners can link the activity of L2 learning to an imaginary or actual community, the L2 learning activity starts to have a special meaning to them and is envisioned in their mind. According to Wenger, imagination is not merely daydreaming or personal fantasy but a source of energy that can sustain learning in an ongoing manner. In such a case, the L2 community is made into something that can be vividly realized by learners.

L2-learning motivation can be maintained or strengthened (illustrated as "enmotivation" in Fig. 6.4) if the L2 motive is integrated with specific goals and participation in L2 communities where the ideal L2 self is created. Conversely, if learners perceive only a vague L2 learning motive, usually initiated by their parents' nudging, then no trace of specific goals or participation is identified. As a result, the learners' perception remains as an L2 motive and the ought-to L2 self. Figure 6.6 represents this gradual retrogressive process as "demotivation" from the ideal to the ought-to L2 self.

6.4.2   L2 Learning Motivation from an AT Perspective: Empirical Research

The application of AT in L2 learning motivation is relatively new. To date, only a few empirical research studies have been reported in academia. In a qualitative study analyzing Chang, a Korean ESL visa student in Toronto, Kim (2010c) presented empirical evidence showing a close connection between AT and the L2MSS.

In the study, Chang, a 25-year-old male student, showed drastic changes from an ought-to L2 self to an ideal L2 self, and also as a learner who possessed a vague L2 learning motive to one with a clear L2 learning motivation. Initially, he passively participated in his ESL class without actively communicating with other ESL students. Chang did not comment on specific learning goals or future use of L2. At the initial stage, he showed externally oriented ought-to L2 self, which pushed him to study English. However, as his ESL learning progressed, Chang gradually developed a friendship with Chinese immigrants and Korean ESL students around him. He created a new learning goal, which was to enroll in a college preparation program (CPP), graduate, and then immigrate to Canada. His new learning goal was aligned with his L2 learning context (i.e., the CPP where he built an excellent peer relationship), and this alignment, in turn, maximized his participation in the CPP and his other learning communities. Thus, the interlink between motive, goal, and participation led to Chang's high-level L2 motivation, which resulted in an ideal L2 self (a college student attending classes in Canada).

Chang's case, described in Kim's (2010c) study, also implies that the social surrounding per se does not lead to an enhanced level of L2 motivation nor does mere exposure to the L2 community guarantee a higher level of L2 motivation. For this, the learner had to create a specific goal and participate in an appropriate study-abroad experience. In Chang's case, although he did not have a specific L2 learning goal, he gradually calibrated his goal toward immigrating to Canada after graduating from his ESL program. His classmates and environment were also aligned with his goals. Thus, when such an alignment among motive, goals, and participation occurs, L2 learners become sensitive to the contextual cues proximal to them and can benefit from these environmental factors. Kim (2010c) emphasizes the importance of aligning these components as follows:

Before the alignment, the beneficial contexts do not stimulate L2 learners' desire to learn the
L2, but with the alignment, L2 learners will notice the gap between their current L2
proficiency and their desirable L2 proficiency.

Kim (2006b) refers to the moment of realizing the linguistic gap as *sensitization*.
He defines sensitization as, "the moment when an L2 learner recognizes the gap
between his or her current L2 proficiency and the desirable L2 proficiency to be
attained" (p. 65). For Chang, his sensitization occurred when he integrated his initial
motive with specific goals and active participation in his L2 communities. In this
regard, it can be stated that sensitization is the process of transformation from motive
to motivation or from an externally oriented ought-to L2 self to an internalized ideal
L2 self.

In another study, Kim (2009b) investigated the interface between the LSMSS and
AT. In this investigation, Kim focused on Joon and Woo, two male ESL visa
students in Toronto, who had different ideal and ought-to L2 selves, as well as
trajectories of the transformational process in their L2 selves. He focused on the
relationship between a motive and a motivation by using Engeström's (1987, 1999a)
AT systems model. The research question was, "How can we understand the ideal
L2 self and the ought-to L2 self concerning Vygotsky's (1978) sociocultural theory
of mind and Engeström's AT framework?"

Joon was a third-year university student at the time of data collection and had a
very close American friend in Korea. He had cultivated a high level of ought-to L2
self across 6 months. When asked about his primary motivation, Joon's answers
were as follows (Kim, 2009b, pp. 281–282):

Excerpt 1: (Second interview, November 2004)
   Interviewer (I): Why are you interested in learning English?
   Joon (J): That's because I need to get a job in Korea. Also, I want to talk with the adoptee,
I mean, my [American] friend in Korea.

Excerpt 2: (Third interview, December 2004)
   J: Of course, getting a job in Korea comes first. And then I want to communicate with my
American friend. I mean without any hesitation.

Excerpt 3: (Seventh interview, April 2005)
   J: Now, in Korea, uh, English has already become a world language, so learning English
is not a matter of personal interest but a must. That's why I learn English.

In the excerpts above, it is noteworthy that Joon consistently emphasized the
instrumental use of learning English: to get a job in Korea, although he frequently
mentioned his desire to communicate with his American friend in Korea. As
explained above, when an L2 learner has internalized the ought-to L2 self, the
learner tends to integrate the specific goals and participation in L2 communities.
The result is the ideal L2 self (see Fig. 6.6). In Joon's case, in the above excerpts, he
consistently stated the need to learn English to get a job. However, his responses to
follow-up interview questions did not confirm the specificity of his job prospects,
nor did it show an increasing interaction with English-speaking communities. The

following excerpts are Joon's response to the question about his future job (Kim, 2009b, p. 283).

> Excerpt 4: (First interview, October 2004)
> J: I'm not sure if this will come true, but, anyways, I would like to work in the New York Stock Exchange.

> Excerpt 5: (Second interview, November 2004)
> J: I think it may not be sufficient to learn English for only a year. I'm planning to apply for a Working Holiday Maker Visa and go to Australia. Maybe in two years?

> Excerpt 6: (Fourth interview, January 2005)
> J: Perhaps, international business. Or hotel management? Now I would like to get a job in a hotel. I'm trying to find some books on the hotel business or hotel management. I don't know what exactly I want to do for a living.

Note that it is entirely understandable for a youth in his early 20s to explore different job prospects, and it would be inappropriate to criticize Joon's lack of a concrete job plan. Instead, the excerpts above present Joon's inconsistency in his job plans. The point is that despite Joon's consistent emphasis on getting a job after learning English in Excerpts 1, 2, and 3, his actual job plan does not show any concreteness and only presents its ephemeral nature. In this regard, Joon may seem to be familiar with the social discourse of English as a global language and may repeat (or "ventriloquate" in Bakhtin's, 1981 terms) this discourse in the above excerpts. From the perspective of L2MSS, Joon seems to exhibit an externally regulated ought-to L2 self that is not yet internalized.

From an AT perspective, based on Joon's comments above, it seems that he formulated two distinct goals in ESL learning: (1) to communicate with other L2 speakers, particularly with his American friend in Korea (sub-goal 1), and (2) to get a job in South Korea (sub-goal 2). As Joon was in an English-speaking environment, his first sub-goal was in line with his communities (particularly his ESL classes). However, his second goal was supported neither by his communities nor by other elements in Engeström's (1987, 1999a) AT system. Joon's activity was mostly centered on ESL classes, not job preparation courses, which shows that none of the community, rules, and division of labor related to the second sub-goal. Thus, we can identify a tension between Joon's (the subject) goal and the components at the bottom in Engeström's model.

Taking Figs. 6.5 and 6.6 into consideration, Joon's case in Kim (2009b) shows that the tension between the upper, essential elements and the lower, expanded elements results in the learners creating an ought-to L2 self and a motive, not a motivation, to learn an L2.

Woo, the other male ESL participant, stayed in a Canadian homestay and built a close relationship with the owner who was a native English speaker. Woo expressed his goal to work at a steel company in Korea in the future. Like Joon, Woo also expressed his instrumental motivation to learn English for his job in the future. However, compared to Joon's vague job prospect, Woo's career goal was specific and precisely elaborated as shown in Excerpt 7 (Kim, 2009b, pp. 285–286).

Excerpt 7: (Second interview, November 2004)
    Woo (W): What I'd like to do in the future is work in the field of steel manufacturing. The steel company, BOSCO [a pseudonym] is, for sure, the top producer of high-quality steel [in Korea] (...) It is not sufficient to sell steel within Korea. So I hope I can get a job in the international sales department of that company and be successful.

Excerpt 8: (Third interview, January 2005)
    W: I'd like to devote myself to that field [i.e., steel manufacturing]. I'd like to sell steel. We cannot sell everything only in Korea; we need to sell all over the world. In that sense, English skill is an important requirement.

Excerpt 9 (Eighth interview, June 2005)
    W: Well, for my job. It is the best tool for my steel exporting job, I mean, employment. My major goal is to get the job.

Excerpts 7, 8, and 9 show Woo's future goal is simple but very specific—to be employed at BOSCO, a steel company in South Korea. Compared to Joon's data in Excerpts 4, 5, and 6, Woo's comments are more internalized and solidly rooted in his career goal. Furthermore, Woo's strong personal relationship with his English-speaking Canadian homestay owner exerted a beneficial impact on his English use and practice. Put differently, Woo actively created a community of practice. In the excerpt below, Woo and his homestay owner's community of English practice is illustrated below (Kim, 2009b, p. 287).

Excerpt 10 (Third interview, January 2005)
    W: At Christmas time, I wrote two Christmas cards and gave one to my homestay mom and the other to her neighbor. Both of them were quite pleased. Of course, I wrote my greeting in English. You know what? She [the homestay owner] checked my English grammar!
    I: (laugh) Oh, did she?
    W: She said she would check whether or not I wrote properly. And she said everything was OK. I said thank you. I felt so happy, because I had this handy opportunity every day.

Note that the above situation might have felt like a humiliating experience for Woo without their mutual friendship and collegiality. On the other hand, it can also be regarded as unwanted criticism by the homestay owner having more linguistic (i.e., English) capital. However, instead of feeling any humiliation, Woo showed his gratitude for her voluntary assistance. Excerpt 10 proves that there was no tension between Woo (the subject) and his community (i.e., the homestay). Thus, in Woo's case, his specific goal (i.e., to work at a steel company) was supported by his active participation in his L2 community (i.e., the homestay). In this case, Woo's externally originated ought-to L2 self had transformed into an internalized, specific ideal L2 self. From an AT perspective, in Woo's AT system, no tension was identified between the upper, basic triangle and the lower, expanded triangle. This resulted in Woo's high level of motivation.

The cases of Joon and Woo, above, show that the degree of internalization and the existence of tension between the upper, essential elements and the lower, expanded elements in Engeström's (1987, 1999a) model make a significant impact on the transformation from the ought-to L2 self to the ideal L2 self as well as that from a motive to a motivation. As Kim (2009b) states, "[w]ithout the support from the community and its related rules and division of labour as defined in Engeström's (1987, 1999a) AT framework, the learner cannot envisage a positive, competent, and promotion-based future L2 self-image" (p. 291).

Compared to Kim's (2009b, 2010c) studies that focused on ESL visa students who stayed in the L2 community for a relatively short period, Kim (2011b) investigated the changing motivations of two recent Korean immigrants to Canada. The participants were highly skilled immigrants and participated in monthly interviews for 10 months. Their monthly interview data were coded and analyzed using Engeström's (1999a) AT system model. Paul and Sandra were of similar ages, and had similar academic backgrounds and previous work experiences. They also resided in the same area in Toronto, the data collection site. They both were in their 30s and were university degree holders. As new immigrants, they were in Toronto for less than 3 months at the time data collection began. Despite the external similarities, Paul and Sandra's motivational trajectories over the 10-month data collection period presented major differences. In Paul's case, his motivation plummeted after the sixth interview, and eventually, a high level of amotivation occurred. On the contrary, Sandra's various subcomponents of motivational constructs were preserved. Kim (2011b) noted the role of life experiences and the education environment and how the participants perceived the impact of these experiences and environment on them. Paul had an accumulated unsuccessful job search experience, which negatively impacted his job-related motivation to learn the L2. At the initial stage, he expressed a firm belief that English proficiency has a direct link to employment. However, despite his moderately high English proficiency and an internationally accredited certificate in his profession, he could not get into the job he had aspired for many months and instead ended up with working part-time (e.g., pizza delivery, telemarketing). Thus, Paul's initial assumption of the efficacy of English proficiency in employment rapidly waned. In the tenth (last) interview, he explicitly negated the link between English and employment. In Engeström's (1999a) AT model, Paul's last interview data presented a variety of tensions among the components in AT.

In Fig. 6.7, note that the object position in the AT model is vacant. It is because Paul did not set up the object of learning, the L2, in his last stage. Since he did not see the merit in learning English anymore, his previous object such as learning English to get a job in Canada disappeared. As human activity is an object-related phenomenon (Kaptelinin, 2005; Leont'ev, 1978), the lack of any object in Fig. 6.7 caused severe conflicts with other components in the AT model. As a result, Paul experienced amotivation in learning an L2. He could not maintain his initial motivation and ended up having a vague motive to learn an L2 dissociated from specific learning goals and for participation in meaningful L2 communities.

Compared to Paul's grim progression in L2 motivation, Sandra's story was significantly different. When asked about the main reason for her immigration, she stated that she wanted to have an enhanced sense of well-being while staying in Canada. Soon after immigration, while working part-time at a sushi restaurant, Sandra started to attend a government-funded ESL program, adult high school credit

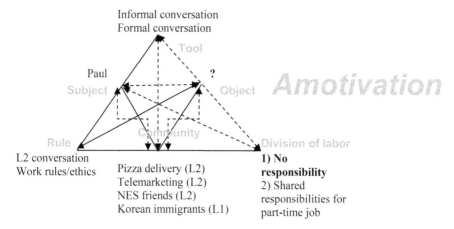

Fig. 6.7 Paul's L2-motivation activity system in the later stage

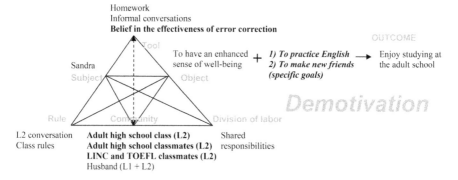

Fig. 6.8 Sandra's L2-motivation activity system in the later stage

courses, TOEFL program, and eventually a certificate program in video film editing. Sandra started to get along with other new immigrants, old-time immigrants in her neighborhood, and English-speaking Canadians whom she met while taking various credit courses and working part-time. Sandra actively participated in L2 communities of practice and appreciated these opportunities to develop her English skills. At a later stage, Sandra became slightly demotivated, as she did not have much chance to receive linguistic feedback. Since Sandra was no longer regarded as an ESL learner in her adult high school credit courses, she did not have feedback on her English although she was exposed more often to L2 interaction with English speakers.

In comparison with Paul''s drastic changes in motivation at a later stage, Sandra did not show such changes. She did not show significant tensions in her activity systems. Figure 6.8 illustrates Sandra's later stage. Note that Sandra's belief in the effectiveness of error correction functioned as a mediational tool (or artifact). Due to her belief, she could develop her English proficiency but at the same time, Sandra's belief conflicted with her L2 community (i.e., adult high school class). The lack of linguistic feedback from her classmates in the adult school created tension with her belief in the effectiveness of English correction. Thus, Sandra experienced demotivation.

Paul's and Sandra's cases prove the usefulness of AT in explaining L2 learning motivation, demotivation, and amotivation coherently. Given the longitudinal nature of L2 learning motivation, the time-consuming nature of L2 learning and the related fluctuation of L2 learning motivation can be systematically addressed using AT. As Kim (2011b, p. 115) argued, "[e]ven if L2 learners were located within similar L2 contexts . . ., the achievement of higher levels of L2 learning motivation by all of the L2 learners could not be guaranteed," and "unless L2 learners understand that their L2 learning activities are efficacious and meaningful to their L2 development, interaction-rich L2 contexts per se may not lead to higher levels of L2 learning motivation" (p. 115).

6.4.3   L2 Learning Demotivation and L2 Teaching Motivation from an AT Perspective

As explained in Sects. 6.2.1 and 6.2.2, most of the previous research was related to L2 learning motivation. In other words, rather than focusing on L2 learning demotivation and L2 teaching motivation, the studies illustrated above focused on L2 learning motivation. Although L2 learning demotivation was explained in the framework of Engeström's AT model (e.g., Kim, 2011b), the main focus was on the overall change in L2 learning motivation, and in the process, either L2 learning demotivation (in Sandra's case in Kim, 2011a) or amotivation (in Paul's case in Kim, 2011b) was explained.

An empirical study on L2 learning demotivation is yet to be conducted. Kim and Kim (2013a) showed the possibility of analyzing L2 learners' demotivation using the framework of Engeström's AT systems model. They argue in their paper, that "reconceptualizing L2 learning demotivation from an AT framework would provide a robust theoretical foundation for better understanding the demotivational process by reflecting on learners' idiosyncratic experience and sociocultural contexts" (Kim and Kim 2013a, p. 143). To show the application of AT in L2 learning demotivation, Kim and Kim (2013a) reanalyzed a learner's case from Lantolf and Genung's (2002) research, where a doctoral student was struggling to learn Chinese as a foreign language in the USA. The student, whose pseudonym is PG, took an intensive summer language course to fulfill her doctoral requirement. PG's demotivational process was coherently explained using Engeström's AT model.

PG's initial motives for enrolling in the Chinese language course were twofold: (1) successfully communicating with native Chinese speakers, and (2) earning a Ph.D. degree by fulfilling her course requirement (i.e., obtaining a satisfactory course grade in one of the language courses offered at her educational institution). Although the second motive had practical importance, PG was mainly motivated by

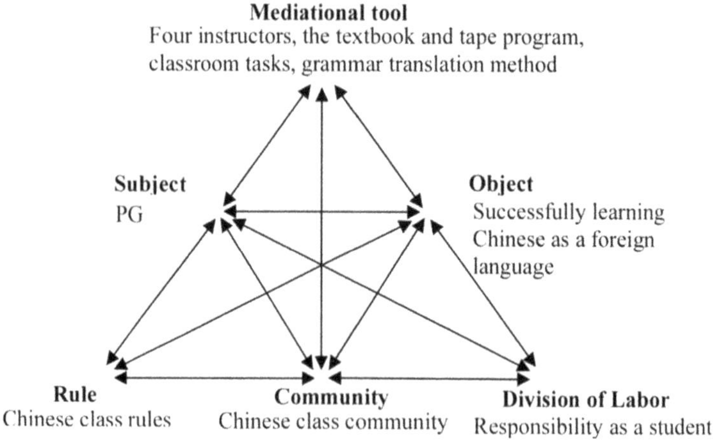

Mediational tool
Four instructors, the textbook and tape program,
classroom tasks, grammar translation method

Subject
PG

Object
Successfully learning
Chinese as a foreign
language

Rule
Chinese class rules

Community
Chinese class community

Division of Labor
Responsibility as a student

Fig. 6.9   PG's Initial L2 learning motivation activity system

the first reason because PG had learned other languages for this communicative purpose. As shown in Fig. 6.9, in PG's initial stage of learning Chinese, we can find no potential conflicts among the subcomponents in Engeström's AT triangular model, and thus she was relatively highly motivated.

However, as the semester progressed, PG gradually experienced learning difficulties and problems resulting from the disparity between her learning object and the other components in her AT. For example, she had problems with her instructors who immediately corrected all the minute errors in students' Chinese sentences and pronunciations. Moreover, PG and all other students were required to conduct translation and transcription exercises in every class. This structured, grammar-translation method started to create severe conflict with her L2 learning object. Her submissive role as a passive learner, obedient to the instructor, was also in conflict with her object. As explained in Sect. 6.4.1, when tension exists between the upper, fundamental triangle and the lower, expanded triangle, a motivation is transformed into a motive, and demotivation arises. Figure 6.10 illustrates this.

Because PG's initial motives were twofold, it was shown that while experiencing demotivation in learning the Chinese language, PG gradually abandoned her first motive of successfully communicating with native Chinese speakers. She only maintained her second motive of fulfilling the language requirement by obtaining a satisfactory course grade. Thus, PG had changed her object accordingly. In Fig. 6.11, the tensions identified in the previous stage were all resolved, and demotivation was also transformed as remotivation. Reflecting on the change in PG's object, the outcome had changed into obtaining a passing grade.

It should be noted that perhaps PG could have abandoned learning an L2 because she experienced tensions among the subcomponents in the AT system. However, by switching her object from "successfully learning Chinese as a foreign language" into "fulfilling the university requirement," PG could be remotivated. Given her urgent need to earn a doctoral degree after fulfilling the language requirement, it might have

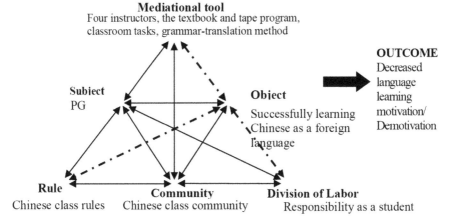

Fig. 6.10 Emerging tensions in PG's L2 learning motivation activity system

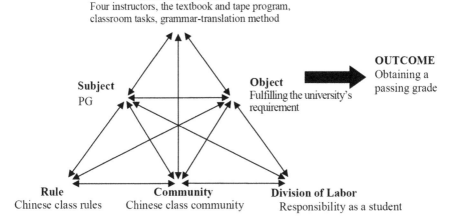

Fig. 6.11 PG's final L2 learning motivation activity system

almost been impossible to abandon the Chinese course entirely. In this regard, Kim and Kim's (2013a) reanalysis of Lantolf and Genung's (2002) study gives a practical implication; in order to not suffer from continued demotivation while learning an L2, it would be better for the learner to be aware of the prime source of conflicts first and then readjust the learning object.

As with L2 learning demotivation study from an AT perspective, studies on L2 teaching motivation have been investigated by using the same orientation. It would be informative to introduce Jang and Kim's (2018) research on young EFL teachers' motivation to teach and Song and Kim's (2016) experienced EFL teachers' cases.

Using Engeström's (1987, 1999a) AT model, Jang and Kim (2018) report on two young in-service English teachers' changes in teaching motivation. In this study, the conflicts between the subject and their contextual factors such as the personal relationship with other colleagues had a significant impact on the teachers' motivation to teach. In case of tension between the teacher and his or her work environment, L2 teaching motivation decreases and the teacher will experience demotivation as well. As stated in the previous section, the conflict between the upper fundamental triangle and the lower, expanded triangle in Engeström's AT model will result in the transformation of a motivation to a motive and will result in demotivation. Furthermore, this conflict exerts a negative impact on the teachers' creativity and maintenance of their ideal L2 teacher self. Supportive colleagues and the work environment will reduce the tension between the upper and lower triangles and also help establish an ideal L2 teacher self.

Similarly, by using Engeström's (1987, 1999a) AT model, Song and Kim (2016) investigated two experienced English teachers in South Korea. They shared a similar amount of teaching experience in the neighboring school district. In this study, it was found that the teachers' beliefs about effective teaching methods played a crucial role in the AT system. Their beliefs functioned as a critical mediational tool for their teaching motivation. Depending on how each teacher has perceived their belief and how they exercised their agency as a language teacher, their teaching motivation progressed differently.

6.5 Motivational Languaging Activities: An Education-Friendly Intervention Method

As briefly stated in Sect. 6.4, Swain (2006, 2010, 2013) developed the concept of languaging, or "the activity of mediating cognitively complex ideas using language" (Swain & Lapkin, 2011, p. 105) while emphasizing the importance of expressing one's thoughts in various cognitively demanding contexts. The underlying assumption of this activity is that such cognitively demanding tasks requiring either L1 or L2 verbalization will enhance the participants' cognitive ability and can also boost their sense of self-worth, particularly for older adults (Lapkin et al., 2010; Lenchuk & Swain, 2010; Swain, 2013). While expressing thoughts, either orally or using written language, we consolidate, modify, and cancel out our previous thoughts. It is for this reason Vygotsky (1978) stated that language is not merely a passive vehicle delivering our thoughts. Our mind is in constant change when expressing our thoughts.

Until recently, languaging activities have been used in cognitive aspects of L2 learning (Swain et al., 2009), but not in emotive-motivational aspects. In L2 learning contexts, particularly in the East Asian context, where English is offered as an obligatory school subject, many students suffer from demotivation (Song & Kim, 2017). Kim (2019) attempted to apply the concept of languaging to enhance students' L2 learning motivation and to prevent their demotivation in learning an L2. The main assumptions in Kim's (2019) research were that if L2 learners have the opportunity to think about their ideal self using the L2, and to communicate such thoughts either orally or in written language, they can increase the level of L2 learning motivation better. In psychology literature, Levav and Fitzsimons (2006) reported that participants' cognitive involvement in a specific task makes the participants better imagine how to do the task in the future. Morwitz et al. (1993) termed a similar phenomenon as the mere-measurement effect. Participation in a task per se can make the participants become more aware of the task and produce an enhanced level of cognitive and emotive involvement.

Based on psychology literature emphasizing the mere-measurement effect and Swain's (2006, 2010) languaging, Kim (2019) developed the notion of motivational languaging activity (MLA) and conducted experiments with three groups of elementary and junior high school students. The MLAs were based on the assumption that the students' efforts to critically review their previous L2 learning and their desirable L2 proficiency in either an oral or a written manner would enhance their sense of motivation. Thus, during a semester (i.e., 14 weeks), the MLAs were conducted seven times, during every other week, with the participants. Each MLA session lasted for 15–20 min for the participants.

During the experiment, the participants were divided into three groups and a control group. They were allotted in one of the following groups: (1) English learning diary group, where they were required to think what they did and learned during their previous English (L2) class, (2) opinion writing group, where after watching a short video clip and reading an exemplary, model case, the participants wrote what they felt, and (3) peer discussion group, where they first watched a short video clip and read an exemplary case and engaged in a peer discussion. In the second and third groups, for the video clip and exemplary case reading materials, Korean celebrities (e.g., famous pop stars, sports stars, and diplomats) were selected, and the participants watched these celebrities delivering lectures, making public speeches or conducting television interviews only in English. After watching and reading these cases, the participants would expect that they can also become like these celebrities after learning English (L2). Thus, it was assumed that the participants could imagine their ideal L2 self as similar to these celebrities, and this will have a beneficial impact on their L2 learning motivation.

To facilitate the participants' creation of their ideal L2 selves, for all three experimental groups, a workbook, *Dream Notebook*, was made through the close collaboration of the researcher and the English instructors. For example, in Fig. 6.12, Mr. Ban Ki-Moon, the former United Nations (UN) Secretary General, was delivering a UN speech in English, and his story related to learning English was briefly introduced. The participants had sufficient opportunities to think of their future and to compare their English learning history and method to those used by celebrities.

To measure the participants' motivational change, Kim (2019) administered two sets of questionnaires at the beginning and the end of the semester. Generally, the results of implementing MLAs over a semester showed that the activities had a positive impact on the students' L2 learning motivation. Elementary school students

Fig. 6.12 Dream notebook sample page (Kim, 2019, p. 87)

showed a greater increase in their motivation than their junior high school counterparts. Specifically, compared to the control group, which did not show any statistically significant increase in motivational subcomponents, the elementary school opinion writing group showed a statistically significant increase in the three subcomponents: the ideal L2 self, attitude toward English learning, and integrativeness. However, in the case of the junior high school group, the result was not straightforward. The junior high school participants showed a statistically significant increase in their ought-to L2 self when they were engaged in the English learning diary activity. The junior high school opinion writing group also presented a statistically significant increase in their cultural interest.

To sum up, the MLA was most effective when the languaging was conducted with oneself through opinion writing. In this case, they were first required to watch exemplary cases from a video clip and read the same ones from *Dream Notebook*. Then they wrote down their impressions in Korean. The fact that their ideal L2 self and integration had increased after the MLAs means that the elementary school students are more willing to become like these exemplary Koreans using ESL/EFL, and the activity of writing down their critical reflections crystalized the elementary school participants' aspiration. Furthermore, in terms of age, younger students were more susceptible to the effect of languaging than older students.

Because Kim's (2019) notion of MLA is relatively new in the field of L2 motivation, a series of studies adopting diverse conditions in MLAs in different educational contexts are being conducted. For example, Y.-K. Kim (2017) used similar MLAs for 334 high school students in the metropolitan city of Seoul across 2 months from September to October 2016 for a doctoral dissertation. Her results also supported Kim's (2019) study that compared the control group and all three experimental groups, showing varying levels of motivational increase. Specifically, the individual writing group's motivational subcomponents increased the best. In this group, students wrote their impressions by responding to a series of questions regarding motivation and attitudes toward English learning after reading exemplary cases. In another study by Lee and Kim (2019), the effectiveness of MLAs for a relatively short period was investigated. For 3 weeks, four different MLAs were administered to 151 high school students. The MLAs used in Lee and Kim's (2019) study, compared to those used in Kim (2019) and Y.-K. Kim (2017), were more intensive in that they were conducted for 50 min in the first week of implementation, and then for 20–25 min in the second and third weeks. Their results also showed that both the experimental groups made significant gains in their subcomponents in L2 learning motivation. In this study, the experimental group that engaged in individual writing and then group discussion yielded greater increases than the group that only engaged in individual writing after watching and reading exemplary cases.

In retrospect, L2 motivation research in the previous generation was mostly descriptive because researchers analyzed the participants' motivational profiles and described their current state of L2 learning motivation. By using a mixture of sophisticated statistical procedures such as factor analysis, regression analysis, and structural equation modeling (SEM), the previous research focused on understanding the learners' motivational characteristics. However, at the same time, a couple of researchers (e.g., Crookes & Schmidt, 1991) have pointed out that this research tradition may not have practical implications that L2 teachers and learners can readily use. In this regard, the application of Swain's (2006, 2010, 2013) concept of languaging to the field of L2 learning motivation showed the possibility of making connections between theory and teaching. Future MLA research will invite more diverse educational settings.

References

Alavinia, P., & Sehat, R. (2012). A probe into the main demotivating factors among Iranian EFL learners. *English Language Teaching, 5*(6), 9–35.

Al-Khalil, M. (2011). Affective, cognitive, and behavioral manifestation of second language motivation in Arabic task-based interaction. Paper presented at the 2011 AAAL Annual Conference, Chicago, U.S.A.

Ames, C. (1984). Achievement attributions and self-instructions under competitive and individualistic goal structures. *Journal of Educational Psychology, 76*, 478–487.

Ames, C. (1992). Classrooms: Goals, structures, and student motivation. *Journal of Educational Psychology, 84*, 261–271.

Bakhtin, M. M. (1981). *The dialogic imagination: Four essays by M. M. Bakhtin.* Austin, TX: University of Texas Press.

Bandura, A. (1993). Perceived self-efficacy in cognitive development and functioning. *Educational Psychologist, 28*, 117–148.

Bandura, A. (1997). *Self-efficacy: The exercise of control.* New York: W. H. Freeman and Company.

Benson, P. (2014). Narrative inquiry in applied linguistics research. *Annual Review of Applied Linguistics, 34*, 154–170.

Block, D. (2003). *The social turn in second language acquisition.* Edinburgh, England: Edinburgh University Press.

Block, D., & Cameron, D. (Eds.). (2002). *Globalisation and language teaching.* London: Routledge.

Bourdieu, P. (1977). *Outline of a theory of practice.* (R. Nice, Trans.). Cambridge, England: Cambridge University Press.

Bourdieu, P. (1991). *Language and symbolic power* (M. Adamson, Trans.). Cambridge, MA: Harvard University Press.

Cole, M. (1996). *Cultural psychology.* Cambridge, MA: Harvard University Press.

Corbin, J., & Strauss, A. L. (2008). *Basics of qualitative research: Techniques and procedures for developing grounded theory* (3rd ed.). Thousand Oaks, CA: Sage.

Covington, M. V. (1984). The motive for self worth. In R. Ames & C. Ames (Eds.), *Research on motivation in education: Student motivation* (Vol. 1, pp. 77–113). San Diego, CA: Academic Press.

Covington, M. V., & Beery, R. G. (1976). *Self worth and school learning.* New York: Holt, Rinehart & Winston.

Crookes, G., & Schmidt, R. W. (1991). Motivation: Reporting the research agenda. *Language Learning, 41*, 469–512.

Davydov, V. V. (1999). The content and unsolved problems in activity theory. In Y. Engeström, R. Miettinen & R.-M. Punamaki (Eds.), *Perspectives on activity theory* (pp. 39–52). New York: Cambridge University Press.

Dewaele, J. (2005). Investigating the psychological and emotional dimensions in instructed language learning: Obstacles and possibilities. *The Modern Language Journal, 89*(3), 367–380.

Dörnyei, Z. (1990). Conceptualizing motivation in foreign language learning. *Language Learning, 40*, 46–78.

Dörnyei, Z. (1994). Motivation and motivating in the foreign language classroom. *The Modern Language Journal, 78*, 273–284.

Dörnyei, Z. (1996). Moving language learning motivation to a larger platform for theory and practice. In R. L. Oxford (Ed.), *Language learning motivation: Pathways to the new century* (pp. 71–80). Honolulu, HI: University of Hawai'i Press.

Dörnyei, Z. (1998). Motivation in second and foreign language classroom. *Language Teaching, 31*, 117–135.

Dörnyei, Z. (2001a). *Teaching and researching motivation.* Harlow, England: Longman.

Dörnyei, Z. (2001b). New themes and approaches in second language motivation research. *Annual Review of Applied Linguistics, 21*, 43–59.

Dörnyei, Z. (2003). Attitudes, orientations, and motivation in language learning: Advances in theory, research, and applications. *Language Learning, 53*(supplementary), 3–32.

Dörnyei, Z. (2005). *The psychology of the language learner: Individual differences in second language acquisition.* Mahwah, NJ: Lawrence Erlbaum.

Dörnyei, Z. (2009). The L2 motivational self system. In Z. Dörnyei & E. Ushioda (Eds.), *Motivation, language identity and the L2 self* (pp. 9–42). Bristol, England: Multilingual Matters.

Dörnyei, Z. (2019). Towards a better understanding of the L2 learning experience, the Cinderella of the L2 Motivational Self System. *Studies in Second Language Learning and Teaching, 9*(1), 19–30.

Dörnyei, Z. (2020). *Innovations and challenges in language learning motivation.* London: Routledge.

Dörnyei, Z., & Csizér, K. (2002). Some dynamics of language attitudes and motivation: Results of a national longitudinal survey. *Applied Linguistics, 23*(4), 421–462.

Dörnyei, Z., Csizér, K., & Németh, N. (2006). *Motivation, language attitudes and globalisation: A Hungarian perspective.* Clevedon, England: Multilingual Matters.

Dörnyei, Z., & Hadfield, J. (2013). *Motivating learning (Research and resources in language learning)*. London: Routledge.

Dörnyei, Z., Henry, A., & Muir, C. (2015a). *Motivational currents in language elearning: Frameworks for focused interventions*. London: Routledge.

Dörnyei, Z., & Kubanyiova, M. (2014). *Motivating learners, motivating teachers: Building vision in the language classroom*. Cambridge, England: Cambridge University Press.

Dörnyei, Z., MacIntyre, P. D., & Henry, A. (Eds.). (2015b). *Motivational dynamics in language learning*. Bristol, England: Multilingual Matters.

Dörnyei, Z., & Ottó, I. (1998). Motivation in action: A process model of L2 motivation. *Working Papers in Applied Linguistics (Thames Valley University, London)*, *4*, 43–69.

Dörnyei, Z., & Skehan, P. (2003). Individual differences in second language learning. In C. J. Doughty & M. H. Long (Eds.), *The handbook of second language acquisition* (pp. 589–630). Malden, MA: Blackwell.

Dörnyei, Z., & Ryan, S. (2015). *The psychology of the language learner revisited*. London: Routledge.

Dörnyei, Z., & Ushioda, E. (2021). *Teaching and researching motivation* (3rd ed.). London: Routledge.

Dweck, C. S. (1986). Motivational processes affecting learning. *American psychologist, 41*, 1040–1048.

Engeström, Y. (1987). *Learning by expanding: An activity-theoretical approach to developmental research*. Helsinki, Finland: Orienta-Konsultit.

Engeström, Y. (1999a). Activity theory and individual and social transformation. In Y. Engeström, R. Miettinen & R.-M. Punamäki (Eds.), *Perspectives on activity theory* (pp. 19–38). New York: Cambridge University Press.

Engeström, Y. (1999b). Innovative learning in work teams. In Y. Engeström, R. Miettinen & R.-M. Punamäki (Eds.), *Perspectives on activity theory* (pp. 377–404). New York: Cambridge University Press.

Erten, I. H. (2014). Understanding the reasons behind choosing to teach English as foreign language. *Novitas-ROYAL (Research on Youth and Language), 8*, 30–44.

Falout, J., Elwood, J., & Hood, M. (2009). Demotivation: Affective states and learning outcomes. *System, 37*, 403–417.

Gao, X. A., & Xu, H. (2014). The dilemma of becoming English language teachers: interpreting teachers' motivation to teach, and professional commitment in China's hinterland regions. *Language Teaching Research, 18*, 152–168.

Gardner, R. C. (1985). *Social psychology and second language learning: The role of attitudes and motivation*. London: Edward Arnold.

Gardner, R. C. (1988). The Socio-educational model of second language learning: Assumptions, findings, and issues. *Language Learning, 38*(1), 100–125.

Gardner, R. C. (2001). Integrative motivation and second language acquisition. In Z. Dörnyei & R. Schmidt. (Eds.), *Motivation and second language acquisition* (pp. 1–16). Honolulu, HI: University of Hawai'i Press.

Gardner, R. C. (2010). *Motivation and second language acquisition: The socio-educational model*. New York: Peter Lang.

Gardner, R. C., & Lambert, W. E. (1959). Motivational variables in second language acquisition. *Canadian Journal of Psychology, 13*, 266–272.

Gardner, R. C., & Lambert, W. E. (1972). *Attitudes and motivation in second language learning*. Rowley, MA: Newbury House.

Gardner, R. C., & MacIntyre, P. D. (1991). An instrumental motivation in language study: Who says it isn't effective? *Studies in Second Language Acquisition, 13*, 57–72.

Gardner, R. C., Masgoret, A.-M., Tennant, J., & Mihic, L. (2004). Integrative motivation: Changes during a year-long intermediate-level language course. *Language Learning, 54*(1), 1–34.

Gardner, R. C., & Smyth, P. C. (1975). Motivation and second language acquisition. *The Canadian Modern Language Review, 31*, 218–230.

Ghadirzadeh, R. Hashtroudi, F. B., & Shokri, O. (2012). Demotivating factors for English language learning among university students. *Journal of Social Sciences, 8*(2), 189–195.

Gillette, B. (1994). The role of learner goals in L2 success. In J. P. Lantolf & G. Appel (Eds.), *Vygotskian approaches to second language research* (pp. 195–210). Norwood, NJ: Ablex.

Hamada, Y. (2008). Demotivators for Japanese teenagers. *Journal of Pan-Pacific Association of Applied Linguistics, 15*(1), 15–38.

Hargreaves, A. (1998). The emotions of teaching and educational. Change. In A. Hargreaves, A. Lieberman, M. Fullan & D. Hopkins (Eds.), *International handbook of educational change* (pp. 558–575). Dordrecht, Germany, Springer.

Hayes, D. (2008). Becoming a teacher of English in Thailand. *Language Teaching Research 12*(4), 471–494.

Heckhausen, H. (1991). *Motivation and action*. New York: Springer.

Heckhausen, H., & Kuhl, J. (1985). From wishes to action: The dead ends and short cuts on the long way to action. In J. Sabini (Ed.), *Goal-directed behavior: The concept of action in psychology* (pp. 134–160). Hillsdale, NJ: Erlbaum.

Higgins, E. T. (1987). Self-discrepancy: A theory relating self and affect. *Psychological Review, 94*, 319–340.

Higgins, E. T. (1998). Promotion and prevention: Regulatory focus as a motivational principle. *Advances in Experimental Social Psychology, 30*, 1–46.

Hochschild, A. R. (1983). *The managed heart: Commercialization of human feeling*. Berkeley, CA: University of California Press.

Igawa, K. (2009). Initial career motivation of English teachers: Why did they choose to teach English? *Shitennoji University Bulletin, 48*, 201–226.

Inbar, O., Donitsa-Schmidt, S., & Shohamy, E. (2001). Students' motivation as a function of language learning: The teaching of Arabic in Israel. In Z. Dörnyei & R. Schmidt (Eds.), *Motivation and second language acquisition* (pp. 297–311). Honolulu, HI: University of Hawai'i Press.

Jang, Hye-Yeong, & Kim, Tae-Young. (2018). A study of English teachers' motivation from an activity theory perspective: Focusing on the school of the future in Seoul and the public middle school. *Secondary English Education, 11*(3), 71–100.

Joongang Ilbo. (2018, January 5th). "Wol 100manwon yeong'eoyoochiwon'eun an makgo"… Gyoyookbu eorinijip yeong'eosueop geumjiyocheon nonran ["They didn't ban English kindergarten spending a million Won a month"… Controversy on the Ministry of Education's ban request for English class in day nursery]. Retrieved January 21, 2019 at https://news.joins.com/article/22260303.

Jung, Sook Kyung. (2011). Demotivating and remotivating factors in learning English: A case of low level college students. *English Teaching, 66*(2), 47–72.

Kaptelinin, V. (2005). The object of activity: Making sense of the sense-maker. *Mind, Culture, and Activity, 12*, 4–18.

Kassabgy, O., Boraie, D., & Schmidt, R. (2001). Values, rewards, and job satisfaction in EFL/EFL. In Z. Dörnyei & R. Schmidt (Eds.), *Motivation and second language acquisition* (pp. 213–237). Honolulu, HI: University of Hawai'i Press.

Keblawi, F. (2005). Demotivation among Arab learners of English as a foreign language. In M. Singhal & J. Liontas (Eds.), *Proceedings of the second international conference on second and foreign language teaching and research* (pp. 49–78). Irvine, CA: The Reading Matrix.

Kikuchi, K. (2009). Listening to our learners' voice: What demotivates Japanese high school students. *Language Teaching Research, 13*(4), 453–471.

Kikuchi, K. (2013). Demotivators in the Japanese EFL contexts. In M. T. Apple, D. Da Silva & T. Fellner (Eds.), *Language learning motivation in Japan* (pp. 206–224). Bristol, England: Multilingual Matters.

Kikuchi, K. (2015). *Demotivation in second language acquisition*. Bristol, England: Multilingual Matters.

Kim, Kyung Ja. (2009a). A comparative analysis of demotivation in secondary English classes. *English Language & Literature Teaching, 15*(4), 75–94.

Kim, Kyung Ja. (2009c). Demotivating factors in secondary English education. *English Teaching, 64*(4), 249–267.

Kim, Kyung Ja. (2018). Factors influencing EFL high school students' motivation and demotivation: Difference by English proficiency. *Secondary English Education, 11*(4), 49–70.

Kim, Tae-Young. (2005). Reconceptualizing L2 motivation theory: Vygotskian activity theory approach. *English Teaching, 60*(4), 299–322.

Kim, Tae-Young. (2006a). Motivation and attitudes toward foreign language learning as socio-politically mediated constructs: The case of Korean high school students. *The Journal of Asia TEFL, 3*(2), 165–192.

Kim, Tae-Young. (2006b). L2 learning motivation from a sociocultural theory perspective: Theory, concepts, and empirical evidence. *English Teaching, 61*(4), 51–76.

Kim, Tae-Young. (2007). Second language learning motivation from an activity theory perspective: Longitudinal case studies of Korean ESL students and recent immigrants in Toronto. Unpublished doctoral dissertation. University of Toronto, Toronto, Canada.

Kim, Tae-Young. (2009b). Korean elementary school students' perceptual learning style, ideal L2 self, and motivated behavior. *Korean Journal of English Language and Linguistics, 9*(3), 461–486.

Kim, Tae-Young. (2009d). The sociocultural interface between ideal self and ought-to self: A case study of two Korean ESL students' motivation. In Z. Dörnyei & E. Ushioda (Eds.), *Motivation, language identity and the L2 self* (pp. 274–294). Bristol, England: Multilingual Matters.

Kim, Tae-Young. (2010a). Socio-political influence on EFL motivation and attitudes: Comparative surveys of Korean high school students. *Asia-Pacific Education Review, 11*, 211–222.

Kim, Tae-Young. (2010b). Reductionism, activity theory, and L2 motivation research: Toward new concepts and definitions. *The SNU Journal of Educational Research, 19*, 87–118.

Kim, Tae-Young. (2010c). Ideal L2 self and sensitization in L2 learning motivation: A case study of two Korean ESL students. *Korean Journal of English and Linguistics, 10*(2), 321–351.

Kim, Tae-Young. (2011a). Korean elementary school students' English learning demotivation: A comparative survey study. *Asia Pacific Education Review, 12*, 1–11.

Kim, Tae-Young. (2011b). Sociocultural dynamics of ESL learning (de)motivation: An activity theory analysis of two adult Korean immigrants. *The Canadian Modern Language Review, 67*(1), 91–122.

Kim, Tae-Young. (2012a). The L2 motivational self system of Korean EFL students: Cross-grade survey analysis. *English Teaching, 67*(1), 29–56.

Kim, Tae-Young. (2012b). An analysis of Korean elementary and secondary school students' English learning motivation and their L2 selves: Qualitative interview approach. *Korean Journal of English Language and Linguistics, 52*, 3–34.

Kim, Tae-Young. (2019). Effect of languaging activities on L2 learning motivation. A classroom-based approach. In M. Haneda & H. Nassaji (Eds.), *Perspectives on language as action* (pp. 80–98). Bristol, England: Multilingual Matters.

Kim, Tae-Young, & Kim, Yoon-Kyoung. (2013a). Reconceptualizing L2 learning demotivation from a Vygotskian activity theory perspective. *English Teaching, 68*(4), 141–163.

Kim, Tae-Young, & Kim, Yoon-Kyoung. (2015). Initial career motives and demotivation in teaching English as a foreign language: Cases of Korean EFL teachers. *Porta Linguarum, 24*, 77–92.

Kim, Tae-Young, & Kim, Youngmi. (2016a). EFL teachers' initial career motives and demotivation in South Korea. *Korean Journal of English Language and Linguistics, 16*(1), 29–52.

Kim, Tae-Young, & Kim, Yoon-Kyoung. (2016b). A quasi-longitudinal study on English learning motivation and attitudes: The case of South Korean students. *The Journal of Asia TEFL, 13*(2), 138–155.

Kim, Tae-Young, & Lee, Yu-Jin. (2013a). Korean students' English learning motivation and demotivation through autobiographic essays: Retrospective reconstruction. *Korean Journal of Applied Linguistics, 29*(1), 37–68.

Kim, Tae-Young, & Lee. Yu-Jin. (2013b). Constructs of Korean graduate students' English learning motivation, demotivation, and remotivation through analyzing retrospective essays. *The Sociolinguistic Journal of Korea, 21*(1), 27–47.

Kim, Tae-Young, & Seo, Hyo-Sun. (2012). Elementary school students' foreign language learning demotivation: A mixed study of Korean EFL students. *The Asia-Pacific Education Researcher, 21*(1), 160–171.

Kim, Yoon-Kyoung. (2017). *The effect of motivational languaging on Korean high school students EFL learning.* Unpublished doctoral dissertation. Chung-Ang University, Seoul, Korea.

Kim, Yoon-Kyoung, & Kim, Tae-Young. (2012). Korean secondary school students' L2 learning motivation: Comparitng L2 motivational self system with socio-educational model. *English Language and Literature Teaching, 18*(1), 115–132.

Kim, Yoon-Kyoung, & Kim, Tae-Young. (2013b). English learning demotivation studies in the EFL contexts: State of the art. *Modern English Education, 14*(1), 77–102.

Kim, Youngmi, & Kim, Tae-Young. (2018). The dynamics of EFL teacher emotion and emotional labor: An exploratory study. *English Language Teaching, 30*(2), 21–41.

King, J. (2015). "It's time, put on the smile. It's time": The emotional labour of second language teaching within a Japanese university. In C. Gkonou, D. Tatzl & S. Mercer (Eds.), *New directions in language learning and psychology* (pp. 97–112), New York: Springer.

Knouzi, I., Swain, M., Lapkin, S., & Brooks, L. (2010). Self-scaffolding mediating by languaging: Microgenetic analysis of high and low performers. *International Journal of Applied Linguistics, 20*(1), 23–49.

Koran, S. (2015). Analyzing EFL teachers' initial job motivation and factors affecting their motivation in Fezalar educational institutions in Iraq. *Advances in Language and Literary Studies, 6*, 72–80.

Korean Educational Development Institute. (2020). 2020 Hankookgyoyook jongdanyeongu: Godeunghaksaeng'eu Gyoyookgeongheomgwa seongjang(II) [2020 Longitudinal research of Korean education: High school students educational experience and development (II)] (RR2020-27). Korean Educational Development Institute: Seoul, Korea. Retrieved March 26, 2021 from https://www.kedi.re.kr/khome/main/research/listPubForm.do.

Kuhl, J. (1987). Action control: The maintenance of motivational states. In J. Kuhl (Ed.), *Motivation, intention, and volition* (pp. 279–291). Berlin, Germany: Springer.

Kubanyiova, M. (2007). *Teacher development in action: An empirically-based model of promoting conceptual change in in-service language teachers in Slovakia.* Unpublished doctoral dissertation. University of Nottingham, England.

Kubanyiova, M. (2009). Possible selves in language teacher development. In Z. Dörnyei & E. Ushioda (Eds.), *Motivation, language identity, and the L2 self* (pp. 314–332). Bristol, England: Multilingual Matters.

Kumazawa, M. (2013). Gaps too large: Four novice EFL teachers' self-concept and motivation. *Teaching and Teacher Education, 33*, 45–55.

Lamb, M. (2007). The impact of school on EFL learning motivation: An Indonesian case study. *TESOL Quarterly, 41*(4), 757–780.

Lamb, M., Csizér, K., Henry, A., & Ryan. S. (Eds.). (2019). *The Palgrave handbook of motivation for language learning.* London: Palgrave Macmillan.

Lantolf, J. P. (Ed.). (2000). *Sociocultural theory and second language learning.* Oxford, England: Oxford University Press.

Lantolf, J. P., & Appel, G. (1994). Theoretical framework: An introduction to Vygotskian approaches to second language research. In J. P. Lantolf & G. Appel (Eds.), *Vygotskian approaches to second language acquisition* (pp. 1–28). Norwood, NJ: Ablex.

Lantolf, J. P., & Genung, P. B. (2002). "I'd rather switch than fight": An activity-theoretic study of power, success, and failure in a foreign language classroom. In C. Kramsch (Ed.), *Language acquisition and language socialization* (pp. 175–196). London: Continuum.

Lantolf, J. P., & Thorne, S. (2006). *The sociogenesis of second language development.* Oxford, England: Oxford University Press.

Lapkin, S., Swain, M., & Psyllakis, P. (2010). The role of languaging in creating zones of proximal development (ZPDs): A long term care resident interacts with a researcher. *The Canadian Journal on Aging, 29*(4), 477–490.

Larsen-Freeman, D., & Long, M. H. (1991). *An introduction to second language acquisition research.* Harlow, England: Longman.

Lee, Hyo-Woong. (1996). Hankook joongodeunghaksaeng'ui taedowa donggiga yeongeohakseup'e michineun yeonghyang [The effects of attitudes and motivation on learning English in Korean secondary school students]. *English Teaching, 52*, 3–34.

Lee, Jinsol, & Kim, Tae-Young. (2018). Novice English teachers' initial career motives and demotivation in South Korea. *English Language and Literature Teaching, 24*(3), 1–20.

Lee, Yeon-Kyung, & Kim, Tae-Young. (2016). Possible teacher self and teachers motivational change: A case study of two Korean English teachers. *Journal of Learner-Centered Curriculum and Instruction, 16*(3), 685–708.

Lee, Yu-Jeong, & Kim, Tae-Young. (2019). The effect of languaging activity on Korean high school students' English learning motivation and metacognitive strategy use. *Secondry English Education, 12*(1), 25–51.

Lenchuk, I. V., & Swain, M. (2010). Alise's small stories: Indices of identity construction and of resistance to the discourse of cognitive impairment. *Language Policy, 9,* 9–28.

Leont'ev, A. N. (1978). *Activity, consciousness, and personality.* Englewood Cliffs, CA: Prentice-Hall.

Levav, J., & Fitzsimons, G. J. (2006). When questions change behavior: The role of ease of representation. *Psychological Science, 17*(3), 207–213.

Locke, E. A., & Latham, G. P. (1990). *A theory of goal setting and task performance.* Eaglewood Cliffs, NJ.: Prentice Hall.

MacIntyre, P. D., Gregersen, T., & Mercer, S. (2016). *Positive psychology in SLA.* Bristol, England: Multilingual Matters.

Markova, A. K. (1990). Ways of investigating motivation from learning in school children. *Soviet Psychology, 28*(6), 21–42.

Markus, H., & Nurius, P. (1986). Possible selves. *American Psychologist, 41*, 954–969.

Meece, J. L., Blumenfeld, P. C., & Hoyle, R. H. (1988). Students' goal orientations and cognitive engagement in classroom activities. *Journal of Educational Psychology, 80*, 514–523.

Miettinen, R. (2005). Object of activity and individual motivation. *Mind, Culture, and Activity, 12* (1), 52–69.

Morwitz, V. G., & Johnson, E. J., & Schmittlein, D. (1993). Does measuring intent change behavior? *Journal of Consumer Research, 29*(1), 46–61.

Muir, C., & Dörnyei, Z. (2013). Directed motivational currents: Using vision to create effective motivational pathways. *Studies in Second Language Learning and Teaching, 3*(3), 357–375.

Nicholls, J. G. (1979). Quality and equality in intellectual development: The role of motivation in edcuation. *American Psychologist, 34*, 1071–1084.

Nicholls, J. G. (1984a). Achievement motivation: Conceptions of ability, subjective experience, task choice, and performance. *Psychological Review, 91*, 328–346.

Nicholls, J. G. (1984b). Concpetions of ability and achievement motivation. In R. Ames & C. Ames (Eds.), *Research on motivation in education* (Vol. 1, pp. 39–73). San Diego, CA: Academic Press.

Nicholls, J. G. (1989). *The competitive ethos and demographic education.* Cambridge, MA: Harvard University Press.

Noels, K. A., Clément, R., & Pelletier, L. G. (1999). Perceptions of teachers' communicative style and students' intrinsic and extrinsic motivation. *The Modern Language Journal, 83*(1), 23–34.

Noels, K. A., Clément, R., & Pelletier, L. G. (2001). Intrinsic, extrinsic, and integrative orientations of French Canadian learners of English. *The Candian Modern Language Review, 57*(3), 424–442.

Noels, K. A., Lou, N. M., Lascano, D. I. V., Chaffee, K. E., Dincer, A., Zhang, Y. S. D., & Zhang, X. (2019). Self-determination and motivated engagement in language learning. In M. Lamb, K. Csizér, A. Henry & S. Ryan (Eds.), (2019). *The Palgrave handbook of motivation for language learning* (pp. 95–115). London: Palgrave Macmillan.

Norton, B. (2013). *Identity and language learning: Extending the conversation* (2nd ed.). Bristol, England: Multilingual Matters.

Norton Peirce, B. (1993). *Language learning, social identity, and immigrant women.* Unpublished doctoral dissertation. University of Toronto, Toronto, Canada.

Norton Peirce, B. (1995). Social identity, investment, and language learning. *TESOL Quarterly, 29*, 9–31.

Oh, Myung-Keun, & Kong, Ji-Hyun. (2000). A study on the Arabic learners' motive and attitudes toward Arab culture. *Foreign Languages Education, 7*(1), 327–353.

Oller, J., Baca, L., & Vigil, A. (1977). Attidues and attainted proficiency in ESL: A sociolinguistic study of Mexican Americans in the Southwest. *TESOL Quarterly, 11*, 173–183.

Ortega, N., & Iberri-Shea, G. (2005). Longitudinal research in second language acquisition: Recent trends and future directions. *Annual Review of Applied Linguistics, 25*, 26–45.

Oxford, R., & Shearin, J. (1994). Language learning motivation: Expanding the theoretical framework. *The Modern Language Journal, 78*(1), 12–28.

Papi, M. (2010). The L2 motivational self system, L2 anxiety, and motivated behavior: A structural equation modeling approach. *System, 38*, 467–479.

Pennington, M. C. (1995). *Work satisfaction, motivation and commitment in teaching English as a second language.* ERIC Document ED 404850.

Ryan, R. M., & Deci, E. L. (2000). Intrinsic and extrinsic motivations: Classic definitions and new directions. *Contemporary Educational Psychology, 25*(1), 54–67.

Ryan, S. (2009). Ambivalence and commitment, liberation and challenge: Investigating the attitudes of young Japanese people towards the learning of English. *Journal of Multilingual and Multicultural Development, 30*(5), 405–420.

Sakai, H., & Kikuchi, K. (2009). An analysis of demotivation in the EFL classroom. *System, 37*, 57–69.

Schmidt, R., & Watanabe, Y. (2001). Motivation, strategy use, and pedagogical preferences in foreign language learning. In Z. Dörnyei & R. Schmidt (Eds.), *Motivation and second language acquisition* (pp. 313–360). Honolulu, HI: University of Hawai'i Press.

Schutz, P. A., & Pekrun, R. E. (2007). *Emotion in education.* San Diego, CA: Academic Press.

Shoaib, A., & Dörnyei, Z. (2005). Affect in lifelong learning: Exploring L2 motivation as a dynamic process. In P. Benson & D. Nunan (Eds.), *Learners' stories: Difference and diversity in language learning* (pp. 22–41). Cambridge, England: Cambridge University Press.

Sivan, E. (1986). Motivation in social constructivist theory. *Educational Psychologist, 21*(3), 209–233.

Skehan, P. (1989). *Individual differences in second-language learning.* London: Edward Arnold.

Skehan, P. (1992). Individual differences in second language learning. *Studies in Second Language Acquisition, 13*, 275–298.

Song, Bongsun, & Kim, Tae-Young. (2016). Teacher (de)motivation from an Activity Theory perspective: Cases of two experienced EFL teachers in South Korea. *System, 57*, 134–145.

Song, Bongsun, & Kim, Tae-Young. (2017). The dynamics of demotivation and remotivation among Korean high school EFL students. *System, 65*, 90–103.

Sugino, T. (2010). Teacher demotivational factors in the Japanese language teaching context. *Social and Behavioral Sciences, 3*, 216–226.

Swain, M. (2006). Languaging, agency and collaboration in advanced language proficiency. In H. Byrnes (Ed.), *Advanced language learning: The contribution of Halliday and Vygotsky* (pp. 95–108). London: Continuum.

Swain, M. (2010). "Talking-it-through": Languaging as a source of learning. In R. Batstone (Ed.), *Sociocognitive perspectives on language use and language learning* (pp. 112–129). Oxford, England: Oxford University Press.

Swain, M. (2013). Cognitive and affective enhancement among older adults: The role of languaging. *Australian Review of Applied Linguistics, 36*(1), 4–19.

Swain, M., & Lapkin, S. (2011). Languaging as agent and constituent of cognitive change in an older adult: An example. *Canadian Journal of Applied Linguistics, 14*(1), 104–117.

Swain, M., Lapkin, S., Knouzi, I., Suzuki, W., & Brooks, L. (2009). Languaging: University students learn the grammatical concept of voice in French. *The Modern Language Journal, 93*(1), 5–29.

Taguchi, T., Magid, A., & Papi, M. (2009). The L2 motivational self system among Japanese, Chinese and Iranian learners of English: A comparative study. In Z. Dörnyei & E. Ushioda (Eds.), *Motivation, language identity and the L2 Self* (pp. 66–97). Bristol, England: Multilingual Matters.

The Canadian Encyclopedia. (2019). Francophone-Anglophone relations. Retrieved January 11, 2019 from https://www.thecanadianencyclopedia.ca/en/article/francophone-anglophone-relations.

Trang, T. T. T., & Baldauf, Jr. R. B. (2007). Demotivation: Understanding resistance to English language learning – The case of Vietnamese students. *The Journal of Asia TEFL, 4*(1), 79–105.

Tremblay, P. F., & Gardner, R. C. (1995). Expanding the motivation construct in language learning. *The Modern Language Journal, 79*, 505–520.

Ushioda, E. (2001). Language learning at university: Exploring the role of motivational thinking. In Z. Dörnyei & R. Schmidt (Eds.), *Motivation and second language acquisition* (pp. 93–126). Honolulu, HI: University of Hawai'i Press.

Ushioda, E. (2003). Motivation as a socially mediated process. In D. Little, J. Ridley & E. Ushioda (Eds.), *Learner autonomy in the foreign language classroom: Learner, teacher, curriculum and assessment* (pp. 90–103). Dublin, Ireland: Authentik.

Ushioda, E. (2007). Motivation, autonomy and sociocultural theory. In P. Benson (Ed.), *Learner autonomy 8: Teacher and learner perspectives* (pp. 5–24). Dublin, Ireland: Authentik.

Ushioda, E. (2013). Foreign language motivation research in Japan: An 'insider' perspective from outside Japan. In M. T. Apple, D. Da Silva & T. Fellner (Eds.), *Language learning motivation in Japan* (pp. 90–103). Bristol, England: Multilingual Matters.

Vygotsky, L. S. (1978). *Mind in society: The development of higher psychological processes.* Cambridge, MA: Harvard University Press.

Vygotsky, L. S. (1987). Thinking in speech. In R. W. Rieber & A. S. Carton (Eds.), *The collected works of L. S. Vygotsky: Problems of general psychology* (Vol. 1). New York: Plenum.

Wang, T., & Malderez, A. (2006). Demotivation: A qualitative study of Chinese English learners at the tertiary level. *Journal of Macau Polytechnic Institute, 2*, 135–147.

Warrington, S. D., & Jeffrey, D. M. (2005). A rationale for passivity and de-motivation revealed: An interpretation of inventory results among freshman English students. *Journal of Language and Learning, 3*(2), 312–335.

Weiner, B. (1992). *Human motivation: Metaphors, theories, and research.* Newbury Park, CA: Sage.

Wenger. E. (1998). *Communities of practice: Learning, meaning, and identity.* New York: Cambridge University Press.

Wertsch, J. V. (1985). *Vygotsky and the social formation of mind.* Cambridge, MA: Harvard University Press.

White, C., & Ding, A. (2009). Identity and self in e-language teaching. In Z. Dörnyei & E. Ushioda (Eds.), *Motivation, language identity, and the L2 self* (pp. 333–349). Bristol, England: Multilingual Matters.

Williams, M., & Burden, R. L. (1997). *Psychology for language teachers: A social constructivist approach.* Cambridge, England: Cambridge University Press.

Yang, Jin-Sook, & Kim, Tae-Young. (2011). The L2 motivational self-system and perceptual learning styles of Chinese, Japanese, Korean, and Swedish Students. *English Teaching, 66*(1), 141–162.

You, C., & Dörnyei, Z. (2016). Language learning motivation in China: Results of a large-scale stratified survey. *Applied Linguistics, 37*(4), 495–519.

Zembylas, M. (2002). "Structures of feeling" in curriculum and teaching: Theorizing the emotional rules. *Educational Theory, 52*(2), 187–208.

Chapter 7
Sociohistorical Genesis of South Korean EFL Learners' English Learning Motivation

As stated in Chaps. 2, 3, and 4, English has long been regarded as a powerful tool for ascending the social hierarchy in (South) Korea.[1] The person who could speak a moderate level of English in Korea could secure a good job and be considered for promotion more readily. Most Koreans, who cannot speak English fluently, feel stressed among those who are more proficient. This frustrates them and causes reluctance to speak in front of others whose English is better than theirs. In this chapter, by considering various sociological factors, it will be argued that Korean English as a Foreign Language (EFL) learners' motivation to learn English is based on their unique traditions, culture, and social environments. Thus, a systematic explanation about Koreans' eagerness to learn English will be explained after we have scrutinized its related five factors.

First, competitive motivation, identified uniquely among EFL learners in South Korea, will be explained. The origin and development of competitive motivation will be the central foci. The second factor surrounding EFL learning in Korea is the concept of "alter ego familism" or learning English for the purpose of advancing the prosperity of student's family and enhancing their social status in relation to other Korean families. The concept of learning English as an insurance or emotional safety net will also be elaborated on while analyzing the status of the English language as the only foreign language in virtually all Korean primary and secondary schools. Currently, students' individual preference or talent for learning a language is largely disregarded, and the attitude of learning English for potential use in the future or simply "just in case" prevails. The third consideration is the learning of English as a type of "Kitsch" or sustainable (but not the best) alternative, replacing authentic

---

[1]It seems obvious that English was regarded as the powerful tool before 1945, but after the foundation of two Koreas in 1948, this view deserves a careful scrutiny. In Chap. 5, it was explained that English is also prioritized in North Korea recently. However, for three decades from the 1950s to 1970s, Russian gained more social recognition than English in North Korea for its diplomatic and political reasons. Thus, the parenthesis in "(South) Korea" refers to this differential consideration between South and North Korea.

© Springer Nature Singapore Pte Ltd. 2021
T.-Y. Kim, *Historical Development of English Learning Motivation Research*,
English Language Education 21, https://doi.org/10.1007/978-981-16-2514-5_7

English instruction offered by qualified native speakers. Then, as the fourth factor, Bourdieu's (1977, 1991) widely recognized concept of cultural capital will be introduced and linked to the learning of English in Korea. From Bourdieu's perspective, the English language instructed to students in Korea can be considered as academic capital with higher value than other languages such as Korean. Finally, "amotivated" EFL learning and its paradoxical results will be approached from the perspective of cultural psychology, with the focus particularly on South Korean mentality, such as collectivism (Choi, 2011a). By analyzing English learning based on these multiple factors, this chapter will conclude that it is necessary to approach L2 learning/teaching (de)motivation by carefully considering the students' and teachers' regional and communal society, cultural tradition, and historical background as well as their individual characteristics or propensity.

7.1 The Motivation Toward Secular Success and the Expansion of Competitive Motivation

As analyzed in previous chapters, even in the preindustrial, feudal dynasty in Korea, it had always been of utmost importance to educate interpreters for the purpose of diplomacy and cross-border trading among neighboring nations. In Goryeo and Joseon Dynasty, *Sayeokwon* (司譯院) was established and fulfilled such a function; in 1883, *Dongmunhak*, established by Müllendorf, did a similar job, and in 1886 *Yookyeong'gongwon*, the Royal Language School, took over the job of Dongmunhak (see Chap. 2). In both *Dongmunhak* and *Yookyeong'gongwon*'s cases, it deserves our attention that the teaching method was mostly the "Direct Method," which emphasized speaking and listening practice without mediating through the students' first language (i.e., Korean). Since King Gojong put an emphasis on learning English as a way to industrialize the preindustrial Korea and import western civilization represented by the U.S. and the U.K., English learning rapidly became popular in late nineteenth century Korea. As stated in Chap. 2, it is recorded in *Joseon Wangjo Silrok* (朝鮮王朝實錄), or Royal Chronicle of the Joseon Dynasty, that King Gojong selected the best candidate for *Yookyeong'gongwon* and proctored the students himself during their English graduation exam. As the former students at *Yookyeong'gongwon* and other missionary school graduates were rapidly hired in various government offices, it was soon believed that English proficiency is the royal road toward employment and prosperity. In fact, this belief might not be sheer exaggeration given that it is found that the customs officers working at Jemulpo (now Incheon, vicinity of Seoul) Customs Office earned a monthly salary four to five times higher than other officers or workers. Upon hearing the news, many Koreans hastily searched for educational institutions where English is instructed. This English craze was intensified by the abolishment of *gwageo* (科擧) test or the traditional officer selection examination in Korea (as well as other Asian countries including China and Vietnam) in 1894 through the Gabo Reform. The students previously preparing for *gwageo* test now eagerly endeavored to find its substitute, and its prominent replacement was the English language.

The memorization of foreign language books represented by classical Chinese literature and application of the foreign language had its long historical lineage in East Asia. For example, it was an essential element in general education in Korea, particularly for the ruling social class called *yangban*. Additionally, in Japan, after the reign of Tokugawa Shogunate from the early seventeenth century to the opening of Japan by the U.S. Admiral Perry in 1853, Confucian literature was predominantly instructed to sons of the then ruling Samurai class in every prefecture across the Japanese archipelago. The young test takers of *gwageo* in Korea must have panicked and felt frustrated once they were notified of the abolishment of the *gwageo* test in 1894. Their panic and frustration provided renewed energy toward English learning. In the new system after the 1894 Gabo Reform, the literacy and oracy of the English language were acclaimed and became the magic "open sesame" for social success in Korea. In some cases, the mass public in Korea widely circulated the dramatic success story of a person who learned English. For example, as presented in Chap. 2, Mr. Lee Ha-Young, from a humble origin with no proper education and special technical skills, met and worked for Dr. Allen, assisting with simple English-Korean translations; he rapidly advanced toward secular success, such as being appointed deputy ambassador to the USA and mayor of Hansung (now Seoul) within 20 years (Jeon, 2006). This miraculous success story of a man of low social class had strengthened the belief (or even myth) of English learning as a ladder for climbing up the social class. In this regard, the motivation to learn English at the turn of the twentieth century is an utterly instrumental one, where English is actually used for employment and sometimes communication in places such as a customs office.

However, in the first half of the twentieth century, Korea experienced severe political unrest. The Eulsa Treaty or the Korea-Japan Protectorate Treaty was signed in 1905 and the Korea-Japan Annexation Treaty on August 22, 1910. The fall of a nation and annexation by Japan led to the perception that Koreans, as the colonized, must not have much opportunity to be appointed as high-ranking government officers, as these positions should be monopolized by Japanese rulers. Thus, in the first decade from 1910 to 1919 before the Samil Independence Movement, learning English was actively suppressed in Korea, and even after 1920, English learning did not imply lively English communication. Japanese officers working at the Government-General of Korea were in charge of English communication for the purpose of international trade. In this social milieu, the English learning during the Japanese Colonization Period gradually acquired another social function: a tool for inward competition for admission to higher educational institutions.

In this sense, the establishment of Kyungsung (or Keijo) Imperial University in 1926 marked a new era of English learning motivation. As explained in the progression of English education in Japan in Chap. 2, the establishment of the 4-year comprehensive imperial university completed the hierarchical structure in the modern education system in Japan. While placing these imperial universities apex, other technical colleges, high schools, middle (or junior high) schools, and primary schools were linearly allocated. This conceptual hierarchy in educational institutions was also implanted in Korea (Lee, 2002). Given this hierarchical structure, the inclusion of English in the entrance exam of Kyungsung Imperial University exerted an impact on the teaching and learning of English in Korea. Before the annexation of Korea and Japan, English functioned as a tool for communication for commerce, trade, and job procurement. However, under colonial Korea, the job prospectus after learning English did not improve for Korean youths; a lion's share of these jobs was offered to the Japanese. Additionally, the opportunity for authentic communication in English was also remarkably limited under colonization.

Despite Koreans' extremely limited opportunity to secure a job or to have authentic English communication, the role of English as a screening tool for high-stakes tests prevailed in the same period. The negative washback effect of Kyungsung Imperial University's admission test was exponential, and English-Japanese translation and Japanese-English translation soon became the norm for the admission tests in other technical colleges and high schools across Korea. The competition for the admission to higher educational institutions was extremely severe. Due to the lack of educational opportunity, only a select few students received tertiary education. A diploma at Kyungsung Imperial University was regarded as a voucher or guarantee toward a decent job. For this reason, English learning during the Japanese Colonization Period had changed its characteristic; it was mainly for the purpose of passing the entrance exam. A prototypical form of competitive motivation surrounding English learning was initiated during this period. It should be noted that competitive motivation is different from instrumental motivation (Gardner, 1985, 2010) in that the former always assumes other colleagues, friends, or classmates with whom the student competed for a small number of seats in higher educational institutions (see Sect. 6.3, Chap. 6). As a motivational subcomponent, it is uniquely identified among Korean students (Kim, 2006, 2010; Kim & Kim, 2016), and the existence of other competitors is assumed in this concept.

After the liberation from Japan in August 1945, Korea was divided into North and South Korea. For the disarmament of the Japanese army, U.S. troops were stationed in the southern part of the Korean Peninsula. Since the official language before the establishment of the government of the Republic of Korea in 1948 was English, only the chosen ones who could speak English and functioned as liaison officers between the U.S. army and the Korean people had an easy channel to information. The same individuals acquired the former Japanese empire's properties seized by the U.S. troops. Their advantageous social status was consolidated by the following Korean War, which lasted more than 3 years. Any Koreans with ambition and a moderate level of English proficiency could have a head start on the road to success in South Korean society. As stated in previous chapters, the rapid economic development, spearheaded by the military style, meticulous system for more than three decades since the 1960s, was also supported by the close political and economic ties between the USA and South Korea.

Against this social background in South Korea, English had been emphasized from two different perspectives. First, English was actually necessary for the after-war reconstruction process and the subsequent developmental process influenced by the USA. In particular, the Park Chung-hee administration, effective from 1961 to 1979 until his sudden assassination, put a constant emphasis on exporting goods to foreign countries, mainly to the USA (McGinn et al., 1980). Thus, ability in English communication was highly anticipated in the corporate companies working with the U.S.-based counterparts. Another type of English, however, became more prominent among Korean students. The school English, similar to *juken eigo* (受験英語) in Japan, was widely practiced among high school students in Korea. All college-bound high school students were required to learn a massive amount of English vocabulary and extensive knowledge in English grammar in preparation for the college entrance exams. Despite the changes in the exam format, in essence, the English exam in this period until 1980 required all high school graduates to take the main entrance exams administered by each university. Overall, compared with the National Academic Ability Test (administered from 1982 to 1993), which was replaced by the College Scholastic Ability Test (from 1994 to present), the English test in the main entrance exam before the 1980s was extremely difficult. To pass such a difficult test, students needed fast reading skills along with extensive knowledge of English grammar and vocabulary. Therefore, the English learning among secondary school students was not toward developing communicative competence but only toward acquiring a high score in English tests. This exam preparation was in fact the continuation of internal competition among compatriots engendered in the Japanese Colonization Period. However, with economic development, many Korean families could increasingly afford their children's university education. Thus, the competitive motivation during the era of economic reconstruction in the latter half of the twentieth century became fiercer than that during the Japanese Colonization Period.

As presented above, the role of English performed two distinctive motivational characteristics in South Korea: instrumental use of English for economic needs and as a scholastic selection tool, accompanied by intense competition among students for better educational opportunities. However, the two types of motivation assume upward social mobility for a better life. Both the instrumental use and the scholastic selection tool focus on having a better life "than the other" people in Korea. The power of English, which affords better job prospects and advancement in workplaces, had been witnessed throughout the history of Korea. From the late nineteenth century's Joseon Dynasty, the first half of the twentieth century under Japanese colonization, and the second half of the same century when Korea presented rapid recovery from the atrocity of the civil war, reconstructed its economy and consolidated its important technological and cultural status in Asia; Koreans' experience has showed them that English proficiency higher "than other compatriots" provides critical advantage. The competitive motivation often found in EFL motivation research (e.g., Kim, 2006, 2010; Kim & Kim, 2016) reflects such shared experiences of most Koreans through modern history. This type of motivation is qualitatively different from instrumental motivation, often defined as the desire to learn English to get a salary benefit or gain admission to a college (Gardner & Lambert, 1972). In this definition, the desire to perform better than other potential competitors has not been hypothesized. Similar to Dweck's (1986) performance goal in her goal-orientation theory, Korean EFL students create a higher level of competitiveness in learning English. If they are not doing better than others, they may not acquire a better score than others, which then results in the failure of obtaining a college admission, particularly the admission to prestigious institutions. If they do not communicate in English better than their other co-workers, they may lose promotion opportunities and eventually be asked to resign from the position. Given this, English learning is often considered as the law of the jungle, and English classes are the jungle in a figurative sense.

Therefore, the motivation uniquely found among Korean students would be a high level of competitive motivation, and this is aimed toward secular success and always assumes the existence of other potential competitors. In the socioeducational situation in South Korea described above, simply acquiring a good test score in English may not be sufficient if other students in the same class earned a better score than the student. Similarly, an office worker's excellent English communication skills would not be acclaimed by his or her superintendent if other colleagues commanded superior English to him or her. This competitive learning context or work environment often engenders belligerent, competitive motivation among learners in Korea.

As explained in Chap. 6, Kim's (2006, 2010) research on EFL motivation among high school students sheds light on the development of competitive motivation in South Korea. Kim published two research articles, and the same subcomponents in EFL learning motivation were measured twice in 2002 and 2006. In both cases, competitive motivation was extracted as one of the motivational subcomponents. Compared with the findings of 2002, those of 2006 indicated that the learners' competitive motivation increased. However, the regression analyses showed that competitive motivation did not affect the participants' English proficiency in a statistically significant manner. This means that no matter how the students perceived other students as potential competitors, it did not affect their English test score either positively or negatively. In other words, although competitive motivation was identified among Korean EFL learners, this did not influence students' English proficiency.

As with other East Asian nations such as China (Lam, Yim, Law, & Cheung, 2004) and Japan (Koike & Tanaka, 1995), English classes in Korea are ample with a competitive atmosphere. The long-standing tradition of *gwageo* test in the Goryeo and Joseon Dynasty was based on Confucianism, which placed a high value on learned men with culture and literacy. The status of *gwageo* was replaced by a college entrance exam, spearheaded by Kyungsung Imperial University in the Japanese Colonial Period, and was succeeded by the other prestigious universities represented by the so-called SKY universities (an acronym of Seoul National, Korea, and Yonsei Universities). Under this traditional thought of study and exam preparation, a person with more knowledge could occupy a better social position, and in general this was true particularly during the war restoration and developmental stage of the nation. However, the neoliberalism initiated by the U.S.-led capitalism rapidly nullified the traditional concept of knowledge, and academic credentialism no longer functioned as effectively in South Korean society as before. Arguably, this new trend identified in twenty-first century Korea would have been initiated by the Asian financial crisis in 1997 and 1998, caused by the collapse of the stock market in Thailand (Kim & Haque, 2002). South Korea was severely affected by this crisis and applied for an emergency bailout fund from the International Monetary Fund (IMF); most Koreans recollect this as "the IMF crisis."

It is noteworthy that the 1997 financial crisis resulted in the dismantling of the stable lifetime employment system under the guise of labor flexibility. Many office workers who had graduated from good-standing universities in Korea faced massive lay-offs, and this cast serious doubts on the efficacy of the academic credentialism that caused extreme competition and engendered subsequent competitive motivation. Before this crisis, life-long employment in the same workplace was an implicit social norm in South Korea; most laborers were full-time workers, and only a small percentage of them were in temporary, unstable positions. Under this relatively stable system before the 1997 IMF crisis, diplomas from a prestigious university meant that the diploma holder is entitled to have a better position at work and the position was virtually occupied permanently. After the financial crisis, this de facto norm was not a given anymore. Many laborers first lost their jobs due to the adverse financial situation at the workplace, and only a modicum of lucky ones could be reemployed, that too with a temporary worker status. Relatively stable job security could not be guaranteed any longer. During this national adversity, persons with a prestigious university diploma were not exempted and their bachelor's or master's degrees could not prevent them from falling into unemployment. The 1997 financial crisis facilitated many Koreans to have a different view on education; instead of a university degree, it was regarded a better preparation for young Koreans to have a unique technical skill by which they can make a living. This new realization toward job security resulted in the influx of technical or vocational high school applications from the late 1990s onward. Thus, the 1997 financial crisis in Korea would be the first instance of questioning the effectiveness of an academic degree, which shattered the ground of competitive motivation that had uniquely functioned in Korea.

Another consideration in the discussion of competitive motivation would be South Korea's economic development. During the economic development stage, an unquestionable tenet was that a diploma from a prestigious university leads to secure employment and to a stable, well-paying job. As the national poverty culminated in the 1950s and 60s in South Korea (Kang, 2001), without submitting such a graduation certificate to potential employers, it would be difficult to have a job at all; in such cases, the jobseekers themselves and their family would experience serious starvation. In such a desperate situation, the diploma, as a physical artifact that can be presented to potential employers, could fulfill the gatekeeping role effectively. A graduation certificate from one of the "SKY" universities was an effective tool for employment. However, as South Korea's economy developed into a mature, stable stage, most Koreans, particularly young generations, do not experience poverty or worry about starving any more. Jobs exist, and job seekers have choices from top-tier companies, which are usually Korea-based conglomerates such as Samsung, Hyundai, or LG Corporation, to second-tier, medium-sized companies, and then third-tier small-sized ones. Most job seekers endeavor to be hired at the top-tier large companies; for this reason, they prepare for the company entrance exam for more than a year, either full-time or part-time, while working at a second or third-tier company. Recent trends also reported that the most desired job among millennials is a government officer's position; once employed, they can find a balance between their personal life and workload (Im, 2018). If unemployed, they can file documents for unemployment insurance, for which the Korean government warrants payment (i.e., 50% of the monthly salary) from a minimum of 3 months to a maximum of 7 months. Thus, in this case, students' high level of English proficiency and their graduation certificate from a prestigious university may not be as valuable compared to their parents' or grandparents' generations. The meaning of having an occupation in this regard changed—from a life-and-death competition for a survival of the fittest toward a choice for a better, affluent lifestyle.

Given the above economic development in the twenty-first century, the high level of competitive motivation identified in Kim's (2006, 2010) research would invite a comprehensive explanation. When considering the minimized effectiveness of a college diploma or graduation certificate, particularly from a prestigious university, Korean students may not need to study English seriously for test-taking purposes toward university admission. The restructuring of the economy after the 1997 financial crisis did not permit any unbridled power of university graduation certificates, and this must have affected students' English learning motivation; they did not need to compete with each other to earn a better score as before. Moreover, the economic development provided jobseekers with a couple of choices, and in this situation, English proficiency did not automatically guarantee a better position at work. As Kim et al. (2019) showed in a recent questionnaire survey, English ability represented by the Test of English for International Communication (TOEIC) functions as a negative gatekeeping device, which means that the minimal score of the TOEIC needs to be met in order to pass the first round of screening for a position. A better score in the TOEIC does not increase the possibility of being hired.

Based on the above situations, why do we still identify a high level of competitive motivation among Korean high school students? Moreover, Kim's (2010) research findings presented that the degree of competitiveness among the students intensified compared with the results of his 2006 research (Kim, 2006). These research findings present a paradoxical situation because we can identify a disparity between the increase of competitiveness among students in Korea and a minimized need of academic credentials and diminishing pressure of employment for bare survival.

First, the parental influence needs to be highlighted to explain this contradiction. In a qualitative study investigating students' perceptions of their own English learning motivation, parental advice and suggestions influence students' positive attitudes in learning English (Kim, 2012a). Moreover, this trend noticeably increased as the students' English proficiency increased. Particularly, the logical explanation of students' fathers for the need to learn English, from their experience at various workplaces, was found to exert a positive influence on students' motivation. Given this, the role of parental influence would be the key factor in determining students' motivation to learn English. Note that the students' parents were educated in the era of economic reconstruction in a poverty-stricken nation. During their parents' adolescence, South Korea of the 1970s and 80s had severe competition at school and workplaces, and this was regarded as the social norm. In South Korea, anyone born between 1954 and 1964, belonging to the baby boomer generation, was exposed to chronic competition. After the Korean War (1950–1953), the baby boomers did not have sufficient nutrition, lacked educational opportunities, and did not enjoy the benefit of economic development, all of which were fully enjoyed by their offspring, Generation X (who were born between the mid-1960s and the early 1980s in South Korea). In the baby boomer generation, the belief in the effectiveness of academic credentials was widely preserved. Only the hardworking students earned admission to prestigious universities, and most of them could get a white-collar office job. As a matter of fact, many of the baby boomers became victims of the 1997 Asian financial crisis and lost their jobs (Im, 2018). In spite of this eventful experience, the baby boomers obstinately adhered to the old paradigm of learning: becoming the ultimate winner in "the battle of exams" will lead to an affluent life in the future. At least these parents' lives somehow proved the effectiveness of this tenet although the 1997 financial crisis had completely overturned it. Above all, they were not cognizant of any alternative way to motivate their sons and daughters than encouraging their competitiveness, which was so effective in their generation.

Another factor intensifying the students' competitiveness would be attributed to school as an educational system. For the high school application process in South Korea, middle school students can select one of various types of high schools: college-bound humanities high school, vocational (e.g., industrial, commercial, and information technology) high school, foreign language high school, arts high school, and science high school. In most high schools, the number of third-year, senior students who gain admission to prestigious universities is of utmost importance for many stakeholders at the high school, such as students, teachers (particularly, school principals), and parents (Kang, 2009). For example, the roll of names is proudly put on public display in front of the high school as a placard, and this becomes the most powerful advertisement for a school. Thus, the number of reputable university admissions is the surest warranty of the following years' student applications. Instead of explaining the school's educational philosophy and teachers' dedication toward each student, the number of "SKY" university admissions will make it easier for most parents of potential students to understand the excellent scholastic performance of the school. Under this educational environment, it would be no surprise that more than 80% of Korean students aspire to attend a 4-year university or want to pursue a postgraduate degree (Yi, 2013). In this regard, high school teachers reiterate and reproduce the importance of *hakbul* or academic credentialism. Through repeated emphasis, teachers implicitly (or sometimes explicitly as well) encourage competition among students. Through ceaseless competition, the students are externally motivated to study harder with the firm belief that such efforts would lead to positive results in university admission; the competition continues and self-reproduces, particularly in the high school context in South Korea. Therefore, in the high school system, students are living in a competitive environment. The information regarding the current years' admissions to a reputed university is rapidly spread over the Internet and this encourages more competition among high schools nationwide. To rank at the top, each high school does its best by emphasizing only on the beneficial effect of competition among students. In this educational milieu, students' level of learning stress from excessive emphasis on competition is rarely addressed, and such clinical symptoms are almost always attributed to personal problems. Korea Statistical Information Service (2016) reported that the prime reason for Korean youths' deaths in 2014 was suicide (7.4 persons out of 100,000), followed by traffic accidents (4.9 out of 100,000).

As stated above, however, the competitive motivation did not have a direct influence on students' English proficiency (Kim, 2010; see also Kim & Kim, 2016). Despite the research findings, it has been observed that competition among Korean secondary school students was encouraged, as was among college-level tertiary students. They were trained in a competitive atmosphere and induced to strive for excellence by comparing them with other supposedly inferior groups of students. The constant comparison with others came as no surprise because they were educated in such a system.

Recently, it has widely been reported that even the students in the same academic department at college try to create a conceptual hierarchy among themselves, depending on their admission types. The undergraduate admission in Korea has diversified, and there are a couple of different admission types: regular admission, rolling-basis admission, special-consideration admission (e.g., students from remote rural areas, those from multicultural background, and those of North Korea defectors), transfer from another tertiary institution, etc. Depending on these admission types, some college students create a conceptual hierarchy and feel unduly superior or inferior depending on their subjective comparative standing in the hierarchy. According to Park and Hwang (2014), the conceptual hierarchy functions even as a sophisticated "caste" system or discrimination mechanism in college. It is noteworthy that the students belonging to the same academic unit try to internally differentiate among themselves. This new trend reflects students' mindset to do better than others to be successful. At the basis of this, despite the paradox between the emphasis of competition in school and the ineffectiveness of it in EFL proficiency in recent years, competitive motivation identified in a previous L2 motivation research (Kim, 2006, 2010; Kim & Kim, 2016) is involved. Park and Hwang (2014) conclude in their report as follows:

> Where do we go for the last destination of this phenomenon? The students in the same department who previously were united under the slogan of university alumni and built their exclusive "castle and moats," are now introducing unduly competition and demarcation among themselves. They do not have any idea how to bond as peer students at the same university. This only results in an endless competition after the countless hierarchical battles for superiority. The aggravation of hierarchy only makes the university a place of solitary confinement that isolates students. In this solitary prison cell, what will be the merit to step on others to be at the top?

The new measure of applying the criterion-referenced assessment in the CSAT effective from 2017 may result in a positive change in the overly competitive English classroom. However, the criterion-referenced assessment is not applied in most subjects in the CSAT, which may limit the scope of positive change in the competitive atmosphere in South Korea. More systematic research will be required in academia to address this recent change in South Korea.

7.2 English Learning as an Insurance and Alter Ego Familism

Kang (2014) reiterates that the enthusiasm toward becoming the upper class had a positive effect on reconstruction of the nation after the Korean War. After the War, the working class endured poor work conditions and kept working to make a living, and at the kernel of this endurance, the parental desire to provide better life conditions for their children existed. As long as their hard work continued, it was believed that their children would enjoy an affluent lifestyle. Through accumulated national experiences from the late nineteenth century, English ability has been equated with one of the royal roads to success.

In some cases, mainly due to the parental desire to make their children succeed in life, the blind belief in the power of English results in negative social phenomena. For example, it was reported that with no scientific basis, parents in Korea had put their children to have a rare surgical operation termed "lingual frenectomy." This operation, known as "tongue-tie release," cuts a band of tissues connecting the underside of the tongue with the floor of the mouth. Originally conducted for patients with tongue-tie, this operation was misused by some South Korean parents who believed their children would pronounce English sounds better by lengthening their tongue by about a millimeter. However, this malpractice was severely criticized because Koreans born and raised in the USA have no difficulty in pronouncing and distinguishing the English phonemes such as /r/ and /l/, which many Koreans have difficulty in pronouncing and distinguishing (Demick, 2002).

Another unique phenomenon in Korea is the *gireogi appa* (goose father) syndrome (see Sect. 4.8, Chap. 4). A *gireogi appa* can be defined as a South Korean man who works in Korea while his wife and children stay in an English-speaking country for the sake of children's education. The term *gireogi*, or goose in English, is used for the goose's migrating habit; often, the father must travel a long distance to meet his family in an English-speaking country (Shin, 2010). It is important to note that the target country is an "English-speaking" one and not one with another foreign language. The family sacrifices the comfort of living together for the sake of their children's English learning and schooling. Those who cannot afford such large amounts of expenditure for the children's extended foreign stay often seek alternative means, such as the English Village, in private English education. Statistics Korea (2014) estimated that English is the elementary school subject that parents spend most of their money on for their children's private education.

These exemplary phenomena are closely associated with the competitive motivation stated in the previous section. Most Korean parents believe that better English proficiency "than others" will provide better lifestyles for their children. In this regard, English proficiency is considered as the tool for internal, intragroup competition. English is considered as economic power (Lee, 2011). As presented in Chap. 4, the term "English divide" is widely circulated among Korean media, and this term emphasizes that the opportunity to receive high-quality English education is rapidly polarized, depending on the student's parents' income level. Even though the South Korean government endeavors to minimize the influence of social class in education, the "English divide" cannot be ignored.

Although there is a widespread belief that English is useful for students' competitive edge in the job market, the actual use of English among workers in labor markets shows a different dimension. In 2011, *Sadanbeupin Hangul Munwha Yeondae* (Hangul Culture United Inc.) investigated the role of English in the Korean society. They recruited 1000 South Koreans from the work population (aged: 25–54), considering geographical region, gender, and age by using a stratified random sampling method. The results presented the participants' actual use of English in their daily lives (W. Choi, 2011b).

> In this survey result, the most notable was the huge disparity between the social expectation and actual use regarding English proficiency. Among the participants, 20.3% responded that they "never" spoke or wrote in English except basic greetings; 20.1% responded that they use it 2–3 times a year. This means that approximately 40% of the participants responded that they rarely use English. Regarding the question of English communication while working with foreigners, 37.8% replied that they never did, followed by 10 minutes a year with 16.7%. In terms of the questionnaire asking about the occasion of using English, 40.1% replied that they "never had such occasion except when they log on to the Internet or jot down an email address." This was followed by 22.5% stating that they use English "when searching for English information through the Web or translating it into Korean." Only 11.9% stated that they need English when "counseling with someone, presenting, lecturing, or giving a proposal."

The above report clearly demonstrates that the need for English proficiency in South Korea is not comparable to the Korean public's general expectations. A similar argument is made by Kim (2005, 2007). He stated that the need for English is not real but simply hypothetical. He stated further that most Koreans spend numerous hours and financial means to learn English not because of an actual, real need but because of a fake need—just in case. Kim (2007) elaborated his argument as follows:

> ... In short, Koreans' English demand is not real but hypothetical. Hypothetical demand reproduces another hypothetical one, and this also reproduces another hypothetical demand, and so on. This vicious circle is the reality of English fever in Korea. The hypothetical demand resulted from the exponential influence of English, but this demand finally seems to have reached the degree of insanity which reflects Koreans' constant feeling of unrest, psychological toadyism, timeserving little culture, ideology promoting excessive competition, commercialism, academic credentialism, and unflagging education fever. The Ministry of Education and presidential candidates often make proposals to upgrade the quality of public English education in order to minimize the negative effect of private English

education. However, this is off the mark, unfortunately. (Kim, 2007, November 21, from Hankook Ilbo)

In the above passage, Kim (2007) argues that the English need in Korea is simply a hypothetical one without firm ground. According to him, the social discourse surrounding English education should be on measuring objective necessity of English learning, not on enhancing the quality of it.

The effort in the Korean society toward English education shows striking similarity to an individual's psyche when applying for insurance. It reflects the mindset of future potential needs despite the unnecessity of much current use. Moreover, the decision of applying for "English insurance" is not made by the students themselves but by their parents. Many Korean parents enforce their children to learn English as early as possible, and sometimes the English education at kindergarten turns out to be a hot national issue (Kim, 2018). At a national level, from the perspective of an insurance metaphor, it can be viewed that the nation, as a decision maker, mandates every student to be insured into a 10-year insurance plan, and this national "English insurance" lasts at least for 10 years from Grade 3 at elementary school to Grade 12 at high school. This group insurance grows from the fear of lagging behind their peers in society. To make every effort to learn English and get a head start is regarded as an unquestionable tenet among Korean students and parents altogether.

In this regard, the belief of efficacy in English in the future is widely shared by parents, schools, and the entire Korean society. This collective frenzy toward English often seems to exhibit "alter ego familism." Familism is defined as a specific type of ideology where the needs of the family as a whole are more important than those of the individual members of the family. Alter ego familism is frequently found in the East Asian culture where Confucian collective values are emphasized. In this culture, an individual's happiness is regarded as a greedy desire, and the public cause overshadows the individual needs (cf. Hofestede, 1980). In this environment, the success or failure of an individual student is not limited to themselves; it is rapidly shared by family members, the community, the school, and the nation. For example, in an international sports event such as the Olympic Games, when an athlete wins a gold medal, the sports anchor often expresses his/her sincere thanks to the athlete. The glory of an individual is equated with that of the family, the society, and the nation. Raised and educated in such a societal atmosphere, the news of a student's gaining admission to a prestigious university rapidly spreads among extended family members, and they all rejoice (despite varying degrees of jealousy). It is because the family members expect the intelligent one will soon exalt the family's honor (Choi, 2011a).

Having undergone the tragic Korean War, those who grew up in the war reconstruction stage did not have much access to higher education, including English education. Thus, many of them ended up as low-paid, temporary, menial laborers. Under these conditions, in a traditionally collective society, if they think that the family's honor was not fully exalted in their current generation, the sublime aspiration to enhance the family honor is succeeded by the next generation. The expectations of the unsuccessful parents are placed on their children, and the parents exert their best to support the children. In the parents' mind, it is often found that their children must have a better life, which is qualitatively different from theirs. Alter ego familism is consolidated under this situation. The success or failure of the children is equated with that of their parents; often many sons fulfill the role of their father's alter ego, and many daughters the role of their mother's alter ego. The children, under parental pressure, do their best at school and sometimes at work to fulfill the unmet dream of their parents. For almost all their infant and adolescent years, these children do not learn to separate themselves from their parents and often the identification with their parents is regarded natural under the pretext of filial duty. Under this milieu, separation anxiety prevails, and the so-called kangaroo/boomerang generation and crowded nest syndrome (Shaputis, 2004) acquire a new meaning in the Korean context. Adding the economic difficulty in times of economic downturn, the Korean kangaroo generation has not learned to separate from their parents because of the strong bond of alter ego familism.

Choi (2011a) stated that in the traditional Korean society, it would not be an easy task to differentiate parents and their offspring because of the close emotional bond between them. Choi argued that it is not uncommon in Korea to find a boxer, after winning the boxing match, with joyful tears calling out to his mother or father loudly. Additionally, in the case of family suicide, it is sometimes reported that the percentage of family suicide of parents with infants or very young children in Korea is significantly higher than that in the western countries (Lee, 2012). All these cases demonstrate that the familial bond in Korea seems remarkably close. In this sense, Choi stated that the "we-ness" in Korea supposes a significant overlap between parents and offspring. Choi further argued that the term "alter ego" or vicarious satisfaction at the sight of one's children's success is a misnomer. It becomes not alter ego but one's own extended ego. The term vicarious satisfaction will make sense only when the parents and the children are separate, individual entities, and it would not be possible if the relationship between them is intermingled and the perception of separation is not clear (Choi, 2011a, pp. 244–245).

It should be noted that at the bottom of this alter ego familism lies competitiveness. Because the social wealth is limited, only "my child" needs to have access to it, and other children from different families should not share it. To exalt the family's honor, only "my" child, who shares "my" gene, should be allowed a spot at a prestigious university or a top-class company in order to gain the access to wealth. If such a spot is allowed to the children of other families, "my" family's safety and wellbeing would be in peril. In this regard, alter ego familism incorporates competitive motivation at its core.

At an individual level, alter ego familism reflects parental desire to provide their children better life conditions than what they had dreamt of and their aspiration for their children to excel in English proficiency compared to others. It should also be noted that alter ego familism can be extended to the level of a nation, and this is often linked to the discourse of national competitiveness. During the process of economic development after the Korean War, particularly during the Park Chung-hee military regime of almost two decades in the 1960s and 1970s, national wealth and prosperity through economic development was a priority for an individual's happiness and wellbeing. The economic drive was re-emphasized in the next decades when the so-called neo-military mogul, President Chun Doo-hwan (tenure: 1980–1988) and his successor President Roh Tae-woo (tenure: 1988–1993) took over the political power, and the 1988 Seoul Olympic Games were successfully held. During the rapid economic development stage, the nation's fate was largely equated with that of its people. After the bare destitution of the war, national development enhanced the overall life conditions of people, and the ideology of nationalism was effective. In the 1990s, when the slogan of neo-liberalism was sweeping over the world as former communist nations were rapidly dismantled, President Kim Young-sam reigned from 1993 to 1997, advocated the idea of national competitiveness under the slogan of *segyehwa* (世界化) or globalization (see Chap. 4). President Kim's motto of *segyehwa* was closely related to English education, in that the globalization of Korea is to export Korean goods to foreign countries and during which, English is mandatory, not optional (Kwon, 2009). At the heart of this ideology of globalization, alter ego familism, if not alter ego nationalism, is involved. The mentality of *segyehwa* seems as follows: Korea, and not any other country, should develop economically, make a head start over other nations, and eventually have a place among world leading nations. In this sublime ideal, English is emphasized as a useful tool for communication.

At the core of alter ego familism at an individual level, "my" family should be better than "other" families, and English is a crucial means to achieve this. Likewise, the alter ego familism modified at a national level equates the nation with one's own family by using the Confucian concept of the one bodiness or trinity of king, teacher, and father (君師父一體). In this time old phrase, one's family is equated with his or her educational community and with the entire nation. In this regard, the extended family metaphor, reflecting the characteristics of a collectivistic society, is involved in this phrase and in the previous slogan of the national development of Korea. After the Korean War, for more than 60 years, alter ego familism functioned effectively and had a beneficial impact on the advancement of most Koreans' life conditions. As stated above, alter ego familism assumes that, at the individual level, one's own family needs to lead a better life than others, and at the national level, "our mother land" should be in a better condition than others. English plays a key role in this process of continued success through crushing "other" families and/or nations.

In summary, English learning has not only an individual meaning but also a collective one. Besides, English learning motivation reflects the family member's collective desire to exalt their family's social status. The meaning of English learning is to achieve personal success to support one's own family. Moreover, this is sublimed to the level of the nation's ideals: advancing to the top developed country in the world. Thus, alter ego familism at individual as well as national levels incorporates the components of competitive motivation.

7.3 English Learning as a "Kitsch"

In Howatt's (2004) literature on the history of foreign language education, only high literati were allowed to learn a foreign language before the industrial revolution; in this regard, foreign language learning was an intellectual amusement among this limited number of populations. Even after the industrial revolution, it was mostly impossible to learn classical Latin or Greek, if one was not from a wealthy family, and the learning of a foreign language in Europe was possible to only the middle (and higher) class. In Korea, the situation of learning a foreign language was not different. Only *yangban*, or high literati, were allowed to learn classical Chinese books represented by the Four Books and the Three Classics (四書三經). The interpreter training courses were also limited to joong'in (中人) or the middle class and were conducted at *sayeokwon* in the Goryeo and Joseon Dynasty (Chung, 2014; Kwon & Kim, 2010). Taking these into our consideration, it would be fair to state that traditionally, the opportunity to learn another language was provided only to those above the middle class, and the people of low working class did not have this opportunity, let alone any educational opportunity.

However, such a traditional education system faced rapid change after the Treaty between Korea and the USA in 1882, and as in the case of His Excellency Lee Ha-Young, persons with a humble family background could ascend to the highest social class as long as they could speak a modicum of English words (Jeon, 2006; see also Chap. 2). In addition, due to the efforts of Western missionaries, various educational institutions across Korea offered English education to many Koreans, and many men of ambition including Mr. Rhee Syngman, who wanted to attain worldly success, exerted every effort to learn English in Christian schools (Kang, 2014). In the entire Korean history, it was the first time that the opportunity to learn was open to all people regardless of their social class. Now foreign language education was not prohibited to the low-class people anymore and became a popular subject for all Koreans. This educational upheaval was a part of the Gabo Reform in 1894, which announced that all Korean people with talent are to be allowed to study and appointed to government posts based on their merit alone, regardless of their social class. The Gabo Reform imbued the ideology of egalitarianism among Koreans, and this enhanced the Korean public's sense of upward mobility; as long as they were making efforts, they could now become part of the higher class with wealth. This egalitarianism is reflected in the boom of English learning in the late nineteenth century.

In this regard, the widespread English learning from the nineteenth century until now seems to have the characteristics of "Kitsch." Originated in German, Kitsch implies (mostly visual) art that is mass produced and appeals to the public, not to the high class. This term is often considered derogatory because it implies that Kitsch work is gaudy and far from sophisticated elite art. According to Kang (2011, pp. 866-867), a Kitsch work is a cheap, mass replica of the genuine product, and this is not a high-class refinement but a "B-class" shoddy imitation. For example, the original *Mona Lisa* by Leonardo Da Vinci cannot be purchased and only be exhibited in the Louvre. However, the printed and copied Mona Lisa can be found and purchased easily, and it does not cost a fortune. Most people, except an absolute destitute, can purchase one or two, as they wish.

Viewed from this perspective, the widespread English education after the nineteenth century shares a remarkable similarity with the concept of Kitsch. Before the modernization period in the Joseon Dynasty, the foreign language represented by classical Chinese characters was only instructed to the high literati class. This can be regarded as the high class, genuine education only for the elite. However, the mass introduction of public education after the Gabo Reform in 1894 ensured that the learning of a foreign language was evenly spread out to all social classes. Moreover, free or affordable English instruction was offered by Western missionaries. Thus, compared with the high cost, limited opportunity to learn Chinese classics only allowed to the highbrows, English instruction can be regarded as the spread of Kitsch.

Particularly, after the Japanese Colonization Period had ended in 1945, the U.S. Military Government (USMG) lasted for 3 years from 1945 to 1948, and its succeeding Korean War (1950–1953) resulted in widening the social gap between only a small number of Koreans who could speak English and most of those who could not. For those who were totally ignorant of English, the images of Koreans who could somehow command a moderate level of English must have evoked complicated emotions—despair and aspiration toward English. Similar to the late nineteenth century when English was desperately needed for modernization by expediting international commerce and diplomacy, English proficiency was enthusiastically welcomed due to the political, military, and economic ties between South Korea and the USA. Although anecdotal, it was not long ago that traffic trespassers who said any gibberish sounding like English and acted as native speakers of English were pardoned by police officers, because the officers could not understand English and were afraid of being involved with intricate diplomatic disputes between the USA and South Korea by "ruffling the feathers" of Americans. Moreover, the pop stars who were either born or raised in the States could easily rise in stardom; whenever they said something in English, even a single English word, many enthusiastic fans (mostly in their teens) would scream in euphoria. In fact, for these teens, the English that the stars uttered must have been a superior language to their Koreans (L1).

The desire to learn and use English is closely linked to the idea of English as Kitsch. The upper class often visit the "inner-circle" countries (e.g., the USA, the U.K., Canada, Australia, New Zealand, and Ireland) to learn English from qualified native speakers of English. A few Koreans tried to give birth in the States because the USA adopts the territorial principle, meaning anyone who is born within U.S. territory will be endowed with U.S. birthright citizenship. According to Bae (2011), U.S. media estimated that more than 10,000 babies were born in the major cities in the USA where the birthright citizenship is offered, and "birth tourists" are visiting these cities for the purpose of "anchoring babies." The reasons for such an eccentric preference for the U.S. citizenship would be multiple, such as avoiding the mandatory military service enforced on virtually all Korean male youths. However, one of the prime reasons would be to have the opportunity to acquire English and be considered as native English speakers. These cases are mainly limited to the upper class who can afford the high cost of living and studying abroad. Given the effectiveness of language acquisition, it would be ideal to be educated in the target language community and to acquire the language naturally or subconsciously, while learning without much conscious effort (Krashen, 1982). In the case of living and studying abroad where English is used on a daily basis, it would be considered as a genuine education or metaphorically a "luxurious, royal learning."

However, the pitfall of this would be that the situation stated above would be allowed only for those who have sufficient financial means or those in special circumstances such as diplomats, foreign correspondences, and study-abroad students in their regular academic program, particularly at graduate school. Most Koreans who cannot go abroad and learn English in an authentic way try to find alternatives to learn English. While saying "stop trying to keep up with the Joneses" to themselves, they would still envy the small number of Koreans who made the attempt in reality. The remaining choice would be less costly but still (somehow) effective education. The desire of the remaining, less-affluent Koreans to learn English is reflected in the private education sector: the burgeoning English conversation institutes for adults, English *hagwons* or cram schools for junior high and high school students, the weekly self-study booklet, distance English learning using phones or video cams over the Internet, and private English tutoring. In public education, after-school English programs can also be considered as an alternative method. All these English learning methods have the characteristics of Kitsch. Although these methods may be alternatives to the costly, genuine study abroad counterparts, students may be able to attain a similar level of proficiency if they make tremendous efforts with a modicum of luck. For this reason, from parents' perspective, despite being Kitsch in nature, they have no other means but to rely on these alternative Kitsch methods.

In the previous section, while explaining alter ego familism, it was argued that South Korean parents equate their children's success with their own because family is regarded as an extended self beyond oneself (Choi, 2011a). Under this collective mentality, Yoon (2016) stated that almost half of Korean parents consider themselves as "edu poor," which is "a South Korean neologism deriving from the words "education" and "poor"" and represents "the financial difficulties faced by families who spend a large portion of their income on their children's education" (Yoon, 2016, para. 1). Yoon (2016) reported that 95.5% of parents with children in elementary school responded that they provided their children with private education. She continued that among parents whose children attended elementary school, "the most common subjects were English (69.3%), while math came in second at 52.6%" (para. 6). At the heart of the mentality of seeking Kitsch English education, Korean parents may have subtle reservations about their upcoming future in terms of insufficient funds to live on after retirement at their old age. Afraid of becoming "edu poor," Korean parents may compromise their children's English proficiency with their financial situation. As mentioned above, for the wealthy upper class, Kitsch English education may not be the attractive first choice because they can actually pursue the "genuine" education abroad. For the remaining majority in South Korea, however, Kitsch English education becomes the only viable option.

While explaining the concept of *simulacrum*, which is a similar concept to Kitsch in that it also means likeness or similarity and the representation or imitation of a person or a thing, Baudrillard (1988) explicated that a simulacrum is only possible in an open society where the social class can be changed, either upwardly or downwardly. In the case of an extremely rigid caste system, the lower-class members do not dare to have the replica or Kitsch of the genuine artifacts. In the Joseon Dynasty, for instance, if their social class is *cheonmin* (賤民) or the lowest "untouchable" class, they do not have the motivation to learn a foreign language at all because they do not have the slightest chance to be appointed as royal translators; from the beginning, they are literally disqualified due to their family origin at birth. However, as stated in previous literature, in late nineteenth century Korea, as the traditional feudal social class system was abolished through the Gabo Reform in 1894, English could be instructed to virtually almost all Koreans and thenceforth the distinction between genuine and Kitsch education had started functioning properly. As early as the late nineteenth century and the early twentieth century, a small number of Koreans had the opportunity to learn and use English in the USA (e.g., Kim, 1916; Sung, 2015), while others did not have many other means but to rely on Kitsch English education such as teacher-centered grammar-translation method in a crowded classroom within Korea. They had hoped to jump to the high social class through the Kitsch method.

It should also be noted that if properly used with meticulous instructional design, Kitsch education could have been and is still effective. Only a few Koreans could ascend the social ladder and become members of the high social class. This rare case has often been associated with the *Dragon Gate* (登龍門) metaphor in East Asia. This metaphor is believed to have originated from the Chinese proverb that if a carp jumps over the Dragon Gate in the Yellow River in Hunan Province, China, it is transformed into a dragon. This metaphor has figuratively been used for thousands of years, justifying students' excessively lengthy efforts to pass *gwageo* test or the royal government official appointment exam. Now, the *gwageo* test had been replaced to many English tests and college entrance exams in South Korea. Because many Koreans still believe that not only authentic English learning in the study abroad context but also domestic Kitsch English education is effective in their English development, many alternative methods of English stated above are spread nationwide as they are regarded as the Dragon Gates.

As Baudrillard (1988) diagnosed, in the postmodern society where mass production is the norm and the ingenuity or creativeness is consumed and reproduced real time, the demarcation between the authentic and the fake (simulacrum or Kitsch) turns obfuscated and is even overthrown. In an extreme case, the fake can acquire the status of authenticity because of its large consumption and familiarity. In this regard, Kitsch English education, in both public and private sectors in South Korea, may not be a failure in the long run and has contributed to South Korea's rapid economic development through English learning, supported by a high level of educational enthusiasm among Koreans (Seth, 2002).

7.4   English Learning as Cultural Capital

It was upward egalitarianism that was spread during the reconstruction period after the Korean War in the 1950s and through the industrialization period after the 1960s under the leadership of President Park Chung-hee (see Chap. 3). One of the Korean proverbs says, "it hurts one's stomach after hearing the news of his or her cousin's buying farmland," which represents the jealousy of close family members' success. A relatively compact territory and dense population in Korea resulted in Koreans' mentality of constant comparison with other neighbors. As many Korean youths became the recipients of English education after the Korean War, they competitively learned English. The total destruction resulted from the atrocious civil war that imbued every Korean with the realization that what is important is not the liquid asset such as savings in the bank or real estate, but intellectual property because the latter cannot be destroyed, even when faced with warfare. Kwon and Kim (2010), Kang (2014), and Kim (2016) stated that even during the Japanese Colonization Period, we can find the enthusiasm to learn English. However, the educational opportunity, particularly that of higher education, was limited only to a select few elite members of society. For this reason, it presents a qualitative difference between the English boom during the Japanese Colonization Period and that after the Korean War when English learning became much more common and open to virtually every Korean.

After 1960, within approximately 30 years, South Korea succeeded in achieving industrialization and is now regarded as one of the new industrializers. Kang (2011) and Yoo (2014) reiterate that it took 200 years for European nations and the USA to complete the process of industrialization, but it took less than 30 years for South Korea to achieve the same feat. Statistics present that in 1962, the nominal GDP per capita in Korea was \$103.88, but in 1989, it reached \$5438.24 (ICEF, 2014), a 54 times growth in 28 years. As of 2018, it is estimated to have reached \$32,774 (International Monetary Fund, 2018 April). Within one generation, Korea transformed its status from one of the poorest nations whose people barely had means to live to the nation having ultra-modern infrastructures and a systematic social insurance system. Underlying this rapid process of compressed development (Whittaker et al., 2007) is the high level of national interest in education, which ICEF (2014) highlights as follows:

> This country invested heavily in education during the second half of the 20th century, and in 2010, spent 7.6% of its GDP on all levels of education—significantly more than the Organization for Economic Cooperation and Development (OECD) average of 6.3%. During that same year, South Korea spent 2.6% on tertiary education, a figure also above the OECD average of 1.6%. (ICEF, 2014, para. 2)

At the core of this expenditure on education exists Koreans' beliefs that every person can be successful as long as he or she studies hard and graduates from a prestigious university. Furthermore, it was widely believed that the diploma bearing the university's name will determine the diploma holder's employment and quality of life in general.

Achieving upward social mobility through *hakbul* or academic credentialism and its subsequent employment opportunity had consolidated the belief in the instrumentality of academic work. However, it seems increasingly difficult for average Korean students to gain admission to prestigious universities by acquiring a good score in the CSAT (called *Suneung* in Korean) and be employed at a large-sized company.

Choi's (2004) research demonstrated that from the perspective of Bourdieu's (1991) cultural capital, one's English proficiency is not the result of an individual student's effort but that of synergistic efforts of all family members. Among the regular school subjects in secondary schools in South Korea such as Korean, English, and math, all included in the CSAT, Choi (2004) highlighted that English is the most seriously affected subject from the economic power of the student's parents. She reasoned that it was because English is still regarded as "the icon of guaranteed success" by many South Koreans. She presented that the confidence in English ability among university students in Korea had been correlated positively with their parents' average monthly income and their standard of living, their parents' academic degree, and their father's occupation. In 2002 when the research was conducted, 29.8% of the students who reported that their parents earned more than five million Won (i.e., $5500) per month responded that they were competent in English. On the contrary, only 9.8% of those who reported that their parents earned less than 1.5 million Won (i.e., $1700) responded that they were English competent. Regarding their father's academic degree, 31.1% whose fathers had a college diploma (or above) stated that they were competent in English, but only 13.9% of the respondents whose fathers had graduated from junior high school (or below) stated the same. Mothers' academic degree presented similar results; 38.9% of the students whose mothers had a college diploma (or above) stated that they were competent in English, but only 12.1% whose mothers had graduated from junior high school (or below) stated the same. Responding to the questionnaire item asking about their father's occupation, 29.7% of the students whose fathers worked in a professional field stated that they were competent in English, but only 5.7% of those whose father was unemployed stated the same.

It should be noted that after 7 years, Choi and Choi (2011) conducted a follow-up study by collecting data from 705 young Korean adults. In this research, they compared the expenses on culture and arts with that of English education according to the participants' perceived social class in South Korea. The results showed that the perceived importance of English, like that of culture and arts, increases as their social class moved from lower to middle and from middle to upper classes. Note that the actual spending on culture and arts decreases as the participants' social class goes down in a statistically significant manner. However, the actual spending on English instruction did not show any statistical difference depending on the social classes. Table 7.1 presents the participants' willingness to spend on culture and arts and English education (Choi & Choi, 2011, p. 228).

Table 7.1 summarizes the participants' willingness to spend, and not their actual spending, as the amount of expenses was not measured. However, it should be noted that regarding culture and arts, the participants' willingness to spend money

Table 7.1 Willingness to spend money (%) on culture, arts, and English education

Item	Culture/arts		English	
How much percentage (%) of your income would you like to spend?	M	s.d.	M	s.d.
Upper Class	10.82	8.856	14.40	9.431
Middle Class	8.98	7.674	13.03	10.127
Lower Class	7.93	7.248	14.31	10.188
Unidentified	6.86	6.934	11.47	9.405
F ($^* < 0.05$)	2.807*		–	

significantly decreased as their social class lowered. For English education, this was not the case. In other words, for the cultural and arts expenditure, the participants had the tendency to increase or decrease expenses based on their perceived social class, but for the English education, they did not want to cut down on the expenses despite their lower social standing. As elaborated in the previous section on Kitsch, the upper class may prefer to make use of English native speakers' private tutoring because they can afford it. The lower class prefer to choose one of various types of Kitsch or simulacrum education such as weekly study guide, private English institute, phone English (i.e., English conversation over the phone), or real-time video English class (particularly after the COVID-19 pandemic).

In Choi and Choi's (2011) research, the crucial question would be "Why do the expenses of English education remain the same regardless of the participants' perceived social class in South Korea?" This implies that English has a high level of cultural capital (Bourdieu, 1977, 1984, 1991). Bourdieu paid attention to unequal distribution of capital and its possession and extended the original concept of capital to intangible preference toward language and cultural heritage. Such cultural and linguistic preference functions as the tool for distinguishing and separating social class, and this preference has exchange value like real capital. He defines the unique preference among members of a society as cultural capital. In the case of English use, it is widely believed in South Korea (as well as many other nations) that those who can speak fluent English are regarded as having a more sophisticated and refined cultural capital than those who cannot. In his book <*Reproduction in Education, Society and Culture*>, Bourdieu (1977) argued that cultural capital, which is subjectively perceived, is consolidated within the boundary of family as one of social systems; in this process of consolidation, the inequality among families is aggravated. Families with means can expedite the process of refining cultural capital whereas those without cannot enjoy such a level of sophistication.

Note that cultural capital of the highbrow does not have inherent, intrinsic value. Rather, cultural capital, widely considered to belong to the high class, is created and strengthens its value mainly through the social convention that places a high value on it. If the social convention reflecting collective consensus of the members of society regards a particular artifact as the (in)visible product having aesthetic value, this artifact acquires the status of cultural capital. For example, from Bourdieu's

(1977, 1984, 1991) point of view, there is no logical reason why we regard classical music as a superior, noble artifact and pop music such as Hip Hop or Reggae as an inferior, secular one. In this regard, the distinction is arbitrary in nature, and such distinction reflects our habitus, coming from our already internalized order of social class. In other words, the cultural capital (which is believed to be) widely circulated among the highbrows does not have any inevitable, inherent, and intrinsic value. It simply reflects an arbitrary difference, and the preference was coincidentally selected by the few in the high class. It can be attributed to the habitus or the individually internalized social structure that the mass consumption of cultural capital of the high social class is enacted, consolidated, and amplified.

As noted above, for job employment, English proficiency has functioned as the crucial criteria. In academia, the situation is not different. For example, it is highly encouraged to offer courses instructed in English for the purpose of enhancing the globalization index useful for the university's world university ranking, administered by Times Higher Education (by Elsevier Ltd) or QS (by Quacquarelli Symonds Ltd.). Moreover, most universities in South Korea emphasize on their professors' writing academic papers in English and publishing them in internationally recognized journals accredited by the Journal Citation Report (by Clarivate, previously Thomson Reuters). All these efforts, from Bourdieu's (1977, 1984, 1991) perspective, would be the process of ritualization and authorization of English as cultural capital (Lee, 2004).

From family, as the first level of socialization, the inheritance of cultural capital begins; in order to expedite such invisible inheritance of English, the family's economic power, parents' occupation, and their social class matter. While going through various social upheavals after the nineteenth century enlightenment era in Korea, Koreans have created a firm belief that English is the most effective tool to import the advanced civilization from the West represented by the USA and is a crucial cultural capital to become fast followers of the newest international trend. Yoon (2002) and Kang (2005) argue that English has transformed its status from the language of aspiration and desire to that of exotic sophistication and eventually to that of power. In South Korea (as well as many other nations in the world), English learning and use has functioned as the powerful, institutionalized cultural capital; in this regard, English learning motivation is the blunt expression of personal desire to acquire cultural capital.

In Sect. 7.1, the concept of competitive motivation and its negative consequences such as an excessive level of unnecessary competition among students in English classes in South Korea (Kim, 2006, 2010) were stated. From Bourdieu's (1984, 1991) point of view, the competition among students may be a natural consequence because English is regarded as one of the most useful cultural capitals. The competition is the external manifestation of the struggle to acquire more capital than others. In addition, the notion of English as cultural capital is strengthened by university admission and job application systems. The imperative necessity to acquire better English test scores in the CSAT and job application process than other candidates aggravates the situation. Thus, the competitive motivation integrated with the concept of English as cultural capital is consistently identified in the EFL classroom in South Korea (Kim, 2006, 2010). It should also be noted that despite the high level of competitive motivation, the research findings strongly demonstrated that the students' competitive motivation was not the significant predictor for their English proficiency (see Sect. 6.3 in Chap. 6). In other words, competitive motivation results from the concept of English as cultural capital. It is also a byproduct of the modernization process in Korea, which reflects intensive academic credentialism (or *hakbul*) and the hypothetical stratification of universities and workplaces among South Koreans.

7.5   The Paradox of Amotivated Students' High English Test Scores

Because of the psychological pressure from parents, teachers, and friends, many school-aged children in South Korea experience varying degrees of stress when learning and studying English. Previous literature presented that the intense competition toward university admission and better job placement lead Korean students to be amotivated English learners (Kim, 2012a). However, it is noteworthy that in the case of high school students and university graduates in South Korea, students' English proficiency is relatively high, even when they are in an amotivated state. These amotivated learners with high English proficiency have not been reported in previous L2 motivation research. The obligatory nature of EFL learning in many Asian contexts may be a part of the explanation for this unique phenomenon; however, in the context of South Korea, *hakbul*-orientation and its related social pressure seems another contributing factor.

In most L2 motivation literature, demotivation becomes prominent as the students' school year increases (Kim, 2012b). Dörnyei and Ushioda (2011) stated that demotivation concerns "*specific external forces* that reduce or diminish the motivational basis of a behavioral intention or an ongoing action" (p. 139, emphasis added). This means that the temporary loss of interest in learning an L2 for the existence of more interesting learning contents than L2 or the gradual loss of interest due to the students' boredom are not regarded as demotivation. However, as presented in Chap. 6, Kim (2012b) and Kim and Seo (2012) argued that the gradual loss of motivational grounds needs to be considered as demotivation. To remedy this confusion, Kikuchi (2015) endeavored to distinguish the concept of demotivator and demotivation. Regarding the former, he states that it is "the specific *internal* and external forces that reduce or diminish the motivational basis of a behavioral intention or an ongoing action" (p. 4, emphasis added) and demotivation concerns "the negative process that pulls learners down," and it is "situational, and demotivated learners can still be motivated again" (p. 5). Amotivation, on the other hand, is defined as "a lack of motivation caused by the realization that "there is no point . . ." or "it's beyond me. . ." (Dörnyei & Ushioda, 2011, p. 140) and is related to "general outcome expectations that are unrealistic for some reason"

(p. 140). It seems that due to the theoretical confusions surrounding the conceptualization of demotivation, systematic research on demotivation and amotivation is still in its nascent stage.

Among research dealing with demotivation and amotivation, what deserves a careful scrutiny in this chapter would be the reason why amotivated learners in South Korea still achieve a relatively high or moderate level of English proficiency. As presented in Chap. 6, I conceptualized L2-learning motivation from an activity-theory perspective and postulated that students remaining in the motive stage may not attain a high level of L2 proficiency. In the motive stage, not the motivation stage, students' motive is not integrated with a specific goal and sense of participation. In this case, they do not have a reference point that can be attained through manageable and visible efforts. In other words, previous studies have assumed that students with motivation, not motives, can achieve a high level of L2 proficiency.

Then, why do amotivated learners, let alone learners with only motives, show a relatively high level of English proficiency in South Korea? As stated above, in the traditional mentality of alter ego familism, students are required to learn English because most of their parents want their children to go to a prestigious university, which is believed to function as an important criterion for securing their job and this will be exalting the family's fame. Given this situation, an essential element of integrative motivation, or "the willingness to be like valued members of the language community" (Gardner & Lambert, 1959, p. 271) in L2 learning may be merely perceived as a remote and abstract ideal. Students learn English not because they want to be like native speakers of English but because of the desire to acquire this cultural capital for pragmatic reasons while competing each other.

In this extreme level of competition to gain a higher English test score that is equated as having more cultural capital stored in an imaginary "bank account," learners have only two choices. First, they may stop learning English and the process of gaining cultural capital gets hindered from that moment and the alter ego familism terminated. Second and a more frequently identified case would be that they may keep studying it half-heartedly with extremely low motivation or amotivation. Amotivated students for various reasons continue learning English without enthusiasm but still achieve a relatively high English proficiency.

In an interview research, Kim (2012a) found that elementary and secondary school students in South Korea kept stating that "English is important," but the degree of their internalization of this discourse showed remarkable individual variability. Even amotivated learners who did not make any meaningful connection between what he or she learned from an English class and his or her personal dream of using English in the future kept learning English lethargically and could gain moderate or sometimes even a high level of English proficiency. The following excerpt presents the case of students who explicitly negated the importance of English.[2]

---

[2]All the exceprts presented in this section were translated into English.

Interview Excerpt 1: Obin Kwon (first year high school student).
Interviewer: Do you think English is important, Obin?
Obin: I don't think English is that important.
Interviewer: Why do you think so?
Obin: Uh... We live in South Korea, It's just ... uh, I can speak Korean well ... I don't think a foreign language is that important ... and I don't want to go abroad either. I may simply end up with staying in Korea, so English is not very important to me. (Kim, 2012a, p. 90).

The above excerpt clearly demonstrates the lack of motivation or amotivation because English learning did not have any personal meaning to the participant, and indeed he saw no point of continuing learning English. Interestingly, Obin, the participant above, had a high level of English proficiency. In the following excerpt, Dongho, another high school participant, showed less internalized necessity of learning English.

Interview Excerpt 2: Dongho Kim (second year high school student).
Interviewer: Do your parents or teachers persuade you to study English?
Dongho: Yes, they do.
Interviewer: Why do you think they keep telling you that it is important?
Dongho: Uh, It's because it is important to earn a good score in school subjects... English is important...
Interviewer: Do you make any efforts to learn English these days?
Dongho: Well, I make a lot of planning for it but don't really do anything.
Interviewer: What kind of planning do you make?
Dongho: Well...., I often think I need to study English harder during vacation, but when the vacation begins, I don't and simply hang around with friends, and that's it. (Kim, 2012a, p. 90)

Again, Dongho scored relatively high in an in-house English test. For these students (and many other EFL students), English may not be perceived differently from any other school subjects. This means that regardless of making meaningful connection between their English learning in the classroom and their future aspiration, they keep studying English. Through conscious efforts to memorize morphosyntactic rules and an extensive vocabulary list, they become skillful in reading English passages and guess the correct meaning rapidly. In this sense, English is learned not for communication but for gaining a high score for their GPAs and eventually for college admission. In Kim and Kim's (2016) research comparing the changing trends of EFL learning motivation and attitudes over 8 years from 2002 to 2010, they found that the overall explanatory power of motivational and attitudinal factors for English proficiency gradually decreased over the 8 years. To be specific, in 2002, 16% of students' EFL proficiency was explained by their EFL learning motivation and attitudes. However, the percentage decreased to 9% in 2006 and to 8% in 2010. This result demonstrates that South Korean students are not much affected by their level of motivation and also strongly suggests the possibility that amotivated learning still can lead to a high level of English proficiency. Kim and Kim (2016) argue as follows:

Korean society and schools circulate and elaborate on the strong need for students to learn English; this may compel students to compete to acquire higher English test scores. In this sense, learning English is regarded as a requisite, not an option, for Korean high school students. The fierce competition appears to stimulate students to achieve a certain level of English achievement without them necessarily being motivated to do so. (Kim & Kim, 2016, p. 150)

Even after high school graduation, the situation does not change. In a recent quantitative research, Kim et al. (2019) investigated 252 Korean jobseekers' perception of English and the standardized English tests such as the TOEIC or OPIc (i.e., Oral Proficiency Interview-computer). They found that Korean jobseekers who were mostly seniors at university or graduates with college diplomas showed a high level of instrumental motivation, competitive motivation, and ought-to L2 self. Note that Korean jobseekers' demotivation had a negative correlation with their English test scores, but their motivation factors did not have statistically significant correlation with the scores. This result is also counterintuitive in that, regardless of their motivation level, their test score did not change. Only demotivational factors had a negative correlation with the test score in a statistically significant manner.

In another study conducted in recent years, it also identified that South Korean college students' English learning motivation did not explain much about their English test score. For example, while investigating 869 undergraduate students in Korea, Kim et al. (2017) found that their L2 proficiency was explained better by EFL learning demotivation than by motivation. Moreover, through structural equation modeling, they found that students' resilience, or the power to bounce back in spite of adversity in learning, had a statistically significant, negative influence on demotivation, but it did not have any significant influence on motivation.

All these findings in South Korea seem to indicate that the students are more sensitive to demotivation than motivation. In other words, students' English proficiency bears a closer relationship with demotivation, the negative counterpart of motivation, whereas their English proficiency had only a weak or no statistical relationship with motivation. Moreover, in the above excerpts, students suffering from amotivation still keep learning English despite their poor study morale.

This Korea-specific, amotivated learning may seem illogical and even counterintuitive; in most previous research in L2 motivation (Dörnyei & Ushioda, 2011; Gardner, 1985, 2010), a high level of motivation has been equated with a high level of L2 proficiency and vice versa. Thus, amotivation or an extremely low level of motivation should mean an extremely low level of L2 proficiency. However, it is not the case in the South Korean context. In order to address this paradoxical situation, the differences in the concept of "self" between Korea and other Western countries need to be elaborated. In cultural psychology comparing the eastern and western concept of mind, Choi and Kim (2011) point out the fundamental difference in understanding minds in the East and the West. In the Western world, the distinction between one's self and others' self is clear, and the notion of self is understood as existing, self-evidently. One's self can be the sole criteria for one's ways of thinking and behavioral pattern (pp. 144–145). In this sense, the western notion of self is "entity-self" (p. 144). However, in the Korean mentality, the aforementioned characteristics of entity-self do not apply. To Koreans, the objectivity and realistic existence of the self does not make much sense. According to Choi and Kim

(2011) and Markus and Kitayama (1991), the Korean concept of mind does not have a clear distinction between me and others and thus the existence of one's self does not stand on firm ground. One's self cannot be the theme of objective investigation since it is always relational; it depends on its relationship with other persons and environment; it is malleable and dynamically evolving. This means that Koreans in general may not try to explain themselves as individuals having "this or that characteristic" but see themselves as individuals with a "greater" tendency of this and "lesser" tendency of that.

While conducting an international comparison study of culture, Hofestede (1991) contrasted individualism and collectivism, and defined them as follows:

> Individualism pertains to societies in which the ties between individuals are loose: everyone is expected to look after himself or herself and his or her immediate family. Collectivism as its opposite pertains to societies in which people from birth onwards are integrated into strong, cohesive ingroups, which throughout people's lifetime continue to protect them in exchange for unquestioning loyalty. (Hofestede, 1991, p. 51)

Kim et al. (1994) argued that Hofestede's (1980) individualist societies focus on "I" whereas collectivist societies on "we." While warning of the oversimplified views on bipolar categorization, they elaborated the distinction as follows:

> According to Hofestede (1980), individualist societies emphasize "I" consciousness, autonomy, emotional independence, individual initiative, right to privacy, pleasure seeking, financial security, need for specific friendship, and universalism. Collectivist societies, on the other hand, stress "we" consciousness, collective identity, emotional dependence, group solidarity, sharing, duties and obligations, need for stable and predetermined friendship, group decision, and particularism. Markus and Kitayama (1991) similarly propose the independent view and interdependent view of the self. They describe individuals who uphold the independent view as being "egocentric, separate, autonomous, idiocentric, and self-contained" (p. 226). Interdependent individuals are "sociocentric, holistic, collective, allocentric, ensembled, constitutive, contextualist, and relational" (p. 227). (Kim et al., 1994, p. 3)

Under this conceptualization of collectivist society, South Korean students' amotivated learning can be explained. Whether they like English or not, they must keep learning it for it is directly related to the emotional welfare of their parents. In alter ego familism, the success of one's children has often been equated with the great pride and joy of their parents. For the collective mentality, each student, as an individual, is not keen on his or her aspiration or wants in school subjects.

Moreover, in the South Korean (as well as most of other EFL countries') education system, English is instructed as a regular, mandatory school subject, and this mandatory learning continues until the students graduate from high school. Many Korean parents start to teach their children English even before they attend elementary school through various means of private education such as private tutoring, English-medium kindergarten, and English education broadcasting. Given this, although the official public English education starts from Grade 3 and continues for 10 years, the years of English exposure must be more than 10 years. Even after college admission, they intermittently learn English mainly for job applications in the future, and the official English test scores are one of the preparatory steps for applying for large-sized, Korea-based conglomerates such as Samsung Electronics, LG Corporation, or Hyundai Motors. Given this, learning English is not a matter of personal choice. It is simply offered to them with no exception.

Under this social milieu, amotivated Korean students achieve a relatively high English test score and proficiency. Regardless of individual students' level of motivation, learning English must be continued, and each student's willingness to continue or not is not considered, if not totally ignored by teachers and parents. Students must learn it because it is simply offered in all Korean elementary and secondary schools. Given this, English learning may be fatalistic; they learn it because they must. English, as a major school subject, exists to be learned.

Explaining the resigned, submissive attitude in Korea, the late columnist, Mr. Lee Gyu-Tae provides the following vignette:

> In spring, seeing a Korean farmer working in the field, a person might casually ask a question like "Why are you planting rice seedlings now?" Many Korean farmers would probably not understand the focus of the question. They would most likely say nothing, responding only with a puzzled expression. The answer might be simple; farmers plant in spring so that they can harvest in autumn. However, it is unlikely that Korean farmers would give such a premature reasoning because they are well aware that they may not have a good harvest in autumn. The actual reason farmers plant in spring is because 'they have to do it now.'

> The 'why' of something does not have much importance to Koreans and rarely interests them. If they were asked any 'how' question, they would easily provide an answer, but 'why' questions are most likely to confuse them. For westerners, when asked a 'why' question, they are likely to be easily able to provide an answer with very clear sources into the bargain. If they are asked why they earn money or work, many of them always seem to have a very clear idea of 'why' they are doing what they do: making money to travel abroad, working to help the needy rather than just living on pension, making money to travel around the world after retirement. . .

> Of course, many Koreans also have goals, such as working to make money to prepare for their wedding, or to buy a condo. However, those things are mostly a pretext based on the basic fact that they do simply work. This is fundamentally different from westerners', whose goals precede work. That is, Korean farmers merely work at the right time in all seasons even without a clear goal.

> Let us assume that a Korean is working in order to purchase a condo. Even if he finally achieves his goal, and purchases it, he will not stop working. He will set another goal such as buying a car for example. Will he stop working after buying the car? Not at all. For Koreans, work is something to do as long as their physical condition allows it. For Koreans, for the questions of 'why', goals are only secondary, minor considerations. Therefore, it is not surprising to observe that most Koreans will continue working even after achieving great wealth. For Koreans, no work equals unhappiness and fear. (translated by the author from Lee, 2000, pp. 33–34)

As explained above, South Korean students simply keep learning mandatory English as determined by learning systems. They learn it because they are required to. The "why" of learning English in this context does not stand, but only "how" and "what" become the main issue of English education. Amotivated but highly proficient English learners in Korea are the natural consequence.

7.6   Chapter Summary

In this chapter, five Korea-specific social phenomena were explained. The origin of competitive motivation can be traced back to the turn of the twentieth century and was intensified through historical, national events including the Japanese Colonization Period and the Korean War. While sustaining adverse life conditions, Korean families consolidated the concept of "alter ego familism" to advance their family's social status. Moreover, because most Korean students competed against each other to acquire better English test scores to be admitted to prestigious universities and have a secure occupation, a social bifurcation occurred surrounding the opportunities that each family could provide to their children. Those who could afford the best English learning method hired native English speakers or went abroad to learn English in authentic communicative environments. However, those who could not choose sustainable alternatives such as attending private English institutes or using telephone English. These phenomena were conceptualized as "Kitsch" English. The "Kitsch" nature in English learning is also linked to Bourdieu's (1991) notion of cultural capital. Due to the perceived higher value of English over that of Korean, English education in both public and private sectors flourished. The establishment of English kindergartens and the study-abroad syndrome explained in Chap. 4 would be the examples of Koreans' consensus of English as cultural capital. This chapter illustrated the Korea-specific situation of amotivated English learning, where students may obtain a high level of English proficiency, even when they are amotivated. It will be extremely difficult not to study English in a competitive, collective social atmosphere, which results in the high English proficiency among amotivated English learners.

The above analyses indicate that English learning motivation and amotivation are generated, maintained, and strengthened as the learners go through and accumulate various life experiences over the years. Their experiences reflect the overall atmosphere in society. Moreover, the parents' opinion toward English learning is often inherited by their children. Therefore, the motivational attitude toward English learning is an inter-generational phenomenon, and hence, sociohistorical and longitudinal analyses on English learning motivation have their own legitimacy.

References

Bae, Ji-Sook. (2011). Korea toughens regulations on anchoring babies, citizenship. Retrieved November 21, 2018 from http://www.koreaherald.com/view.php?ud=20110109000252.

Baudilliard, J. (1988). *Selected writings* (M. Poster, ed.) Stanford, CA: Stanford University Press.

Bourdieu, P. (1977). *Reproduction in education, society, and culture* (trans. R. Nice). London: Sage.

Bourdieu, P. (1984). *Distinctions: A social critique of the judgement of taste.* Cambridge, MA: Harvard University Press.

Bourdieu, P. (1991). *Language and symbolic power* (trans. G. Raymond & M. Adamson). Oxford, England: Polity.

Choi, Sang-Chin. (2011a). *Hankookin'ei simrihak [The psychology of Koreans]*. Seoul, Korea: Hakjisa.

Choi, Sang-Chin, & Kim, Ki-Beum. (2011). *Moonwhasimrihak [Cultural psychology]*. Paju, Korea: Jisiksaneupsa.

Choi, Set-Byol. (2004). An investigation of English proficiency in Korean society from the cultural capital perspective: Focusing on college students' English learning and views on excellent English speakers. *Ewha Journal of Social Sciences 11*, 5–21.

Choi, Set-Byol, & Choi, Yu-Jung. (2011). The meaning and structure of Korean English from the cultural capitalism perspective: Comparison with cultural art. *The Korean Association for Cultural Sociology, 10*, 207–252.

Choi, Won-Hyeong. (2011b, January 9). Does English have competitive edge? Only used when logging on in reality! Retrieved July 29, 2018 from http://www.hani.co.kr/arti/culture/religion/510014.html

Chung, Kwang. (2014). *Joseonsidae'eui oikook'eo gyoyook [Foreign language education in the Joseon Dynasty]*. Seoul, Korea: Gimyeongsa.

Demick. B. (2002, April 8). A snip of the tongue and English is yours! Retrieved November 12, 2018 from https://archive.is/20061210222056/http://www2.gol.com/users/coynerhm/a_snip_of_the_tongue_and_english.htm#selection-207.0-207.42.

Dörnyei, Z., & Ushioda, E. (2011). *Teaching and researching motivation* (2nd ed.). Harlow, England: Pearson.

Dweck, C. (1986). Motivational processes affecting learning. *American Psychologist, 41*(1), 1040–1048.

Gardner, R. C. (1985). *The social psychology and second language learning: The role of attitude and motivation*. London: Edward Arnold.

Gardner, R. C. (2010). *Motivation and second language acquisition: The socio-educational model*. New York: Peter Lang.

Gardner, R. C., & Lambert, W. E. (1959). Motivational variables in second-language acquisition. *Canadian Psychology, 13*(4), 266–272.

Gardner, R. C., & Lambert, W. E. (1972). *Attitudes and motivation in second language learning*. Rowley, MA: Newbury House.

Hofestede, G. (1980). *Culture's consequences: International differences in work related values*. Beverly Hills, CA: Sage.

Hofestede, G. (1991). *Cultures and organizations: Software of the mind*. London: McGraw-Hill.

Howatt, A. P. R. (2004). *A history of English language teaching* (2nd ed.). Oxford, England: Oxford University Press.

ICEF. (2014). High performance, high pressure in South Korea's education system. Retrieved November 23, 2018 from http://monitor.icef.com/2014/01/high-performance-high-pressure-in-south-koreas-education-system/.

Im, Hong-Taek. (2018). *90nyeonsaeng'i onda [There come the ones born in the 90s]*. Seoul, Korea: Whale Books.

International Monetary Fund. (2018 April). Report for selected countries and subjects: South Korea. Retrieved November 25, 2018 from https://www.imf.org/external/pubs/ft/weo/2018/01/weodata/weorept.aspx?pr.x=34&pr.y=8&sy=2017&ey=2018&scsm=1&ssd=1&sort=country&ds=.&br=1&c=542&s=NGDPD%2CPPPGDP%2CNGDPDPC%2CPPPPC&grp=0&a=.

Jeon, Bong-Gwan. (2006). Lee Ha-Young daegam'eui yeong'eo choolsegi [Chronicle of His Excellency Lee Ha-Young's success in English learning]. Retrieved December 8, 2018 from http://shindonga.donga.com/Library/3/02/13/105895/4.

Kang, Joon-Mann. (2009). *Ipsijeonjeang janhoksa [The atrocious history of college entrance exam]*. Seoul, Korea: Inmulgwasasangsa.

Kang, Joon-Mann. (2011). *Teukbyeolhan nana daehanminkook [Special country: The Republic of Korea]*. Seoul, Korea: Inmulgwasasangsa.

Kang, Joon-Mann. (2014). *Hankook'ingwa yeong'eo [Koreans and English]*. Seoul, Korea: Inmulgwasasangsa.

Kang, Nae-Hee. (2005). Research papers: English education and its social import in colonial Korea. *In/Outside, 18*, 262–293.

Kang, Seoghoon. (2001). Globalization and income inequality in Korea: An overview. Paper presented at FDI, Human Capital and Education in Developing Countries Technical Meeting (13-14 December 2001) Paris: OECD. Retrieved December 9, 2018 from http://www.oecd.org/dev/2698445.pdf.

Kikuchi, K. (2015). *Demotivation in second language acquisition: Insights from Japan.* Bristol, England: Multilingual Matters.

Kim, Dong Sung. (1916). *Oriental impressions in America.* Cincinnati, NH: The Abingdon Press.

Kim, Miso, Choi, Duk-In, & Kim, Tae-Young. (2019). South Korean jobseekers' perceptions and (de)motivation to study for standardized English tests in neoliberal corporate labor markets. *The Asian EFL Journal, 21*(1), 82–106.

Kim, So-Hyun. (2018, September 26). South Korea to review banning English education for preschoolers. Retrieved November 13, 2018 from http://www.koreaherald.com/view.php?ud=20180925000067.

Kim, S.-H., & Haque, M. (2002). The Asian financial crisis of 1997: Causes and policy responses. *Multinational Business Review, 10*(1), 37–44.

Kim, Tae-Young. (2006). Motivation and attitudes towards foreign language learning as socio-politically mediated constructs: The case of Korean high school students. *The Journal of Asia TEFL, 3,* 165–192.

Kim, Tae-Young. (2010). Socio-political influences on EFL motivation and attitudes: Comparative surveys of Korean high school students. *Asia Pacific Education Review, 11,* 211–222.

Kim, Tae-Young. (2012a). Hankook chojoongdeunghaksaengdeul'eui yeong'eo hakseupdonggi mit je 2eoneo jaa boonseok: Jeongseongjeok interview jeopkeunbeop [An analysis of Korean elementary and secondary school students' English learning motivation and their L2 selves: A qualitative interview approach.] *Korean Journal of English Language and Linguistics, 12*(1), 67–99.

Kim, Tae-Young. (2012b). The L2 motivational self system of Korean EFL students: Cross-grade survey analysis. *English Teaching, 67*(1), 29–56.

Kim, Tae-Young. (2016). Iljegangjeomgi yeong'eogyoyook'eui sahoigyoyookjeok yangsang boonseok: Chosun, Dongailbo gisareul joongsimeuro [An investigation of socio-educational aspects of English education during the Japanese Colonization Period: Focusing on Chosun Ilbo and Dong-A Ilbo]. *Studies in English Education, 21*(1), 179–210.

Kim, Tae-Young, & Kim, Yoon-Kyoung. (2016). A quasi-longitudinal study on English learning motivation and attitudes: The case of South Korean students. *The Journal of Asia TEFL, 13*(2), 72–161

Kim, Tae-Young, Kim, Youngmi, & Kim, Ji-Young. (2017). Structural relationship between L2 learning (de)motivation, resilience, and L2 proficiency among Korean college students. *The Asia-Pacific Education Researcher, 26*(2), 397–406.

Kim, Tae-Young, & Seo, Hyo-Sun. (2012). Elementary school students' foreign language learning demotivation: A mixed methods study of Korean EFL context. *The Asia-Pacific Education Researcher, 21*(1), 160–171.

Kim, U., Triandis, H. C., Kâgitcibasi, C., Choi, S.-C., & Yoon, G. (Eds.). (1994). *Individualism and collectivism: Theory, method, and applications.* Thousand Oaks, CA: Sage.

Kim, Yeong-Myeong. (2005). *Sinhankookron: Danilsahoi hankook, keu bitgwa geurimja [Theory of New Korea: Korea as unidirectional society – Its light and darkness].* Seoul, Korea: Ingansarang.

Kim, Yeong-Myeong. (2007). Yeong'eo yeolpoongeul jamjaewooryeomyeon [How to calm English frenzy]. Retrieved August 12, 2018 from http://news.hankooki.com/lpage/opinion/200711/h2007112118551324370.html.

Koike, I., & Tanaka, H. (1995). English in foreign language education policy in Japan: Toward the twenty-first century. *World Englishes, 14*(1), 13–25.

Korea Statistical Information Service. (2016). 2016nyeon cheonsonyeon tonggye [2016 youth statistics]. Retrieved December 8, 2019 from http://www.kostat.go.kr/portal/korea/kor_nw/2/6/5/index.board?bmode=read&aSeq=353501.

Krashen, S. D. (1982). *Principles and practice in second language acquisition.* New York: Pergamon.

Kwon, Oryang. (2009). The current situation and issues of the teaching of English in Korea. *Ritsumeikan Language and Culture Studies, 21*(2), 21–34. Retrieved November 12, 2019 from http://www.ritsumei.ac.jp/acd/re/k-rsc/lcs/kiyou/pdf_21-2/RitsIILCS_21.2pp21-34KWON.pdf.

Kwon, Oryang, & Kim, Jeong-Ryeol. (2010). *Hankook yeong'eogyoyooksa [History of English education in Korea].* Seoul, Korea: Hankookmunwhasa.

Lam, S.-F., Yim, P.-S., Law, J. S. F., & Cheung, R. W. Y. (2004). The effects of competition on achievement motivation in Chinese classrooms. *British Journal of Educational Psychology, 74* (2), 281–296.

Lee, Gyoo-Tae. (2000). *Hankookin'eu him 2 [Power of the Koreans 2].* Seoul, Korea: Sinwonmunhwasa.

Lee, Heung-Soo. (2011). *Yeong-eoga gyeongjeda: Yeong'eo'eui gwageowa hyeonjae, geurigo mirae [English is economy: Past, present, and future of English].* Seoul, Korea: English Moumou.

Lee, Hyeon Jung. (2012). 'The parent-child suicide pact' and the concept of the family in East Asia: A cross-cultural approach of South Korea, China and Japan. *The Journal of Korean Studies, 40*, 187–227.

Lee, Jeong-Kyu. (2002). Japanese higher education policy in Korea during the colonial period (1910-1945). *Education Policy Analysis Archives, 10*(14), Retrieved from http://epaa.asu.edu/epa/v10n14.tml/.

Lee, Seungryul. (2004). Yeong'eo'eui jegookgwa yeong'eogyoyook'eui jeongchiseong [The empire of English and the politics of English education]. *Bigyomunhak, 33,* 323–338.

Markus, H. R., & Kitayama, S. (1991). Culture and the self: Implications for cognition, emotion, and motivation. *Psychological Review, 98,* 224–253.

McGinn, N. F., Snodgrass, D. R., Kim, Y. B., Kim, S.-B., & Kim, Q.-Y. (1980). *Education and development in Korea.* Cambridge, MA: Harvard University Press.

Park, Sung-Hwan, & Hwang, Yoon-Jeong. (2014, July 1). Gamhi Yonseidae dongmoongeorinun nondeul. . . [Those who dare say Yonsei university alumni. . .]. Retrieved November 12, 2018 from http://www.hani.co.kr/arti/society/society_general/644939.html.

Seth, M. J. (2002). *Education fever: Society, politics and the pursuit of schooling in South Korea.* Honolulu, HI: University of Hawai'i Press.

Shaputis, K. (2004). *The crowded nest syndrome: Surviving the return of adult children.* Olympia, WA: Clutter Fairy.

Shin, Hyunjung. (2010). *"Gireogi Gajok": Transnationalism and language learning.* Unpublished doctoral dissertation, University of Toronto, Ontario, Canada.

Statistics Korea. (2014). 2013nyeon sagyoyookbi josagyeolgwa [Survey result of private education expenses in 2013] Retrieved August 14, 2014 from http://kostat.go.kr/portal/korea/kor_nw/2/13/1/index.board?bmode=read&bSeq=&aSeq=311886&pageNo=1&rowNum=10&navCount=10&currPg=&sTarget=title&sTxt=.

Sung, Hyun-Kyung. (Ed.). (2015). *Kyungsung elite'eui mangook yuramgi [The global sojourn of elites in Kyungsung].* Seoul, Korea: Hyunsilmoonhak.

Whittaker, D. H., Zhu, T., Stturgeon, T. J., Tsai, M. H., & Okita, T. (2007 December). Compressed development in East Asia [ITEC Working Paper Series, 07-29 December 2007]. Retrieved November 24, 2018 from http://www.itec.doshisha-u.jp/03_publication/01_workingpaper/2007/07-29-FINAL-Whittaker%20etal-itecwp.pdf.

Yi, C. C. (Ed.). (2013). *The psychological well-being of East Asian youth.* Dordrecht, Germany: Springer.

Yoo, Simin. (2014). *Na'eui hankookhyeondaesa [My modern Korean history].* Seoul, Korea: Dolbaege.

Yoon, Ji-Kwan. (2002). The oppression of English: Its origin and structures. *In/Outside, 12,* 10–32.

Yoon, Young-Mi. (2016). Almost half of S. Korean parents consider themselves "edu-poor." Retrieved November 21, 2016 at http://english.hani.co.kr/arti/english_edition/e_national/748517.html.

Chapter 8
Conclusion

This chapter focuses on the historical development of English learning motivation in Korea. In Chaps. 2, 3, and 4, the historical genesis of English learning motivation was investigated through the paths of significant historical events. Chapter 5 analyzes the progression of English education and the prime motive in China, Japan, and North Korea, respectively. Chapter 6 focuses on the recent advancement of English learning motivation in South Korea, including L2 motivation research influenced by activity theory, demotivation, teacher motivation, students' competitive motivation, and the motivational languaging activity. Chapter 7 highlights five unique sociopsychological factors that created, maintained, and strengthened English learning motivation in (South) Korea.

As argued in the Introduction, the primary concern in this book is the role of sociocultural contexts surrounding each L2 learner. In particular, how sociopolitical events had intricate relations with the macroeconomy in a nation. Such social events influence L2 learners and their families, and for this reason, the conceptualization of individual learners with cognition and emotion is not sufficient. They are constantly influenced by society and cannot be separated from their family, friends, school community, neighborhood, and administrative district. In this regard, this book-length investigation resonates with Ushioda's (2009) argument of the "person-in-context relational view" in understanding the emergent nature of motivation. She expressed her view as follows:

> [I]t seems that in much existing research on language motivation, context or culture is located externally, as something pre-existing, a stable independent background variable, outside the individual. It is either the object of our attitudes and perceptions, or a determinant of our behaviour. The unique local particularities of the person as self-reflective intentional agent, inherently part of and shaping her own context, seem to have no place in this kind of research. (Ushioda, 2009, p. 218)

Based on Ushioda's (2009) argument, English learners in Korea do not exist in a vacuum. The desire to learn English was incubated from the discourse of English as the steppingstone toward upper social class. English was (and is) perceived as a useful tool for being admitted to a prestigious university and hired in a large

© Springer Nature Singapore Pte Ltd. 2021
T.-Y. Kim, *Historical Development of English Learning Motivation Research*,
English Language Education 21, https://doi.org/10.1007/978-981-16-2514-5_8

conglomerate or at a government office. At the core of this perception lie the century-long diplomatic relations with the USA and other industrialized western nations. Additionally, the domestic contexts unique in Korea, such as *hakbul*, or academic credentialism, and rapid economic development, should be considered in understanding Korea-specific competitive motivation. In other words, the English culture in Korea, which is inseparable from its history, society, and economic situations of each era, generated and influenced Koreans' unique mentality regarding English teaching and learning. In understanding English learning and teaching (de)-motivation in Korea as well as other EFL countries around the globe, the longitudinal sociohistorical view needs to be considered as a crucial factor, not as a constant static in the background. This "person-in-context" view is the main argument encompassing the current volume.

8.1 Summary

Since the Korea-U.S. Treaty of Peace, Amity, Commerce, and Navigation was ratified in 1882, the English language had been perceived as the "golden key" to employment and social success. The Korean government supported training experts in a foreign language to modernize the nation, and young Korean youths who aspired to be employed as civil servants were enrolled in the Royal Language School. Additionally, starting in the 1880s, Christian missionaries, mostly from the USA, started to establish missionary schools across Korea. Despite the purpose of missionary schools to propagate Christianity in Korea, Koreans eager to learn English started attending them.

Because the Korean government hired foreign instructors at the Royal Language School, the teaching subjects were instructed in English. Similarly, the language of instruction at foreign missionary schools was English. Thus, it is noteworthy that in the nineteenth and the early twentieth century, the method of instruction in English education in Korea was typically English immersion, where students are required to speak and write in English to express themselves.

However, 35 years of the Japanese Colonization Period in Korea resulted in the rapid retrogression in English education. This period also instilled the notion of competitive motivation among Koreans in English learning. It may be a natural consequence to find various levels of instrumental motivation in learning a foreign language. However, in the case of Korean students' learning English during the Japanese Colonization Period, the purpose of language learning is not primarily related to authentic communication with English speakers. Instead, the prime reason for learning English was to excel among other students in college entrance exams. In Chap. 2, it was argued that the creation of *hakbul*, or academic credentialism, can be traced back to the establishment of Kyungsung (or Keijo in Japanese) Imperial University, founded in 1924. As the graduates of this university were offered a high-rank position in the Government-General of Korea under Japanese rule, Koreans aspired to be admitted. Under this socioeducational context, the role of

English and its learning was rapidly transformed from instrumental motivation (which represents the desire to be employed at a secure position by using English for communication) to academic, competitive motivation for university admission purposes. Note that in this qualitative transition, the communicative competence was not the priority; while vying for the limited admission quota, the internal competition among compatriots was emphasized.

As presented in Chap. 3, even after the liberation from Japan in 1945, the overall situation of English learning and its motivation did not change significantly. The outbreak of the Korean War and the restoration period after the civil war prevented the Ministry of Education of Korea from introducing a communication-based English curriculum in secondary schools. Moreover, the military government by President Park Chung-hee emphasized economic development through systematic economic plans, which resulted in rapid growth in the South Korean economy. In the 1970s and 80s, the industrial transition from a poverty-stricken agricultural nation to a substantial industrial nation required quick and reliable measures to select a new workforce in South Korea. In this social milieu, college diplomas started to function as a warranty for the holders' intellectual potentials; universities in South Korea were placed hierarchically. Graduates from top-tier universities had better opportunities to be interviewed and hired, whereas those from less prestigious schools increasingly had fewer opportunities. As such, the competition to be admitted to prestigious universities became fiercer every year. Because English was continuously included as one of the crucial subjects for college entrance exams, high school students developed reading comprehension skills and memorized complicated morphosyntactic rules. As the entrance exams did not measure speaking and listening proficiency, students' priorities were placed on reading and grammar. As their parents and grandparents had during the Japanese Colonization Period, Korean students in the 1970s and 80s learned English mainly for internal competition with their peers. A similar situation reflects Koreans' desire to ascend to the elite social class by having better opportunities in higher education and employment (Lee, 2017; Seth, 2002). With this socioeconomic situation in South Korea, the competitive motivation among young students became fiercer, and English learning was mainly for preparing for college entrance exams or job placement tests.

The situations illustrated in Chap. 4 showed different historical trajectories after the 1990s. The deep-rooted test-orientation until the 1980s gradually faced significant changes at the end of the decade. Being the host of major international sports events such as the 1988 Seoul Summer Olympic Games turned a new page in English education in South Korea. Additionally, the *segyehwa* or globalization policy after the inauguration of former president Kim Young-sam made Koreans realize the importance of communicative competence in English (Song, 2012). This renewed attention started to be reflected in the national curriculum, which led to the launch of the sixth and seventh National Curricula, effective from 1992 to 2007 (Kim & Kim, 2019). Elementary English education was introduced nationwide in 1997 (Kwon, 2000). With the preparation phase during the policy of globalization during the tenure of President Kim Young-sam, starting in 1997, Grade 3 and 4 elementary school students received one class-hour (i.e., 40 min) English instruction, and Grade 5 and 6 students received two class-hour instructions. Based on the critical period hypothesis (cf. Birdsong, 1999), elementary English education focused on developing students' speaking and listening proficiency (Ahn et al., 2015). Despite significant problems such as the lack of systematic preparation in implementing elementary English instruction nationwide (Min, 2007) and increasing spending on private English education (Ministry of Education, 2018), it is thought that "elementary school English has a positive long-term effect" in terms of students' English proficiency (Kwon, 2005, p. 49).

Chapter 4 also reports various English-related social changes at the turn of the century. For example, pro-English policies are explained including the Teaching English in English (TEE) certificate (Lee, 2011), the English Village in various local government levels (Choi, 2011), the English Program in Korea (EPIK) (Lee, 2015), and the Jeju Global Education City (JGEC) (Jeong & Kwon, 2018). Various social phenomena also expedited the above political movement. Koreans witnessed the TOEIC frenzy associated with the university admission policy (Kang, 2011), and Mr. Bok Geo-il argued for the adoption of English as an official language in South Korea (Bok, 1998, 2002). The study abroad and goose father syndrome also gained social recognition in South Korea (Chow, 2012). All these changes around the twenty-first century necessitated the changing perception toward English among Koreans. In previous generations, English functioned as a selection tool for college admission and job recruitment, and because of this internal use of English, literacy skills, and not speaking and listening proficiency, were measured. However, due to the increasing needs of international communication, the previous paradigm of English education could no longer be maintained. South Koreans now pay more attention to speaking and listening proficiency in English. Fundamental changes in competitive motivation, however, are not identified; the previous method of a paper-and-pencil based English test is gradually being replaced by a speaking and listening test. However, in both cases, students compete with each other to put themselves in higher standing. The recent adoption of criterion-referenced test in the CSAT may alleviate the competitive atmosphere among Korean students, but this speculation will require more academic research.

Chapter 5 expands the scope of analysis to neighboring countries of South Korea. English gradually spread in the southern part of China. With drastic fluctuations in the perception of learning English, Chinese people initially had an ambivalent attitude toward English (and other Western languages), which was affiliated with the traditional concept of Sinocentrism, or the notion of China as the only Central Flowery (中華) country in the world. However, despite the refusal to accept the languages of so-called Western barbarians, Western nations continued to expand their political influence in China. English education in China became widespread due to the contribution of missionary schools across China (Deng, 1997). After the establishment of *Tongwen Guan*, the Interpreter's College (Bolton, 2002) eventually replaced the role of *keju* or traditional imperial examination for appointing civil servants at the end of the nineteenth century. Through major historical events such as the collapse of the Qing Dynasty, the establishment of the Republic of China in 1912, and the People's Republic of China in 1949, English was increasingly regarded as a prime tool for enlightening the public and introducing the advanced Western civilization. Despite political turmoil due to the Cold War and Cultural Revolution, English, in general, was instructed to Chinese students. After the Open Door Policy by Deng Xiaoping in 1978, English instruction was expedited and is now state-controlled in the form of the College English Test.

In the case of Japan, English was rapidly introduced after the Peace Treaty with the USA in 1854. Except for a relatively short period at the end of World War II, English was consistently taught in Japan, as it was regarded as the language of modernization. Thus, the attitude toward English education in Japan did not meet the kind of significant resistance witnessed in China. Instead, Japan adopted utilitarian attitudes toward English. Translation and interpretation from English to Japanese were prioritized, and as a result, the traditional grammar-translation method has been preferred. However, recent educational innovations are found in English education: elementary English education is introduced first to fifth and sixth-year and then to third and fourth-year elementary school students, and native English-speaking teachers are invited to Japan (Sasaki, 2008).

Compared with the motivation to learn English in China and Japan, North Korea's situation seems drastically different. Although instrumental reasons to learn English are observed in most parts of the world, due to the long-standing diplomatic dispute with the USA and South Korea, the analysis of English learning and its related motivation in North Korea requires a different understanding. In Chap. 5, it was emphasized that in North Korea, English education, as a part of socialist education, highlighted the concept of *Juche* or self-reliance, glorified the dictatorship of the Kim family, and reiterated their antipathy toward the USA and South Korea because they are the representative nations threatening North Korea's national security (and spreading U.S. imperialism). However, after the reign of Kim Jong-un from 2011, notable changes are identified in English education. Vilification toward the USA and South Korea dramatically reduced, and the ideological contents justifying socialism and the monopoly of the Kim family were replaced with more practical, everyday contents. Although these are notable changes, because North Korea does not have active diplomatic and economic relations with most Western nations, students in the North may not have an authentic need to learn English; they have extremely little chance of meeting foreign nationals (Baik, 1994). Thus, it can be concluded that English education is mostly consumed for internal use among North Koreans. For example, English is included as one of the test subjects for college entrance exams, and it is also used for the dissemination of the *Juche* ideology among North Korean students.

Chapter 6 introduces recent theoretical advances in L2 motivation research. The former part of this chapter starts with a summary of previous dominant research in L2 motivation, such as Gardner's (1985) socioeducational model and Dörnyei's (2005, 2009) L2 motivational self-system. After examining the conceptual compatibility between Gardner's and Dörnyei's theories, Chap. 6 focuses on context-specific L2 learning demotivation in East Asia by introducing Falout et al.'s (2009) and Kim and Kim's (2013) research. Recent interest in L2 teacher motivation and emotional labor are also included in Chap. 6, covering various cases of L2 teacher (de)motivation in the USA and Egypt (Kassabdy et al., 2001), Iraq (Koran, 2015), Japan (Kumazawa, 2013; Sugino, 2010), Slovakia (Kubanyiova, 2009), and South Korea (Song & Kim, 2016). As a new research methodology, L2 motivation research invited various large-scale, meta-analytic studies, and the third part of this chapter deals with 13,391 Hungarian L2 learners (Dörnyei et al., 2006), more than 10,000 Chinese EFL learners (You & Dörnyei, 2016), and 6301 Korean EFL elementary school students (Kim & Seo, 2012). Competitive motivation, consistently identified among South Korean students and a central theme of investigation throughout this book, was explained with close analysis of Kim's (2006a, 2010a) and Kim and Kim's (2016) consecutive, quasi-longitudinal studies. It was noteworthy that the predictability of motivation and attitudes in students' English proficiency decreased longitudinally. This phenomenon was attributed to the exam-oriented Korean society; regardless of motivation and attitude toward English, students are forced to learn English and exhibit their best abilities in English tests.

The latter part of Chap. 6 highlights the Activity Theory (AT) analysis of L2 learning motivation and demotivation. Influenced by Vygotsky's (1978, 1987) sociocultural theory, it was argued that AT has the potential to approach L2 motivation by paying particular attention to the interaction among language, learner, and the learning environment. Engestrom's (1987, 1999) AT triangle is explained, and *motives, needs, and motivation* (AT-inspired concepts relevant to motivation) are introduced with visual illustrations for conceptualizing and distinguishing these crucial concepts. Then, the relationship between the L2 motivational self-system and AT-based L2 motivation theory is illustrated by using Kim's (2009, 2010b) previous work. Additionally, empirical research (mainly conducted in South Korea) is introduced with representative interview excerpts (Kim, 2006b, 2009, 2010c) and a series of AT system models (Kim, 2011a; Kim & Kim, 2013). This chapter concludes with Motivational Languaging Activities (MLAs), a practical educational intervention to increase the level of students' L2 learning motivation. Influenced by Swain's (2006, 2010, 2013) idea of cognitive languaging, or "the activity of mediating cognitively complex ideas using language" (Swain & Lapkin, 2011, p. 105), MLAs were practical efforts to expand Swain's cognitive languaging to the area of L2 learning motivation. In general, MLAs were proven effective in enhancing students' levels of motivation (Kim, 2017b, 2019; Lee & Kim, 2019).

Chapter 7 focuses on Korea-specific, socioeducational considerations in English learning motivation. Five factors were illustrated: competitive motivation, alter ego familism, "Kitsch" English, English as cultural capital, and amotivated English learning. Since the introduction of English in the nineteenth century, English has secured its status as a useful tool for ascending the social hierarchy in Korea. During the Japanese colonization from 1910 to 1945 and the Korean War from 1950 to 1953, English was increasingly perceived as a powerful tool to gain access to the savvy, sophisticated Western lifestyle. Thus, the competitive motivation explained in various chapters throughout this volume needs to be approached from longitudinal perspectives. The English fever was engendered through the modernization process in (South) Korea, and with limited financial means within a household, only one or two children were chosen to receive higher education, including the study of

English. In this case, the collective mentality of alter ego familism is created where the parental expectation is channeled through their offspring. The success or failure of the children is often equated with that of their parents, and parents endeavor to provide the best opportunity to receive high-quality education to achieve or maintain a high status for their family in the community. It is apparent that traditional Confucian ideology influences the close family bond. In this collective societal atmosphere, educational opportunity is often regarded as a family investment. A family without financial means cannot provide the best English education, which is represented by studying abroad in English-speaking countries or private English tutoring with native English speakers. Alternative methods such as a private English institute or an English Village are explained as "Kitsch," which is effective though not considered authentic. All these Korea-specific phenomena reflect the idea of English as cultural capital (Bourdieu, 1977, 1991). To acquire upward social mobility, students compete with each other to improve their English proficiency, which is crucial cultural capital. As the competition becomes fiercer (Kim, 2006a, 2010a; Kim & Kim, 2016), students' motivation and attitudes do not function as significant predictors for their English test scores, and high English proficiency of amotivated English learners is reported in recent research in South Korea (Kim, 2012a, 2012b).

8.2 Prospect of English Learning Motivation

As the central theme of our investigation is English learning motivation, the chapters in the present volume have focused on what types of motivational constructs have existed in English learners in Korea from historical perspectives. In this section, a foreseeable future trend in English learning motivation will be explained. The first subsection will introduce two opposing directions in English learning motivation: one is passive attitudes negating the need for learning English, and the other is intensifying competitive motivation to learn English. In the second subsection, a long-term prospect of learning English will be explained, paying close attention to the recent technological advances represented by Information Technology.

8.2.1 Opposite Directions in the Motivation/Demotivation Continuum

Learning a foreign language is always related to the power of the language. Chan (2016) considers five categories in deciding "powerful languages" around the globe: geography (countries spoken, land area, and inbound tourists), economy (GDP, GDP/capita, exports, foreign exchange market, and special drawing rights [SDR] composition), communication (native speakers, L2 speakers, family size, and outbound tourists), knowledge and media (internet content, feature films, top-500 universities, and academic journals), and diplomacy (IMF, UN, World Bank, and Index of 10 Supranational organizations [e.g., IOC, OECD, FIFA]). In Chan's (2016) "Power Language Index," English is ranked at the top, and Korean is in 16th place. In Chan's categorization, although the term "powerful" may be perceived as subjective, it still shows the relative importance of teaching English to most Korean students.

However, South Korea has developed its economic power in the global market, and GDP per capita has increased exponentially—from $64.1 in December 1955 to $33,346 in December 2018 (CEIC, 2019). As explained in Chaps. 3 and 4, the rapid economic development in South Korea was spearheaded with the dictatorial leadership of President Park Chung-hee at the sacrifice of democracy. For this reason, there exist pros and cons regarding the dictatorial regime in South Korea. In terms of economic prospects, due to the increasing purchase power of South Koreans, many tourist attractions provide Korean pamphlets, and global websites such as Amazon, Apple, Google, and Netflix offer Korean-language websites. Moreover, Korean pop culture is shared and enjoyed among youth globally. For example, BTS, the K-pop superstar "idol group" is estimated to have generated $3.54 billion for South Korea annually and $1.26 billion as an added value every year (Hyundai Research Institute, 2018). High-speed internet, Korean pop music, movies, drama, cosmetics, and fashion represent the Korean Wave, or *Hallyu* (韓流), which has spread internationally and is already becoming a global phenomenon (Kim, 2007a).

South Korea's economic and cultural development seems to influence students' English learning motivation and attitudes. An increasing number of students have started to create an attitude of "why bother to learn English?" As the Korean language gains recognition, its younger generation may question the legitimacy of learning English. New information and world news are instantly translated into Korean, and most Koreans will be notified of important developments by merely scrolling down Naver or Daum apps (two major portal apps in South Korea). The use of smartphones and information technology infrastructure in South Korea expedites the above modern trend. "Then why do we need to learn English?" our students often ask us. In Bourdieu's (1991) terms, the cultural capital surrounding the Korean language has increased, although it is still incomparable to that of English. Average Koreans can lead their lives only speaking Korean as Kim (2005, 2007b) argued that the need for English learning is not real but simply hypothetical. Almost limitless internet contents are uploaded, shared, and consumed in Korean. Free translation apps can alleviate the burden of translation: without knowing the basic vocabulary, they can travel to foreign countries with the support of translation apps installed on their smartphones.

Given this, English instruction offered at school can be easily regarded as a graduation requirement to secondary school, or one of the many school subjects needed to pass college entrance exams. To such students, traditional concepts of integrative or instrumental motivations lose their ground. If they do not want to live in a foreign country, integrative motivation is ineffective in maintaining their interest in learning English as a foreign language. Additionally, instrumental motivation, if all information is simultaneously translated and disseminated through the internet platform, will no longer be valid. Thus, students do not see the merit of learning English.

This speculation is confirmed in the case of amotivated students in Japan. Although Japan experienced the "Lost Decade," a severe economic recession from 1991 to 2001, and suffers from an aging population, it had enjoyed economic development and cultural prosperity in the latter half of the twentieth century (similar to the current situation in South Korea described above). The "why bother" attitude toward learning English has been identified in Japan: this passive, sometimes negative attitude is termed *Uchimuki* (内向き), or "an allegedly inward-looking tendency among young Japanese people" (Yashima, 2013, p. 37). In this attitude, students are not enthusiastic about learning English, studying, or working abroad because "going abroad does not necessarily benefit students in securing good jobs" (p. 37). As Japan is the third largest in the world by its national GDP, and the second largest developed country, Japanese students are prone to creating the attitude of *Uchimuki*, consolidating passive attitudes toward learning English. As reported by Falout et al. (2009), Japanese students show varying degrees of demotivation in learning English, and this passive attitude seems to be one of the potential factors. A similar attitude to *Uchimuki* may be found and consolidated among South Korean students: students will increasingly refuse to learn English as they do not see any benefits. As a result, demotivation to learn English will be on a constant increase.

At the end of the motivational continuum, however, still lies an unprecedentedly high level of motivation to learn English. As stated in Chaps. 3 and 4, the rate of university attendance among Korean youth increased exponentially for the last 70 years after the Korean War. The Ministry of Education of Korea reported that the number of South Korean students from kindergarten to high school fell by 167,000 in 2017 (Kim, 2017a). Korean universities are expected to face a student enrollment crisis due to the shrinking student population. High school students can gain admission to college relatively quickly compared to their parents' generation. As the admission quota remains the same, students can be admitted to college as long as they do not aim for the top-tier schools.

These macro changes in population structure in South Korea may result in positive changes in education. Severe competition for college admission may be alleviated, and students may receive individual attention at school due to the decreased number of students in class. However, this has not been realized yet. At the core of this phenomenon, the competitive motivation is still valid among students aiming for prestigious universities. In the previous generation, the Confucian tradition in Korean society suppressed female students' university admission. Moreover, high school students from lower-income family background did not commonly pursue higher education and instead sought practical career pathways. The current situation in South Korea is drastically different: approximately 70% of high school graduates pursue tertiary education, and since 2005, female students' college admission rate has consistently exceeded that of male students. As of 2018, rates were 73.8% for females versus 65.9% for males (Lee, 2019).

At the superficial level, enthusiasm toward tertiary education seems to have elevated the overall level of education in South Korea. However, given the nature of competitive motivation, the desire to learn English and other school subjects comes from the desire to enhance one's chance of being admitted to a prestigious university and be employed in a secure, high-paying job. Thus, in twenty-first century Korea, as most high school students are advancing to tertiary education, a college diploma is not sufficient. Only graduation certificates from prestigious universities will increase the chance of employment—other second- or third-tier universities cannot compete. At present, 70% of high school students attend university, and this number has started to decrease. This means that in general the gaining admission to university will be easier than now because Koreans start to critically reconsider the effectiveness of tertiary education for employment. At the same time, however, this also means future competition for admission to the most prestigious universities will be intense, and the role of English as a major subject in the CSAT will continue to be prioritized. Chapter 4 introduces the recent trend of the CSAT toward a criterion-referenced testing format. Although the adoption of a criterion-referenced test in the English section may alleviate the excessive level of competition among students and the cost of private education in South Korea, the fluctuating difficulty level in the English section each year will continue to be a significant problem. Because the prediction of the difficulty level is not easy (even for the testing experts), Korean high school students and their parents who prepare for the CSAT cannot disregard the importance of English (Yang, 2018). In sum, as Kim's (2006a, 2010a) and Kim and Kim's (2016) previous research proved, the competitive motivation toward English, particularly in the CSAT, becomes aggravated because English is still perceived as a powerful tool for college admission and employment.

In the future, some students will continue to learn English mainly to communicate with speakers in other nations, and through such authentic communication, they may achieve self-actualization and bridge the gap between their actual L2 self and the ideal L2 self (cf. Dörnyei, 2005, 2009). In previous literature focusing on elementary school students (Kim, 2011b), results showed various levels of motivation, such as intrinsic, extrinsic, integrative, and instrumental. Additionally, elderly English learners in South Korea over 60 years old showed a high level of motivation toward English learning; their prime motive was self-actualization (Kim & Kim, 2015). Considering the diverse population that can be categorized as English learners, their types of motivation must be taken into account. However, in the twenty-first century, while predicting future trends related to English education, central themes of investigation will focus on the opposite directions of demotivation versus high level of competitive motivation. In this line of a motivational continuum, at one end, there are students refusing to learn English; at the other end, students dominated by competitive motivation endeavor to learn English to increase their test scores in the CSAT (Fig. 8.1).

The gap between the two ends of this continuum may be widened in the future. As technological development is expedited and automatic translation is widespread, students will show an increasing trend of neglecting English-learning, showing only minor enthusiasm. In contrast, students who understand the value of English

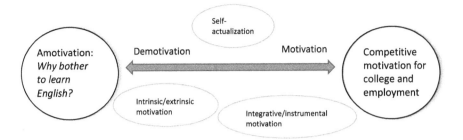

Fig. 8.1 The motivational continuum

proficiency as cultural capital for their future will exert efforts to maximize their English test scores for the CSAT or other English tests (such as the TOEIC or IELTS). Therefore, future trends in the distribution of the student population will show a bimodal distribution in their motivational levels. Two major groups of students will be identified: amotivated/demotivated group versus competitively motivated group. For the existence of students having communicative motivation, cultural exchange motivation, or the desire for self-actualization, minor groups of students will be placed in the middle. However, given the number of students, the vast majority of them in South Korea (and many other nations in East Asia) will be located at one of the ends of the motivational continuum.

8.2.2   The Influence of Information Technology at the Dawn of the Digital Age

As the main focus of this book is to analyze the historical progression of EFL learning motivation in Korea, the prospect of English learning and its related motivation would be beyond the scope of the present volume. However, the previous chapters proved that the socioeconomic environment has consistently influenced EFL learning motivation that faces both students and teachers. Foreseeable changes in language education will be closely connected to the learner's mindset about learning English. The most imminent technological advance is the development of artificial intelligence (AI) technology. For the last couple of decades, various subfields in TESOL and applied linguistics have flourished, and these academic disciplines include information and communications technology (ICT), computer-assisted language learning (CALL), multimedia-assisted language learning (MALL), flipped learning, blended learning, and automatic translation. With these tremendous technological developments supported by high-speed wireless internet, it is not unusual to find foreign tourists who use translation apps such as WayGo, Papago, Google translation, iTranslate, and TripLingo. They speak their first language into the phone, and the apps can successfully convey the intended message to the speakers of a different language. The widespread use of smartphones across the globe will expedite the use of automatic translation through related apps. These translation apps are often incorporated with visual aids and realized as augmented reality. For example, Google Glass, an optical display in the shape of a pair of glasses that displays textual and visual information, can install various translation apps to facilitate communication between different language users or patients having trouble communicating (Dingfleld et al., 2017). At this point, all these IT devices are called "wearable devices," but it is not unimaginable to predict that wearable devices could evolve into "insertable devices" (into one's body) that enable instant understanding of texts or verbal messages written in foreign languages. In 2018, a news blog, entitled "Thousands of Swedes are inserting microchips under their skin," reported that more than 4000 Swedes inserted microchips under their skin with the major function of executing financial transactions (NPR, 2018). This would be an irreversible trend in our civilization; the size of the microchip will likely be dramatically small, with an exponentially increasing capacity. Results will affect the future of traditional foreign language instruction, mainly conducted in the school classroom; it may face drastic decreases, if not extinction.[1]

This foreseeable change will present a qualitatively different horizon in learning and teaching an L2 learner in a traditional classroom. Most students may have doubts about learning an L2 while witnessing the convenient use of translation apps. A typical question voiced might be, "Why do I need to learn English (as a foreign language)? All I need is my smartphone and the translation app." Teachers will be able to defend their rationale to continue their L2 instruction for a short time; they might argue for the legitimacy of learning an L2 due to the inaccuracy of the apps or the possibility of misinterpreting the intended message. However, apps are constantly being improved, and translation apps can manage various topics. Moreover, the accuracy rate of the apps will approximate to perfection in the future. L2 teachers' primary duties would face transformational changes at school. Instead of teaching the language contents, they may need to find the best apps equipped with the most user-friendly interfaces and the fewest errors in interpretation. As Rogers (1961) stated half a century ago, the teacher will become not an authority figure transmitting knowledge but a facilitator of learning. With professional support from L2 teachers or facilitators, learners will select the apps suitable for their intended communicative purposes. These apps can be used for simultaneous translations while reading a document written in a foreign language or real-time interpretation for conversations with speakers of a different language. In this future scenario, the role of L2 learning motivation may face fundamental reorientation; it may not be L2 "learning" motivation but the motivation to choose the best app for an L2.

With the support of technology, students can acquire knowledge in English without much difficulty in decoding messages. As long as students can choose the appropriate app for their purposes, the linguistic difficulty itself would not create

---

[1] After the COVID-19 pandemic, the traditional concept of schooling has rapidly been transformed. Hybrid instructions having online and offline education are often identified, and even entirely online education via video conferencing apps such as Zoom is found in both public and private education.

much of a psychological barrier between the L2 text and the students. Given this, technological advances will continue to contribute to egalitarianism by decreasing the information gap caused by the lack of foreign language proficiency. In the near future, the social issues related to English learning, such as competitive motivation, the Gireogi gajok, or the goose family syndrome, will disappear.

References

Ahn, Tae Yeon, Kim, Tae eun, & Roh, Won Kyung. (2015). Research on the gap between elementary and middle school classroom instruction: An analysis of the English classroom. *Journal of Learner-Centered Curriculum and Instruction, 15*(5), 159–186.

Baik, Jonghak Martin. (1994). *Language, ideology, and power: English textbooks of two Koreas.* Unpublished doctoral dissertation. University of Illinois at Urbana-Champaign, IL, U.S.A.

Birdsong, D. (1999). *Second language acquisition and the critical period hypothesis.* Mahwah, NJ: Lawrence Erlbaum.

Bok, Geo-il. (1998). *Gookje'eo sidea'eui minjok'eo [National language in the age of global language].* Seoul, Korea: Moonji.

Bok, Geo-il. (2002, February 5). Yeong'eo yeolpoong ireotge bonda [I see English fever like this]. In Donga Ilbo.

Bolton, K. (2002). Chinese Englishes: From Canton jargon to global English. *World Englishes, 21* (2), 181–199.

Bourdieu, P. (1977). *Reproduction in education, society, and culture* (trans. R. Nice). London: Sage.

Bourdieu, P. (1991). *Language and symbolic power* (trans. G. Raymond & M. Adamson). Oxford, England: Polity.

CEIC. (2019). South Korea GDP per capita: 1953-2018. Retrieved January 19, 2020 from https://www.ceicdata.com/en/indicator/korea/gdp-per-capita

Chan, K. L. (2016). Power language index: Which are the world's most influential languages? Retrieved January 19, 2020 from http://www.kailchan.ca/wp-content/uploads/2016/12/Kai-Chan_Power-Language-Index-full-report_2016_v2.pdf

Choi, Yoon-Hwa. (2011). The effect of a short immersion program at English Village on elementary school students' motivation at different English proficiency levels: A Gardner's AMTB based analysis. *English Language Teaching, 23*(2), 181–199.

Chow, S. (2012, August 22). The Korean "goose family" phenomena: Educational migrants. Retrieved January 12, 2020 from https://globalprosperity.wordpress.com/2012/08/22/the-korean-goose-family-phenomena-educational-migrants/

Deng, P. (1997). *Private education in modern China.* London: Praeger.

Dingfield, L., Kassutto, S., & Dine, J. (2017). Use of Google Glass to enhance communication education. *Journal of Pain and Symptom Management, 53*(2), 390–391.

Dörnyei, Z. (2005). *The psychology of the language learner: Individual differences in second language acquisition.* Mahwah, NJ: Lawrence Erlbaum.

Dörnyei, Z. (2009). The L2 motivational self system. In Z. Dörnyei & E. Ushioda (Eds.), *Motivation, language identity and the L2 self* (pp. 9–42). Bristol, England: Multilingual Matters.

Dörnyei, Z., Csizér, K., Németh, N. (2006). *Motivation, language attitudes and globalisation: A Hungarian perspective.* Clevedon, England: Multilingual Matters.

Engeström, Y. (1987). *Learning by expanding: An activity-theoretical approach to developmental research.* Helsinki, Finland: Orienta-Konsultit.

Engeström, Y. (1999). Activity theory and individual and social transformation. In Y. Engeström, R. Miettinen & R.-M. Punamaki (Eds.), *Perspectives on activity theory* (pp. 19–38). New York: Cambridge University Press.

Falout, J., Elwood, J., & Hood, M. (2009). Demotivation: Affective states and learning outcomes. *System, 37*, 403–417.

Gardner, R. C. (1985). *Social psychology and second language learning: The role of attitudes and motivation.* London: Edward Arnold.

Hyundai Research Institute (2018, December 17). Bangtan Sonyeondan (BTS)'s gyeongjejeok hyogwa [Economic effect of BTS]. Retrieved January 19, 2020 from http://hri.co.kr/board/reportView.asp?numIdx=30107&firstDepth=1&secondDepth=1&thirdDepth=

Jeong, Seungmo, & Kwon, Sangcheol. (2018). Debates of global competitiveness and selective education over international school education: The case of Jeju Education City. *The Journal of Korean Urban Geographical Society, 21*(3), 17–33.

Kang, Joon-Mann. (2011). *Teukbyeolhan nara daehanminkook [Special country: The Republic of Korea].* Seoul, Korea: Inmulgwasasangsa.

Kassabdy, O., Boraie, D., & Schmidt, R. (2001). Values, rewards, and job satisfaction in EFL/EFL. In Z. Dörnyei & R. Schmidt (Eds.), *Motivation and second language acquisition* (pp. 213–237). Honolulu, HI: University of Hawai'i Press.

Kim, Da-sol. (2017a, August 31). South Korean students fall by 167,000 this year. Retrieved January 19, 2020 from http://www.koreaherald.com/view.php?ud=20170831000321

Kim, Jeongmee. (2007a). Why does Hallyu matter? The significance of the Korean Wave in South Korea. *Critical Studies in Television: The International Journal of Television Studies, 2*(2), 47–69.

Kim, Tae-Young. (2006a). Motivation and attitudes towards foreign language learning as socio-politically mediated constructs: The case of Korean high school students. *The Journal of Asia TEFL, 3*, 165–192.

Kim, Tae-Young. (2006b). L2 learning motivation from a sociocultural theory perspective: Theory, concepts, and empirical evidence. *English Teaching, 61*(4), 51–76.

Kim, Tae-Young. (2009). The sociocultural interface between ideal self and ought-to self: A case study of two Korean ESL students' motivation. In Z. Dörnyei & E. Ushioda (Eds.), *Motivation, language identity and the L2 self* (pp. 248–273). Bristol, England: Multilingual Matters.

Kim, Tae-Young. (2010a). Socio-political influences on EFL motivation and attitudes: Comparative surveys of Korean high school students. *Asia Pacific Education Review, 11*, 211–222.

Kim, Tae-Young. (2010b). Reductionism, activity theory, and L2 motivation research: Toward new concepts and definitions. *The SNU Journal of Educational Research, 19*, 87–118.

Kim, Tae-Young. (2010c). Ideal L2 self and sensitization in L2 learning motivation: A case study of two Korean ESL students. *Korean Journal of English and Linguistics, 10*(2), 321–351.

Kim, Tae-Young. (2011a). Sociocultural dynamics of ESL learning (de)motivation: An activity theory analysis of two adult Korean immigrants. *The Canadian Modern Language Review, 67*(1), 91–122.

Kim, Tae-Young. (2011b). Korean elementary school students' English learning demotivation: A comparative survey study. *Asia Pacific Education Review, 12*, 1–11.

Kim, Tae-Young. (2012a). Hankook chojoongdeunghaksaengdeul'eui yeong'eo hakseupdonggi mit je 2eoneo jaa boonseok: Jeongseongjeok interview jeopkeunbeop [An analysis of Korean elementary and secondary school students' English learning motivation and their L2 selves: A qualitative interview approach.] *Korean Journal of English Language and Linguistics, 12*(1), 67–99.

Kim, Tae-Young. (2012b). The L2 motivational self system of Korean EFL students: Cross-grade survey analysis. *English Teaching, 67*(1), 29–56.

Kim, Tae-Young. (2019). Effect of languaging activities on L2 learning motivation. A classroom-based approach. In M. Haneda & H. Nassaji (Eds.), *Perspectivees on language as action* (pp. 80–98). Bristol, England: Multilingual Matters.

Kim, Tae-Young, & Kim, Yoon-Kyoung. (2013). Reconceptualizing L2 learning demotivation from a Vygotskian activity theory perspective. *English Teaching, 68*(4), 141–163.

Kim, Tae-Young, & Kim, Yoon-Kyoung. (2015). Elderly Korean learners' participation in English learning through lifelong education: Focusing on motivation and demotivation. *Educational Gerontology, 41*(2), 120–135.

Kim, Tae-Young, & Kim, Yoon-Kyoung. (2016). A quasi-longitudinal study on English learning motivation and attitudes: The case of South Korean students. *The Journal of Asia TEFL, 13*(2), 72–161

Kim, Tae-Young, & Kim, Youngmi. (2019). EFL learning motivation in Korea: Historical background and current situation. In M. Lamb, K. Csizér, A. Henry & S. Ryan (Eds.), *Palgrave Macmillan handbook of motivation for language learning* (pp. 411–428). Cham, Switzerland: Palgrave Macmillan.

Kim, Tae-Young, & Seo, Hyo-Sun. (2012). Elementary school students' foreign language learning demotivation: A mixed study of Korean EFL students. *The Asia-Pacific Education Researcher, 21*(1), 160–171.

Kim, Yeong-Myeong. (2005). *Sinhankookron: Danilsahoi hankook, keu bitgwa geurimja [Theory of New Korea: Korea as unidirectional society – Its light and darkness]*. Seoul, Korea: Ingansarang.

Kim, Yeong-Myeong. (2007b). Yeong'eo yeolpoongeul jamjaewooryeomyeon [How to calm English frenzy]. Retrieved August 12, 2018 from http://news.hankooki.com/lpage/opinion/200711/h2007112118551324370.html

Kim, Yoon-Kyoung. (2017b). *The effect of motivational languaging on Korean high school students EFL learning*. Unpublished doctoral dissertation. Chung-Ang University, Seoul, Korea.

Koran, S. (2015). Analyzing EFL teachers' initial job motivation and factors affecting their motivation in Fezalar educational institutions in Iraq. *Advances in Language and Literary Studies, 6*, 72–80.

Kubanyiova, M. (2009). Possible selves in language teacher development. In Z. Dörnyei & E. Ushioda (Eds.), *Motivation, language identity, and the L2 self* (pp. 314–332). Bristol, England: Multilingual Matters.

Kumazawa, M. (2013). Gaps too large: Four novice EFL teachers' self-concept and motivation. *Teaching and Teacher Education, 33*, 45–55.

Kwon, Oryang. (2000). Korea's education policy changes in the 1990s: Innovations to gear the nation for the 21st century. *English Teaching, 55*(1), 47–91.

Kwon, Oryang. (2005). The effect of elementary school English education on Korean high school students' English abilities. *English Teaching, 60*(3), 49–66.

Lee, Esther. (2019, July 1). 13nyeonjjae namhaksaengboda daehak mani ganeun hankook yeohaksaeng [Female students in Korea go to college more than male students in 13 straight years]. Retrieved January 19, 2020 from https://news.joins.com/article/23511999

Lee, Hueng-Soo. (2011). *Yeong'eoga hyeongjeda: Yeong'eo'eui gwageowa hyeonjae, geurigo mirae [English is economy: Past, present, and future of English]*. Seoul, Korea: English Moumou.

Lee, Kyung-Sook. (2017). *Siheom kookmin'eui tansaeng [The birth of exam-oriented people]*. Seoul, Korea: Pooreunyeoksa.

Lee, Young Shik. (2015). Innovating secondary English education in Korea. In B. Spolsky & K. Sung (Eds.), *Secondary school English education in Asia* (pp. 47–64). London: Routledge.

Lee, Yu-Jeong, & Kim, Tae-Young. (2019). The effect of languaging activity on Korean high school students' English learning motivation and metacognitive strategy use. *Secondry English Education, 12*(1), 25–51.

Min, Chan-Kyoo. (2007). Innovative English education curricular and the strategies of implementation in Korea. In Y.-H. Choi & B. Spolsky (Eds.), *ELT curriculum innovation and implementation in Asia* (pp. 101–129). Seoul, Korea: Asia TEFL.

Ministry of Education (2018). 2017nyeon cho, joong, go sagyoyookbi josa gyeogwa balpyo [Report of elementary, middle, and high school private education expenditure in 2017]. Retrieved December 21, 2018 from https://www.moe.go.kr/boardCnts/view.do?boardID=294&boardSeq=73506&lev=0&searchType=null&statusYN=W&page=1&s=moe&m=0503&opType=N.

NPR. (2018, October 22). Thousands of Swedes are inserting microchips under their skin. Retrieved January 17, 2020 from https://www.npr.org/2018/10/22/658808705/thousands-of-swedes-are-inserting-microchips-under-their-skin

Rogers, C. (1961). *On becoming a person.* Boston: Houghton Mifflin.

Sasaki, M. (2008). The 150-year history of English language assessment in Japanese education. *Language Testing, 25*(1), 63–83.

Seth, M. J. (2002). *Education fever: Society, politics, and the pursuit of schooling in South Korea.* Honolulu, HI: University of Hawai'i Press.

Song, Bongsun, & Kim, Tae-Young. (2016). Teacher (de)motivation from an Activity Theory perspective: Cases of two experienced EFL teachers in South Korea. *System, 57,* 134–145.

Song, Jae Jung. (2012). South Korea: Language policy and planning in the making. *Current Issues in Language Planning, 13*(1), 1–68.

Sugino, T. (2010). Teacher demotivational factors in the Japanese language teaching context. *Social and Behavioral Sciences, 3,* 216–226.

Swain, M. (2006). Languaging, agency and collaboration in advanced language proficiency. In H. Byrnes (Ed.), *Advanced language learning: The contribution of Halliday and Vygotsky* (pp. 95–108). London: Continuum.

Swain, M. (2010). "Talking-it-through": Languaging as a source of learning. In R. Batstone (Ed.), *Sociocognitive perspectives on language use and language learning* (pp. 112–129). Oxford, England: Oxford University Press.

Swain, M. (2013). Cognitive and affective enhancement among older adults: The role of languaging. *Australian Review of Applied Linguistics, 36*(1), 4–19.

Swain, M., & Lapkin, S. (2011). Languaging as agent and constituent of cognitive change in an older adult: An example. *Canadian Journal of Applied Linguistics, 14*(1), 104–117.

Ushioda, E. (2009). A person-in-context relational view of emergent motivation, self and identity. In Z. Dörnyei & E. Ushioda (Eds.), *Motivation, language identity and the L2 self* (pp. 215–228). Bristol, England: Multilingual Matters.

Vygotsky, L. S. (1978). *Mind in society: The development of higher psychological processes.* Cambridge, MA: Harvard University Press.

Vygotsky, L. S. (1987). Thinking in speech. In R. W. Rieber & A. S. Carton (Eds.), *The collected works of L. S. Vygotsky: Problems of general psychology* (Vol. 1). New York: Plenum.

Yang, Do-Woong. (2018, August 27). Yeong'eo jeoldaepyeonggaro yeong'eo gonggyoyook deo mooneojeotda [Due to the criterion-referenced English test, public English education is being collapsed]. Retrieved January 20, 2020 from http://www.kyosu.net/news/articleView.html?idxno=42522.

Yashima, T. (2013). Imagined L2 selves and motivation for international communication. In M. T. Apple, D. Da Silva & T. Fellner (Eds.), *Language learning motivation in Japan* (pp. 35–53). Bristol, England: Multilingual Matters.

You, C., & Dörnyei, Z. (2016). Language learning motivation in China: Results of a large-scale stratified survey. *Applied Linguistics, 37*(4), 495–519.